HISTORICIZING MODERNISTS

Historicizing Modernism

Series Editors

Editorial Board

Historicizing Modernism challenges traditional literary interpretations by taking an empirical approach to modernist writing: a direct response to new documentary sources made available over the last decade.

Informed by archival research, and working beyond the usual European/American avant-garde 1900–45 parameters, this series reassesses established readings of modernist writers by developing fresh views of intellectual contexts and working methods.

Series Titles

Arun Kolatkar and Literary Modernism in India, Laetitia Zecchini
British Literature and Classical Music, David Deutsch
Broadcasting in the Modernist Era, Matthew Feldman, Henry Mead and Erik Tonning
Charles Henri Ford, Alexander Howard
Chicago and the Making of American Modernism, Michelle E. Moore
Ezra Pound's Adams Cantos, David Ten Eyck
Ezra Pound's Eriugena, Mark Byron
Great War Modernisms and The New Age *Magazine*, Paul Jackson

James Joyce and Absolute Music, Michelle Witen
James Joyce and Catholicism, Chrissie van Mierlo
John Kasper and Ezra Pound, Alec Marsh
Katherine Mansfield and Literary Modernism, edited by Janet Wilson, Gerri Kimber and Susan Reid
Late Modernism and the English Intelligencer, Alex Latter
The Life and Work of Thomas MacGreevy, Susan Schreibman
Literary Impressionism, Rebecca Bowler
Modern Manuscripts, Dirk Van Hulle
Modernism at the Microphone, Melissa Dinsman
Modernist Lives, Claire Battershill
The Politics of 1930s British Literature, Natasha Periyan
Reading Mina Loy's Autobiographies, Sandeep Parmar
Reframing Yeats, Charles Ivan Armstrong
Samuel Beckett and Arnold Geulincx, David Tucker
Samuel Beckett and the Bible, Iain Bailey
Samuel Beckett and Cinema, Anthony Paraskeva
Samuel Beckett's 'More Pricks than Kicks', John Pilling
Samuel Beckett's German Diaries 1936–1937, Mark Nixon
T. E. Hulme and the Ideological Politics of Early Modernism, Henry Mead
Virginia Woolf's Late Cultural Criticism, Alice Wood
Christian Modernism in an Age of Totalitarianism, Jonas Kurlberg
Samuel Beckett and Experimental Psychology, Joshua Powell
Samuel Beckett in Confinement, James Little
Katherine Mansfield: New Directions, ed. by Aimée Gasston, Gerri Kimber and Janet Wilson
Modernist Wastes, Caroline Knighton
The Many Drafts of D. H. Lawrence, Elliott Morsia
Samuel Beckett and the Second World War, William Davies
Judith Wright and Emily Carr, Anne Collett and Dorothy Jones
Ezra Pound's Washington Cantos and the Struggle for Light, Alec Marsh

Upcoming titles

Historical Modernisms: Time History and Modernist Aesthetics, edited by Jean-Michel Rabaté and Angeliki Spiropoulou

HISTORICIZING MODERNISTS

Approaches to 'Archivalism'

Edited by
Matthew Feldman, Anna Svendsen and Erik Tonning

BLOOMSBURY
NEW DELHI • LONDON • OXFORD • NEW YORK • SYDNEY

BLOOMSBURY INDIA
Bloomsbury Publishing India Pvt. Ltd
Second Floor, LSC Building No. 4, DDA Complex, Pocket C–6&7,
Vasant Kunj, New Delhi 110070

BLOOMSBURY, BLOOMSBURY ACADEMIC INDIA and the Diana logo are trademarks of Bloomsbury Publishing Plc

First published in India 2025
First published in Great Britain 2021

Cover design by Eleanor Rose

This edition published with permission from Bloomsbury Publishing Plc,
50 Bedford Square, London, WC1B3DP, UK

A catalogue record for this book is available from the British Library.
A catalog record for this book is available from the Library of Congress.

ISBN: 978-93-61318-23-8

Series: Historicizing Modernism

Typeset by Integra Software Services Pvt. Ltd.
Printed in India by Manipal Technologies Limited, Manipal

For Naomi and Barnaby

iustitia, in qua virtutis est splendor maximus

CONTENTS

ILLUSTRATIONS

PREFACE

This book series is devoted to the analysis of late nineteenth- to twentieth-century literary modernism within its historical contexts. *Historicizing Modernism* therefore stresses empirical accuracy and the value of primary sources (such as letters, diaries, notes, drafts, marginalia or other archival materials) in developing monographs and edited collections on modernist literature. This may take a number of forms, such as manuscript study and genetic criticism, documenting interrelated historical contexts and ideas, and exploring biographical information. To date, no book series has fully laid claim to this interdisciplinary, source-based territory for modern literature. While the series addresses itself to a range of key authors, it also highlights the importance of non-canonical writers with a view to establishing broader intellectual genealogies of modernism. Furthermore, while the series is weighted towards the English-speaking world, studies of non-Anglophone modernists whose writings are open to fresh historical exploration are also included.

A key aim of the series is to reach beyond the familiar rhetoric of intellectual and artistic 'autonomy' employed by many modernists and their critical commentators. Such rhetorical moves can and should themselves be historically situated and reintegrated into the complex continuum of individual literary practices. It is our intent that the series' emphasis upon the contested self-definitions of modernist writers, thinkers and critics may, in turn, prompt various reconsiderations of the boundaries delimiting the concept 'modernism' itself. Indeed, the concept of 'historicizing' is itself debated across its volumes, and the series by no means discourages more theoretically informed approaches. On the contrary, the editors hope that the historical specificity encouraged by *Historicizing Modernism* may inspire a range of fundamental critiques along the way.

Matthew Feldman
Erik Tonning

ACKNOWLEDGEMENTS

Deriving from an international conference in the University of York hosted by Bloomsbury, the Norwegian Study Centre and the Department of Foreign Languages in the University of Bergen, this volume approaches modernism via the employment of various types of primary source material: correspondence, manuscripts and drafts, memoirs and production notes, reading notes and marginalia, and all manner of useful contextualizing sources like news reports or eyewitness accounts. In bringing together a diversity of approaches to this 'historicizing' theme, the editors are grateful to Bloomsbury Academic for supporting the Historicizing Modernism/Modernist Archives conference hosted at the University of York's Norwegian Study Centre, 17–19 May 2018. Colleagues at Bloomsbury have been supportive of this project from the start, and we would like to pay special tribute to David Avital, Ben Doyle and Lucy Brown for their continued support of this volume and the two series from which it derives. Additional thanks go to Wassim Rustom for his assistance with earlier drafts towards this volume, and to the Bloomsbury production team for help with the final edition. The editors would also like to single out the patience and professionalism of Viswasirasini Govindarajan across the copy-editing process, for which we are immensely grateful.

INTRODUCTION TO HISTORICIZING MODERNISTS: APPROACHES TO 'ARCHIVALISM'

Matthew Feldman

It is now commonly accepted that there was something that set modernism off from artistic movements which it eclipsed, or the post-modernism that has succeeded it. In the case of literary modernism, this is often described as aesthetic experimentalism, particularly in terms of narrative structure and interiority of description. An apt overview is provided by the opening sentences of *The Bloomsbury Companion to Modernist Literature*:

> Literary modernism is characterized by dazzling experimentation, perplexing narrative and poetic form, and often by contradictory aesthetic and ideological tendencies the desire to 'make it new' is combined with a nostalgic yearning for a lost and at times primitive past; the admiration for technology and science is paired with a suspicion of the dehumanizing threat; and although modernist writing can often be radically progressive and even revolutionary in political and sexual terms, it also frequently expresses a fascination with and allegiance to far-right traditionalist and even totalitarian ideologies.[1]

Modernism, then, contains multitudes. Yet it also bears a visible mark, in its manifestations from the later nineteenth to the later twentieth century, of indeterminacy, of formal innovation, and of turning inward to make sense – or not, as the case may be – of the bewildering changes engendered by the modern world.[2]

This bare-bones characterization begs the question: just what is it to 'historicize' modernism? In the chapters to follow, the ensuing responses – and practices – vis-à-vis this question are naturally multifaceted, for in one sense historicizing may be defined simply as 'representing or treating as history'. Admittedly, the latter, contentious term can indicate both 'the past' and 'representations of the past'. In this tension one may recall the prefatory injunction of Kant's foundational work of the Enlightenment, *The Critique of Pure Reason*, of which Modernist Studies itself remains an (even if unwitting or begrudging) heir: 'Human reason has the peculiar fate in one species of its cognitions that it is burdened with questions which it cannot dismiss, since they are given to it as problems by the nature of reason itself, but which it also cannot answer, since they transcend every capacity of human reason.' As Kant already discerned the past may not be objectively recoverable, but objects from the past certainly are; as are events, able to be inter-subjectively[3] documented or contemporaneously attested (as with court eyewitness testimony). It is to these material traces that historicism traditionally attends. But again, how does this relate to thinking about modernism?

Before essaying some suggestions in answer to this relationship, however, a few words about what historicizing modernism is *not*, particularly in the wake of the oft-identified 'archival turn' of primary-source engagement over the last generation.[4] Despite the close reading and poststructuralist theorizing still influential in the study of modernism, *The Oxford Handbook of Modernisms* observes that 'a general "archival turn" is nonetheless altering the shape of Modernist Studies'. This tendency in modernist criticism, contends James Knapp, 'has regrounded much scholarly debate in the archive as a corrective to ahistorical theorizing'.[5] Finn Fordham conditionally agrees, rightly adding that contemporary modernist scholars are 'not "beyond an archival turn", but within the force of its swerve, and so we shall be for some time. This is a condition we should not only get used to, but also one we should respond to by imagining, finding out, and testing different ways of making use of it.'[6]

Historicizing Modernists presents an exemplary case study of Fordham's palimpsestic 'Modernist Archive'. Contributions to this volume are all historicist engagements with modernist literature. That is to say, whether providing historical context, examining the literary compositional process, or source-based transcription and annotation, this approach to criticism seeks corroboration by objects and information outside the source text. This demands neither a replacement nor closing down of contrasting literary-critical readings, but instead self-reflexively inclines towards stepping back from the published text to examine the contexts helping to shape it. This return to para-texts, drafts and other recoverable contextual evidence can in turn facilitate new textual understandings – raising perspectives of influence, working methods or historical pressures that contribute to advancing our knowledge of both work and author.

An essential ingredient separating the above, recent tendency from a much older and better-established New Historicism in Modernist Studies is that 'the literary canon' seems to remain an important starting point. Whereas New Historicism 'is interested in history as represented and recorded in written documents' and tends towards a '*parallel* study of literature and non-literary texts' (my italics), what I have termed modernist 'archival criticism' tends to centre around recognized, oftentimes critically lauded, writers, presented in Part I of this collection.[7] Sidestepping the vicissitudes of canon formation, contemporary modernist manuscript scholars tend to gravitate towards canonical authors like Ezra Pound, Samuel Beckett, Virginia Woolf, Gertrude Stein or James Joyce. One reason for this is obvious: known authors frequently leave behind sizeable literary estates, which are then acquired by well-funded research centres.

The value of primary sources – ranging from texts of all kinds to physical and digital objects – may be shared by both approaches, as is 'the new historicist commitment to viewing the object or the anecdote within a larger connective social web'. Similarly, continues Amy E. Earhart: 'New historicism perceives literature as located within a historical, cultural, and social matrix and that this matrix allows for a deep reading of the text in question. At the same time, the scholar is to maintain a self-reflexive critical stance in relation to the text.'[8] Yet for the more recent archival criticism, the mediation of institutions and power relations tends to be much less an object of theorizing, and indeed concern; and instead of submerging the text into a network of contextual associations and ideological faultlines, a guiding assumption is that context also illuminates craft. New historicism may well be understood as 'resolutely anti-establishment'; in the words of one recent study, this includes

> established visions of the archive as the embodiment of state authority and law; as a fetish that acts as a substitutive gratification for the impossibility of 'truth' as an 'organized' index that materially contextualizes man's consciousness; and as the censored contents of the unconscious speaking through a parapraxis.[9]

By contrast, different types of archival work included here are to some degree predicated upon 'the establishment' for canon formation, funding for research trips, manuscript access and even scholarly collaboration (for esoteric authors rarely have multiple scholars working on them, and their estates and/or unpublished papers are less uniformly collected into holding libraries).

If New Historicism is an imperfect precursor and descriptor of this recent tendency, the same goes for the more Marxist-oriented Cultural Materialism. The emphasis on neglected contexts and recovering alternative histories again bears some important similarities with more recent archival criticism. Yet the latter's political commitments appear less explicit, and are often accompanied by a wariness towards grand narratives – even literary-critical or theoretical grand narratives. The new archival criticism is characterized by pragmatism and specificity rather than political engagement. Nonetheless, there is an important impetus here from Cultural Materialist approaches in bringing lesser-known modernist writers into sharper focus, for Cultural Materialism is helpfully wary of the canon. By inviting scholars to look beyond the 'greats' of modernisms past, Cultural Materialism has reinvigorated our focus on many of modernism's networks and everyday interactions. Furthermore, Cultural Materialsm, and its offshoot, cultural studies, 'does not limit itself to "high" cultural forms' but extends to 'forms like television and popular music and fiction'. Canonical modernist authors are precisely those '"high" cultural forms' downplayed by cultural materialism which also (like its 'American counterpart', New Historicism) has tended to research Shakespearean or early modern subjects – rather than those since the printing revolutions of the late nineteenth century, when books and journals started to circulate widely in an age of 'mechanical reproduction'.[10]

Both movements, finally, seemed to have waned over the last generation as another essential ingredient to archival criticism continues to wax exponentially: the digital revolution. Finn Fordham has rightly observed that the digital humanities has 'combined' with a 'historical turn' over the last generation, while Earhart adds that 'new historicist scholars who perceived the archive as the space of scholarship [also] viewed the digital as a tool for enacting the ideal of textual inclusion'.[11] Thanks to digital photography and document scanning, reproduced documents can be obtained without physically visiting a holding library or archive. An emailed request for PDF scans uploaded online now makes it possible to consult 'archives' on an android phone or Kindle anywhere in the world. Increased emphasis on collaboration – including shared transcriptions, photographs and other methods – also comes to the fore. At the same time, a collapsing of geographical strictures has likewise been beneficial for archival criticism: not many scholars around the world are able to physically (let alone repeatedly) get to, say, the Beinecke archives in New Haven, Connecticut, or to the Beckett International Foundation holdings in Reading, UK. A digital library of unpublished materials, available mere clicks away, has doubtless been amongst the greatest impetuses in this new archival criticism, or 'archivalism'.

As an *amuse bouche* for the chapters comprising this volume – in their own ways and across the many tributary specialisms in Modernist Studies (e.g. Pound, Woolf or Beckett Studies) – this introduction liberally refers to previous volumes in Bloomsbury's *Historicising Modernism* and *Modernist Archives* series. *Historicising Modernism* is now entering its tenth year and has seen the release of more than two dozen analytical volumes on modernist authors and their contexts, with most editions reissued in paperback.[12] The editors, Professor Erik Tonning and I, alongside our colleague and friend Dr David Tucker, had all carried out archival studies long before 2011. We met as PhD students working in the archives on Samuel Beckett, and Erik and I launched a seminar series on the latter called 'Samuel Beckett: Debts and Legacies'. We felt that these archival approaches were well-established in Beckett Studies, but far less so in other sub-disciplines in Modernist Studies. Accordingly, we worked with David Avital (then of Continuum Books) to launch a pan-modernism series geared towards neglected materials and the way in which this can have a transformative impact on specific authors like Woolf or Yeats (for instance, two early studies in the series from 2013, Alice Wood's *Virginia Woolf's Late Cultural Criticism* and Charles Armstrong's *Reframing Yeats*), and upon Modernist Studies more generally (as with Dirk van Hulle's 2014 tour de force of genetic criticism, *Modern Manuscripts: The Extended Mind and Creative Undoing from Darwin to Beckett and Beyond*).

One starting point was that an overemphasis upon 'theory', broadly understood, had taken some attention away from texts themselves and their production, and that these detailed textual histories often challenged or problematized the theoretical lenses trained upon modernist texts. We have therefore provided a forum for analysis of neglected or unpublished materials, while also tempering some of the more expansive theorizing by rooting *Historicizing Modernism* in primary sources and unpublished materials.[13] In this way, our largest accomplishment may have been in providing a platform, and bringing together, otherwise overlooked scholarship and methodological perspectives centred upon making empirically robust, even falsifiable, claims *before* more traditional acts of literary interpretation, and assuming the utility of connecting those acts with such claims as far as possible. Our goal, then, has been to provide a visible platform for previously unmoored archival volumes on modernist authors, their context/s and related questions (like inter-medial studies, notably extending to 'radio modernism' – as in Dinsman's 2017 *Modernism at the Microphone* and the edited *Broadcasting in the Modernist Era* of the year before). When we started out, nearly a decade ago, there felt like a glut of highly theoretical modernist series – often with university presses – but far fewer fora available for archival studies, let alone the wholescale reproduction of archival materials.

The latter is at the forefront of our partner series, *Modernist Archives*. More documentary in scope, this series was launched in 2015 and now contains nine volumes taking in genetic editions mapping the compositional process, unpublished manuscripts, annotated scholarly editions, and the 'grey canon' of archival correspondence, notebooks and more.[14] As it complements the series editors' Preface in the frontmatter to this edition, the remit of *Modernist Archives* series bears reproducing here. It attempts to delimit some of the parameters now associated with the 'archival turn' in the study of modernism over the last generation:

> Archival excavation and detailed contextualization are becoming increasingly central to scholarship on literary modernism. In recent years, the increased accessibility and dissemination of previously unpublished or little-known documents and texts have led to paradigm-shifting scholarly interventions on a range of canonical authors (Beckett, Eliot, Joyce, Pound and Woolf, among others), neglected topics (the occult, 'primitivism', fascism, eugenics, book history, the writing process), and critical methodologies (genetic criticism, intertextuality and historical contexts). This trend will surely only increase as large-scale digitization of archival materials gathers pace and existing copyright restrictions gradually lapse.[15] *Modernist Archives* is a book series that aims to channel, extend and interrogate these shifts by publishing hitherto unavailable or neglected primary materials for a wider readership. Each volume also provides supporting, contextualizing work by scholars, alongside a critical apparatus of notes and references.
>
> The impetus for *Modernist Archives* emerges from the editors' well-established series, *Historicizing Modernism*. While *Historicizing Modernism*'s focus is analytical, *Modernist Archives* will make accessible edited and annotated versions of little-known sources and avant-texts. The monographs and edited collections in *Historicizing Modernism* have revealed the extent to which contemporary scholars are increasingly turning towards archival and/or unpublished material in order to reconfigure understandings of modernism, in its broader historical rootedness as well as in its compositional methodologies. The present series extends this empirical and genetic focus.

> Understanding and defining such primary sources as a broad category extending to letters, diaries, notes, drafts and marginalia, the *Modernist Archives* series produces volumes that not only unearth significant unpublished material and provide original scholarship on this material, but also develop cutting-edge editorial presentation techniques that preserve as much information as possible in an economical and accessible way. Also of note is the potential for the series to explore collections pertaining to the relations between literary modernism and other media (radio, television), or important cultural moments. The series thus aims to be an enabling force within modernist scholarship.
>
> It is becoming ever-more difficult to read this extraordinary period of literary experimentation in isolation from contextualizing archival material, sometimes dubbed the 'grey canon' of modernist writing. The difficulty, we suggest, is something like a loss of innocence: once obviously relevant materials are actually accessible, they cannot be ignored. They may challenge received ideas about the limits or definition of modernism; they may upend theoretical frameworks, or encourage fresh theoretical reflection; they may require new methodologies, or revise the very notion of 'authorship'; likewise, they may require types of knowledge that we never knew we needed – but *there they are.*
>
> However, while we are champions of historical, archival research, *Modernist Archives* in no way seeks to influence the results or approaches that scholars in this area will utilize in the exciting times ahead. By commissioning a wide range of innovative and challenging editions, this series aims to once more 'make strange' and 'make new' our fundamental ideas about modernism.[16]

Put simply, both series start from an empirical grounding and historical context, championing the importance of primary source materials in approaching the study of modernist authors. In this more empiricist tradition, then, one reason for archival approaches to modernism – or more narrowly, of *Historicizing Modernists* – is simply that the material is *there.* 'There' includes both specialized reading rooms with privately held collections and, increasingly in the third decade of the twentieth century, materials presented digitally and/or online.

Already in the early 1990s Jerome McGann had coined the term 'digital archive', and had played a leading role in incorporating computer-based methods in the study of literature through the University of Virginia's Institute for Advanced technology in the humanities. Only a year later 'the archive' also became a subject for critical theory, as famously announced in Jacques Derrida's 1994 *Archive Fever*: 'do we already have at our disposition a concept of the archive? a concept of the archive which deserves this name? which is one and whose unity is assured? Have we ever been assured of the homogeneity, of the consistency, of the univocal relationship of any concept to a term or to such a word as 'archive'?'[17] Yet this is far from New Historicists' approach to manuscript study, which Stephen Greenblatt has described as more of 'a practice rather than a doctrine'. Thus while a theorist like Derrida asks who could 'inhabit this unusual place, this place of election where law and singularity intersect in privilege', scholars familiar with prosaic days in records room grasp, perhaps pre-theoretically, that 'the Archive is made from selected and consciously chosen documentation from the past and also from the mad fragmentations that no one intended to preserve and that just ended up there'.[18] True, 'the archive' is all this, but also a space to gather materials; make intellectual connections and have ideas; to get research tips or do favours; to photograph and document items; to follow rules and archivists; to mix (some form of) twenty-first-century technology to search – and perhaps find – (usually modern) manuscripts for consultation; excitement and boredom.

'There' may have a temporal dimension as well. In so far as the period of literary 'modernism' is more comfortably historicized from the late nineteenth to the mid-twentieth century,[19] lapsing copyright restrictions (often after a period of seventy years) and the growing availability of online primary sources surely make this current moment the 'golden age' of manuscript study. An excellent example of the latter is the Beinecke's digitization of multiple modernist works by Joseph Conrad, including all 210 handwritten folios of his canonical text, *Heart of Darkness*.[20] It is a painful irony that the field – plagued by job insecurity and a wider scepticism about the value of the humanities – is enjoying the fruits of this 'golden age' at the worst possible time professionally. Likewise, the ubiquity of computer writing and editing, perhaps coincidentally, emerged just as the embers of modernism were being extinguished with works like Russell Hoban's underrated *Riddley Walker* or Samuel Beckett's superlative late trilogy, *Company, Ill Seen Ill Said* and *Worstward Ho*.

Whether such archivalism is biographical or chronological; whether engaging with materials as different as handwritten letters or ledgers of book sales; and whether the undertaking is what Chris Ackerley has termed 'validity in annotation',[21] or the more intertextual approach to reading notes and commonplace notebooks taken in the bulk of chapters below, what these approaches share is an interest in linking published texts with evidence – frequently archival, but always empirically underpinned – beyond its covers. That is to say, in providing historical context, examining the literary compositional process or engaging in letter- or source-based transcription, this approach to criticism seeks *corroboration* by objects and information outside the text. This entails neither a replacement nor closing down of contrasting literary-critical readings, but instead inclines towards moving back from the published text to examine the scaffolding that helps to build it. This stepping backward to different types of 'blueprints', in turn, facilitates new textual understandings – raising perspectives of influence, working methods or historical context that can often lead to redoubled advances in knowledge of the 'construction' in question.

Like the vexed question of archivalism, entire bookshelves have been devoted to the question of just what 'modernism' is (or better, 'was' – for few still contend that artistic modernism persists in the twenty-first century; or at least without non-hyphenated modifiers like 'late' or 'liquid'). Surely any account would do well to heed Alexander Howard's opening injunction in his book on Charles Henri Ford that, quite apart from being a 'notoriously difficult term to define', the term 'modernism' remains the 'most nebulous of notions' and 'continues to recede from our view'. For Howard, this view extends beyond the traditional 1945 watershed by at least a generation.[22] Extending even further both temporally and beyond the usual European and Anglophone scenes, Alys Moody and Stephen Ross's superb *Global Modernists on Modernism: An Anthology* traces literary modernism's reach as extending both temporally beyond 1945 and geographically beyond the usual European and Anglophone scenes, to 1970s Fiji and Zaire, 1980s India and Syria, and even post-Tiananmen China. In turn, this assessment chimes with the 'expansive' tendency of the new Modernist Studies, as identified by Mao and Walkowitz 'in what we might think of as temporal, spatial, and vertical directions'. They continue:

> As scholars demonstrate the fertility of questioning rigid temporal delimitations, periods seem inevitably to get bigger (one might think of 'the long eighteenth century' or 'the age of empire'). Meanwhile, interrogations of the politics, historical validity, and aesthetic value of exclusive focus on the literatures of Europe and North America have spurred the study (in the North American academy) of texts produced in other quarters of the world or by hitherto little-recognized enclaves in the privileged areas. In addition to these temporal and spatial expansions, there has been what we are calling here a vertical one, in which once quite sharp boundaries between high art and popular forms of culture have been reconsidered: in which canons have been critiqued and reconfigured; in which works by members of marginalized social groups have been encountered with fresh eyes and ears; and in which scholarly inquiry has increasingly extended to matters of production, dissemination, and reception.[23]

There can be no doubt that recent studies have expanded our understanding of modernism's relationship to ethnicity, gender, sexuality, postcolonialism – such that these are rarely now called 'other modernisms' as they were just a dozen years ago. These too are modernisms, but in less familiar contexts than the white, male and Eurocentric canon formation that first gave us 'the modern' over a century ago.

Yet if history is being returned to these neglected subjects and their ground-breaking work – exemplified by Arun Kolatkar's Indian 'art of assemblage' modernism from the later 1960s – history cuts both ways. That is to say, modernism did have a back story, as historicists are keen to point out.[24] As Finn Fordham points out, modernism entered everyday use in the early twentieth century as a religious, specifically Catholic, pejorative description of evolutionism in doctrine, and became adopted by avant-garde writers and thinkers as a counter-cultural badge of decadence and bohemian sacrilege. At the same time that John Middleton Murry was offering a now-domesticated definition of modernism in 1911 as artistic forms that pierce 'the outward surface of the world, and disengages the rhythms that lie at the heart of things, rhythms strange to the eye, unaccustomed to the ear, primitive harmonies of the world', Fordham reminds us, '[b]etween 1907 and 1930 there were over 350 references to the term in *The Times*: ninety per cent of these refer to the theological context of Modernism; the remainder feature in articles on architecture, music or literature'.[25] As Erik Tonning's paradigm-shifting *Modernism and Christianity* contends, this was often a productive tension, one born of the appreciation, in Europe and North America at least, that Christianity could be attacked or embraced, but never ignored. In this case, recent works in new Modernist Studies serve to return historical context to the cultural ubiquity of Christianity, whether in terms of David Jones' Catholic modernism in his later writings, or in Jonas Kurlberg's study of T. S. Eliot and the Moot's attempted modernistic 'revitalization of Christianity' around the Second World War.[26]

Many of these and other modernist cultural engagements are registered in ground-breaking titles published by the *Historicizing Modernism* series. For instance, the movement from 'little magazines' like the New Age to publishing houses like the Woolfs' Hogarth Press a generation later is also a history of modernist publishing.[27] So too with developments in education and other modernist arts such as painting and music – to empirically-approached thematic issues relating to gender and colonialism.[28] Yet to date, pride of place in the *Historicizing Modernism* series has been given to single-author studies of both central figures to narratives of modernism like Katherine Mansfield and Samuel Beckett,[29] as well as oft-neglected writers like T. E. Hulme, Mina Loy and Thomas MacGreevy.[30] Given his centrality to the development of Anglophone modernism, it should come as little surprise that Ezra Pound is well-represented in the *Historicizing Modernism* series, ranging from Pound's intertextual readings and later work towards *The Cantos*,[31] to the charged world of Pound's fascist politics in two works by Alec Marsh.[32] Some of these debates are revisited in Chapters 3 and 4 of this volume, with Marsh taking the *longue durée* and Ehtee drilling down into mid-1930s correspondence. While these and other chapters will be briefly discussed below, it bears noting, as a declaration of interest, that I have long contended Pound's fascist connections have been sanitized by his leading defenders – or put another way, an exemplar of the kind of work archival criticism entails is engaging Pound's still-misunderstood embrace of fascism, which is charted in his archive.[33]

The first two chapters of *Historicizing Modernists* form a different dyad on another canonical modernist author: Virginia Woolf. Commencing with this leading modernist author underscores how different 'archivalist' approaches to the same author can nonetheless produce markedly different results. Michèle Barrett's 'WoolfNotes: Virginia Woolf's Reading and Research Notes Online' examines the last major collection of unpublished Woolf materials. Preserved in archives in Britain and the United States, these extensive notes show that far from being an untutored genius Woolf was a lifelong, diligent researcher. The notes demonstrate a range of erudite areas and deploy languages other than English – Greek, French, Italian, German. The WoolfNotes project brings these to light, and the process of digitizing these archival materials has been driven by the twin objectives of visual authenticity, with regard to the material text, and readability of the finished images. The edition discussed in this chapter is being constructed so as to facilitate further interactive developments in the future. Barrett's chapter discusses some of the intellectual and practical issues at stake in such a project.

Natasha Periyan's chapter then examines how such material is applied to empirically-based interpretative readings. To do so Chapter 2, 'The Biopolitics of *Mrs Dalloway*: Intelligence and Sentiment', draws on archival and genetic material to offer a Foucauldian biopolitical reading of Woolf's *Mrs Dalloway*. This 1925 novel was produced during a transitional political moment: set during the first Baldwin Conservative government and published during the second Baldwin Conservative government, it was mostly drafted during the first minority Labour government. As corroborated by contemporaneous sources, this period of political upheaval is registered in the text's critique of intelligence and sentiment. These are both qualities, in turn, associated with class politics and meritocratic discourses – as well as with literary traditions, either in well-rehearsed arguments surrounding modernist difficulty or in the eighteenth-century novel of sympathy. As this chapter emphasizes, Woolf's biopolitical critique is enacted through a classificatory narrative of an imperialistic ruling elite, while wrestling with ambivalent assessments of the novel's lower-class 'intelligent' characters. Periyan argues Woolf's depiction of Clarissa Dalloway engages with stereotyped notions of female intelligence and recasts archetypal models of female sensibility, as Woolf scrutinizes the limitations of sympathetic engagement with the 'lower class as victims'. The novel's thematic depiction of intelligence and sentiment is paralleled by its affective qualities, as *Mrs Dalloway* reaches for a new standard of modernist affect that foregrounds a new standard of aesthetic response demanding of both the intelligence and the emotions.

As the following pair of chapters show, a decade later both 'intelligence and the emotions' were at play in Ezra Pound's turn to fascism in the 1930s. In a provocative third chapter by Svetlana Ehtee, '"[E]s die höchste Zeit ist" to Reconsider Ideology: Ezra Pound and Nazi Germany', poses the question of how extreme Pound's radical right politics became between the wars. For Ehtee, Pound, a self-proclaimed literary activist, believed that both the Federal Reserve and the Bank of England had a monopoly over the control of the value of money and, therefore, the ability to alter its buying power. If these institutions were governed by 'big Jews,' as Pound increasingly feared by the mid-1930s, then everyday finance capitalism was in the hands of 'usurers' – the notorious subject of Pound's 'Canto XLV', 'Usura', and scores of texts to follow. As Pound explained in a 1934 letter to Lieutenant-Colonel Graham Seton Hutchison, a writer, British army officer and fascist activist: 'anti banks is anti se{m}ite' [*sic*]. Unlike Pound's obsession with Mussolini and the influence that the meeting with 'The Boss' had on the poet, Pound's efforts to influence Hitler's propaganda machine have been culpably overlooked by scholars. Given the fact that Hutchison, with whom Pound corresponded between 1934 and 1936, fostered relationships with high-ranking Nazis – even extending to speculation that he was a Fifth Columnist for Nazi Germany – Ehtee maintains that Pound's connections to the Third Reich deserve much greater scholarly attention. In undertaking this work, Chapter 3 reveals the contours of Pound's pro-Nazi efforts before the Second World War, and shows how the poet's support for Hitler's Germany extended into, and beyond, the Second World War.

Also taking as its subject Pound's correspondence, Alec Marsh tacks a different approach in Chapter 4, opting for the *longue durée* in Pound's generation-long correspondence with Olivia Rossetti Agresti. 'Will This Yowling Never Cease? The Pound/Agresti Correspondence and the Changing Scope of Ezra Pound Studies' also engages the issue of scholarly annotation, comparing Archie Henderson's *"I Cease Not to Yowl" Reannotated*, with an earlier edition of the Pound / Olivia Rossetti Agresti letters in 1998 by Demetres Tryphonopoulos and Leon Surette, entitled *"I Cease Not to Yowl": Ezra Pound's Letters to Olivia Rossetti Agresti*. Henderson began to compile what is now a vast corrective – which is still ongoing, and available for purchase – in response to the 1998 edition's inadequate and sometimes uncomprehending annotation. As Marsh sets out, the initial annotators failed to understand the Pound they were meeting in these letters. A generation later, Henderson began what has become, in Marsh's view, the most important work on Pound published in this century. Marsh's survey of this text and its historical contexts, providing an invaluable commentary on the Pound/Agresti letters but also on the many other editions of Pound correspondence from the 1950s, also sheds crucial evidential light on Pound's difficult late Cantos. To understand this new, fascist Pound, Marsh argues, scholars must reluctantly follow Henderson by delving into aspects of the Master many had not wished to know.

Chapter 5 then shifts focus to another right-wing modernist author in '*Useful Knowledge* beyond the Beinecke: Gertrude Stein Reading Discourses of Democracy and Nationalism in *Life Magazine* and *The Literary Digest*'. Isabelle Parkinson commences from the recognition that Yale's Beinecke archive – home to most of Pound's papers – has also loomed large in Stein scholarship, particularly since Ulla Dydo's painstaking work to situate Stein's writing practice as the nexus of an everyday life reflected in the archive's materiality of drafts, notes and clippings. The significance of the Beinecke material, alongside the important feminist investment in an attention to the quotidian, means that, for Parkinson, Stein's personal life has often been important in examinations of her work. This chapter moves from the personal into public culture by following the documents out of the context with which Stein was engaged as a reader. The weekly magazines *Life* and *The Literary Digest* (1890–1938) made important reading for Stein in the production of works included in her 1928 collection *Useful Knowledge*. Indeed, both these sets of documents, indexed in but absent from Stein's archive, are refracted in her texts. Often understood as representing Stein's very personal coming-to-terms with her American identity, Parkinson argues that *Useful Knowledge* is much more about Stein's interwar reading – one representing her 'everyday' as a reader of the broadcast print texts, aimed at an expanding transatlantic educated class and responding directly to a new era of mass democracy. This chapter then turns to the way Stein's 'Three Leagues' (1919) and 'Woodrow Wilson' (1920), in particular, mediate popular discourses of democracy in the American weeklies. In these short pieces, published in *Useful Knowledge* as exemplary of her Americanness, Stein writes as a reader of the American periodicals she was to take across her forty-three years as a Parisian expat, revealing the power of the popular press in constructing modernist readings of individual subjects as national subject.

The connection of the individual to collective is also central to Chapter 6, 'Clashes over Transcendence: T. S. Eliot and Karl Mannheim through the Lens of Programmatic Modernism'. Amidst heightened societal turmoil, Jonas Kurlberg reveals how a small group of intellectuals that called themselves 'the Moot' gathered between 1938 and 1947 in order to catalyse a Christian cultural revolution. Drawing upon correspondence, records and other archival documents, Kurlberg highlights that interest in the Moot rests not only in its ambitions but also in the calibre and diversity of its members. One of the Moot's more compelling sub-plots, for instance, is the interaction between Karl Mannheim – the eminent Hungarian sociologist and secular Jew – and T. S. Eliot, famed poet, nationalized Briton and Anglo-Catholic. In this chapter, Kurlberg analyses their ultimately competing visions for the future of no less than 'Western Civilization' itself. Both Eliot and Mannheim lamented the loss of transcendence in the wake of modern secularization and its purportedly colossal impact upon social cohesion in Western civilization. Sharing in this diagnosis, both came to see religion as a social force on which any future cultural re-construction depended. Considering the alternatives at hand, fascism and communism, both deemed a renewed Christendom within liberal democracy to be preferable to quasi-religious totalitarian ideologies. Nevertheless, Kurlberg demonstrates that Eliot repeatedly resisted Mannheim's calls for greater central planning in favour of fostering organic growth of society and culture, arguing that it is precisely their divergent dispositions to the transcendent that lies behind their conflicting views.

Jumping squarely into the terrain of late modernism a generation later, Chapter 7 reads Samuel Beckett's 1966 *Ping* in light of the theory and practice of film editing, specifically, Eisenstein's theory of overtonal montage. As Anthony Paraskeva sets out in '*Ping* and Overtonal Montage', Beckett wrote *Bing* in French (translated into English as *Ping*) only a year after editing *Film*, his only professional experience with cinema. Albeit neglected by scholars to date, there are several references in Beckett's letters to the process of editing *Film* on a moviola, the film industry standard editing machine until the 1970s. Intriguingly, during post-production on *Film*, Beckett formed a close friendship with the film's editor, Sidney Meyers, who had written critical essays on the 'the similarity between literary editing and film editing'. Accordingly, in considering this new technology in relation to Beckett's oeuvre, Chapter 6 argues that *Ping* resembles the sound of the interlocking metal parts of a moviola. To make this case, Paraskeva argues that similarities extend to serial permutations of words and phrases, repeated in various combinations, acquiring a cellular quality, as though the narrative eye were scanning a strip of film frame-by-frame to locate the point of suture at which the cut is made. The frequent recurrence of the word 'white' suggests the clear blank frame at the end of a take, when light enters the camera. The logic of interconnecting phrases of sensuous abstraction, of qualities of white, heat, light – and the elision of primary narrative qualities of plot, character, action (there are no verbs) – directly evokes, in this account, Eisenstein's theory of overtonal montage. As Paraskeva shows, this is described in an article in *Close Up*, where the cut is made not on primary expressive qualities of plot, movement or action, but on secondary sensuous qualities of heat, drought, thirst, liquidity.

The focus shifts in part two of this collection, away from canonical modernists like Stein, Woolf, Pound and Beckett, towards lesser-known figures and previously neglected themes. Amongst the most central – at a day-to-day level for modernist authors, at least – is the role of religion, and specifically Christianity, as an inescapable social and cultural backdrop. In Chapter 8, Thomas Berenato examines the role of Catholicism in the work of the English-Welsh painter-poet, David Jones. Assigned to 'battalion nuclear reserve', Jones (1895–1974) saw the worst of the Battle of Pilckem Ridge, in July and August 1917, from behind the front lines. But these grimmest days of the First World War would inspire a poem Jones began in the mid-1930s after completing a draft of his first book, *In Parenthesis* (1937), about the Somme, July 1916, in which he had been wounded. In the view of 'David Jones's "Balaam business": The Poetics of Forgiveness after Passchendaele', this new work, *The Book of Balaam's Ass*, attempts expiation of survivor's guilt. It celebrates the 'baptism by cowardice' of one Private Shenkin (Private Jones in the drafts, which are brought to bear in this chapter), a Chaplinesque antihero who emerges from the horror unscathed thanks to his good misfortune to fall into a shell-hole during the assault. Although Jones 'abandoned' the thirty-five-page typescript, 'as it would not come together', he nonetheless included two fragments as the first and last items in his final book, *The Sleeping Lord* (1974). As Berenato emphasizes, Tom Goldpaugh, the most recent editor of Jones's unpublished poetry, has shown that Jones built his poems from the inside out by splitting them open and stuffing material of other origin inside. Goldpaugh argues that almost everything Jones wrote after *In Parenthesis* belongs to a single, vast devotional-type work, the relationship of whose parts to the whole Jones reconceived down the decades. The instance of a new page of verse, and its accompanying footnotes, that Jones added to the *Balaam's Ass* typescript in 1971 serves as Berenato's point of departure for a global account of Jones's compositional practice, based upon analysis on documents in the Jones archives at the Burns Library, Boston College and the National Library of Wales, Aberystwyth.

Yet any archival scholar will recognize navigating the referencing systems of these and similar research institutions can be no mean feat. As Chapter 9 reminds us, finding aids is a key – if often overlooked – part of the research process. Taking as his source material the wealth of modernist magazines now available for scholarly study, Archie Henderson suggests a definition of the 'modernist archive', as conventionally conceived, and to suggest how the definition may be expanded so as to incorporate a whole range of collections, both physical and digital, that might not ordinarily be thought of as part of a modernist author's archive. According to 'Modernist Archives and Little Magazine Networks', authors whose archives would be broadened under such a definition would include T. S. Eliot, Ezra Pound, Wyndham Lewis and a number of others. Using sample issues of the *Little Review* and *Poetry Magazine*, back files of which have been digitized and made available online, Henderson analyses the contents of the selected issues to illustrate how they might be linked with each other, with the authors published by them, and with other periodicals that might be considered to be part of the 'modernist network'. To date, *British Poetry Magazines 1914–2000: A History and Bibliography of 'Little Magazines'*, compiled by David Miller and Richard Price in 2006, is the only book indexing twentieth-century literary magazines by geographical location, subject, name and title. Yet with an additional mapping programme and a more refined and detailed topical classification system, it could be possible to visualize an author's connections with cities, connections with various magazines, and the magazine's connections with one another. As one scholar has queried, 'in a question parallel to that of social network mapping: how "connected" was Pound to London, to the international reviews, to wealthy benefactors?' As models for this proposed kind of visualization, Henderson draws upon multiple archival and library lists of right-wing periodicals where such geographical and topical analysis and mapping have already been carried out.

Amongst the most notable writers to emerge from 'little magazines' of the modernist era, in Chapter 10 Gerri Kimber turns to another author undergoing a scholarly reassessment – like David Jones, in large measure through archival engagement. 'Modernist (Dis)location: The Case of Katherine Mansfield' takes as its subject the genesis and development of the *Edinburgh Edition of the Collected Works of Katherine Mansfield*, incorporating a broader discussion on the repositioning of Mansfield within the modernist literary canon as a result of the edition. Until the Edinburgh edition, there had never been a true scholarly edition of Mansfield's writing, with the exception of the five volumes of her letters published by Oxford University Press between 1984 and 2008. This state of affairs led to Kimber's new edition, comprising all of Mansfield's essays, reviews, translations, parodies, poetry and personal writing. A significant amount of new material was uncovered in various archives, and incorporated into all four volumes. Particular attention is given to the cultural landscape Mansfield had grown up with in New Zealand – and chose to dislocate herself from – which underwrote her European view of modernity from a postcolonial viewpoint. In much of her work she merged both concepts, as she experimented and honed her skills as a writer. In incorporating everything Mansfield wrote, as this chapter emphasizes, the Edinburgh edition maps Mansfield's development as one of Britain's key exponents of literary modernism, redefining her status within the modernist canon, and regenerating scholarship in this iconic New Zealand writer.

Literary high modernism then gives way to (very) late modernism with the timely reminder that 'gossip makes the world go around' – a truism no less relevant, and perhaps even more so, during the modernist era. This is the subject of Alexander Howard's chapter, 'Gossip from Abroad, or, Why Historicize Modernism?' Taking this unorthodox approach – while again, moored to unpublished materials and contemporaneous sources – Howard considers what a theoretical understanding of gossip might bring to scholarly understandings of the modernist archive. Providing a backdrop to this exploration are archives from a range of important, yet largely overlooked, late modernist and proto-postmodernist cultural producers (and premier gossipers). Chapter 11 then asks just what the contents of the archives of avant-garde cultural producers such as Charles Henri Ford and Parker Tyler reveal about the various ways in which modernism did and did not develop. The argument Howard advances is that a thoroughgoing appraisal of the archives of overtly queer figures of Ford and Tyler's ilk tells much about the overarching trajectory of Anglo-American modernism. It also charts the various ways in which these and other assorted late modernists sought to break away from the sorts of theoretic and creative strictures of many prominent (high) modernists. Structured around a series of detailed case studies drawing in equal measure on freshly unearthed documents and original close readings, Howard argues that writers such as Ford and Tyler found creative, collaborative means with which to subtly undercut what they perceived to be problematically gendered, pre-existing modes of modernist cultural production (as found in the work of older writers such as T. S. Eliot and Ezra Pound). Further to that, Chapter 11 argues that talkative and networked writers like Ford and Tyler paved the way for writers and thinkers now commonly associated with postmodern art and literature. In this sense, Howard posits that a properly historicized reading of the voluminous and rich archives of Ford and Tyler provides the critical means to not only historicize modernism, but to historicize many of the crucial things that came after modernism.

As this suggests, one of the scholarly benefits prized by archival critics is the ability to recover previously marginalized voices. This is likewise the perspective obtained by Chapter 12, 'Expanding the Archives of the Queer Harlem Renaissance: Richard Bruce Nugent's Unpublished Modernism'. In 1926, David Deutsch recounts, Richard Bruce Nugent published one of the first explicitly queer Harlem Renaissance texts, 'Smoke, Lilies and Jade,' in the short-lived journal *Fire!!* Condemned by older Renaissance writers because of its highly stylized, decadent references to same-sex intimacies, Nugent's long-overlooked work has recently been excavated in several scholarly and popular volumes reviewed in this chapter. Building upon these, Deutsch argues that although Nugent is still portrayed as an imitator of late nineteenth-century European queer styles, his still-yet-to-be published archive makes unmistakeable a deft handling of modernist narrative techniques. Attention is then trained on Nugent's story 'Lunatique', published as a short sketch in *Gay Rebel of the Harlem Renaissance* (2002), within its original context as a section of his unpublished novel 'Uranus in Cancer'. Here, Deutsch finds, in particular, that Nugent employs familiar modernist defamiliarizing techniques to depict the interstices of 'queer' and 'normal' desires in multi-racial American contexts. This archival reclamation illustrates how Nugent values same-sex, mixed-race non-monogamous relationships, which evidence a form of queer loyalty to one particular but non-exclusive romantic partner. Chapter 12 closes by suggesting that Nugent's work can help to theorize a useful queer loyalty to our modernist archival studies – a loyalty that defies engaging an archive through totalizing or too monogamous approaches to literary classifications so as to avoid myopically rigid interpretations and critical receptions.

The volume then closes with a fascinating reflection upon the construction and dissemination of these pivotal 'critical receptions' with Miranda Dunham-

Hickman's 'Q. D. Leavis, Archives, and the "Art of Living"'. Grounded in the work of the pioneering Cambridge critic Q. D. Leavis, Chapter 13 meditates on occlusions and archives – the ways that materials placed as 'archival' with respect to a certain system are positioned, so as to be hidden from view – though they can mark factors essential to the development and workings of that system. In materials related to the construction of a certain text, often they witness what can feel like an occluded matrix, Dunham-Hickman argues. In this respect the work of Q. D. Leavis, co-founder of *Scrutiny* and author of *Fiction and the Reading Public*, whose archive this chapter references, itself represents the exemplar of such a matrix – a still generally unrecognized body of source material importantly shaping the work of the group associated with the periodical *Scrutiny* and its legacy – and in turn 'the rise of English', the field this group did so much to build. Amongst other notable supporters, Marshall McLuhan valorized Leavis's work in approaching the modernist novel, particularly for attending to 'ground' as well as 'figure' in the cultural environment in which novels were constructed and received. The essay considers the place of such a 'ground', or matrix, in Q. D. Leavis's intellectual trajectory, as well as her development as a public intellectual. Chapter 13 then closes by framing a methodological question about how, in future, archival researchers might handle a newly available set of archival materials associated with Leavis herself. In doing so it also invites us, as modernist scholars, to reflect upon our own practices in the expanding, inclusive territory of archival criticism to which *Historicizing Modernists: Varieties of 'Archivalism' in Modernist Studies* is dedicated.

Notes

1 Ulrika Maude, 'Introduction' to *The Bloomsbury Companion to Modernist Literature*, ed. Ulrika Maude and Mark Nixon (London: Bloomsbury, 2018), p. 1.
2 For a superlative, concise documentary overview of the period, see Steven Matthews, ed., *Modernism: A Sourcebook* (Basingstoke: Palgrave, 2008).
3 Immanuel Kant, *Critique of Pure Reason*, trans. Paul Guyer (Cambridge: Cambridge University Press, 1998 [1781]), p. 99. See also Kant's 'Conjectural Beginning of Human History', in *Toward Perpetual Peace and Other Writings on Politics, Peace, and History*, trans. David L. Colclasure (New Haven: Yale University Press, 2006), 'But creating a historical account entirely out of speculations does not seem much better than drafting the plan for a novel. Indeed, such an account could hardly be called a conjectural history, but rather only a fabricated history', p. 24.
4 A good overview is provided in Naomi Milthorpe, 'Archives, Authority, Aura: Modernism's Archival Turn', *Papers on Language and Literature* 55/1, pp. 3–15.
5 James Knapp, cited in Finn Fordham, 'The Modernist Archive', in *The Oxford Handbook of Modernisms*, ed. Peter Brooker, Andrzej Gąsiorek, Deborah Longworth and Andrew Thacker (Oxford: Oxford University Press, 2010), p. 47.
6 Fordham, 'The Modernist Archive', p. 53.
7 Peter Barry, 'New Historicism and Cultural Materialism', in *Beginning Theory: An Introduction to Literary and Cultural Theory* (Manchester: Manchester University Press, 2002), pp. 174–5.

8 Amy E. Earhart, 'The Era of the Archive: The New Historicist Movement and Digital Literary Studies', in *Traces of the Old, Uses of the New: The Emergence of Digital Literary Studies* (Ann Arbor: University of Michigan Press, 2015), cited pp. 54, 40.
9 Cited in James Gifford, James M. Clawson and Fiona Tomkinson, 'Introduction' to 'Archives & Networks of Modernism', in *Global Review: A Biannual Special Topics Journal* 1/1 (2013), p. iv.
10 See John Brannigan, *New Historicism and Cultural Materialism* (Basingstoke: Palgrave Macmillan, 1998), Part 1; see also Barry, 'New Historicism and Cultural Materialism', pp. 183–4.
11 Cited in Fordham, 'The Modernist Archive', p. 48; and Earhart, 'The Era of the Archive', p. 51.
12 See details for the *Historicizing Modernism* series, www.bloomsbury.com/uk/the-many-drafts-of-d-h-lawrence-9781350139688/ (all websites last accessed 26 July 2020).
13 See, for example, Elliot Morsia, *The Many Drafts of D. H. Lawrence: Creative Flux, Genetic Dialogism, and the Dilemma of Endings* (London: Bloomsbury, 2020); and Michelle E. Moore, *Chicago and the Making of American Modernism: Cather, Hemingway, Faulkner, and Fitzgerald in Conflict* (London: Bloomsbury, 2020).
14 See, respectively, Wayne Chapman, ed., *W.B. Yeats's Robartes-Aherne Writings: Featuring the Making of His 'Stories of Michael Robartes and His Friends'* (London: Bloomsbury, 2018); Thomas Goldpaugh and Jamie Callison, eds., *David Jones's The Grail Mass and Other Works* (London: Bloomsbury, 2018); Mark Byron and Sophia Barnes, *Ezra Pound's and Olga Rudge's* The Blue Spill: *A Manuscript Critical Edition* (London: Bloomsbury, 2019); Stephanie J. Brown, ed., *Edith Ayrton Zangwill's* The Call: *A New Scholarly Edition* (London: Bloomsbury, 2019); Pamela L. Caughie and Sabine Meyer, eds., *Man into Woman: A Comparative Scholarly Edition* (London: Bloomsbury, 2020); Michael T. Davis and Cameron McWhirter, eds., *Ezra Pound and 'Globe' Magazine: The Complete Correspondence* (London: Bloomsbury, 2015); John Goody and Adrian Osbourne, eds., *The Fifth Notebook of Dylan Thomas: Annotated Manuscript Edition* (London: Bloomsbury, 2020); and Thomas Berenato, Anne Price-Owen and Kathleen Henderson Staudt, eds., *David Jones on Religion, Politics, and Culture: Unpublished Prose* (London: Bloomsbury, 2018).
15 With respect to the notoriously restrictive Joyce Estate, for instance, the 'James Joyce Digital Archive' declares in the 'Copyright and Permissions' section of the website: All of James Joyce's works published during his lifetime and everything unpublished as of 1 January 2012 (including all presently 'lost' or 'mislaid' documents) are in the public domain. Other public domain items include 'The Earliest Sections of Finnegans Wake', ed. M. J. C. Hodgart (James Joyce Review, February 1957), *Scribbledehobble: The Ur Workbook for Finnegans Wake*, ed. Thomas E. Connolly (Evanston: Northwestern University Press, 1961), A First-Draft Version of Finnegans Wake, ed. David Hayman (Austin: University of Texas Press, 1963) and the various volumes of the Letters (London: Faber and Faber, 1957, 1966). (http://www.jjda.ie/main/JJDA/JJDAhome.htm.)
16 Series editors' preface to *Modernist Archives*, www.bloomsbury.com/uk/series/modernist-archives/.
17 See Earhart, 'The Era of the Archive', pp. 42ff; and Jacques Derrida, *Archive Fever: A Freudian Impression*, trans. Eric Prenowitz (London: University of Chicago Press, 1996), p. 33.
18 Cited in Earhart, 'The Era of the Archive', p. 61.

19 See, for example, David James, 'Introduction' to *The Legacies of Modernism: Historicising Postwar and Contemporary Fiction*, ed. David James (Cambridge: Cambridge University Press, 2011), pp. 8ff; and Alex Latter, *Late Modernism and The English Intelligencer* (London: Bloomsbury, 2017).
20 See, respectively, K. Paul *Saint-Amour Modernism and Copyright* (Oxford: Oxford University Press, 2010); and Yale University's Beinecke Rare Book and Manuscript Library, digitization of Joseph Conrad's 210 handwritten folios towards Heart of Darkness (*c.* 1899–1902), https://brbl-dl.library.yale.edu/pdfgen/exportPDF.php?bibid=2014001&solrid=3436993.
21 Chris Ackerley, 'The "Distinct Context of Relevant Knowledge": Beckett's "Yellow" and the Phenomenology of Annotation', in *Beckett and Phenomenology*, ed. Ulrika Maude and Matthew Feldman (London: Bloomsbury, 2011), ch. 11.
22 See Alexander Howard, *Charles Henri Ford: Between Modernism and Postmodernism* (London: Bloomsbury, 2017), pp. 1–2.
23 Douglas Mao and Rebecca L. Walkowitz, 'The New Modernist Studies', *PMLA* 123/3 (May 2008), pp. 737–8.
24 See Laetitia Zecchini, *Arun Kolatkar and Literary Modernism in India* (London: Bloomsbury, 2014), ch. 4.
25 Finn Fordham, 'Between Theological and Cultural Modernism: the Vatican's *Oath against Modernism*, September 1910', *Literature & History* 22/1 (Spring 2013), cited pp. 9, 18.
26 See Erik Tonning, *Modernism and Christianity* (Basingstoke: Palgrave, 2014); and Jonas Kurlberg, *Christian Modernism in the Age of Totalitarianism* (London: Bloomsbury, 2020). See also Chrissie van Mierlo, *James Joyce and Catholicism: The Apostate's Wake* (London: Bloomsbury, 2019).
27 See Paul Jackson, *Great War Modernisms and* The New Age *Magazine* (London: Bloomsbury, 2014); and Claire Battershill, *Modernist Lives: Biography and Autobiography at Leonard and Virginia Woolf's Hogarth Press* (London: Bloomsbury, 2014). For different approaches to modernist 'little magazines', for instance, note the different databases and materials compiled in Britain (www.modernistmagazines.com) as against that in the United States (http://modjourn.org); see also the International Dada Archive, www.lib.uiowa.edu/dada/.
28 See, respectively, Natasha Periyan, *The Politics of 1930s British Literature: Education, Class, Gender* (London: Bloomsbury, 2019); Rebecca Bowler, *Literary Impressionism: Vision and Memory in Dorothy Richardson, Ford Madox Ford, H.D. and May Sinclair* (London: Bloomsbury, 2018); David Deutsch, *British Literature and Classical Music: Cultural Contexts 1870–1945* (London: Bloomsbury, 2017); Michelle Witen, *James Joyce and Absolute Music* (London: Bloomsbury, 2019); Caroline Knighton, *Modernist Wastes: Recovery, Re-Use and the Autobiographic in Elsa von Freytag-Loringhoven and Djuna Barnes* (London: Bloomsbury, 2020); and Anne Collett and Dorothy Jones, *Judith Wright and Emily Carr: Gendered Colonial Modernity* (London: Bloomsbury, 2021).
29 For studies of Mansfield, see Janet Wilson, Gerri Kimber and Sue Reid, eds., *Katherine Mansfield and Literary Modernism* (London: Bloomsbury, 2014); and more recently, Aimée Gasston, Gerri Kimber and Janet Wilson, eds., *Katherine Mansfield: New Directions* (London: Bloomsbury, 2020). For works on Samuel Beckett, see Mark Nixon, *Samuel Beckett's German Diaries, 1936–1937* (London: Bloomsbury, 2011); David Tucker, *Samuel Beckett and Arnold Geulincx: Tracing a 'Literary Fantasia'* (London: Bloomsbury, 2014); Anthony Paraskeva, *Samuel Beckett and Cinema* (London: Bloomsbury, 2018); Iain Bailey, *Samuel Beckett and the Bible* (London: Bloomsbury, 2015); John Pilling, *Samuel*

Beckett's More Pricks Than Kicks: *A Strait of Two Wills* (London: Bloomsbury, 2014); Joshua Powell, *Samuel Beckett and Experimental Psychology* (London: Bloomsbury, 2020); William Davies, *Samuel Beckett and the Second World War* (London: Bloomsbury, 2020); and James Little, *Samuel Beckett and Confinement* (London: Bloomsbury, 2020).

30 See Henry Mead, *T.E. Hulme and the Ideological Politics of Early Modernism* (London: Bloomsbury, 2017); Sandeep Parmar, *Reading Mina Loy's Autobiographies: Myth of the Modern Woman* (London: Bloomsbury, 2014); and Susan Schreibman, ed., *The Life and Work of Thomas MacGreevy: A Critical Reappraisal* (London: Bloomsbury, 2014).

31 See, respectively, David Ten Eyck, *Ezra Pound's Adams Cantos* (London: Bloomsbury, 2014); Mark Byron, *Ezra Pound's Eriugena* (London: Bloomsbury, 2016); and Michael Kindellan, *The Late Cantos of Ezra Pound: Composition, Revision, Publication* (London: Bloomsbury, 2019).

32 See Alec Marsh, *John Kasper and Ezra Pound: Saving the Republic* (London: Bloomsbury, 2017); and more recently, idem., *Ezra Pound's Washington Cantos and the Struggle for Light* (London: Bloomsbury, 2021).

33 See Matthew Feldman, *Ezra Pound's Fascist Propaganda, 1935–1945* (Basingstoke: Palgrave, 2013); and 'The "Pound Case" in Historical Perspective: An Archival Overview', in *Politics, Intellectuals and Faith: Essays by Matthew Feldman*, ed. Archie Henderson (ibidem-Verlag: Stuttgart, 2020).

Part I

HISTORICIZING CANONICAL MODERNISTS

1

WOOLFNOTES: VIRGINIA WOOLF'S READING AND RESEARCH NOTES ONLINE

Michèle Barrett

Introduction

The digital edition – available online at WoolfNotes.com – of Virginia Woolf's lifetime reading and research notes aims to expand our knowledge of Woolf by revealing the extent to which her writing, both fiction and non-fiction, was indebted to her personal research on social, historical, economic, political and imperial issues. Her considerable experience of empirical and historical research was occluded, as also was her formal education, both during her lifetime and for many years after her death. Virginia Woolf herself preferred to hide her education and scholarly labours from view, and her widower, family and estate continued to prioritize her reputation as a natural literary genius and 'highbrow' author.

The WoolfNotes project will change understanding of Woolf by providing the materials that correct misleading myths, which have come from conservative and radical scholars alike, about her life and work. The project is a collaboration between two Woolf scholars; it builds on Brenda Silver's authoritative summary of the reading notebooks, published as *Virginia Woolf's Reading Notebooks* in 1983 by Princeton University Press and now available online from the University Press of New England, and secondly my own distinctively historical and sociological approach to Woolf's writing, as found in *Virginia Woolf: Women and Writing* (1979 and still in print), the Penguin edition *of A Room of One's Own and Three Guineas* (1993 and currently a Penguin Modern Classic), and various articles and papers, including 'Virginia Woolf's Research for *Empire and Commerce in Africa* (Leonard Woolf, 1920)', published in *Woolf Studies Annual* in 2013.

This chapter describes the project of digitizing Woolf's reading and research notes, explaining the extent of the materials. It emphasizes the importance of these notes in correcting the myth (partly self-generated) that Woolf was uneducated. It reprises Brenda Silver's definitive account of the contents of the sixty-seven reading notebooks, and explains that the WoolfNotes project will present the facsimiles on screen in conjunction with Silver's authoritative index. The reading notebooks, and Silver's commentary, form the heart of the WoolfNotes project. I have, however, been able to add research materials that do not fit the definition of a reading notebook as such. These include Woolf's extensive research notes on imperialism and international trade. They also include two idiosyncratic notebooks: the *Agamemnon* notebook, which she constructed as a crib for reading in Greek, and a quirky index she made of the contents of Edward Arber's eight-volume anthology of English literature.

WoolfNotes.com project description

Virginia Woolf's habit when reading for work – reading 'seriously', as she put it – was to make notes as she read.[1] The notebooks in which she made notes from her reading total sixty-seven volumes. The original notebooks themselves are in three archives, thirty-three in the Woolf papers at the University of Sussex in the UK, thirty-three in the Berg Collection at the New York Public Library (NYPL), and the remaining one at the Beinecke Library at Yale. Many are in a fragile condition, and many are difficult to read as she was not writing for anyone else and her handwriting, which can be a struggle at the best of times, verges at times on the unreadable. They are easier to read if you know what each one is about, and in 1983 Brenda Silver published detailed summaries of the contents of each of the notebooks. In the currently available digital edition, we have juxtaposed facsimiles of the original notebooks with Silver's summaries of their contents. In addition, the project has added some less well-known notebooks and other manuscripts containing a variety of Woolf's studies and research into classical, historical and factual sources.

Virginia Woolf's notes were usually made by hand in ink. She liked to use coloured inks, frequently turquoise but also purple, and royal blue. The notes on imperialism included in this edition are on 8" by 5" index cards, made of thin paper rather than thick card. The Monks House archive in Sussex contains several stacks of these note cards. Some cards are typed, often with corrections in her distinctive handwriting. There are two main categories of notes, quotations from books, and materials extracted from Consular reports.

The first phase of the project was a complex and lengthy process of working with the three separate archives to scan the original notebooks in order to create high-resolution images. In 2017, I established the permissions and did the preparatory work, then in 2018–19 the scanning was done by all three archives. Apart from time and technical challenges of liaising with different archives, we were concerned to acquire technically compatible images in order to present consistent quality throughout. The technical director of the project, Gilly Furse of Osprey Websites, provided oversight and, where necessary, mentoring of the scanning. All of the archives used manuscript scanning systems which make images with an overhead camera, either flat for loose leaf pages, or in a book cradle and sometimes under glass to weight certain bound volumes. The different archives have achieved good though not exactly similar high-resolution images. Sussex and the NYPL, the archives containing the majority of the manuscripts, use colour reference cards which enable colour fidelity to be checked and corrected if necessary.

To date we have created roughly 7000 images of Woolf's notes. The raw scans of the reading notebooks were completed first, and scans of the index cards of research notes added subsequently. These files, not surprisingly, occupy many gigabytes of raw data, which is the basis for the post-processing in which scans are photoshopped into high-resolution final images for the website. The raw images plus processed versions require considerable disk space extending into terabytes counting all versions of files; this requires storage, upload/download transfers and backup technologies for the project.

The third element of the project is construction of the website itself. The design was worked out at the beginning with the technical director of the project. The website is naturally fairly data-heavy, built in a Content Management System (CMS). Copyright for the whole compilation was cleared with the Woolf Estate; the website is to be free access, based in the UK, and available to the general public. The first online version is scheduled for late 2021, although it may take some time to process and get all the content up.

Debunking the myth of the 'untutored genius'

For background, let me mention the place of 'the social system' in Woolf's writings. In June 1923, thinking about what she was attempting to accomplish with *Mrs Dalloway*, Virginia Woolf declared in her diary that 'I want to criticize the social system, & to show it at work, at its most intense'.[2] The WoolfNotes project uncovers the ways in which Woolf studied what she called 'the social system', and how she learnt to understand how it worked, which was the precondition for showing how it worked in her fiction.

That 1923 diary entry, chosen by Leonard Woolf for his 1953 selection, did not prevent commentators from insisting that there was actually *no* social content in her novels.[3] A. J. P. Taylor pronounced her novels 'irrelevant for the historian'.[4] Malcolm Bradbury, writing in 1970, said that 'for Virginia Woolf consciousness is intuitive and poetic … the flux has no marked social origin'.[5] Walter Allen, in his 1965 survey of the English novel, said that Woolf's characters were 'aesthetes' whose intelligence and self-consciousness weaved a close sieve through which 'the greater part of the common experiences of life will not pass'.[6] Elizabeth Hardwick, writing in 1974 about *The Waves*, complained that there was no plot, no characters and no verisimilitude, that 'her novels aren't interesting'.[7]

These critics are at odds with Virginia Woolf's intentions about showing the social system at work. From the 1970s and 1980s, the interpretative pendulum was to swing in the other direction, with Virginia Woolf appropriated as a radical critic of a modern patriarchal and class-dominated social system. I believe the first British statement of this sociological interpretation was my PhD thesis of 1976, and a publication in 1978, arguing that Woolf's fiction contained a critique of war, religion, academic institutions and the middle-class family.[8] In the sociological language of the time, I concluded that Virginia Woolf's novels contain a fundamental criticism of bourgeois patriarchal society, suggesting that 'although the attack is launched mainly from a feminist perspective it encompasses to some degree a left wing critique of the class system'. In my PhD I outlined the ways in which this underlying critical social agenda had been disguised by her writing's modernist form, private codes of meaning and mystical orientation.

American feminists pushed the issue more strongly, in the course of the 1970s and 1980s, than I did in my collection of Woolf's writings on women,[9] claiming Woolf unambiguously as a heroine of feminism.[10] These issues became contested and, in my judgement, feminist readings of Woolf as a radical eco-warring socialist courted the danger, as I have argued previously,[11] of exaggerating the radicalism of a deeply ambivalent political subject. Underlying this debate is the fact that Woolf left much of her explicit content about the 'social system' on the cutting room floor. The progressive drafts of *The Waves*, for instance, show that her text becomes increasingly more abstracted from personal social experiences. But they remain present in an oblique manner, and can be traced to her own understanding of the mechanics of how social systems 'work'. The development of this understanding is unveiled in the research materials published in WoolfNotes.com, which is surveyed below.

Evidence from Woolf's reading notes: Brenda Silver's research

Since the 1983 publication of Brenda Silver's authoritative account of the sixty-seven holograph volumes of Virginia Woolf's reading notebooks, it has been clear that they constitute an enormous repository of information about how she amassed information about the subjects on which she was to write.[12] Her reading covered a wide range of subjects in history, anthropology, biography, science and journalism. There are also more predictable literary sources across a number of languages. Since their publication in the 1970s, Woolf scholars as well as the general public have become increasingly interested in Woolf's easily available *Diaries* and *Letters*. Since then, Silver's catalogue of reading notebooks, pointing to material held in archives at Sussex (the Monks House Papers held at The Keep), the Berg Collection at the NYPL, and the Beinecke Library at Yale,[13] has been less used than it deserves.

Silver's preface to the original edition of the *Reading Notebooks* in 1983 summarizes the contents of the notebooks:

> The majority of the entries in these volumes are those Woolf made when reading for reviews, for critical or biographical essays, for her own information about a subject, or for background for a book. Two notebooks contain early translations and comments on Greek and Latin literature; one, notes for *Flush*; eleven, notes for *Three Guineas*; eight, notes for *Roger Fry: A Biography*; and three, notes for the history of English literature that was to open with 'Anon' and 'The Reader'. Other notebooks trace the development of single essays, of the ideas about novels that resulted in 'Phases of Function', of the eighty or so starts she claimed

> to have made on the first *Common Reader* and the three years she spent on *The Common Reader: Second Series*.[14]

Silver goes on to emphasize the importance of the notes:

> Even the briefest glance at the reading notes is enough to show their crucial role in Woolf's growth as critic, biographer, historian, and feminist, and the seriousness she brought to her tasks. No matter what the subject, no matter how long or short the piece, she sought out the relevant letters and diaries, biographies and autobiographies, histories and criticism – both contemporary and modern – that would place the work and its author in their literary and cultural contexts.[15]

Silver further quotes Woolf's 1938 comment about her thirty-year stint writing reviews for the *Times Literary Supplement*: that she 'was made to read with a pen and notebook, seriously'.[16] Woolf's notebooks chart the development of this serious reader, providing a detailed record of what she read and what she thought of it, for her own novels and essays, for her own interest, as well as for commissioned book reviews. The notebooks enabled her to record facts, and quotations, as well as to comment on what she was reading. Silver had previously shown, in publishing Woolf's draft essays 'Anon' and 'The Reader', that the reading notebooks include materials (in notebooks 16 and 21) for her last and unfinished project – a book ranging across the whole of English literature 'as' (Woolf noted in her diary) 'I've read and noted it'.[17]

Silver, in her 1983 *Reading Notebooks*, quotes Woolf's note on Goldsmith's *The Vicar of Wakefield*: 'The social machinery seems to have imposed a pretty sharp mould upon 18th Cent. Fiction.'[18] Silver's account of the notebooks shows, beyond his daughter's inheritance of Leslie Stephen's social, indeed sociological, analysis, Woolf herself moving towards a more critical stance towards social and political institutions. Sir Leslie Stephen was Virginia Woolf's father and an important influence on her early reading and education. In her earliest diaries she describes him bringing her books she wanted to read, and giving her the run of his library. Many of his own copies of books can be found in her library, now housed at the University of Washington at Pullman. Leslie Stephen arranged for her to attend the King's College London Ladies Department from 1897 (she was aged fifteen), where she studied History, German, Greek and Latin.[19]

The scholarly side of Woolf's note-taking

I have recently examined the extensive notes Woolf made when acting as a research assistant for Leonard Woolf in 1917–18.[20] This exciting collection, discussed by Wayne Chapman in 1998,[21] forms a significant part of WoolfNotes.com. This material, in Virginia Woolf's hand in the Leonard Woolf archive at Sussex, consists of empirical information about international trade and about British imperialism, particularly in Africa. The notes clarify that Virginia Woolf was extremely knowledgeable about these subjects; in turn, this new view paves the way for new readings of key texts such as *Night and Day* and *The Waves*. It seems likely that this large collection of original materials compiled by Virginia Woolf will alter the ways in which we understand her fiction and non-fiction with regard to questions of imperialism, economics and politics.

A closer look at these 1917–18 materials is useful. These notes are composed of over 700 8" × 5" folios, mainly in her own hand – or typed and corrected in her hand – used in Leonard Woolf's *Empire and Commerce in Africa* (1920). The research materials include Virginia Woolf's notes from substantial publications about European imperialism in Africa: Wylde's *Modern Abyssinia*, Lugard's T*he Rise of Our East African Empire* and many others. She read and made notes on extensive French and Italian sources, and also displayed a flourishing scholarly style of footnoting.

These works on imperialism include her hundreds of pages of notes on international trade at the end of the nineteenth century, and its bearing on colonial power relations. Virginia Woolf read, gutted and quoted from British consular reports – literally starting at the Argentine Republic and ending with Zanzibar. Much of the material she copied was quantitative indications of imports and exports. Her notes from the 1897 report on Trebizond (Turkey), concerning the massacre of Armenians in the 1890s, throw new light on this issue, as it is represented in *Mrs Dalloway*. Using her research notes on British Consular Reports from Turkey, concerning the Hamidian massacres of the 1890s, we can reconsider the Armenian question raised in this novel. As I suggest below, we can say at the least that Clarissa Dalloway's ignorance of the facts was not shared by her author.

Woolf's style of note-taking differed from the synthesizing summaries her husband produced of the materials they read for *Empire and Commerce*. Her notes for that project, on the other hand, revelled in the immediacy of exact quotation and in a directly literary apprehension of the language she was reading. In a reminiscence of her brother Thoby as a student, Woolf wrote: 'He was not, as I was, a breaker off of single words or sentences – not a note-taker – he was much more casual and rough and ready and comprehensive.'[22] The voice of Bernard in *The Waves* shares this habit with his author: 'I keep my phrases hung like clothes in a cupboard, waiting for someone to wear them.'[23] Woolf's practice in her reading notebooks was to use both forms, combining direct quotation with personal response and commentary.

In my 2013 article, I discuss why Virginia Woolf undertook this research for Leonard Woolf's book on imperialism. The likeliest answer is that it was considered therapeutic work after a major breakdown. A life-long scholar, who as a teenager was reading ambitious works of history and philosophy, the habit of reading and researching was reassuring to her. It was her own writing that caused anxiety, not reading and taking notes about the work of other people. Even many years after her death, Leonard Woolf did not see fit, discussing that book in his autobiography, to acknowledge the contribution she had made to *Empire and Commerce*.[24] Why, however, was she so keen to hide both her formal education and the amount of serious research that underlies her fiction? It was a stance that her husband, her family and the estate have appeared to support over the years. Hence the myth that she was simply a genius who sprang from nowhere.

Woolf's education and scholarly habits of study

We now know that Woolf's repeated claim to have been educated solely through her father's library is untrue, and that she studied several subjects at Kings College London Ladies Department.[25] The library she inherited from Leslie Stephen has been preserved at Washington State University in Pullman. This large collection of the Woolfs' own books provides another useful source of information about her education and reading.[26] Evidence of her adolescent studies in Greek can be found in her own library, which includes an annotated Homer. In similar vein, her reading notebooks include passages copied in the original Greek, alongside her attempts at translations. The Woolf library also holds Virginia Stephen's copy of Hakluyt's *Principal Navigations, Voyages, Traffics and Discoveries of the English Nation*. This calf-bound and name-plated edition includes a piece by Francis Drake that Virginia Woolf used as the basis for her description of Santa Marina in *The Voyage Out* (1915). Although Virginia Woolf did not annotate her books, her husband has left extensive comments at the back of many of their books.

The discovery by Christine Kenyon Jones and Anna Snaith that Virginia Stephen (later Woolf) had studied History, German, Greek and Latin at the King's College Ladies Department in Kensington in 1897–1901 was published in 2010. It opens up exploration of the historiography she encountered from Professor Laughton at King's, which has now been analysed by Clara Jones.[27] The fact that she took formal exams in German at King's – in both of which she secured an Upper Second – is intriguing in light of her outsider stance about universities.[28] Woolf's persistent claim, in private correspondence as well as in well-known public statements, that she had not been educated was therefore mendacious. Her experience as a detailed and dogged empirical researcher has also been minimized in her authorial profile as an inspirational genius. Woolf is an unreliable narrator of her own life, as a comparison between the argument of *A Room of One's Own* and her own strikingly different financial behaviour illustrates.[29] Access to Woolf's notebooks and manuscripts can shed light on apparently seamlessly inspired writing passages which are, in actuality, underlain by considerable literary or historical scholarship.

Example: Woolf's notes on Wordsworth

Woolf's reading notebooks document and illustrate the life of a professional writer. They are absolutely capacious. To take one tiny but interesting question – what did Virginia Woolf think about the poet Wordsworth? We know that she published an essay on his sister Dorothy in the context of thinking about illness.[30] We also know that in 1906, under the cloak of anonymity in the *Times Literary Supplement*, she reviewed Wordsworth's *Guide to the Lakes*, admiring 'the terse veracity of the poet's prose' – whilst jibbing slightly at the fact that he 'condescends more than a poet should' in giving tips on accommodation to travellers.[31] Apparently she was paid £9.7s for her review, announcing to Violet Dickinson that it was 'the largest sum I have ever made at one blow'.[32] In 1911 she wrote, with a typical mix of seriousness and humour, to Saxon Sydney-Turner: 'I am reading the Prelude [The Prelude, by Wordsworth]. Don't you think it one of the greatest works ever written? Some of it, anyhow, is sublime: it may get worse.'[33]

What, over a lifetime, did Woolf think of Wordsworth's poetry? There are seventeen references in the Pullman catalogue to books by or about Wordsworth that were in the Woolfs' personal library. Some of these are signed by or bookplated to Virginia Woolf, including two copies of *The Prelude*. If we search Brenda Silver's text we find that Wordsworth occurs in seven of Woolf's reading notebooks: 9, 20, 24, 30, 35, 38 and 47. This last (47) casts some interesting light on the question. It is a large notebook, containing twenty-eight entries and running to nearly seventy pages. Brenda Silver dated its contents to the period 1923/24. There is only one page on Wordsworth, and she is back to *The Prelude*, reading Book 7, the section entitled 'Residence in London'. On this page Woolf made two notes underneath substantial quotations from the poem, the first showing how she saw her work as a fiction writer, and the second her work as a critic.

> The matter that detains us now may seem,
> To many, neither dignified enough
> Nor arduous, yet will not be scorned by them,
> Who, looking inward, have observed the ties
> That bind the perishable hours of life
> Each to the other, and the curious props
> By which the world of memory and thought
> Exists and is sustained

Underneath this extract, Woolf has written: 'Good quotation for one of my books'.

Albeit passed over by Silver, the second extract that she has copied out is as follows:

> But though the picture weary out the eye,
> By nature an unmanageable sight,
> It is not wholly so to him who looks
> In steadiness, who hath among least things
> An under-sense of greatest; sees the parts
> As parts, but with a feeling of the whole.

To this passage Woolf has added, in her own voice: 'This shd. [should] be true of criticism.'

This folio also presents us with an issue that has determined the format of the digital edition. Underneath the 'good quotation for one of my books' line is another, about Wordsworth's language, and it is very difficult to read, although 'nicety' has been suggested by Stuart Clarke. Silver leaves it out in her book; yet in the digital edition, the reader is free to decipher it in their own time. The difficulty of reading Woolf's handwriting, particularly when she was writing solely for her own eyes, makes the prospect of a full transcription of the materials difficult. As time goes by, transcriptions of sections or individual notebooks will appear, but it is not feasible to provide a full transcription at this point. Clara Jones, of King's College London, is now a member of the WoolfNotes team and a rolling programme of solicited transcriptions from Woolf scholars, which she and I will curate, will be added to the edition over time. The function of the WoolfNotes project is to make these materials available to everyone, with the enormous benefit of juxtaposing them with Brenda Silver's index. On a screen it will be possible to read the original text side by side with the summary that enables the reader to make the best sense of it.

As suggested above, Brenda Silver's 1983 review of the *Reading Notebooks* facilitates many fascinating insights into Woolf's reading and research. In taking a different methodological tack, the digital edition of WoolfNotes.com takes the opportunity to add a selection of other relevant Woolf manuscripts. As these are less well-known, some examples follow.

The Agamemnon Notebook

One significant highlight is the *Agamemnon Notebook*, a unique item relating to Woolf's reading of Aeschylus. This is held in the Berg Collection at the NYPL. It is an extraordinarily evocative thing, paying tribute to Woolf's abiding interest in Greek and also to her fearlessly individual approach to book making and binding. The book is like one of those crib texts with the original on one side and a translation on the other; in this case, she has pasted the original on the right and the translation on the left. The contents have been padded out with cut-up pieces of printed paper, presumably to fit the hard cover she has chosen.

The classicist Yopie Prins has explained exactly how Woolf made it:

> To make this book, Woolf cut up an older Greek edition of the play (published in 1831 by Charles James Blomfield) and pasted the printed text into the right side of each page. On the left side she transcribed by hand, in variously black and blue ink from her fountain pen, a prose translation from Professor Arthur Verrall (published in 1904, an annotated edition with Greek and English on facing pages). Woolf wrote at the time, 'I am making a complete edition, text, translation & notes of my own – mostly copied from Verrall, but carefully gone into by me.' Unpublished and unauthorized, her private 'edition' was less a translation than a transcription, to which Woolf added a few variations with occasional marks and remarks in the margins, commenting on passages of interest or defining Greek words that she had underlined and looked up in the Greek-English dictionary. After several months of trying 'to make out what

> Aeschylus wrote' and 'master the *Agamemnon*', Woolf was pleased to proclaim in her diary, 'I now know how to read Greek quick (with a crib in one hand) & with pleasure.'[34]

Yopie Prins has published a substantial and fascinating discussion of Woolf's *Agamemnon* notebook, now forming a section of her book *Ladies Greek*. She has agreed (pending publisher's approval) to make her essay available on the WoolfNotes website as a companion to and interpretation of this unique notebook.[35]

Woolf's notes from historical sources and their use in her fiction

As the name suggests, the WoolfNotes digital edition is more broadly titled than Silver's account of the 'reading notebooks'. This is because it includes materials that do not meet the criteria for a reading notebook as such, but are nonetheless germane to Woolf's reading practice (or to her research notes). Another example is the index she made for herself of items of interest in an anthology of English literary and historical writing. The anthology was Edward Arber's *An English Garner: Ingatherings from Our History and Literature*, published in eight volumes between 1877 and 1896, and it is described, in Anne Olivier Bell's accompanying archival note, as 'Reprints of English literary texts between Caxton and Addison'.[36] Woolf has used the flyleaf to announce its title, in the turquoise ink used throughout the book: *Arber's English Garner*. Turning to the title page, she repurposed an address book for her index: The Commercial 'Where Is It?' No 61, published by John Walker & Co Ltd. She stuck a stationery label on the spine, with *Arber* on it. Each entry in the index includes the topic, in alphabetical order, and many then attach a date; all entries give the volume of the anthology and the page reference.

The items that Woolf decided to index, for easy reference to a large group of sources, throw light on her historical interests. The book starts with the first entry under A, 'Angling, Secrets of, J.D. 1631/1.141'. This is a reference to *The Secrets of Angling*, a long pastoral poem eventually attributed to John Dennys, which was published posthumously in four editions, ranging from 1613 to 1652. Further entries under A include 'Army, Ranks in British, 1630 1.463' [i.e. vol 1 of Arber], while also on the Army there is 'Army Rations in time of Eliz: 2.206'. There are also two entries on America: 'America, annals of to 1633. 2. 287' and 'America, Present State of, 1624. 2. 285'. The important category for Woolf of 'anonymous' appears on this page as 'Anonymous, 17th Cent.poems. 3. 395'. Anne Boleyn gets three references, to her coronation, to the verses at her coronation, and to the 'triumph at Calais & B[oulogne]'.

The letter C in Woolf's curious index to Arber's *Garner* begins with 'Carriers Cosmography. 1. 223 account of Inns re. 1637'. This is a reference to John Taylor's guide to the inns and lodgings where carriers of things and people on different routes around the country could be found. This directory was itself also alphabetical, going through the various English towns from St Albans, whose carriers arrived every Friday in London and were to be found at the Peacock in Aldersgate, to York, whose carriers lodged at The Bell without Ludgate.

This 'C' page of Woolf's index also contains several entries related to her interest in early modern maritime exploration, for example, 'Cavendish Voyage round world 2.117'. In turn, 'Cowley, A. Drinking in Drake's Chair 2. 269' is a reference to Abraham Cowley's Ode of 1663 'Sitting and Drinking in the Chair, made out of the Reliques of Sir Francis Drake's Ship'.[37] The index is significant in that some of these materials get worked into her novels – readers of Woolf's *Orlando* will not be surprised by an entry for 'Frost, Great. 1608 1. 77'. The dramatic description of the great frost in London in 1608 in *Orlando* takes many of its compelling details from Thomas Dekker's pamphlet 'The Great Frost' (Cold Doings in London. A Dialogue.) which was included in Arber's anthology.[38] Richard Hakluyt's compilation of maritime narratives in his *The Principall Navigations, Voiages, Traffiques and Discoueries of the English Nation* (1589–1600) had been read and loved by Woolf since her teenage years and was used by her to add colour to her fiction. Woolf's beloved Hakluyt makes several appearances in the Arber index. Under H, naturally enough, we find 'Hakluyt. R. Acct of Trade with Levant 1.20'. Many narratives of voyages occur under the letter V, including several to be found in Hakluyt's collection.

Inclusion of Woolf's idiosyncratic index to Edward Arber's *An English Garner* raises some of the editorial and technical issues posed by digital editions. Woolf has used a small bound book for it, while many of her notebooks are loose leaved. Some she has covered or bound herself. The archive materials include not only repurposed bound books (or their covers), and loose pages, but also informally created books with cuttings or other material stuck into them; groups of pages connected by treasury tags, rusting paperclips and punched hole systems. No less than six notebooks in the Berg collection have been partially jacketed with the boards of a Robert Graves book, *The Feather Bed* – presumably lying around at the Hogarth Press at a convenient moment. The objective in making the digital edition has not been simply to indicate the range of the content of Woolf's notes, which usually are found on the recto pages of bound or looseleaf notebooks, but to reproduce Woolf's notes as material texts. This democratizes scholarship and allows for anyone to interpret them online. This has meant that the items have been scanned as objects, including covers, endpapers and miscellaneous notes on otherwise blank verso pages. The first of our two most important objectives has been visual authenticity, and these materials have ben represented exactly as found in the archive. The second important objective has been readability, since Woolf's handwriting can be difficult to read.

Empire and Commerce *notes for Leonard Woolf*

The development of the WoolfNotes project makes available a fascinating collection of research notes on imperialism and international trade, as noted above, made by Virginia Woolf during the 1917/18 period. She read a wide variety of books, writing by hand or typing detailed notes, which are now in Leonard Woolf's papers in Sussex. This work was initially intended for a book on International Trade, and for, one he did subsequently write, *Empire and Commerce in Africa* (1920).

Virginia Woolf's notes were to assist her husband with the book that he was writing for the Fabian Society. Materials were collected and analysed for a general work on international trade, but the book ultimately published was a more focused account of imperialism in Africa, especially the northern and eastern parts of the continent. The Woolfs conducted extensive international research in order to give a global context for this study of Africa.

These research notes total 783 folios, approximately 8" × 5" in size. They shed light on Virginia and Leonard Woolf's relationship as well as the ideas they shared about British imperialism. They also reveal Virginia Woolf to be a meticulous, even slightly pedantic scholar. The research notes include an enormous amount of empirical information about international trade, including many hand-drawn tables. They demonstrate her facility with factual data, often disguised in her fiction.

The quotation cards

The first category of index cards is materials that found their way into the text of Leonard Woolf's *Empire and Commerce in Africa.* These consist of a pile, an inch or so high, of thin cards, mainly consisting of quotations from the books that Virginia Woolf consulted. These include works such as the *Memoirs of Francesco Crispi* (in three volumes), F. D. Lugard's *The Rise of Our East African Empire* (in two volumes), P. L. McDermott's *British East Africa* and Augustus Wylde's *Modern Abyssinia.* In addition to works in English, Virginia Woolf made extensive notes (in French) from a book by Jean Darcy, and from Alfred Rambaud's book on Jules Ferry. She also made notes in Italian from Lincoln de Castro's *Nella Terra Dei Negus: pagine raccolte in Abissinia.* These longhand notes were organized into regional and thematic classifications, added in the top right-hand corner in Leonard Woolf's handwriting.

These notes run to a total of 117 sides of notecards. Of these, sixty-seven are in her handwriting and approximately fifty typed notecards can also be attributed to her. Virginia Woolf's reading notes, in this collection, are mainly in the form of carefully referenced quotations rather than summaries of arguments. One of Leonard Woolf's significant sources of evidence was a book by the French historian Jean Darcy: *France et Angleterre: Cent Années de Rivalité Coloniale: L'Afrique* (1904). Virginia Woolf's extensive notes from Darcy include some with an altogether scholarly style of footnoting. One handwritten quotation from Darcy is embellished with two footnotes, in superior script and underlined in the text, in French, citing such mundane British sources as the *Daily Chronicle* and *The Times.*

This run of index cards includes one that has clearly been made by Leonard Woolf; it is distinguishable from Virginia Woolf's notes as he made summaries of arguments rather than simply copying out quotations, and he has typed in his own subject headings at the top. For his chapter on 'Tunis and Tripoli' Leonard

Woolf relied heavily on the memoirs of Francesco Crispi, particularly the third volume, published in 1914. The extensive research notes on this source are all made in Virginia Woolf's hand. Similarly, F. D. Lugard looms large in *Empire and Commerce*, in terms of both his actions and his personal values. Leonard Woolf went to the trouble of sorting out his contentious strategy, and discusses his movements in some detail. Virginia Woolf seems to have read Lugard's long memoir with an eye to finding quotations illustrating his imperialist attitudes.

These materials on imperialism in Africa provide striking evidence of a Virginia Woolf even more incensed by British imperialism than her publicly anti-imperialist husband. They show her familiarity with the rhetoric of imperialism, and with its poor historical record. Her research on these materials was extensive, but the amount of background reading that she undertook on the global economic context of imperialism in Africa in the 1890s was still more so. This work involved not just reading and making notes from discursive books on the subject, but ploughing through factual reports, made by British consular officials around the world, in turn representing a considerable amount of quantified empirical data.

Virginia Woolf's summaries of Consular Reports

The second category, larger than the 117 index cards that were to be used in *Empire and Commerce*, consists of the notes that Virginia Woolf made from British Consular Reports around the world, when the project was defined broadly as 'International Trade'. These include lengthy quotations and detailed reproductions of information – presented in tabular form – covering imports and exports, immigration and other subjects. In total there are 666 folios, in Virginia Woolf's own hand, of notes from these British Consular Reports on international trade.

These notes are largely made up of quotations, mostly, though not exclusively, from British official consular reports. They contain a great deal of factual information – particularly about imports and exports during the 1890s, the period of the 'scramble for Africa'. According to the National Archives, these reports take up fifteen metres of their own shelves, and many UK libraries hold copies. We know from correspondence that Sydney Webb arranged for the Woolfs to use the copies held at the London School of Economics and Political Science.

In compiling this information, Virginia Woolf frequently copied it out by hand in tabular form. As with materials used in *Empire and Commerce*, these notes are typically in longhand, although some are typed, and usually carry in the top right-hand corner of Leonard Woolf's classification of the subject matter (occasionally this is in Virginia Woolf's hand). The reports themselves are printed chronologically, but Virginia Woolf's research notes, and hence the WoolfNotes project, follow alphabetical order. Starting with the Argentine Republic, Virginia Woolf made several note cards from an 1893 Consular Report. All her notes are properly referenced, in this instance with an underlined Cons Rep Argentine Republic no 1147–1893.

Several cards relate to general trade statistics. They are usually defined, in Leonard Woolf's hand, by themes such as 'Commercial Treaties' or the 'Foreign Trade'. Other cards cover specific trading issues. Under the headings of 1889–90, 'Frozen meat,' Virginia Woolf has copied out, from the1893 Consular Report, the following prosaic details:

> Another large item was 662,000 Kilos of frozen cattle. The frozen sheep export trade has developed immensely, from 12,000 carcasses in 1887 to 20,000 carcasses in 1890. Of exports under this head England took about one-fourth, & Brazil took most of the fallow, fat, preserved tongues, preserved meat, all the frozen cattle, & nearly all the frozen sheep.

On the material transcribed, there are no comments, other than the choice of what she was copying. The collection runs on with notes on Bulgaria, Chile, China, 'Corea', Costa Rica, Cuba, Denmark, Ecuador, Egypt and a large section of ninety-five folios of comments on France. Leonard Woolf has headed an opening page 'France Trade of France for past 12 years Consular Report 1889. No 622. Important for French Colonial Policy and Statistics.' General statistical information is presented here, as in another hand-drawn table by Virginia Woolf, on the 'Value of French Trade with Chief Commercial Nations Exports', this section itemizing trade with the UK, Belgium, Germany and the United States. Somewhat amateurishly, she has not left enough space for the far right column of 1898. This table underlines the emphasis that was later to appear in *Empire and Commerce* on the last decade of the nineteenth century.

These records pile on: the sixty-three pages on Germany are followed by Greece, Guatemala, Hayti [VW's spelling], Holland and Italy, which takes these notes, counting only those in Virginia Woolf's own hand, to 391 sides. Woolf's thirty-nine cards on Japan, nine on Mexico, and through Morocco, Nicaragua, Norway, Paraguay, Persia, Portugal, 'Roumania' – are all in modest numbers until we reach Russia with forty-eight pages. The notes run on through Serbia, Siam, Spain, Sweden, Switzerland, Tunis and to Turkey. From Turkey to Uruguay and to the United States, which devotes several notes to America's acquisitions of new states, for example, Hawaii and 'Porto Rico'.

The collection concludes with Zanzibar, whose imports and exports in a tabular form were faithfully copied out by Virginia Woolf from the 1902 Consular Report. The country column on the left starts with 'British India' and 'German East Africa', an emphasis that well concludes this immense series of notes about international trade. Zanzibar provides a fitting end to the series, linking all this broad contextual research on international trade with the more precise, and more political, research that Virginia Woolf undertook for Leonard Woolf's *Empire and Commerce in Africa*.

Virginia Woolf refrained from making summaries of arguments, or commenting on what she was reading, simply copying out passages or tables that had attracted attention. This is very different from the way in which she made notes when she was reading for herself rather than for Leonard's work, as is shown in a comparison between these research notes and her own reading notebooks. She was acting as a research assistant for his work on imperialism and her notes are in the scholarly tradition. Her own creative notes are alive and interactive, full of summaries and summative comments, with quotations bound into her responses to what she was reading.

Example: Reference to Armenia in Mrs Dalloway

By way of extended conclusion, it is worth focusing on one particular instance of knowledge that Virginia Woolf gained from her research on the Consular Reports. This material may help to reconsider the controversial issue of the portrayal of the Armenian question in *Mrs Dalloway*. Virginia Woolf made forty-six sides of notes on consular reports from Turkey, which largely centred on Britain's lack of competitiveness, in particular the lack of salesmen and failure to guarantee prices for freight, which their competitors did. In hindsight, the decline of the Ottoman Empire can be seen in these reports, spanning from 1890 to the mid-1890s and covering the then Ottoman-held Aleppo, Beyrout, Damascus, Jerusalem, Palestine and Tripoli.

One noteworthy report contains a reference to the massacres of Armenians in 1894–96. Virginia Woolf copied this passage from the Trebizond consular report of 1897. Trebizond [now Trabzon] on the southern coast of the Black Sea was at the western end of the Silk Route, where many of the 1894–96 Armenian Massacres occurred. This violent episode from the end of the Ottoman Empire is sometimes considered a precursor to the Armenian genocide of the First World War period.

As is now well known, the massacres of this period were brutal. The historian Mark Levene describes an Armenian demonstration in Constantinople, put down with extreme ferocity 'the Hamidian regime in effect having given the "mob" the green light to kill with impunity'. 'Beginning in Trabzon [Trebizond], the killings ebbed back and forth across all of eastern Anatolia … before culminating in one particularly grizzly assault in Urfa [in December 1896] in which not only was there a general massacre in the Armenian quarter but some 3000 people, who had taken refuge in its cathedral, were burnt to death when it was torched with kerosene.'[39]

Virginia Woolf's consular source notes 'Commerce in 1896 was almost completely paralysed by the gravity of the political situation', and that 'a specific review of the trade of the year wd. scarcely serve any useful purpose'. But the report was more concerned with the weakness of British trade competitiveness against Germany and Austria. Leonard Woolf classified it as '1896 Trebizond Turkey Germ. Competn.'; considering only its significance for trade, Virginia Woolf, however, registered the human significance of these events.

The reference to the Armenians in *Mrs Dalloway* takes on new relevance in light of these materials. It is after lunch. Richard Dalloway has given his wife some red and white roses, and is going out. 'He must be off', he said, 'getting up'. 'Some Committee?' she asked, as he opened the door. 'Armenians', he said; or perhaps it was 'Albanians'. Dalloway returns with a pillow and a quilt, repeating a doctors prescription for an hour's complete rest after luncheon. Clarissa Dalloway then muses:

> He was already half-way to the House of Commons, to his Armenians, his Albanians, having settled her on the sofa, looking at his roses. And people would say, 'Clarissa Dalloway is spoilt.' She cared much more for her roses than for the Armenians. Hunted out of existence, maimed, frozen, the victims of cruelty and injustice (she had heard Richard say so over and over again) – no, she could feel nothing for the Albanians, or was it the Armenians? but she loved her roses (didn't that help the Armenians?) – the only flowers she could bear to see cut. But Richard was already at the House of Commons; at his Committee, having settled all her difficulties. But no; alas, that was not true.[40]

Trudi Tate has argued, in a challenge to what she sees as 'current feminist thinking' about the novel, that Woolf is here both satirizing and condemning Clarissa Dalloway's 'preposterous' childishness and refusal of responsibility.[41] Like Mrs Ramsay, Mrs Dalloway is a complex figure for feminists. Women's ignorance is part of the cultural structure that took Britain to war. Tate suggests that June 1923, when *Mrs Dalloway* is set, was the key moment in Britain's long history of betrayal of the Armenians. Richard Dalloway, after giving his wife the roses, then goes off to the committee that negotiates their fate. Tate argues that the historical setting of *Mrs Dalloway* is very precise, that Virginia Woolf was well informed about the Armenian issues, and has written a text 'judgmental of her [CD] and of her entire class'.[42]

Woolf also specifically records Clarissa Dalloway musing 'She could not think, write, even play the piano. She muddled Armenians and Turks; loved success, hated discomfort, must be liked; talked oceans of nonsense: and to this day, ask her what the Equator was, and she did not know'.[43] By comparison there can be no possibility that Virginia Woolf herself muddled Armenians and Turks; we know she was actually extremely well-informed on this topic.

Biographically, the issue went deeper than Consular Reports. In 1906 Virginia Stephen, aged twenty-four, travelled with her siblings to Greece and Turkey. Arriving in Athens her diary reveals a very romantic Hellenophile: 'like a free English woman I will deal deliberately with the days adventures, whether they are significant or irrelevant. And after all, every step is on sacred ground.'[44] The Stephen family, mounted on donkeys, climbed Mount Pentelicos in Greece, described by Virginia Stephen in her 1906 diary.[45] Thoby and Adrian had taken a month to get there on horseback, travelling through Montenegro, Dalmatia and Albania. Thoby Stephen returned to England while the others continued on to Constantinople and, as we now know, Vanessa was to be taken ill with appendicitis and Thoby had contracted typhoid, from which he died back in London.[46]

Arriving in Constantinople, on the deck of the boat at 6 am to watch the dawn, Virginia Stephen was bowled over by the sight of Santa Sophia, 'like a treble globe of bubbles frozen solid, floating out to meet us'.[47] Later during this visit, she wrote a diary entry on the subject of faith, business and life, the context of a contentious remark about the Armenian conflict:

> There is faith enough; & business enough; & life enough to keep both eddying swiftly along the stream. No one who has visited the Mosques & the bazaars can doubt the force of the current. But at the same time, no one knows exactly where it tends; a dozen stories of the place show that it can take a subterranean channel, & it was not ten years ago that the Turks and Armenians massacred each other in the streets. So perhaps if it were your lot to spend your life here you might think your station one of some risk – as a resting place beneath a volcano.[48]

Thus the Consular reports Virginia Woolf was researching ten or so years later were describing places she knew and had visited – indeed, had an emotional connection with, and this formed part of the knowledge that she brought to bear when dealing with the representation of Armenians, in *Mrs Dalloway*. It might be relevant, too, that Leonard Woolf, for whom she was doing the research in 1917–18, had a strong interest in the Armenian genocide. In his autobiography he described Gladstone's campaign against the Hamidian massacres of the 1890s: 'I was fourteen years old at the time and it was my first profound political experience.' Invoking a teacher whose 'passionate indignation had a great effect on me', he recalled that 'I could almost see the helpless Armenians being bayoneted by the Turkish soldiers and the women and children fleeing and floundering through the snowdrifts'.[49] As this suggests, Virginia Woolf surely knew the difference between the Armenians, about whom she had read such a lot, and Albanians, whose country her brothers had ridden through on the ill-fated trip of 1906.

That example, which I have drawn from the rather enigmatic British consular reports from Turkey that Virginia Woolf worked on in 1917/18, helps our thinking about the issue of the Armenians in *Mrs Dalloway*. Woolf's comprehensive research notes clarify that she was not ignorant and uneducated, entirely the reverse. The function of WoolfNotes is to bring these connections to light, facilitating further study and thinking about her literary work. Beverly Schlack's book, *Continuing Presences: Virginia Woolf's Use of Literary Allusion*, published in 1979, provided many interesting identifications.[50] There is more interest now in the hinterland of scholarship that underlay her fiction, and in the range and depth of her own reading, for example, in modern editions of Woolf work, such as the one from Cambridge University Press, or Barbara Lounsberry's studies of the diaries that she read as well as of her own diaries.[51]

In this chapter I have merely sketched some examples where knowledge of her own reading and research notes casts new light on how we interpret her literary work. In the case of Woolf, the relationship between her final texts and their predecessors and sources is often ambiguous and occluded. Some of her work is graced with an academic apparatus, as we find in *Three Guineas* and *Flush*; in other cases, for example, the Preface to *Orlando*, factual veracity is mocked. This writer, comparing the claims of history and fiction, declared that 'where truth is important, I prefer to write fiction'.[52] We may not accept the distinction, or agree that a choice must be made. The late Julia Briggs, writing in 2006 about *Orlando*, gestures towards a complexity in Woolf's writing that the WoolfNotes project aims to help us appreciate:

> Behind Woolf's fiction, as always, lay an extraordinary range of reading, a weight of serious thought and knowledge, worn so lightly that we are scarcely aware of it: the butterfly wing of fiction, fantasy and imagination are, after all, always underpinned by the stone arches of history and politics, and clamped together with the iron bolts of fact.[53]

Author's Note

I would like to thank Brenda Silver, a collaborator on this project, for her work on the reading notebooks. She provided not only summaries of the notebooks, but invaluable context and commentary. The idea of the WoolfNotes.com project was to bring her original scholarship (published in 1983) alive, using the technology now at our disposal, by presenting it alongside the contents of the notebooks themselves, making them publicly available. Her contribution to this project, which we began working on in 2016, has been essential, and much appreciated. I would also like to thank the technical director of the project, Gilly Furse, of Osprey Websites, whose contribution – on both the technical and research side – has been critical to its viability and success. Clara Jones has now joined the team and I am grateful to her for our continuing collaboration in Woolf studies. Other colleagues, including Nadia Atia, Catherine Lee and Victoria Walker, have made contributions for which I am very grateful. I am also grateful to Matthew Feldman for his editorial suggestions. My thanks also to Sarah Baxter and Sarah Burton at the Society of Authors, and to Virginia Nicholson on behalf of the Woolf Estate, who have given permission for this project to be realized. The materials in Sussex have been made available through the work of Fiona Courage, Rose Lock, Karen Watson and others: I would particularly like to thank Tim Evenden for his heroic labours in the digitization suite at The Keep. At the NYPL, my thanks to Joshua McKeon and Lyndsi Barnes at the Henry W and Albert A Berg Collection, and to Eric Shows and Thomas Lisanti of Permissions and Reproduction services there. Thanks also to Paul Civitelli at the Beinecke Rare Book and Manuscript Library at Yale University. This project has been supported financially by the Leverhulme Trust, the British Academy and the School of English and Drama at Queen Mary University of London, and I am grateful to them all.

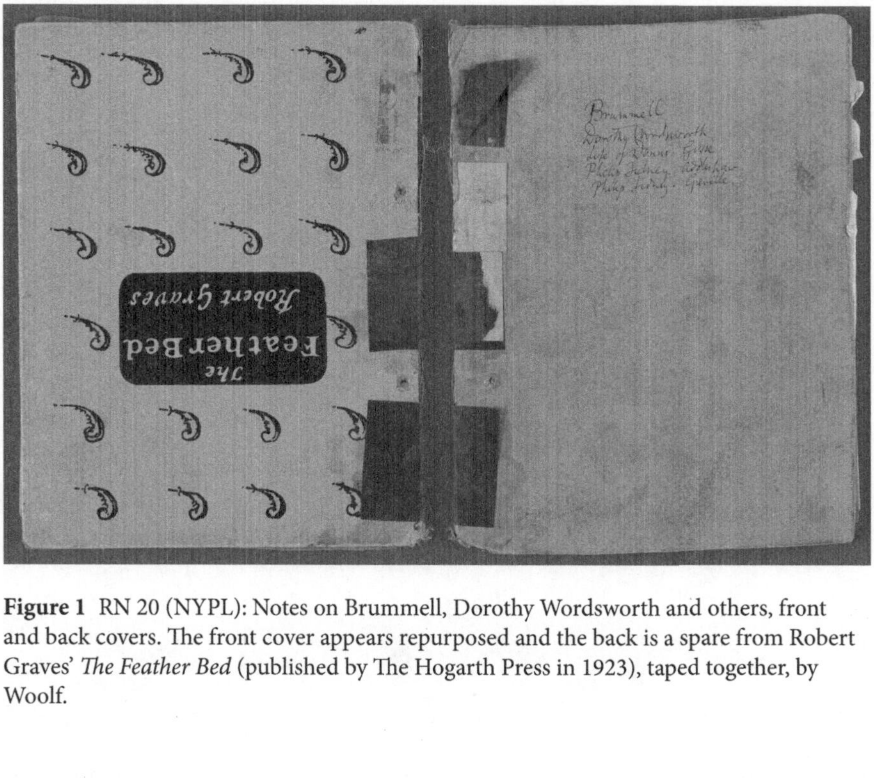

Figure 1 RN 20 (NYPL): Notes on Brummell, Dorothy Wordsworth and others, front and back covers. The front cover appears repurposed and the back is a spare from Robert Graves' *The Feather Bed* (published by The Hogarth Press in 1923), taped together, by Woolf.

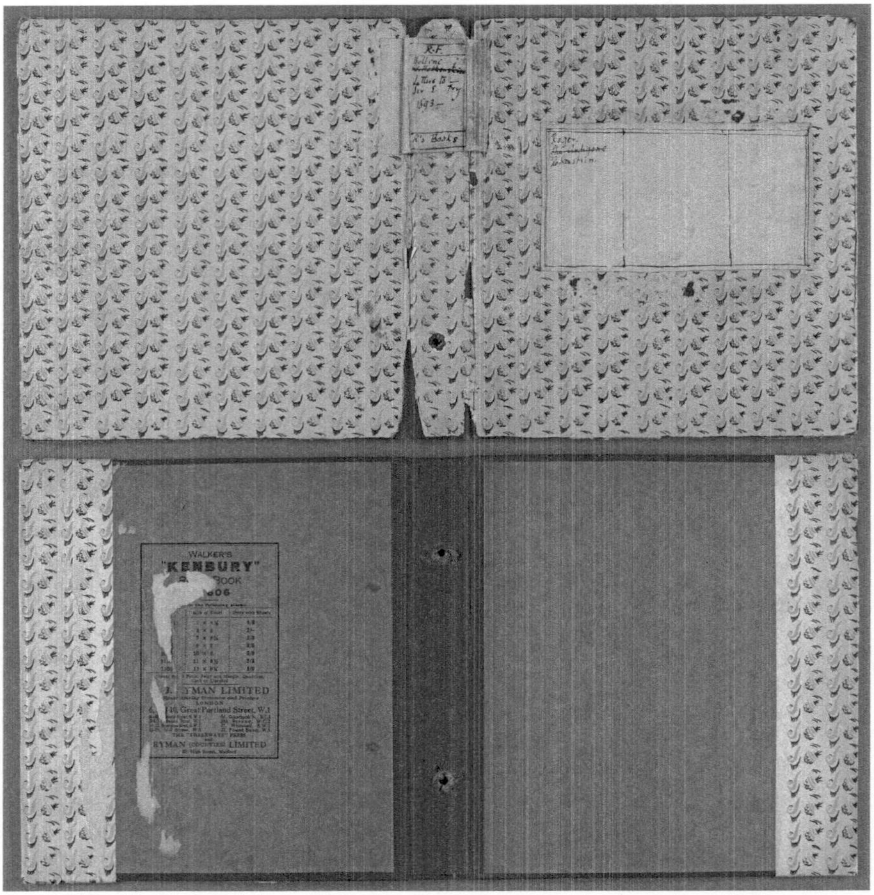

Figure 2 RN 61 (Sussex): Notebook cover made by Woolf by re-covering a hardback book with a contemporary style of decorative paper, possibly from the Hogarth Press or Omega workshop. The paper is pasted over onto the insides, and labels placed by Woolf on the spine and front cover.

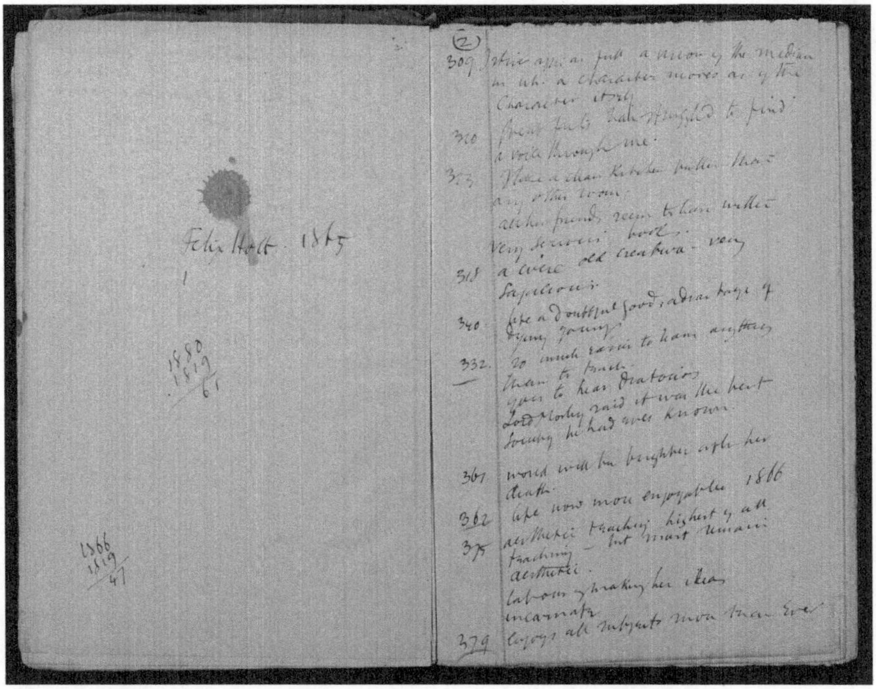

Figure 3 RN 41 (Sussex): Notes on George Eliot. Woolf was reading J. W. Cross's *Life* of Eliot. On the verso page, she has made notes calculating Eliot's age. (*Felix Holt* was published in 1866, when Eliot was forty-seven and in 1880 she married and died, aged sixty-one.)

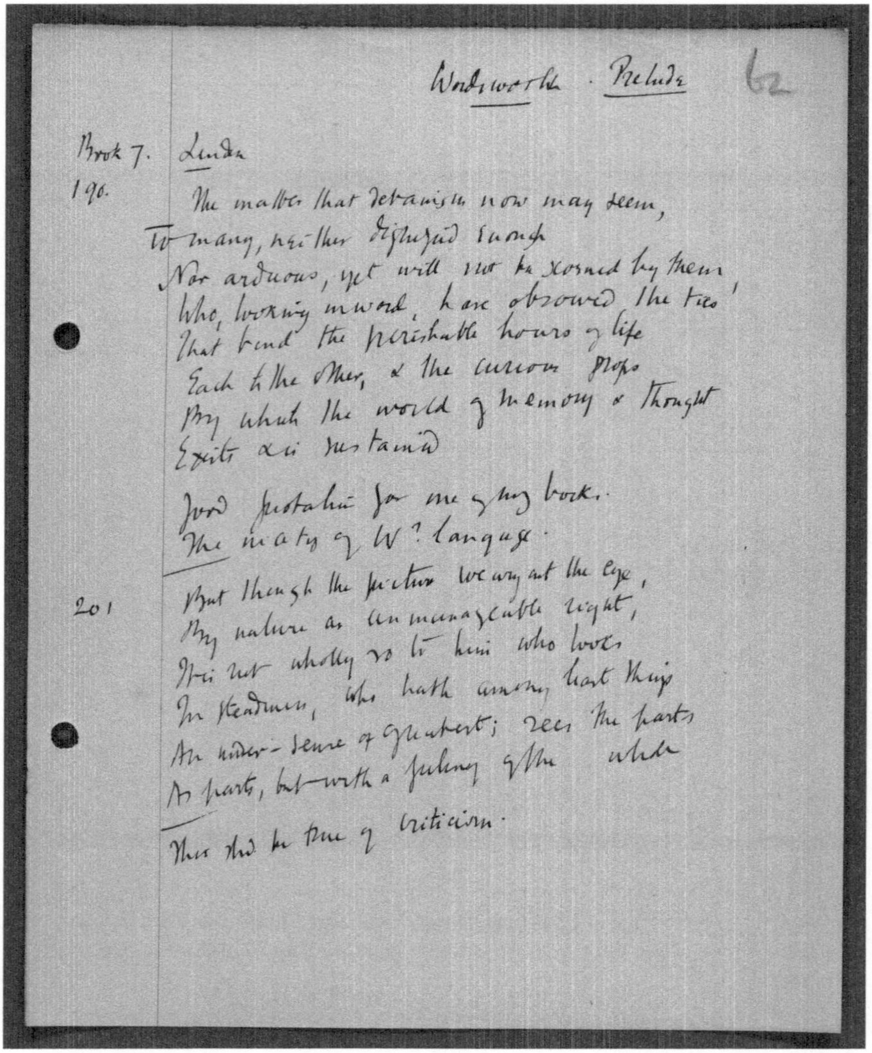
Wordsworth · Prelude 62

Book 7. London

196. The matter that detains us now may seem,
To many, neither dignified enough
Nor arduous, yet will not be scorned by them,
Who, looking inward, have observed the ties
That bind the perishable hours of life
Each to the other, & the curious props
By which the world of memory & thought
Exists & is sustained

Good quotation for one of my books.
The majesty of W.'s language.

201 But though the picture weary out the eye,
By nature an unmanageable sight,
It is not wholly so to him who looks
In steadiness, who hath among least things
An under-sense of greatest; sees the parts
As parts, but with a feeling of the whole

This shd be true of criticism.

Figure 4 RN 47 (Sussex): In a notebook of mixed subjects, Woolf has copied out two sets of lines from Wordsworth's *The Prelude* with the comments *'Good quotation for one of my books'* and *'This shd.* [should] *be true of criticism'*.

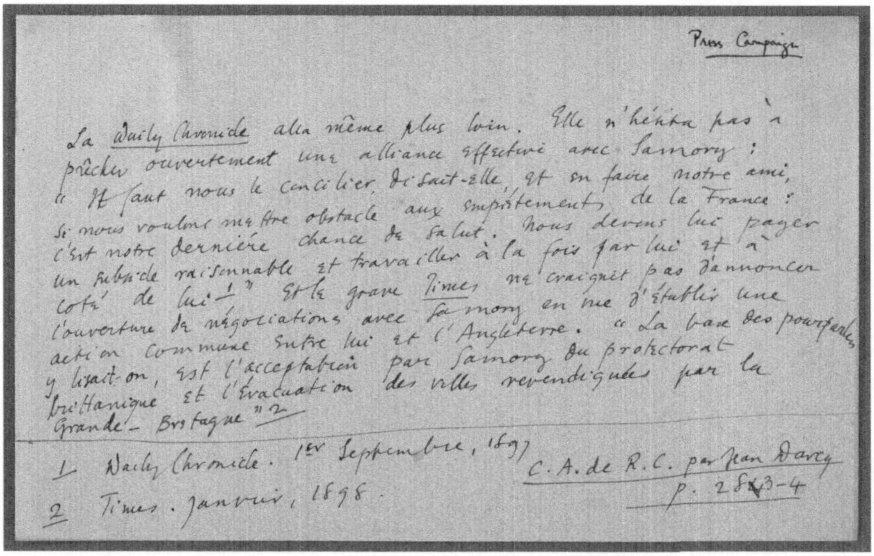
Press Campaign

La Daily Chronicle alla même plus loin. Elle n'hésita pas à prêcher ouvertement une alliance effective avec Samory : « Il faut nous le concilier, disait-elle, et en faire notre ami, si nous voulons mettre obstacle aux empiètements de la France : c'est notre dernière chance de salut. Nous devons lui payer un subside raisonnable et travailler à la fois par lui et à côté de lui.1 » Et le grave Times ne craignit pas d'annoncer l'ouverture de négociations avec Samory en vue d'établir une action commune entre lui et l'Angleterre. « La base des pourparlers y lisait-on, est l'acceptation par Samory du protectorat brittanique et l'évacuation des villes revendiquées par la Grande-Bretagne »2

1 Daily Chronicle. 1er Septembre, 1897

2 Times. Janvier, 1898.

C.A. de R.C. par Jean Darcy
p. 283-4

Figure 5 *Empire and Commerce* cards (Sussex): Notes on *France Et Angleterre: Cent Années de Rivalité Coloniale* by Jean Darcy [France and England: A Hundred Years of Colonial Rivalry]. Leonard Woolf has classified the note as 'Press Campaign'.

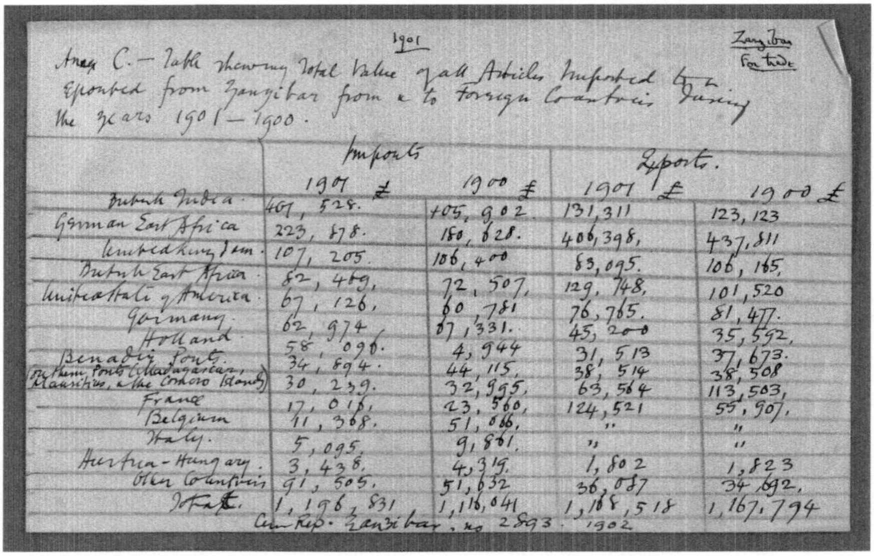

1901

Zanzibar For trade

Anex C. — Table showing Total Value of all Articles Imported to & Exported from Zanzibar from & to Foreign Countries during the years 1901–1900.

	Imports 1901 £	Imports 1900 £	Exports 1901 £	Exports 1900 £
British India	401,528	405,902	131,311	123,123
German East Africa	223,878	180,828	406,398	437,811
United Kingdom	107,205	106,400	83,095	106,165
British East Africa	82,469	72,507	129,748	101,520
United States of America	67,126	60,781	76,765	81,477
Germany	62,974	87,331	45,200	35,592
Holland	58,096	4,944	31,513	37,673
Benadir Ports	34,894	44,115	38,514	38,508
Southern Ports (Madagascar, Mauritius, & the Comoro Islands)	30,239	32,995	63,564	113,503
France	17,016	23,560	124,521	55,907
Belgium	11,368	51,866	"	"
Italy	5,095	9,861	"	"
Austria-Hungary	3,438	4,319	1,802	1,823
Other Countries	91,505	51,632	36,087	34,692
Total £	1,196,831	1,116,041	1,168,518	1,167,794

Con. Rep. Zanzibar, no 2893. 1902

Figure 6 *Empire and Commerce* cards (Sussex): A table made by Woolf of the value of trade between Zanzibar and elsewhere (British India, German East Africa, etc.), based on British Consular Reports. Leonard Woolf's classification is 'Zanzibar, For[eign] trade').

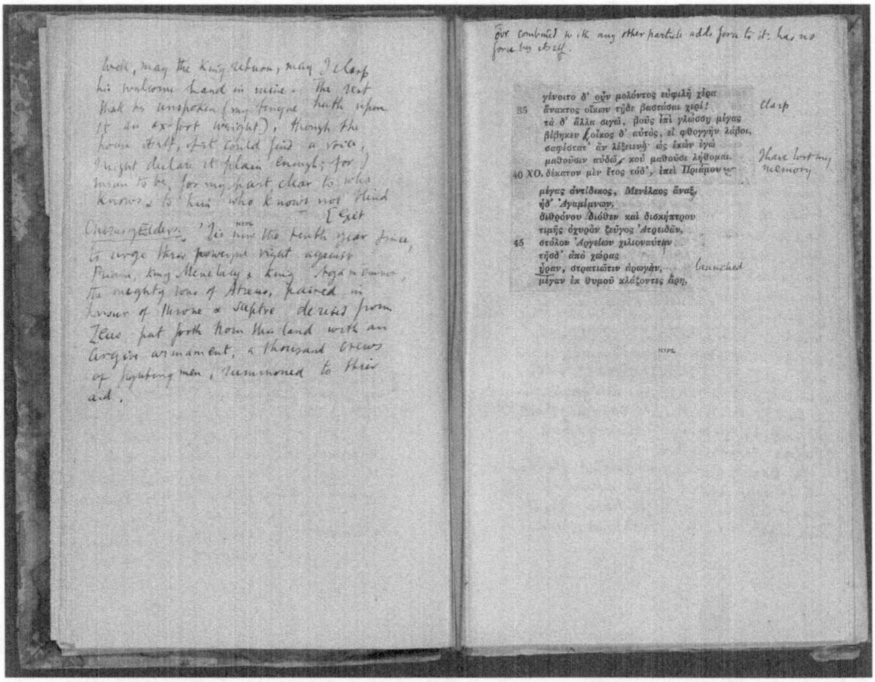

Figure 7 The *Agamemnon Notebook* (NYPL): Notes and crib made by Woolf of Aeschylus's play *Agamemnon*, using the original Greek and Verrall's translation.

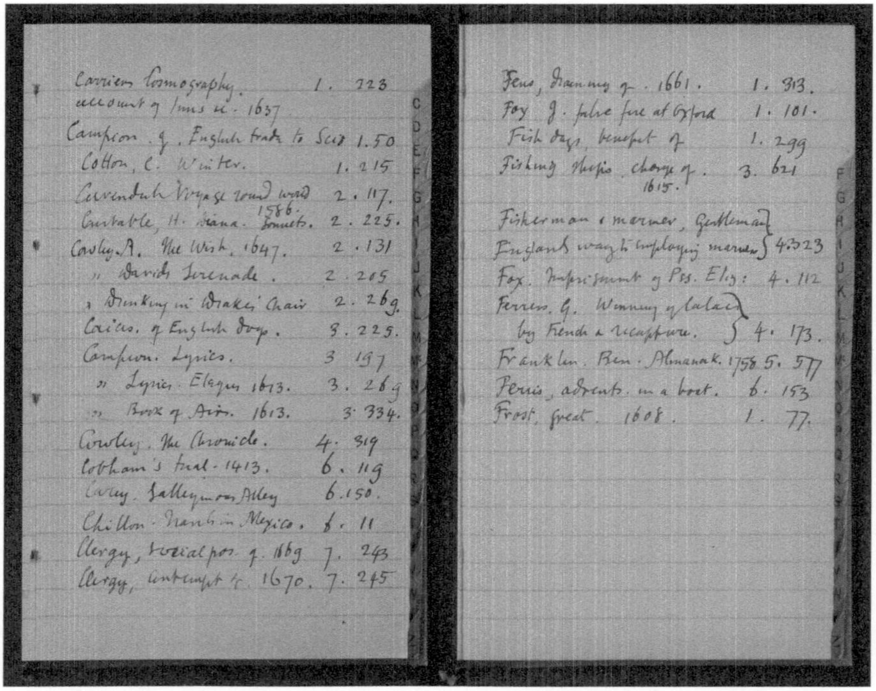

Figure 8 Notebook re Edward Arber's *An English Garner* (Sussex): Two pages of Woolf's own index of selections from Arber, pages C and F.

Notes

1 Virginia Woolf, *The Diary of Virginia Woolf – Vol. 5: 1936–41*, ed. A. O. Bell (Harmondsworth: Penguin, 1985), p. 145.
2 Virginia Woolf, *The Diary of Virginia Woolf – Vol. 2: 1920–1924*, ed. A. O. Bell and A. McNeillie (Harcourt and Brace, 1978), p. 243.
3 Virginia Woolf, *A Writer's Diary: Being Extracts from the Diary of Virginia Woolf*, ed. Leonard Woolf (London, The Hogarth Press, 1953).
4 A. J. P. Taylor, *English History, 1914–45* (Oxford: Clarendon, 1966), p. 311.
5 Malcolm Bradbury, 'The Novel in the 1920s', in *The Twentieth Century, Vol. 7, Sphere History of English Literature*, ed. B. Bergonzi (London: Sphere, 1970), p. 199.
6 Walter Allen, *The English Novel* (Harmondsworth: Penguin, 1965), pp. 47–351.
7 Elizabeth Hardwick, *Seduction and Betrayal: Women and Literature* (London: Weidenfeld, 1974), p. 136.
8 Michèle Barrett, 'A Theory of Modernism and English Society between the Wars: With Particular Reference to Virginia Woolf' (University of Sussex: D.Phil Thesis, 1976); and 'Towards a Sociology of Virginia Woolf Criticism', *The Sociological Review* 26 (1978), now posted on www.michelebarrett.com (all websites last accessed 7 March 2020).
9 Michèle Barrett, *Virginia Woolf: Women and Writing* (London: The Women's Press, 1979).
10 See, for example, Jane Marcus, V*irginia Woolf and the Languages of Patriarchy* (Bloomington and Indianapolis: Indiana University Press, 1987).
11 Michèle Barrett, 'Introduction' to *A Room of One's Own* and *Three Guineas* (Harmondsworth: Penguin, 1993), pp. ix–xlix.
12 Brenda R. Silver, *Virginia Woolf's Reading Notebooks* (Princeton: Princeton University Press, 1983), www.dartmouth.edu/~library/digital/publishing/books/silver-virginia-1983/.
13 Archives at Sussex (the Monks House Papers held at The Keep); see also the Berg Collection at the New York Public Library; as well as the Beinecke Library at Yale.
14 Silver, *Virginia Woolf's Reading Notebooks*, p. xi. Silver's introductory essay is included in WoolfNotes.com. The mention in this paragraph is to two reading notebooks related to this literary historical project; in the index to the book, and in Silver's 1979 article, these notes are identified as being in three reading notebooks: 16, 21 and 37 (Note also that WoolfNotes.com does not use roman numbers.)
15 Ibid., pp. xi–xii.
16 Woolf, *The Diary of Virginia Woolf – Vol. 5*, p. 145.
17 Brenda Silver, 'Anon and the Reader', *Twentieth Century Literature* 25/3–4 (1979), pp. 356–441; and Woolf, *The Diary of Virginia Woolf – Vol.* 5, p. 180.
18 Silver, *Virginia Woolf's Reading Notebooks*, p. 9.
19 Ibid., p. 10; see also Virginia Woolf, *A Passionate Apprentice: The Early Journals, 1897–1909*, ed. Mitchell A. Leaska (London: Hogarth Press, 1990), pp. 5–134.
20 Michèle Barrett, 'Virginia Woolf's Research for Empire and Commerce in Africa (Leonard Woolf, 1920)', *Woolf Studies Annual* 19 (2013).
21 Wayne K. Chapman '"L.'s Dame Secretaire": Alix Strachey, The Hogarth Press and Bloomsbury Pacifism. 1917–1960', in *Women in the Milieu of Leonard and Virginia Woolf: Peace, Politics and Education* (New York, Pace University Press, 1998).
22 Virginia Woolf, *Moments of Being: Unpublished Autobiographical Writings of Virginia Woolf*, ed. Jeanne Schulkind (London: Chatto & Windus, 1976), p. 119.

23 Woolf, *The Waves* (Harmondsworth: Penguin, 1992), p. 167.
24 Leonard Woolf, *Downhill All the Way* (New York: Harcourt Brace, 1967), p. 83.
25 Christine Kenyon Jones and Anna Snaith, '"Tilting at Universities": Woolf at King's College London', *Woolf Studies Annual* 16 (2010), pp. 1–44.
26 Michèle Barrett, 'Leonard and Virginia Woolf's Library at Washington State University', *Bulletin of the Virginia Woolf Society of Great Britain* 35 (2010), pp. 7–11.
27 Clara Jones, *Virginia Woolf: Ambivalent Activist* (Edinburgh: Edinburgh University Press, 2016), pp. 31–2.
28 Michèle Barrett, 'Bayreuth and Berlin: The Voyage Out and the Place of German in Woolf's Writing', in *The Voyage Out: Centenary Perspectives*, ed. Sarah M. Hall et al. (London: Virginia Woolf Society of Great Britain, 2015).
29 Michèle Barrett, 'Introduction' to *A Room of One's Own* and *Three Guineas*, pp. ix–xlix.
30 'Dorothy Wordsworth', in *The Essays of Virginia Woolf, Vol. 5*, ed. Stuart Clarke (London: The Hogarth Press, 2009), pp. 113–21.
31 Anonymous [Virginia Woolf], *Times Literary Supplement*, 15 June 1906; See also *The Collected Essays of Virginia Woolf*, ed A. McNeillie, Vol. 1 (London: Harcourt Brace Jovanovich, 1989), pp. 105–9.
32 Woolf, *The Flight of the Mind: The Letters of Virginia Woolf – Vol.1: 1888–1912*, ed. Nigel Nicolson and Trautmann (London: Hogarth Press, 1975), p. 232.
33 Ibid., p. 460.
34 Yopie Prins, *Ladies' Greek: Victorian Translations of Tragedy* (Princeton: Princeton University Press, 2017), 'Chapter One: The Spell of Greek: Virginia Woolf's Agamemnon Notebook', p. 36.
35 Ibid., pp. 35–56.
36 Edward Arber, *An English Garner: Ingatherings from Our History and Literature* (London: E. Arber, 1877–96).
37 Cowley's Ode hangs on the back of Drake's chair, which had been made from timbers of the Golden Hind, and was donated to the Bodleian Library in Oxford by John Davies, the keeper of Deptford's naval stores. See www.bodleianlibs.tumblr.com, 'the chair that sailed around the world'.
38 Virginia Woolf, *Orlando*, ed. Michael Whitworth (Oxford: Oxford University Press, 2015), p. 200.
39 Mark Levene, *Genocide in the Age of the Nation-State, Vol 2: The Rise of the West and the Coming of Genocide* (London: I.B. Tauris, 2005), p. 306.
40 Virginia Woolf, *Mrs Dalloway* (Harmondsworth: Penguin, 1992), p. 120.
41 'Mrs Dalloway and the Armenian Question', in *Modernism, History and the First World War*, ed. Trudi Tate (Manchester: Manchester University Press, 1998), p. 154.
42 Ibid., p. 167.
43 Woolf, *Mrs Dalloway*, p. 134.
44 Woolf, *A Passionate Apprentice*, p. 321.
45 Ibid., pp. 326–7.
46 The death of Thoby Stephen is discussed in Quentin Bell, *Virginia Woolf: A Biography: Vol 1 Virginia Stephen* (London: The Hogarth Press, 1972), pp. 109–10.
47 Woolf, *A Passionate Apprentice*, p. 347.
48 Ibid., p. 357.
49 Leonard Woolf, *The Journey Not the Arrival Matters: An Autobiography of the Years 1939–1969* (London: The Hogarth Press, 1969), p. 388.

50 Beverly Ann Schlack, *Continuing Presences: Virginia Woolf's Use of Literary Allusion* (University Park and London: Pennsylvania State University Press, 1979).

51 The general editors of the Cambridge University Press edition of Woolf are Susan Sellers and Jane Goldman. Barbara Lounsberry has written a sequence of books on Woolf's diary readings as well as on her writing. See *Becoming Virginia Woolf*; *Virginia Woolf's Modernist Path*; and *Virginia Woolf: The War without, the War Within* (Gainesville: University Press of Florida, 2014, 2016, 2018, respectively).

52 Virginia Woolf, *The Pargiters*, ed. Mitchell A. Leaska (London: Hogarth Press, 1978), p. 9.

53 Julia Briggs, *Reading Virginia Woolf* (Edinburgh: Edinburgh University Press, 2006), p. 160.

2

THE BIOPOLITICS OF *MRS. DALLOWAY*: INTELLIGENCE AND SENTIMENT

Natasha Periyan

> L. has been telling me about Germany, & reparations, how money is paid. Lord what a weak brain I have – like an unused muscle. He talks; & the facts come in, & I can't deal with them. But by dint of very painful brain exercises, perhaps I understand a little more than Nelly of the International situation. And L. understands it all – picks up all these points out of the daily paper absolutely instantly, has them connected, ready to produce. Sometimes I think my brain & his are of different orders. Were it not for my flash of imagination, & this turn for books, I should be a very ordinary woman. No faculty of mine is really very strong.
>
> But its [sic] a question of work. I am already a good deal pulled together by sticking at my books: my 250 words of fiction first, & then a systematic beginning, I daresay the 80th, upon the Common Reader, who might be finished in a flash I think, did I see the chance to flash & have done with it. But there's a lot of work in these things. [...] And should I demolish Richardson? whom I've never read. Yes, I'll run through the rain into the house & see if Clarissa is there. But thats [sic] a block out of my day, a long long novel.[1]

Woolf's August 1924 diary entry above was written as she was finishing the first draft of *Mrs. Dalloway* and in the process of writing *The Common Reader*. The entry is embedded within biopolitical discourses that reflect a politics based on, as Foucault describes, a concern with optimizing the 'aptitudes' of the population.[2] Woolf's struggle to understand the 'International situation' is framed in terms of an intelligence test. The concept of 'intelligence' was absorbed into psychology from nineteenth-century evolutionary biology and perceived 'cognition as essentially layered or graded'.[3] Woolf demonstrates a sensitivity to this graded model of intelligence as she attempts to establish her intellect on a scale, framed in gender and class terms: she notes that 'I understand a little more than Nelly' (her servant), but less than her husband, whom she credits with superior powers of synthesis and assimilation. Woolf performs 'very painful brain exercises' to work her 'weak brain' in terms which recall the mental acrobatics reminiscent of the intelligence test while evidencing an autodidact commitment to work, as if resolving not to think about the relative strength of her faculties and to commit instead to a rigorous programme of self-education.

Woolf had links to Francis Galton, the inspiration for the first generation of intelligence testers. Her father's family, the Stephen family, were included as a case study in *Hereditary Genius* (1869), where Galton first expounded his theory of the inherited nature of intellectual ability, with a focus on the male line. Galton's principles provided a model which could readily assimilate psychometric testing: by about 1908 Anglo-Saxon investigators became aware of Binet's intelligence test, and by 1921 Kurt Danziger notes that intelligence tests formed part of the discipline of psychology.[4] Woolf's Bloomsbury circle was familiar with the intelligence debate: in September 1924, the books' pages of the *Nation and the Athenaeum* edited by Leonard Woolf, included Marjorie Strachey's review of the *Report of the Consultative Committee on Psychological Tests of Educable Capacity and Their Possible Use in the Public System of Education*. Strachey's article echoes Woolf's perception of the intelligence test as manifesting a form of intellectual acrobatics in her suggestion that intelligence tests 'are known to most people as a particularly trying kind of parlour game'.[5] Strachey argues nonetheless that 'it will not do to pooh-pooh it airily, as a modern fad, without taking the trouble to investigate it' and takes seriously the possibilities that intelligence testing could hold for education.[6] She finds the Report 'disappointing' but welcomes its recommendations that intelligence test results are only interpreted by trained psychologists, and that the Advisory Body should work with university psychology departments to research the uses of intelligence tests further.[7]

The Report was published in a climate where the Left was calling for 'secondary education for all' in a system that was increasingly envisaged in tripartite terms following the findings of the 1924 Report, and the 1926 Hadow Report which proposed a secondary system structured around the grammar, the technical and the secondary modern school.[8] Wooldridge identifies the progressive elements in the meritocratic model which 'offered a means of reconciling elitism with democracy'.[9] George Bernard Shaw's 1910 manifesto *Socialism and Superior Brains* suggests how one form of elitism was replaced with another, however. Shaw describes social democracy as 'the paradise of the able man' that could take industry 'out of the hands of brutes and dullards' pivoting social reform around intellectual ability.[10] As the 1924 Report suggests, intelligence tests could be used by the state to facilitate programmes of educational reform; indeed, as Wooldridge identifies, the intelligence test offered a mechanism for the establishment of a meritocratic political order, implemented by the competitive examination and the scholarship ladder.[11]

Latent within Woolf's diary entry is also the influence of a biopolitical order founded in sentiment. Just as in the late nineteenth and early twentieth centuries the intelligence test facilitated a social order founded in a meritocracy of intellect, in the eighteenth and nineteenth centuries capacity was framed in terms of an ability to receive impressions and feelings. Kyla Schuller examines the biopolitics of impressibility in nineteenth-century American literature, wherein the capacity of different populations to be affected by feeling was held to be delineated along racial and gender lines. She argues that 'Sentimentalism [...] is a broad regulatory technology in which neurological and emotional tendencies play important roles in reconciling the impressible body to its role in a biological population, rather than a narrower aesthetics and politics of the moral aptness of emotional identification.'[12] Schuller's analysis resonates with Todd's description of a 'meritocracy of feeling' as she describes the 'difficulty relating class and sensibility' for writers of the eighteenth century.[13] While some writers suggested that sensibility was 'equalizing since it occurred in all ranks', others associated it as a 'property more or less exclusively of the higher and more genteel orders'.[14] Woolf's comment that without her 'imagination' she would be 'a very ordinary woman' suggests a self-effacing susceptibility to the very characterizations of female intelligence to which she was opposed. Lorraine Daston describes how the early modern period naturalized the notion that the female intellect was in opposition to the capacity for abstract reason, an ideology which persisted well into the eighteenth century.[15] Women's mental landscape was founded on the contention that intellectual traits were determined by their purportedly cold, moist bodily complexion which, as Ian Maclean notes, were more subject to 'metamorphosis'.[16] Daston examines how this 'metamorphosis' was held to facilitate women's greater imaginative capacity: '[s]ensory impressions, stamped upon the brain as a seal upon wax [...] adhered more easily, distinctly, and durably in the soft, humid female matter than in that of the hot, dry male'.[17]

Woolf's intention to read Samuel Richardson's *Clarissa*, the archetypal model of female sensibility in sentimental literature, as she was drafting *Mrs. Dalloway* suggests how her own Clarissa is a reframing of an intertextual source. Woolf would have been familiar with the novel through her father, Sir Leslie Stephen, who edited *The Works of Samuel Richardson* (1883). Richardson's work was paradigmatic of a broader tradition of the literature of sympathy, shaped by the principles of Hume and Smith. As John Mullan notes, Hume and Smith were 'sceptical' about the powers of reason, positioning it as subservient to the passions.[18] For Leslie Stephen the anti-rationality of Smith's theory of sympathy with its emphasis on imaginary identification and spectatorship offered a 'standard of morality [which] seems to be too fluctuating to serve any intelligible purpose'.[19] For Hume, principles of sympathy extended out into a broader social philosophy: 'pleasure or uneasiness in the characters of others' is equivalent to an 'extensive concern for society'.[20]

Social organization and sympathy in Woolf's work have been explored in recent analyses which have variously marginalized and foregrounded class politics. Kirsty Martin decentres class from her analysis of sensibility in a focus on 'sensory entanglement' and embodied emotion, while Clara Jones analyses how Smith's model of sympathy elucidates the 'Introductory Letter', arguing that Woolf exposes the limits of sympathetic engagement as a form of cross-class political involvement. Jones comments that Woolf points instead to the need to establish a 'new ideal of identification galvanised with the language of political solidarity'.[21] Raymond Williams interprets Bloomsbury's alignment to political standards of sympathy and solidarity in the context of a biopolitics of intelligence. He argues that Bloomsbury's political action was directed towards reform of a 'short-sighted and stupid' ruling class, arguing that this occurred through 'very strong and effective feelings of sympathy with the lower class as victims'.[22] Bloomsbury, Williams suggests, 'relates to a lower class *as a matter of conscience*: not in solidarity'.[23] The class politics of *Mrs. Dalloway* are of particular significance given its immediate political context. Trudi Tate identifies that the novel is set during the first Baldwin Conservative government, published during a second Baldwin government, and mostly drafted while Labour's first minority government was in power.[24]

I argue that the transitional political moment of *Mrs. Dalloway* is registered in the text's biopolitical critique of intelligence and sentiment. This is enacted through a classificatory narrative voice that echoes the mechanism of the intelligence test as Woolf exposes the 'stupidity' of a ruling elite while wrestling with the concept of meritocracy. *Mrs. Dalloway* recasts models of female sensibility to interrogate the social and aesthetic paradigms of sympathetic alignment. The text scrutinizes the limitations of sympathetic engagement with the 'lower class as victims' through an aesthetic register that ironizes discourses of sentimentality as Woolf reaches for a new standard of modernist affect.

My historicist approach is indebted to the pioneering work of scholars including Michèle Barrett and Brenda Silver, whose previous research elucidates how Woolf's reading is felt in the politics of her texts, and whose WoolfNotes project will facilitate archival approaches that will deeply enrich understandings of Woolf's work.[25] My methodological approach is facilitated by Woolf's diaries, which contain a close commentary of her political reactions and working processes. Cross-referencing dates and comments in Woolf's diary against the dating of Woolf's evolving manuscript enables an understanding of how *Mrs Dalloway*'s debate between intelligence and sentiment sharpened in relation to political crisis, while examining Woolf's novel through critiques Woolf made in *The Common Reader*, drafted (as Woolf's diaries and literary manuscripts reveal) as she wrote *Mrs Dalloway*, demonstrates a line of continuity between Woolf's essays and novels that enable new aesthetic readings. The chapter's fully contextualized approach to close-reading, which draws on previously unconsidered parliamentary records, periodicals, educational reports and medical texts, elucidates how the text's biopolitics are constructed in a cultural context where intelligence and sentiment were categories with live political and aesthetic implications.

A shifting political clime is registered in *Mrs. Dalloway*. Lady Bruton is keen to employ Richard Dalloway to write her family history once he is no longer in government: 'all the papers were ready for Richard down at Aldmixton whenever the time came; the Labour Government, she meant'.[26] The final party scene foregrounds the political classes and includes a portrait of the 'ordinary' (189) Prime Minister. In this episode, the novel's debate between the biopolitics of sympathy and intelligence finds its focus through Sally Seton: 'Cleverness was silly. One must say simply what one felt' (210). The debate between sentiment and intellect is reprised in the novel's final moments: '"Richard has improved. You are right," said Sally. "I shall go and talk to him. I shall say good-night. What does the brain matter," said Lady Rosseter, getting up, "compared with the heart?"' (213). Sally Seton's affirmation of 'the heart' rather than 'the brain' is not in Woolf's original drafting of the closure dated to 9 October 1924, which moves straight from Richard Dalloway's perception of his daughter to Peter Walsh's observation of Mrs. Dalloway.[27]

Woolf's diary notes that she started the party scenes on or around 7 September 1924 and her notebook records that she completed drafting them on 9 October 1924, the date that the Labour government was defeated by 166 votes on a Liberal enquiry into the Campbell Case, which precipitated Labour's defeat at the polls on 29 October 1924.[28] On 17 October, Woolf recorded her frustration with events: 'owing to the defeat of the Govt. in the Campbell Case, we are now condemned to a dose of lies every morning; the usual yearly schoolboys wrangle has begun'.[29] In revising the novel in November 1924 to January 1925, when Woolf records waiting for her proofs, Woolf added in Sally's polarization between the 'brain' and the 'heart'. The narrative coding in these additions suggests a critique of a complacent ruling class. Earlier in the party, Peter finds that 'After all these years he really could not call her "Lady Rosseter"' (205). The switch of narrative identification from 'Sally' to 'Lady Rosseter' signals a subtle shift in focalization, from Peter Walsh to the narrator. Anna Snaith identifies the 'indeterminacy' that free indirect discourse allows, noting that dichotomies of 'character/narrator' become 'blurred' through the device and suggesting the political potential of such narrative choices.[30] In this instance, the shift in focalization signalled through the identification of Sally as Lady Rosseter, implicates her affirmation of sentiment, rather than intellect, as part of a wider aristocratic order which marginalizes intellectual power.

The novel's narrative is seemingly absorbed in the classificatory drive of the intelligence test as the mental capacity of characters is repeatedly assessed. This sharpens into a political critique through Richard Dalloway. Peter Walsh and Sally Seton 'bond' (84) in their opinion of Richard's limited intelligence. Clarissa recalls Sally's assessment of Richard's mental ability, considering 'Sally Seton saying that Richard would never be in the Cabinet because he had a second-class brain' (133). At the party Sally reflects on this failing: 'Richard Dalloway not in the Cabinet. He hadn't been a success, Sally supposed?' (205). Trudi Tate notes the perception that Baldwin was a 'nonentity leading to a very dull government', suggesting that Richard's 'inability to get in the cabinet [...] would have been a failure of some magnitude'.[31] In the light of the perceived mediocrity of the Baldwin government, Marjorie Strachey's observation in her review of the 1924 Haldane Report seems pointed: 'have they [intelligence tests] ever been tried on subjects *known* to be intelligent, such as Cabinet Ministers?'[32] Peter Walsh similarly identifies Richard's lack of intelligence:

> a thorough good sort; a bit limited; a bit thick in the head; yes; but a thorough good sort. Whatever he took up he did in the same matter-of-fact sensible

> way; without a touch of imagination, without a spark of brilliancy, but with the inexplicable niceness of his type. He ought to have been a country gentleman – he was wasted on politics. He was at his best out of doors, with horses and dogs – how good he was, for instance, when that great shaggy dog of Clarissa's got caught in a trap and had its paw half torn off, and Clarissa turned faint and Dalloway did the whole thing; bandaged, made splints; told Clarissa not to be a fool. That was what she liked him for perhaps – that was what she needed. 'Now, my dear, don't be a fool. Hold this – fetch that,' all the time talking to the dog as if it were a human being. [...] Seriously and solemnly Richard Dalloway got on his hind legs and said that no decent man ought to read Shakespeare's sonnets because it was like listening at keyholes [...] The only thing to do was to pelt him with sugared almonds – it was at dinner. But Clarissa sucked it all in; thought it so honest of him; so independent of him; Heaven knows if she didn't think him the most original mind she'd ever met! (83–4)

The free indirect discourse absorbs the public-school parlance associated with the upper classes in terms such as 'thorough good sort'. This 'niceness of his type' is counterbalanced by Peter's classification of Richard as 'limited', 'thick'. Richard's identification of Clarissa as a 'fool' is ironized in the context of Peter's determinations of Richard's intelligence. Through Peter, Woolf aligns Richard with an evolutionary scale of intelligence as he opines about Shakespeare's morality 'on his hind legs'. Darwin's *The Descent of Man* identified 'numberless gradations' of 'mental powers' between animal and man and, as Danziger argues, 'the category of biological/evolutionary intelligence was deployed to rationalize the grading of human groups in a hierarchy of excellence'.[33] The blurring of the line between animal and human being is suggested as Peter remembers Richard 'talking to the dog as if it were a human being'. Richard similarly talks to human beings as if they were dogs in his infinitive instruction to Clarissa: 'Hold this – fetch that', the latter typically a command given to a dog. The term 'pelt' punningly suggests not simply Peter showering Richard with almonds, but an animal skin. The metaphor is structurally linked to Peter Walsh's previous reminiscence of Richard Dalloway helping Clarissa's dog after it injures its paw, but it also echoes and inverts Septimus Warren Smith's nightmarish vision of evolutionary degeneration in Regent's Park: 'It was horrible, terrible to see a dog become a man! [...] Why could he see [...] into the future, when dogs will become men? It was the heat wave presumably, operating upon a brain made sensitive by eons of evolution' (76).

Septimus's intelligence is a particular focus of the narrative. Rezia is depicted as awed by his intelligence and his manager, Mr Brewer, 'thinking very highly of Smith's abilities' (95), considers him one of his 'ablest young fellows' (95). The narrator offers a more ambivalent appraisal of Septimus's mental capacity:

> To look at, he might have been a clerk, but of the better sort; for he wore brown boots; his hands were educated; so, too, his profile – his angular, big-nosed, intelligent, sensitive profile; but not his lips altogether, for they were loose; and

> his eyes (as eyes tend to be), eyes merely; hazel, large; so that he was, on the whole, a border case, neither one thing nor the other; might end with a house at Purley and a motor car, or continue renting apartments in back streets all his life; one of those half-educated, self-educated men whose education is all learnt from books borrowed from public libraries, read in the evening after the day's work, on the advice of well-known authors consulted by letter. (93)

The draft manuscripts of *Mrs. Dalloway* demonstrate Woolf's considered choice of words in her description of Septimus. She experimented with the phrases 'an ordinary case' and '~~a strange case~~' before settling on 'border case', a phrase that grants Septimus an indeterminate place that resonates with both his sanity and intelligence.[34] The 1924 Report repeatedly explores the use of the intelligence test to help in determining the classification of 'borderline cases' of pupils in diagnosing mental deficiency and in deciding success in the scholarship examination – a suggestive context for understanding Septimus, whose autodidact background implies lack of access to secondary education.[35] In 1924, Theo Hyslop, Woolf's former doctor, published *The Borderland,* which explores the 'danger' of a population of hysterics, neurasthenics, visionaries, eccentrics and mentally deficient who occupy a 'borderland' 'between sanity and insanity'.[36] Hyslop's eugenicist conviction determined that democratic educational reform was 'resulting [in] the sacrifice of mental health to the acquirement, not of wisdom, but of mere knowledge'.[37] He links the meritocratic era of intelligence to a misguided policy of state investment in education: 'This is, indeed, a brain age, but it is also an age when not only are the ratepayers penny wise and pound foolish, but their unfortunate progeny are apt to be months learning and years defective'.[38]

Hyslop's work also evidences anxiety about the 'the immense hordes of those who are permitted to live as free citizens' in the guise of the borderlanders who occupy an unregulated hinterland, uncontrolled by 'the legal provisions' that govern the clinically insane.[39] Matthew Thomson explores the 1918 Representation of the People Act in the context of the 1913 Mental Deficiency Act, noting the 'ongoing concern over redefining the boundaries of responsible political citizenship' which 'should be seen as an important part of the context in which mental deficiency came to be regarded as a serious social problem'.[40] The case of the shell-shocked soldier suggested the porousness of the boundary between mental health and mental illness.[41] Parliamentary debate over expanding the franchise included the proposition that those who had resided in a prison, asylum or workhouse for thirty days or more should be disqualified from voting, until it was pointed out that this would unfairly disenfranchise shell-shocked soldiers.[42]

Through the identification of Septimus, the autodidact, shell-shocked soldier, as a 'border case' Woolf embodies anxieties surrounding the process of 'adjusting to democracy' that pivot around the education, intelligence and mental capacity of an expanding electorate.[43] The narrator's physiognomic, 'diagnostic' gaze that appraises Smith's intellect does so in terms which recognize indirection and indeterminacy in his appearance.[44] He has an 'intelligent' profile belied by a pair of 'loose' lips that are echoed later in the text by the 'loose-lipped' (128) female vagrant encountered by Richard Dalloway. Donald J. Childs argues that loose lips are a eugenical signal in Woolf's work and associates Woolf, the narrator and Bradshaw with an 'unchallenged pattern of eugenical values'.[45]

While there is ambiguity in the narrator's treatment of Septimus and the pride, ambition and delusory romantic instincts that propel his self-education, *Mrs. Dalloway* repeatedly satirizes eugenicist values. The eugenicist association of class with intelligence is, as I have demonstrated, a particular target of the narrative. Woolf's satire of Hugh Whitbread as the public school type is oriented around the arrogance of racial privilege in his punning name: white breed. There is irony also in the portrait of Lady Bruton, who is embarked on a eugenicist project to encourage emigration to Canada while, as the narrator identifies, being deficient in 'the logical faculty' herself (198). The imperial project is figured in *Mrs. Dalloway* as the preserve of a stupid ruling elite. Through Septimus and Miss Kilman, Woolf depicts a meritocratic politics sacrificed to imperialism. As 'one of the first to volunteer' (95), Septimus would have belonged to the A1 class of recruits; as Mr Brewer recognizes the war 'took away his ablest young fellows' (95). Like Septimus, Miss Kilman's intelligence is recognized by other characters; Richard Dalloway thinks her 'very able' (14) and Elizabeth Dalloway regards her as 'frightfully clever' (144). Miss Kilman's German origins mean that just when she 'might have had a chance at Miss Dolby's school, the war came' she 'had to go' (136).

The novel's intersection of class and gender politics lies at an ambivalent faultline surrounding female intelligence in its depiction of Clarissa. Clarissa Dalloway assesses her own intelligence in relation to Miss Kilman: 'she was never in the room five minutes without making you feel her superiority, your inferiority' (14), and Miss Kilman similarly thinks Clarissa a 'Fool! Simpleton!' (138). Clarissa Dalloway is both a vehicle for Woolf's feminist critique of the cultural underestimation of female intelligence and a target of her class critique of an intellectually moribund ruling order. Clarissa is aligned with stereotypical accounts of female intelligence:

> Not that she thought herself clever, or much out of the ordinary. How she had got through life on the few twigs of knowledge Fräulein Daniels gave them she could not think. She knew nothing; no language, no history [...] Her only gift was knowing people almost by instinct, she thought, walking on. (11)

The quotation explores a debate between intelligence – or being 'clever' – and instinct. Kurt Danziger argues that in late nineteenth century animal psychology, instinct and intelligence were opposed as evolutionary biology and psychology evolved a distinction between the superior quality of behaviour developed through individual learning and adaptability, and the inferior association of instinctive behaviour based on inherited patterns.[46] Turn-of-the-century psychologists and philosophers including Henri Bergson and William James continued to examine the relationship between intelligence and instinct. Through Clarissa, Woolf observes an association of female intelligence with instinct as a consequence of a lack of education ('the few twigs of knowledge Fräulein Daniels gave them'). Clarissa's association of instinct with social prowess reflects eighteenth-century discourses which perceived the essence of the female intellect as its sociability.[47] In *Emile*, Rousseau describes the intellect of Sophy as a feat of social adaptability: 'it is the sort of mind which calls for no remark as she never seems cleverer or stupider than oneself' and Mullan assesses Richardson's novels as envisaging 'a responsive feminine sensibility as the best embodiment of social instinct'.[48] Peter Walsh's characterization of Clarissa Dalloway as '[t]he perfect hostess' (69) embeds her within this model of social intelligence.

In the passage above, the repetition around the verbs 'think' and 'knew/know' stylistically amplifies the focus on Clarissa's intellectual capacity. The narration is focalized through Clarissa in the free indirect discourse that reflects the colloquial intensity of Clarissa's voice as she reflects on her educational training ('she could not think') before shifting to the diegetic voice of the narrator in the phrase 'she thought' to create a distancing effect from Clarissa's estimation of her 'gift' for instinctive understanding as a form of 'knowing'. Elsewhere in the narrative this claim for an instinctive understanding of others is called into doubt in ways which reflect upon the politics of sympathy in the text. John Mullan argues that Woolf's intertextual source both depicts displays of sympathy and problematizes sociability, arguing that 'exceptional reaches of sympathy[,] are set against a world of twisted or broken communications'.[49] This resonates with the politics of sympathy as reflected in *Mrs. Dalloway*, where Clarissa's claims of 'instinctive' knowledge of others are troubled as Peter Walsh reflects on his earlier conversation with Clarissa: 'It was unsatisfactory, they agreed, how little one knew people' (168).

Clarissa's instinctive 'knowing' of others is put under pressure in the novel's paradigmatic moment of sympathetic engagement when Clarissa Dalloway fe
herself united to Septimus Warren Smith on hearing of his death: 'She felt some
very like him – the young man who had killed himself' (204). Martin acutely
the 'sensationalist', 'melodramatic' terms of Clarissa's bodily identificatio
Septimus, as opposed to the 'fragmented pathos' of the description of his s
Attention to *The Common Reader*, drafted as Woolf wrote *Mrs. Dalloway*
that this moment can be read as part of the text's critical assessment of
An analysis of *The Common Reader*'s aesthetic critique of emoti
how an ironized sentimental register undermines Clarissa's claims
sympathy. The devastating sparseness to the description of Sep
resonates with Woolf's analysis of ancient Greek literature's ca
emotion in 'On Not Knowing Greek'. The essay engages with
impersonality as it argues that 'It is obvious in the first place th
is the impersonal literature'.[51] Via a caesura, the essay associat
with literary status: 'Greek is the impersonal literature; it is
masterpieces' (37). The Greeks were able to express em
they 'could say, as if for the first time, "Yet being dead th
It is possible to assess the measure of Woolf's own arb
models of emotion from the passage she cites, which is

freighted with a stately dignity summoned through a sophisticated, oxymoronic formula. The conditions of the age are held to account for the change in the literary expression of emotion: in 'the vast catastrophe of the European war our emotions had to be broken up for us, and put at an angle from us, before we could allow ourselves to feel them in poetry or fiction' (34). The War Poets could thus only speak in a 'sidelong, satiric manner [...] It was not possible for them [...] to speak simply of emotion without being sentimental' (34). The distinction Woolf draws between 'emotion' and 'sentiment' and her advocacy of the former alongside her suspicion of the latter resonates with Michael Bell's analysis of the degradation of the term 'sentiment' in the early twentieth century. From its 'honorific' status in the enlightenment, it 'dwindled to a term of near abuse referring to mawkish self-indulgent and actively pernicious modes of feeling'.[52] A modernist anxiety surrounding sentimentality is evident in 'The Patron and the Crocus' (also in *The Common Reader*) which maintains that the literary patron's most 'useful work' is in 'bracing a writer against sentimentality on the one hand and a craven fear f expressing his feeling on the other. It is worse, he will say, and perhaps more nmon, to be afraid of feeling than to feel too much' (209).

Voolf's efforts to distinguish between sentiment and 'emotion' or 'feeling' offer through which to understand the emotional affect of *Mrs. Dalloway* and the essay's role as an aesthetic guide to the novel. Woolf's diary expresses n for the expression of emotion while writing *Mrs. Dalloway*. On 19 June wondered: 'One must write from deep feeling, said Dostoevsky. And Am I writing The Hours from deep emotion?'[53] Woolf's concern for ' and 'deep emotion' marks her project off from more superficial eeling, and in the context of her paradigmatic intertextual source nction from the eighteenth-century novel of sentiment and the ition. Bell describes the 'apparently decisive break' from the on of the eighteenth century in the modernist era and argues ers were concerned with 'the transformation of sentiment erion of true feeling'.[54] The 'sentimental' is explored in *Mrs.* through the perspective of Peter Walsh. Peter is dismissive sentimentality: 'Clarissa had grown hard, he thought; nto the bargain' (54). Other characters reflect on their ugh the lens of Peter Walsh's approbation. Clarissa al attitude to sentimentality implicitly directed at owed him words: "sentimental," [...] A book was timental. "Sentimental," perhaps she was to be ion and quotation marks objectify the term as tes and aesthetic tastes. In the novel's final n Peter's assessment of her: 'Peter would 'he would think her sentimental – he

hetic identification with Septimus nmentary from Peter Walsh's epiction of Septimus Warren

Smith, Peter Walsh attempts to stop his mental projections of a dead body that he imagines in an ambulance passing him in the street. The narrative structure of *Mrs. Dalloway*, which juxtaposes the description of Septimus's death with Peter's sighting of the ambulance, encourages the reader to identify this body as Septimus's. Peter imagines the body 'stretched on a shelf with a doctor and a nurse …' (166). The ellipses break off his reflections as he chastises himself for his imaginative projections: 'but thinking became morbid, sentimental, directly one began conjuring up doctors, dead bodies; a little glow of pleasure, a sort of lust, too, over the visual impression warned one not to go on with that sort of thing any more – fatal to art, fatal to friendship' (166). Via Peter Walsh, Hume's emphasis on the spectacular nature of sympathy is derided as a revelling in lurid details of death. Peter Walsh's forestalling of his own imaginings, which he decries as 'morbid' and 'sentimental', frames a set of aesthetic criteria through which to consider Clarissa's identification with Septimus. She is surely guilty of a 'lust […] over the visual impression' (166) when she reflects:

> Always her body went through it, when she was told, first, suddenly, of an accident; her dress flamed, her body burnt. He had thrown himself from a window. Up had flashed the ground; through him, blundering, bruising, went the rusty spikes. There he lay with a thud, thud, thud in his brain, and then a suffocation of blackness. So she saw it. (202)

The phrase 'so she saw it' emphasizes the 'visual impression' Clarissa has formed and encourages a connection with Peter Walsh's comments. There is a melodramatic excess to the description in the onomatopoeic repetition of 'thud' and in the metaphorical burning body and dress which evokes the funeral pyre. The funereal language continues in phrases such as 'wreathed about with chatter' (202). In the original narration of Septimus's death, no description is given of Septimus's body, beyond Sir William Bradshaw's description of it as 'horribly mangled' (165). The details Clarissa imagines of the body punctured by the spikes of iron railings imply a 'morbid' (166) revelling in the gruesome nature of the death. As John Mullan describes, sentimental literature was characterized by Hume's principles of sympathetic sociality as well as a language of sentiment and feeling. He notes that Hume, Richardson and Sterne 'committed to […] a language of feeling for the purpose of representing necessary social bonds; all discover in their writing a sociability which is dependent upon the communication of passions and sentiments'.[55] Woolf, however, recasts a moment of sympathetic identification as a moment not of sociability but rather as an appropriation of another's experience for the purposes of self-validation: 'She felt glad that he had done it; thrown it away while they went on living' (204). The addition of the phrase 'He made her feel the beauty; made her feel the fun' in the US edition of the text reinforces the narcissistic ends of sympathetic engagement.[56]

As Martin's work on the rhythms of sympathy in *Mrs. Dalloway* suggests, the text is interested in moments of alignment between different characters. As in the case above, however, the novel detaches sympathy from the language of sentimentalism. The novel's use of narrative echoing, as opposed to overt emotional identification, engages with the politics of sympathetic engagement in jarring, morally queasy terms. Both Septimus's death and Clarissa's imaginative summoning of it are paralleled through encounters with unnamed characters. In the moments before Septimus's suicide, he notices that 'Coming down the staircase opposite an old man stopped and stared at him' (164) while Clarissa similarly observes an old lady in the middle of her reverie on Septimus's death: 'She parted the curtains; she looked. Oh, but how surprising! – in the room opposite the old lady stared straight at her!' (204). Both the old man and the old lady are ambiguous figures which invite an array of interpretations, as images of mortality perhaps, or moments of connection or even confrontation. The similarity of these two encounters links Clarissa and Septimus while the seeming imperviousness of both the old man and the old lady as neutral observers sets into relief the melodramatic terms of Clarissa's sympathetic attachment to Septimus with an emotional register that is far odder and harder to classify.

The scene of Clarissa's identification with Septimus is tonally polymorphous. As well as moments of melodrama, there are also moments of comedy that critique discourses of impressibility. These bodily discourses are comically summoned by Woolf, when on hearing of the news of a 'young man' who had killed himself, Clarissa enters a 'little room' (201) where the Prime Minister and Lady Bruton had met. She observes the shape of their buttocks on the sofa cushions: 'The chairs still kept the impress of the Prime Minister and Lady Bruton, she turned deferentially, he sitting four-square, authoritatively' (202). The image is comical, but it also materializes the figurative usage of the term that is employed later in the same passage to more sinister effect. The physical impression of buttocks upon cushions as an act of force upon a passive surface is transposed to the metaphysical realm of the human mind as Clarissa reflects on Sir William Bradshaw as 'forcing your soul [...] if this young man had gone to him, and Sir William had impressed him, like that, with his power, might he not then have said (indeed she felt it now), Life is made intolerable; they make life intolerable, men like that?' (203).

Schuller argues that impressibility is signified on a sliding scale with white and female bodies culturally held to have a greater capacity for receiving emotional impressions, while 'civilized', white men only exhibit impressibility to a controlled degree as 'sex difference [...] secures the stability of civilization'.[57] Where Schuller emphasizes race and sex as the categories through which 'nineteenth-century biopower consolidated in a sentimental mode that regulated the circulation of feeling throughout the population and delineated differential relational capacities of matter, and therefore the potential for modern evolutionary progress', for Woolf, health is a significant coordinate around which impressibility operates: 'Naked, defenceless, the exhausted, the friendless received the impress of Sir William's will' (113).[58] In Schuller's analysis of nineteenth-century literature, the capacity for impressibility signifies 'modern evolutionary progress'; in *Mrs. Dalloway*, the vulnerability of the mentally ill body and its capability of receiving impressions renders it susceptible to eugenic control via Bradshaw's medical practice. He works to ensure that 'unsocial impulses, bred more than anything by the lack of good blood, were held in control' (113) in his nursing homes in Surrey and restricts breeding among the mentally ill: 'Sir William not only prospered himself but made England prosper, secluded her lunatics, forbade childbirth, penalised despair, made it impossible for the unfit to propagate their views until they, too, shared his sense of proportion' (110).

The novel's engagement with a biopolitics of health is significant in relation to the specific historical moment at which *Mrs. Dalloway* is set. There is some critical debate surrounding the historical significance of the novel's setting on a Wednesday in 'the middle of June' (6), which it is possible to date to Wednesday 20 June 1923.[59] Although David Bradshaw suggests that Woolf sets her novel on an '*imaginary* Wednesday in June 1923, not on Wednesday 20 June', there is a historical specificity to the novel's events that suggests a documentary basis for Woolf's social critique.[60] Two events in the novel occurred not on Wednesday 20 June 1923, but the previous day: Tuesday 19 June 1923. The resolution of the Surrey vs. Yorkshire cricket match that Peter Walsh reads about in the 'stop press' (179) occurred on 19 June after a three-day match. Similarly, the Bill that Clarissa observes Sir William Bradshaw discussing with Richard Dalloway dates the novel:

> He was talking to Richard about that Bill probably, which they wanted to get through the Commons. [...] They were talking about this Bill. Some case Sir William was mentioning, lowering his voice. It had its bearing upon what he was saying about the deferred effects of shell shock. There must be some provision in the Bill. (200–1)

David Bradshaw suggests that Bradshaw is lobbying to have the power to forcibly intern shell-shocked ex-servicemen.[61] It is possible to get a precise sense of the debates surrounding the treatment of the mentally ill through attention to Hansard records. On Tuesday 19 June 1923, the Mental Treatment Bill was transferred to the House of Commons from the House of Lords, a detail that parallels Bradshaw's concern to get the Bill 'through the Commons'. In the first reading of the Bill in the House of Lords, the Mental Treatment Bill was noted as having 'the chief purpose [...] to provide that a patient suffering from incipient *mental* disorder may be received for *treatment* without certification'. The mental instability of those who are 'mad by reason of accident occurring either at home or during the recent war in an act of heroism on the battlefield' was acknowledged in discussions. The Bill was also an opportunity to discuss eugenic controls. One speaker suggested this was 'germane to the subject' arguing that 'lunacy' had to be considered not merely in relation to a 'temporary cure' but 'with regard to the [...] principle of seeing whether it is not possible by some wise and humane means to extirpate from our race the curse under which, if we do not conquer it, we shall ourselves be ultimately destroyed'.[62]

Woolf's diary contains no entry for the 20 June 1923, but it does, however, contain a lengthy entry for the 19 June 1923. This is the entry in which Woolf considers the expression of emotion in her text and identifies her ambition for the novel as shaped by political and social concerns: 'In this book I have almost too many ideas. I want to give life & death, sanity & insanity; I want to criticise the social system, & show it at work, at its most intense – But here I may be posing.'[63] The oblique reference to the Mental Treatment Bill of 1923 in *Mrs. Dalloway* suggests that Woolf displaces events from Tuesday 19 June 1923 – the date upon which she articulates her social ambitions for the novel – onto the following day, indicating the centrality of a critique of the biopolitics of the state to her social critique.

Sir William Bradshaw is the figure through whom the novel's biopolitics of intelligence and impressibility unite. He offers the novel's fullest expression of meritocratic advancement: unlike the 'second-class' (133) Richard Dalloway and the 'ordinary' (189) Prime Minster, Bradshaw had 'won his position by sheer ability (being the son of a shop-keeper)' (105) and Clarissa identifies him as 'extraordinarily able' (201). While Septimus's mental ability is associated with culture and reading, Bradshaw's intellect is not defined through a sensitivity to culture and the arts. He is a philistine who 'never had time for reading' and resents 'cultivated people who came into his room and intimated that doctors, whose profession is a constant strain upon all the highest faculties, are not educated men' (108). The novel devalues the proponent of 'this exacting science' (109) who has expertise over a realm which, as the narrator archly suggests, 'has to do with what, after all, we know nothing about – the nervous system, the human brain' (109–10). Woolf's intention to explore 'sanity & insanity [...] to criticise the social system' emerges through Bradshaw as a critique of a medical meritocracy that is closely allied to an intellectually moribund political class, and advances a eugenic ideology to coerce the impressible sick.[64]

Coda: Intelligence, sentiment and modernist reading

The debate between sentiment and intelligence reverberates interestingly across reviews of *Mrs. Dalloway*, suggesting that the terms of the novel's biopolitical critique were also relevant to modernist reading practices which explored the roles of intelligence and sentiment. Richard Hughes comments on the novel as evidencing Woolf's 'masterly and masterful intellect', calling it an 'intellectual triumph'.[65] J. F. Holms finds that 'Mrs. Woolf has culture and intelligence' but disparagingly argues that 'most of the book, despite its pure and brilliant impressionism, is sentimental in conception and texture, and is accordingly aesthetically worthless'.[66] Edwin Muir found that *The Common Reader* demonstrates Woolf's 'intelligence', while she 'uses her sensibility [...] in [...] *Mrs. Dalloway*'.[67] Muir's separation between the two qualities of intelligence and sentiment along generic lines stands in tension with the simultaneous creative process behind the two works. This creative process signals an affinity between the thematic debates of *Mrs. Dalloway* and Woolf's conception of the ideal approach to reading. Woolf herself engages with the relative merits of intelligence and sentiment in reading literary texts in her 1931 essay, 'The Love of Reading' which examines Richardson's *Clarissa*. The essay argues

> reading [...] is a complex art. It does not merely consist in sympathising and understanding. It consists, too, in criticising and in judging. [...] But if this process of judging and deciding is full of pleasure it is also full of difficulty.[68]

In this context, the stylistic devices of *Mrs. Dalloway* – its demands on the intelligence and its critique of the limits of sensibility – serve a metatextual purpose. In *Mrs. Dalloway*, Woolf engages with the archetypal eighteenth-century model of female sensibility and eighteenth-century reading practices that foreground sentiment and sympathy. In her reworking of her intertextual source, Woolf not only advances a biopolitical critique of the state and ironizes stereotyped notions of the female intellect, as I have argued, but also foregrounds a new standard of aesthetic response that demands both the intelligence and the emotions.

Notes

1 Virginia Woolf, *The Diary of Virginia Woolf Volume II 1920–1924*, ed. Anne Olivier Bell (London: Hogarth Press, 1978), p. 309.
2 Michel Foucault, *The History of Sexuality Vol 1: An Introduction*, trans. Robert Hurley (London: Penguin Books, 1976), p. 141.
3 Kurt Danziger, *Naming the Mind: How Psychology Found Its Language* (London: Sage, 1997), p. 69.
4 Ibid., p. 71, p. 66.
5 Marjorie Strachey, 'Intelligence Tests', *Nation and the Athenaeum*, 6 September 1924, pp. 695–6 (cited p. 695).
6 Ibid., p. 695.
7 Ibid., p. 696.
8 Denis Lawton, *Education and Labour Party Ideologies, 1900–2001 and Beyond* (London: Routledge, 2005), p. 30.
9 Adrian Wooldridge, *Measuring the Mind: Education and Psychology in England, c. 1860–c. 1990* (Cambridge: Cambridge University Press, 1994), p. 175.
10 George Bernard Shaw, *Socialism and Superior Brains* (1910), www.marxists.org/reference/archive/shaw/works/brains.htm (all websites last accessed 8 June 2020).
11 For critiques of meritocracy, see Michael Young, *The Rise of the Meritocracy 1870–2033* (London: Thames & Hudson, 1958); Jo Littler, *Against Meritocracy: Culture, Power and Myths of Mobility* (London: Routledge, 2017).
12 Kyla Schuller, *The Biopolitics of Feeling: Race, Sex, and Science in the Nineteenth Century* (Duke University Press: Durham; London, 2018), p. 9.
13 Janet Todd, *Sensibility: An Introduction* (London: Methuen, 1986), pp. 13, 12.
14 Ibid., p. 13.
15 Lorraine Daston, 'The Naturalized Female Intellect', *Science in Context* 5/2 (1992), pp. 209–35.
16 Ian Maclean, *The Renaissance Notion of Woman: A Study in the Fortunes of Scholasticism* (Cambridge: Cambridge University Press, 1980 [1995]), p. 42.

17 Daston, 'Naturalized Female Intellect', p. 216.
18 John Mullan, *Sentiment and Sociability: The Language of Feeling in the Eighteenth Century* (Oxford: Oxford University Press, 1998 [2000]), p. 49.
19 Leslie Stephen, *History of English Thought in the Eighteenth Century in Two Volumes Vol. II* (London: Smith, Elder & Co., 1876), p. 75.
20 Cited in Mullan, *Sentiment and Sociability*, p. 34.
21 Kirsty Martin, *Modernism and the Rhythms of Sympathy: Vernon Lee, Virginia Woolf, D.H. Lawrence* (Oxford: Oxford University Press, 2013), pp. 8, 20; Clara Jones, *Virginia Woolf: Ambivalent Activist* (Edinburgh: Edinburgh University Press, 2016), p. 133.
22 Raymond Williams, 'The Bloomsbury Fraction', in *Culture and Materialism* (London: Verso, 2005 [1980]), pp. 165–89 (cited p. 173).
23 Ibid., p. 174.
24 Trudi Tate, *Modernism, History and the First World War* (Manchester: Manchester University Press, 1998), p. 162.
25 Brenda R. Silver, *Virginia Woolf's Reading Notebooks* (Princeton: Princeton University Press, 1983), www.dartmouth.edu/~library/digital/publishing/books/silver-virginia-1983/; Michèle Barrett, 'Virginia Woolf's Research for *Empire and Commerce in Africa* (Leonard Woolf, 1920)', *Woolf Studies Annual* 19 (2013), pp. 83–122.
26 Virginia Woolf, *Mrs Dalloway* (London: Penguin, 1996), p. 122.
27 Notebooks of Virginia Woolf, The British Library, London, UK, Vol. II, f.113r, Add MS 51045.
28 Woolf, *Diary II*, p. 312.
29 Ibid., p. 318.
30 Anna Snaith, *Virginia Woolf: Public and Private Negotiations* (Basingstoke: Palgrave Macmillan, 2000), p. 71.
31 Tate, *Modernism*, p. 162.
32 Strachey, 'Intelligence Tests', p. 696.
33 Danziger, *Naming the Mind*, p. 70.
34 Notebooks of Virginia Woolf, The British Library London, UK, Vol. I, f101r, Add MS 51044.
35 Board of Education, *Report of the Consultative Committee on Psychological Tests of Educable Capacity and Their Possible Use in the Public System of Education* (London: HM Stationery Office, 1924), pp. 84; 90; 92; 94; 118; 150; 152; 160.
36 Theophilus Bulkeley Hyslop, *The Borderland* (London: Phillip Allan & Co, 1924), p. 1.
37 Ibid., p. 116.
38 Ibid., p. 117.
39 Ibid., pp. 1, 9.
40 Matthew Thomson, *The Problem of Mental Deficiency: Eugenics, Democracy and Social Policy in Britain c. 1870–1959* (Oxford: Clarendon Press, 1998), p. 54.
41 Ibid., p. 99.
42 Ibid., p. 52.
43 The phrase 'adjusting to democracy' is from Thomson, p. 6.
44 Donald J. Childs, *Modernism and Eugenics: Woolf, Eliot, Yeats, and the Culture of Degeneration* (Cambridge: Cambridge University Press, 2001), p. 56.
45 Ibid., p. 56.
46 Danziger, *Naming the Mind*, p. 71.
47 Daston, 'Naturalized Female Intellect', p. 216.
48 Cited in Daston, 'Naturalized Female Intellect', p. 217; Mullan, *Sentiment and Sociability*, p. 4.

49 Ibid., p. 61.
50 Ibid., p. 102.
51 Virginia Woolf, *The Common Reader: Volume I* (London: Vintage, 2003), p. 23. Further references will be from this edition and cited parenthetically in the text by page number.
52 Michael Bell, *Sentimentalism, Ethics and the Culture of Feeling* (Basingstoke: Palgrave, 2000), p. 2.
53 Woolf, *Diary II*, p. 248.
54 Bell, *Sentimentalism, Ethics*, p. 160.
55 Mullan, *Sentiment and Sociability*, p. 2.
56 E. F. Shields, 'The American Edition of "*Mrs. Dalloway*"', *Studies in Bibliography*, Vol. 27 (1974), pp. 157–75 (p. 171).
57 Schuller, *Biopolitics of Feeling*, p. 62.
58 Ibid., p. 5.
59 See David Bradshaw, 'Explanatory Notes', in Virginia Woolf, *Mrs. Dalloway*, ed. David Bradshaw (Oxford: Oxford University Press, 2000), pp. 166–84 (cited pp. 183–4).
60 Ibid., p. 183.
61 David Bradshaw, 'Introduction', in *Mrs. Dalloway*, p. xvii.
62 Hansard 'Mental Treatment Bill' (3 May 1923), https://api.parliament.uk/historic-hansard/lords/1923/may/03/mental-treatment-bill-hl.
63 Woolf, *Diary II*, p. 248.
64 Ibid., p. 248.
65 Robin Majumdar and Allen McLaurin, eds., *Virginia Woolf: The Critical Heritage* (London: Taylor & Francis, 1975), p. 167.
66 *Critical Heritage*, pp. 169, 171.
67 Ibid., pp. 184, 185.
68 Virginia Woolf, 'The Love of Reading', in *The Essays of Virginia Woolf, Volume V 1929–1932*, ed. Stuart N. Clarke (London: Hogarth Press, 2009), pp. 272–3.

3

'[E]S DIE HÖCHSTE ZEIT IST' TO RE-CONSIDER IDEOLOGY: EZRA POUND AND NAZI GERMANY

Svetlana Ehtee

Three and a half decades ago, the critic Charles Bernstein raised the issue of the ethical implications of Ezra Pound's anti-Semitic and fascist views in his talk at the Pound Centennial Observance at Yale University (31 October–2 November 1985).[1] According to Bernstein's retrospective impressions, the topic and tone of his lecture were not widely appreciated:

> I was just about the youngest person invited to speak, and the only Jewish one; it didn't seem a coincidence that I was also the only person to raise the question of Pound's fascism at this occasion. The spirit of the supposedly academic event was set by the Pound's [*sic*] daughter asking us to observe several minutes of silence in honor of the anniversary of her father's death, which coincided with the Yale event. In keeping with this reverential spirit, the tone of the event was solemn and studiously respectful. In contrast, my speech would have seemed boisterous and structurally irreverant [*sic*]; though insofar as this was so it was oddly more in the mood of the putative subject. [...] After the event, at which it was made clear to me that I should not have spoken the way I did (not a new problem for me however), I wasn't surprised that Yale Review turned the piece down. While they may have had other reasons to reject it, since it was advocating an approach to poetry antipathetic to their aesthetic agenda, I couldn't help but interpret it as an extension of the reception I had gotten at the centennial.[2]

Though the academic climate has changed since the Pound centennial conference, with much having been written on the topic of Pound's unsavoury political views and inexcusable biases in the intervening years, the increasing digitization of relevant and otherwise unpublished library holdings challenges our understandings of the still-underappreciated extent of Pound's support of fascism.

To date, over thirty biographies and biographical accounts of Pound have been published.[3] As early as 1960, in his part-biography, part-critical analysis of Pound, G. S. Fraser tackled the same issues that the 'Pound enterprise'[4] still finds debatable today.[5] How should we interpret Pound's socio-political endeavours?

What implications do Pound's fascist positions have for the evaluation of his work? The early biographies of Pound, framed by formalist approaches then prevalent in literary studies, greatly shaped the scholarly understanding of the poet's oeuvre during the 1970s. However, these biographies also paved the way for contemporary biographers who still, in the second decade of the twenty-first century, turn a blind eye to the extent of Pound's anti-Semitism and fascism. Many have argued that Pound scholarship is torn between critics assessing Pound's oeuvre by exculpating his allegiances or, in turn, by condemning him and disregarding his work.[6]

Steered by Hugh Kenner's monumental *The Pound Era*, subsequent biographies of Pound have often selectively used biographical information, ignoring the poet's political ideas and the effect of his views upon his work. Since the goal of critics before the mid-1970s was understandably to secure Pound's place as a leading modernist writer and craftsman, they focused mostly on Pound's experimental poetics. This is reflected in the words of Charles T. Davis who writes in the first edition of *American Literary Scholarship* (1963) that 'the amount of scholarship devoted to the man [Pound] and his work indicates the continued improvement of his reputation, despite his unhappy political history'.[7] Indeed, Pound's early biographers were faced with the challenging task of writing about a poet whose reputation had already been tarnished by his wartime activities and subsequent confinement to a mental asylum for over twelve years.

While the shift from formalist studies to politically based perspectives has certainly influenced how we read Pound's work in the twenty-first century, it has also exposed a stagnation of attention to the topics which Pound scholars still consider 'off limits'. This stagnation is evident in biographer Alec Marsh's unsparing questions:

> How could such a great modern artist hold such apparently reactionary views? Was he a traitor as the U.S. Government alleged? Was he, in fact, insane? [...] Above all, how could such a good and generous man, as his life repeatedly attests, be gripped by such passionate hatreds as to make his name synonymous in many people's minds with 'fascism' and 'anti-Semitism'? Finally, what is the proper relation between poetry and politics?[8]

Marsh is here as perceptive as Fraser was in 1960: these queries are still pressing in the case of Pound studies. While the amount of Pound's unpublished correspondences suggests that there is enough untapped information to provide impartial and comprehensive answers to the questions related to the poet's socio-political ideas, critical assessments have often fallen short of venturing into the archives, unearthing new evidence, or simply avoiding *a priori* assumptions.

Pound's obsession with Mussolini and the influence that his meeting with 'The Boss' clearly had upon him have been widely researched in the context of the archive. Most recently, Matthew Feldman has put a finer point on Pound's radical right socio-politics in *Ezra Pound's Fascist Propaganda, 1935–45* (2013), and has faced severe and sometimes punitive scholarly backlash as a result. By unearthing several thousand radio items missed or undocumented by Poundians, Feldman's study serves as a reminder that one should not underestimate the poet's involvement in Fascist Italy's propaganda. Another recent addition, Catherine Paul's *Fascist Directive: Ezra Pound and Italian Cultural Nationalism* (2016), has shown the influence that Italian cultural heritage had on Pound's view of Mussolini's Fascist regime and the poet's own support of the latter. These two indispensable studies complement each other in their effort to elucidate Pound's Fascist thinking by employing new archival evidence and by showing the kinds of implications the poet's socio-political ideas have had on his work, respectively.

In contrast to the recent scholarly interest in Pound and Italian Fascism, Pound's efforts to influence and support Hitler's war propaganda have been unjustly overlooked by biographers and scholars alike. Since *The Cantos* were written over a period of more than fifty years—encompassing two world wars and their devastating aftermaths—the epic reflects these developments in history as well as the ensuing changes in Pound's own life and beliefs. It is unsurprising then that *The Cantos* contain little-noted lines indicating Pound's approval of Nazi tactics. In addition, several key epistolary exchanges that Pound maintained chronicle the poet's Nazi sympathies. Pound's letters to Graham Seton Hutchison, William Joyce and James Strachey Barnes touch on the poet's willingness to serve the Nazi or the Salò Republic cause through propaganda efforts.

Pound's support for the Nazi regime becomes evident in a passage from Canto 51 citing excerpts from a speech by Rudolf Hess, one of 'Hitler's most fanatical supporters',[9] which was broadcasted from Königsberg, a Prussian city now belonging to Russia. The aim of Hess's speech was to justify the purge of the Night of the Long Knives on 30 June 1934 in which the Nazis carried out a series of executions to solidify Hitler's leadership. In this speech, delivered on 8 July 1934, Hess re-affirmed his allegiance to Hitler, and announced that the party's unity had been restored as a result of the purge.[10] Donned in his party uniform, the Deputy Führer also claimed that the Reich's domestic and foreign policy was one of peace, which, of course, was received with scepticism by many outside of Germany because of the violence which the speech was intended to justify.[11] In Canto 51, Pound juxtaposes Hess's speech with 'Geryone', the personification of usury he borrowed from Dante.[12] Hess's speech, on the other hand, is depicted as a divine message ('Deo similis quodam modo') according to which '[z]wischen die Volkern erzielt wird/a modus vivendi' ('the way of life should be achieved between the peoples', my translation).[13] I would not go as far as Robert Casillo in 'Ezra Pound, L. A. Waddell, and the Aryan Tradition of "The Cantos"', however, in which he claims that Pound is suggesting that Hitler is 'the king' who proclaims the aforementioned lines from the 'King's mountain, an oracular place'.[14] As well, I am also not convinced by David Moody's claim that 'the whole passage [...] must be in his [Geryon's] voice'[15] since I find that there is a clear distinction in this passage between the narrator who is said to be '[t]hus speaking in Königsberg', that is, Rudolf Hess, and Geryone's usurious song identified later in the passage ('sang Geryone' and 'I am Geryon [*sic*] twin with usura'). Furthermore, this shift in narrative voice is suggested not only by the punctuation (after a sequence of three consecutive full stops, the narrative switches to Geryone's song indicated by the series of consecutive semi-colons) but also by the very message of Hess's speech, which Pound praises, and Geryone's song, which Pound denounces.

An earlier version of Canto 51, collected in Bacigalupo's *Posthumous Cantos*, further supports my argument that Hess's words are envisioned as a separate entity in the text and that Pound did indeed agree with the Deputy Führer's statements. In the version documented by Bacigalupo, Pound not only cites more extensively from the broadcast, but also identifies Hess as the broadcaster ('Hess, Königsberg 34') and does not include the fragment in the final version in which he mentions Geryone. Moody's argument that Pound equates Geryone's evil with Hess's is thus simply not plausible. In fact, in the version documented in Bacigalupo's book, Pound himself comments on Hess's words with an exclamatory 'Yes!' and expresses his agreement: 'es die höchste Zeit ist' ('it is high time'; my translation):

> 'Das endlich eine wirkliche Verständigung
> zwischen den Völkern erzielt wird'
> Hess, Königsberg 34
> Yes! es [*sic*] die höchste Zeit ist.
> [...]
> Es ist die höchste, das endlich, zwischen die Völkern, eine
> Verständigung ...[16]

Furthermore, in 'The Text as Process and the Problem of Intentionality', Hans Walter Gabler documents that Pound's approval of Hess's broadcast was evident even in the note attached to the manuscript of Canto 51: 'In the typed note possibly excerpted from a newspaper report, Pound encircles the opening phrase and emphatically repeats in pencil "Yah es die hoschste Zeit ist"'.[17] In '[a] marginal note added in ink', as Gabler notes, Pound wrote: 'Follows lgty [*sic*] murder of Dollfuss'.[18] Indeed, in a 26 July 1934 letter, only a day after Dollfuss's murder, Pound informed Graham Seton Hutchison, a writer, military theorist and fascist activist, of what he discerned to be silver linings:

> The murder of Dolfus [*sic*] is a damn shame, but might give
> a good deal of support to the wilder and less proven parts
> of yr/ interpretation of Albert.
> In any case the Brit. Press does NOT mention it,
> have just read that Thyssen has left the nazi party.

CHEERS

Regardless of Pound's learning of the Austrian Chancellor Engelbert Dollfuss's murder by an Austrian Nazi, the poet's support of Hess was unfaltering. Pound must have also known that, at the time of the broadcast, Hess was already serving as the Deputy Führer of the German Nazi Party, the position he held from 1933 to 1941. And while I agree with Moody that at the time it was not obvious that Hitler would annex Austria four years later, Pound's own writing proves that he did know of Dollfuss's murder, that he must have seen through Hess's peace-speech, and that he himself was openly supporting a Nazi in writing. After all, Pound revised Canto 51 but chose to retain Hess's words, removing only Hess's name and the date of his speech.

Pound's unpublished correspondence with British army officer Lieutenant-Colonel Graham Seton Hutchison (1890–1946) also exposes Pound's leanings.[19] This exchange, held between 1934 and 1936, sheds light on the poet's willingness to write fascist propaganda.[20] Hutchison founded the National Workers' Movement in 1933, but the party was later renamed the National Socialist Workers' Party and still later in 1936 the National Workers' Party.[21] It is significant to mention that, according to Stephen Dorril, *Der Stürmer* reported in 1935 that Nazi agents were sent to London to form a branch of Rosenberg's *Nordische Gesellschaft*.[22] This was, according to Dorril, the beginning of the Nordic League in Britain. Nick Toczek further argues that the MI5 believed that the Nordic League was 'directed from Berlin'.[23] Given that Hutchison fostered relationships with high-ranking Nazis[24] and that there was speculation that he was 'in German pay, as a publicist',[25] Pound's connections to Hutchison and to the Third Reich certainly deserve greater scholarly attention than they have received.[26]

The most illuminating study of Pound's correspondence with Hutchison and one of the most thorough investigations of the poet's Nazi allegiances to date appeared in Gavin Bowd's *Fascist Scotland* (2013), even though the book only briefly mentions the correspondence, discussing it on six of its 306 pages. Within scholarship devoted to Pound, there are only cursory mentions of this correspondence in Noel Stock's *The Life of Ezra Pound* (1970), Hugh Witemeyer's edition of *Pound/Williams: Selected Letters of Ezra Pound and William Carlos Williams* (1996), and Michael T. Davis's and Cameron McWhirter's edition of *Ezra Pound and 'Globe' Magazine: The Complete Correspondence* (2015).[27] The only other work providing a short description of the Pound/Hutchison correspondence and including one of their letters is Roxana Preda's edition of *Ezra Pound's Economic Correspondence, 1933–1940* (2007).[28] To make matters more complicated, the archivist at the Beinecke Library who catalogued these letters misspelled Hutchison's surname on the original letters. The additions in pencil the archivist made at the beginning of most letters read 'Hutchinson', so critics may have been misled to believe that the person in question was the Hutchinson of Hutchinson & Co, the publisher who printed Mussolini's *My Autobiography* as well as a number of the Lieutenant-Colonel's own works. The fact that Pound himself misspelled Hutchison's surname on a number of occasions has certainly contributed to the confusion.

Since Hutchison, much like Pound, believed that his work was suppressed by publishers due to its didactic nature and controversial subject matters, their correspondence focuses largely on the reasons behind such alleged suppression. Hutchison's body of work provides abundant evidence of what these controversial topics included. In *Footslogger: An Autobiography* (1931), for example, Hutchison writes of his correspondence with 'Hitler's favourite author', Ernst Jünger, and of Jünger's praises of Hutchison's work.[29] Unlike *Footslogger*, which captures Hutchison's 'drift to Nazism',[30] *Meteor* (1933) reads like a Nazi-propaganda-infused anti-Semitic litany against the 'Jewish financial system, which is enslaving the world'.[31] 'We have faith in ourselves and our race', Hutchison continues, to fight the 'unscrupulous, greedy alien financiers to whom are joined other unscrupulous careerists'.[32] The way forward, according to the Lieutenant-Colonel, was for people to join the aforementioned pro-Nazi National Workers' Party of Great Britain, which he founded in 1933 under the slogan 'King-Race-Empire'.[33] In addition, Hutchison's fascist beliefs were close to Pound's own views, so that, unlike many of Pound's other epistolary exchanges, their letters show reciprocal encouragement as well as mutual interest in socio-political topics and economic theories.[34] Hutchison was so supportive of Pound's programme of economic reform[35] that the poet granted him permission to incorporate extensive passages from *ABC of Economics* into his 1934 novel *Blood Money*.[36]

Even though Hutchison later, in the 1940s, abandoned Nazism and switched allegiance to the Scottish National Party, which was in itself radical, he publicly expressed his fascist activism at the time of his exchange with Pound.[37] What is even more important for understanding Pound's politics is that Hutchison fostered 'links with Hitler and the Nazis',[38] to the extent that there was speculation that he was a 'great friend of Hitler' and that he worked as a publicist for the Germans.[39] For example, in his multi-volume *Diaries* (1973), Sir Robert Bruce Lockhart, a British diplomat and secret agent during the Second World War, noted in a 1933 journal entry that Hutchison was close to Hitler:

> Graham Seton Hutchison, the writer and author of *The W Plan*, etc. [...] is a great friend of Hitler. He speaks German well and has been writing up Germany. He has been doing this for some years, wrote a pamphlet on German wrongs in Silesia, and I remember Bernstorff telling me at the time that he was paid by the Germans and asking me if he was worth the money.[40]

Similarly, in diaries by the Reichsleiter Alfred Rosenberg, the notorious Nazi ideologue, Hutchison reportedly informed the Führer of what he considered to be threats to the Reich.[41] In May 1934, for example, Rosenberg remarked on a letter by Hutchison, which was then forwarded to Hitler himself, in which the British Lieutenant-Colonel discloses a private conversation he had in Berlin with a German diplomat, banker and nephew to the former Ambassador to the United States, Count Albrecht von Bernstorff (who is also mentioned as a connection between Lockhart and Hutchison in the aforementioned *Diary* entry). In this letter, Hutchison writes of Bernstorff's treasonous claim that 'a terrible collapse [of the Third Reich] will follow'.[42] According to Rosenberg, Hitler responded that, 'if this statement could be verified, he [the Führer] would take action against B[ernstorff] and impose the toughest penalties'.[43] Hutchison must have been a trustworthy Nazi informant: Bernstorff was later sent to a concentration camp for helping persecuted Jews and was ultimately executed by the Gestapo in 1945.[44]

While there is no evidence Pound knew of Hutchison's connections to Rosenberg, he certainly did know that the Lieutenant-Colonel took the initiative in communicating his socio-political views to Rudolf Hess, Reich Deputy Führer, as well as to Hitler himself. In a letter to Pound dated 12 November 1934, Hutchison raised his connection to the Nazi leader when discussing the then-demilitarized Saar territory:[45]

> Re Frogs. Important. Intense propaganda going on
> among inhabitants of former devastated areas. Recruits from
> these districts inflamed by propaganda are being sent to Metz
> for intensive training. I have personal knowledge. They
> are being told the Hun is at the gate. The Metz Corps
> are those prepared to march to the Saar. *I've sent informat-*
> *ion to Adolf of course.* (emphasis added)

Had he not been cognizant of this connection from the onset of their correspondence, Pound certainly became aware of Hutchison's connections to Nazi Germany in mid-1934: 'I've written to Germany, General [Karl] Haushofer, highly intelligent, stupendous worker, adviser of Hess, broadcasters and orientalists. Deeply interested to read your philosophic basis.'[46] Haushofer, a German general and geo-politician, was not only a long-time 'adviser' but also a devoted teacher and 'surrogate father' to Rudolf Hess.[47] Haushofer's 'geopolitical' ideas, as they are now known, contributed to the Nazi pursuit of *Lebensraum* (or living space), later used by the Nazis to explain Hitler's expansionism no less than the Third Reich's political violence.[48] Haushofer met Hitler through Hess in the Spring of 1920[49] and, although he evidently opposed Hitler's virulent anti-Semitism (given that his own wife, Martha Haushofer, was half-Jewish), the connection Haushofer-Hess-Hitler has been well-documented.[50] Stirred by an opportunity to spread his socio-political views, Pound quickly responded with enthusiasm: '{IF} [ill del] Haushofer can correspond in english, we cd/ correspond direct,/[ill del] I cd/ send you carbons./[ill del] I can have 'em send him my ABC is he read eng/ tho' he is prob/beyond that ... '[51] Even though scholars have yet to explore Pound's relationship with Haushofer, what is evident is that Hutchison served as a link between Hess's advisor and Pound: 'I've written Haushofer get in touch with/you. Both he and his wife write and read perfect Eng-/lish.'[52]

This correspondence further suggests that Pound conceived of Hutchison as an intermediary between himself and the Führer. Pound repeatedly prompted Hutchison to encourage Hitler to adopt the poet's economic theories. By the mid-1930s, Pound was able to look past Hitler's mania in order to secure his support of the 'economic LIGHT'.[53] With a view to promoting his hybrid economic ideas, Pound assured Hutchison that '[s]urely NOW is the moment for them [Germans] to announce a REAL/economic reform'.[54] Pound seems to be suggesting that such an economic agenda would bring Hitler more followers ('Plenty of the best lads will rally/ and will combat/ anti=ADOLF PROPAGANDA IF he can be got to broadcast/a little economic news').[55] Yet, he did not stop there. Pound must have also believed that the German leader could serve as an appropriate propagator of this economic programme and thus communicated that Hitler 'can be made/ simpatico [Italian for "likable"]'.[56] Naturally, Pound envisioned himself as the architect of propaganda for such an economic plan: 'Re Adolf and what I can do. IF anybody in Germany will/announce an honest economic programme I will do my damndest/to get news of it printed straight'.[57] Just over a month later, Pound was already excited about the prospects of a larger, economically enlightened Germany:

> WHEN Adolf HHHHHHHHHHHHHHHHHHHHHHHHHHHHHHHHH
> HHHHHHHHHHHHHHHHHHHHHH [*sic*] really starts bucking the
> banks, the world will gather too him/ and there will
> be more of this MeinFuhrer bizniz/ OUTSIDE Hunnland.[58]

Although some have argued that Pound believed he was 'anti-banks' and not actually anti-Semitic – mostly following Pound's claim that not all usurers were Jewish – his words to Hutchison prove that the poet equated the Jews with financial institutions by this time.[59] As a matter of fact, Pound even suggested diverting the media attention from 'pogroms' and 'racial prejudice' to economics in order to avoid negative press:

> I DONT see how germany [*sic*] can get a break

[ill del] UNLESS Adolph proclaims a an [*sic*] UNAMBIGUOUS economic

> reform. Something absolutely clear an anti[ill del]banks
> anti banks is anti se{m}ite. if [*sic*] you like [ill del] but it is
> the only viable form. And it doesn [*sic*] NOT give the kike
> a chance to howl about pog{r}ums and rac{e} prejudice.[60]

Indeed, Pound's letters to Hutchison between 1934 and 1936 show how Pound was clearly aware of anti-Semitism in mid-1930s Germany:

> Interminably to continue/ [A. R.] {O}rage is probably just as worried
> about yr/ open anti semitism as you are about his not
> patting Adolf/[61]

Given the information provided in Pound's letters to Hutchison, I have to disagree with Tim Redman that 'Pound was not aware of the horror that the Germans were perpetrating at the same time he was making the broadcasts [1940–45]'.[62] The Pound/Hutchison letters show that Pound was aware of the violent tactics by the Nazis as early as 1934. Pound's views of violence perpetuated by fascists were in actuality frequently expressed in his letters to Hutchison. As Pound explained to the Lieutenant-Colonel in a letter from 9 November 1934: '[t]ime to [have] pogrums [*sic*] is WHEN YOU/ have the power'. By this time Germany had established a totalitarian regime of persecution and murder of political opponents and had established the first concentration camps.[63]

The similarities between Pound's views and 1930s Nazi propaganda force a reconsideration of the narrative surrounding Pound's wartime efforts and a re-evaluation of the political underpinnings of his work. For example, the notion that jazz musicians are somehow connected to a Jewish conspiracy was an idea Pound entertained as early as the 1930s. This belief was perfectly aligned with Nazi propaganda which also claimed that jazz was 'black' because it originated in predominantly African American communities, and was perceived as 'Jewish' since many advocates of jazz in Germany were Jews.[64] In a letter to Hutchison from June 1934, Pound cautioned the Lieutenant-Colonel: 'Note that the NEGOR [*sic*] MUSIC monopoly in the U.S. <u>is</u> in the/hands of jews, and that [ill del] pore marse nigguh [*sic*] is exploited thereby'.[65] In drawing a conspiratorial connection between drugs, jazz, Jews and world domination, Pound here engages in a well-known strain of Nazi propaganda. The so-called 'Nigger-Jew jazz' phrase was concocted by Nazi ideologues to persuade the public that 'degenerate' Jews 'contained a significantly large proportion of negroid blood' leading them to enjoy this 'atonal modernist music'.[66] This was presented as evidence of a systematic plot by the Jews to contaminate the minds of the 'racially pure'.

At the start of the Second World War, Joseph Goebbels, the Reich Minister of Propaganda of Nazi Germany, started a radio campaign mainly aimed at the British public 'in an attempt to reverse the damage done by the BBC to the Germans'.[67] These broadcasts were hosted by the expatriate Irish-American William Joyce, better known as 'Lord Haw Haw', a co-founder of the pro-Nazi National Socialist League in Britain. The programme Joyce hosted was titled 'Germany Calling', which, interestingly, included American-type jazz music tailored to Nazi ideology in addition to expected propaganda-infused commentaries. The lyrics to well-known jazz songs were re-written according to Nazi propaganda and then performed on air. For example, the lyrics to the popular song 'I've Got a Pocketful of Dreams' were rendered as 'Gonna save the world of Wall Street, / gonna fight for Russia, too, / I'm fightin' for democracy, / I'm fightin' for the Jew', performed by 'Charlie and His Orchestra' (*Charlie und Sein Orchester*) and broadcasted in autumn 1941.[68] According to J. J. Wilhelm, Pound started listening to Joyce's programme in 1940 and later began a correspondence with the notorious broadcaster.[69] As indicated by their correspondence, Pound must have interpreted Lord Haw Haw's propaganda scheme as a confirmation that Britain was, indeed, governed by Jews; that jazz music was another medium used by the Jewry to brainwash the English-speaking West; and that Soviet Jews, Hitler's great enemy, were plotting the demise of other nations in their conspiracy to take over the world.[70]

After the Allied forces entered mainland Italy in 1943, the moment marking the beginning of the demise of Mussolini's regime, German soldiers quickly seized control of the Italian north. This culminated in the creation of the Salò Republic, or *Repubblica Sociale Italiana* (September 1943–May 1945). The Nazis established Mussolini as the leader of the RSI on Lake Garda. Even though this was obviously a Nazi-backed puppet regime, Pound was not dissuaded from continuing his efforts in support of *Il Duce*. During this time, Pound was close friends with a fellow EIAR broadcaster and ardent Fascist Major James Strachey Barnes (1890–1955), better known as the 'Italian Lord Haw Haw'. Barnes was an anti-Semitic British national who lived in Italy and broadcasted pro-Fascist propaganda, much like Pound.[71] Barnes had met Mussolini several times and was, like Pound, under the watchful eye of MI5 from the 1930s due to his fervent support of Fascism.[72] Barnes was such a prominent figure in Fascist Italy that when, on 27 September 1930, he married Buona Guidotti, he received congratulations from both the Pope and Mussolini.[73]

Also known under his Italianized name of 'Giacomo', Barnes kept diaries from January 1943 to May 1945 in which he not only details his everyday life, but also describes the lives of other like-minded people in Italy, including Pound. It is through Barnes's diary that we learn of the details of Pound's long walk from Rome northwards, towards the Salò Republic. As the Allied forces made their way from Salerno, where they initially landed on 9 September 1943, Pound snuck through the front lines.[74] Since Pound had been indicted for treason by the United States in July 1943, he clearly wanted to avoid being captured by the Allies. Though much has been written about Pound's trek from Rome, less interest has been shown about the issue that the Fascist authorities apparently prepared a fake passport to protect the poet from approaching Allied forces. We learn from Barnes's diary that he personally delivered Pound's fake Italian passport to the German Embassy: 'Went to the German Embassy with Ezra Pound's false passport & asked them to look for him & give it to him', Barnes writes.[75] We must ask ourselves how important Pound would have been for the fascists if, in the midst of the Allied attack, a false passport was delivered for him at no less than a German Embassy? With the exception of a few brief mentions, however, scholars have unaccountably overlooked Pound's relationship with Barnes.[76]

While Pound's connections to and relationships with fascist groups deserve further investigations and a book-length study, the question of whether Pound was an anti-Semitic fascist must be answered in the affirmative. And while an increasing number of academic publications have been attempting to illuminate Pound's life and work, it seems that an alarming number of scholars are not yet ready to acknowledge and accept Pound's politics at face value.[77] Arguably, new archival research necessitates an equally rigorous understanding of historical and ideological contexts that must accompany the more subjective interpretations of poetry. How do scholars and readers reconcile historical narrative with Pound's canonical aesthetics? This is certainly not a new question; however, recent archival research pushes modernist scholarship to continue working towards new understandings. As historians have recently shown, the English-speaking world was far better informed about Germany's anti-Jewish attitude than previously thought. As early as in June 1931, Faber & Faber published Christopher Turner's

English translation of General Erich Ludendorff's *Weltkrieg droht auf deutschem Boden* as *The Coming War*, in which Ludendorff describes Germany's 'self-emasculation' at the Treaty of Versailles and calls for the German people to 'take the sword to regain their liberty' against 'supernational forces' and 'their Jewish mentality'.[78] Just two years later, in 1933, Otto Katz's *The Brown Book of the Reichstag Fire and Hitler Terror* was translated into English and published in London. The book listed forty-five concentration camps in Germany and claimed that there were between 35,000 and 40,000 prisoners held within.[79] Perhaps the most telling evidence was that several hundred foreign journalists reported on Kristallnacht, the event which marked 'a dramatic turning point in the way Nazism was perceived' and 'effectively ended whatever attractions Nazism had earlier held for ordinary people and their governments'.[80] Returning to Charles Bernstein's words which opened this chapter, and in light of the archival evidence discussed herein, it seems that the crucial question we should be asking ourselves is whether it is our job to understand Pound as the person and poet he was or the person he was apart from his greatness as an artist and critic. Only after we have learned the true extent and nature of Pound's ideology will we be able to meaningfully contribute to the cognate discussion of the practical implications of reading, studying or teaching the works of a poet who is championed by so many fascist movements today.[81]

Notes

1 For a more detailed account of the Centennial Observance, see Peter Viereck's 'Pound at 100: Weighing the Art and the Evil', *The New York Times* (29 December 1985), p. 3. See also Hugh Witemeyer's review of the conference, which devotes a paragraph to Bernstein's paper: 'The Yale Centennial Conference', *Paideuma* 15/1 (Spring 1986), pp. 123–8.

2 The full speech is available at: http://writing.upenn.edu/epc/authors/bernstein/essays/poundbern.html. This talk was later partially published in Bernstein's *My Way: Speeches and Poems* (Chicago: University of Chicago Press, 1999).

3 See Svetlana Ehtee, 'Biographies, Biographical Accounts, and Memoirs of Ezra Pound', http://ezrapoundsociety.org/index.php/biographies-of-ezra-pound.

4 Donald Davie, *Ezra Pound* (Chicago: The University of Chicago Press, 1975), p. 5.

5 This essay comes out of my PhD Dissertation, 'After Ez Stirred Up That Hornets['] Nest: Ezra Pound's Politics of "Open" Poetry', completed at the University of New Brunswick, Canada, in 2020. I was greatly aided by Sara Dunton, Demetres Tryphonopoulos, Archie Henderson, and Alec Marsh, who have read various drafts of this paper and provided invaluable suggestions. Finally, completing this paper would have been impossible without Matthew Feldman's patience, support and expertise.

6 William Chace argued that there are three camps in Pound scholarship. The first group focuses largely on formalistic analyses which provide no 'reference to his [Pound's] ideas', while the second camp 'analyze[s] his ideas without reference to his work' by making 'scathing attacks'. The third camp does Pound 'the greatest disservice of all' by simply agreeing with Pound. (*The Political Identities of Ezra Pound & T. S. Eliot* (Stanford, CA: Stanford University Press, 1973), p. 4). David

Heymann, furthermore, wrote about the problems one encounters in dealing with a poet such as Pound: 'His [Pound's] supporters have tended in the past to depict him in terms most favourable to him – to emphasize the power of his poetry – but have ignored some of the paramount concerns – economic and political – that plagued him during a major portion of his life. Conversely, there are those more interested in the fact that he was an anti-Semite, a drumbeater for Hitler and Mussolini, than they are in coming to terms with his poetry' (*Ezra Pound: The Last Rower, A Political Profile* (New York: The Viking Press, 1976), p. x).

7 Charles T. Davis, 'Pound', in *American Literary Scholarship*, ed. James Woodress (Durham, NC: Duke University Press, Vol. 1963, no. 1, 1965), p. 173.

8 Alec Marsh, *Ezra Pound* (London: Reaktion Books, 2011), p. 11.

9 James Douglas-Hamilton, *The Truth about Rudolf Hess* (Edinburgh: Mainstream Publishing, 1993), p. xxxxvii.

10 It is significant to note that the following lines from Canto 104 echo that very same speech Hess gave in Königsberg: '"Good chaps" said Schmidt/"damn shame we have to fight "em'. Hate is not born in the trenches/nor among 2nd. lieutenants'. Ezra Pound, *The Cantos of Ezra Pound* (New York: New Directions, 1996), p. 759. I am grateful to Archie Henderson for bringing this information to my attention.

11 *Office of United States Chief of Counsel For Prosecution of Axis Criminality, Nazi Conspiracy and Aggression* (Washington: United States GPO, 1946), p. 810.

12 Carroll F. Terrell, *A Companion to the Cantos of Ezra Pound* (Berkeley and Los Angeles: University of California Press, 1980), p. 199.

13 Pound, *The Cantos of Ezra Pound*, p. 251.

14 Robert Casillo, 'Ezra Pound, L. A. Waddell, and the Aryan Tradition of "The Cantos"', *Modern Language Studies* 15/2 (1985), p. 78.

15 David Moody, *Ezra Pound: Poet. A Portrait of the Man and His Work, Vol II: The Epic Years 1921–1939* (Oxford: Oxford University Press, 2014), p. 233.

16 Massimo Bacigalupo, *Posthumous Cantos* (Manchester: Carcanet, 2015), p. 54.

17 Hans Walter Gabler, 'The Text as Process and the Problem of Intentionality', *TEXT* 3 (1987), p. 114.

18 Gabler, 'The Text as Process and the Problem of Intentionality', p. 115.

19 Hutchison published several works of fiction and non-fiction; alongside *Footslogger* and *Meteor*, some of Hutchison's most well-known works include *Arya* (1934), *Your Verdict* (1934) and *The Master Book of Secrets and Secret Societies* (1937), which he published under the pseudonym 'Graham Seton'.

20 'Ezra Pound Collection', American Literature Collection, Beinecke Rare Book and Manuscript Library, Yale University, New Haven, CT, YCAL MSS 43, box 23, folders 1025–1027; 'Ezra Pound: Correspondence of Ezra Loomis Pound, poet, (b. 1885, d.1972) and Lt-Col. Graham Seton Hutchison, writer, (b.1890, d.1946)', Western Manuscripts, British Library, London, UK, Add MS 74270. Copyright © 2020 by Mary de Rachewiltz and the Estate of Omar S. Pound. Used by permission.

21 Gavin Bowd, *Fascist Scotland* (Edinburgh: Birlinn, 2013), p. 53.

22 Stephen Dorril, *Blackshirt: Sir Oswald Mosley and British Fascism* (London and New York: Viking, 2006), p. 425.

23 Nick Toczek, *Haters, Baiters and Would-Be Dictators: Anti-Semitism and the UK Far Right* (London: Routledge, 2015), p. 220.

24 Bowd, *Fascist Scotland*, p. 50.

25 Sir Robert Bruce Lockhart, *The Diaries of Sir Robert Bruce Lockhart: 1915–1938*, ed. Kenneth Young (New York: St. Martin's Press, 1973), p. 257.

26 Hutchison wrote a 'Foreword' to Victor E. Marsden's pamphlet *Jews in Russia: with Half Jews and 'Damped' Jews: With a List of the Names of the 447 Jews in the Government of Russia on the Establishment of the Soviets* (London: The National Workers' Party of Great Britain, 1920, reprinted in 1936). Marsden became notorious for his English translation of *The Protocols of the Learned Elders of Zion*, published posthumously in the early 1920s. *The Protocols* were alleged minutes from a meeting of Jewish conspirators who had plotted to take over the world by pushing it into war. I am greatly indebted to Archie Henderson who brought this information to my attention.

27 K. K. Ruthven writes that Pound recommended Hutchison's novels (*Ezra Pound as Literary Critic*, London: Routledge, 1990, p. 125) but he does not mention nor delve into the correspondence.

28 Lieutenant-Colonel Hutchison's surname has often been misspelled in print: in Preda's edition of *Ezra Pound's Economic Correspondence, 1933–1940* (Gainesville, FL: University Press of Florida, 2007) Hutchison is referred to as 'Hutchinson' (see p. 137 (notes), p. 270 (index), p. 297 and 299 (index)); David Moody also misspells Hutchison's surname in his *Ezra Pound, Poet: A Portrait of the Man & His Work, Vol. II: The Epic Years, 1921–1939* (Oxford: Oxford University Press, 2014), p. 377 (notes). Unfortunately, even newer publications, such as Graham Macklin's 2020 book *Failed Führers: A History of Britain's Extreme Right* (London and New York: Routledge), which mentions Pound's 21 May 1936 letter to Hutchison, misspell Hutchison's surname in the same manner.

29 Bowd, *Fascist Scotland*, p. 51.

30 Ibid.

31 Graham Seton Hutchison, *Meteor* (London: Hutchinson & Co, 1933), pp. 274–5.

32 Hutchison, *Meteor*, p. 275.

33 See 'Ezra Pound Collection', YCAL MSS 43, box 23, folder 1027.

34 As Bernhard Dietz duly notes, Hutchison published his anti-Semitic manifesto in 1936 under the title *Truth. The Evidence in the Case. On the Political Influence of the Jews* (London: np, 1936). See Dietz, *Neo-Tories: The Revolt of British Conservatives against Democracy and Political Modernity (1929–1939)* (London: Bloomsbury Academic, 2018), p. 258. I am thankful to Archie Henderson for sharing this information and to Ian Copestake who kindly sent me the book in question.

35 Pound believed that both the Federal Reserve and the Bank of England had a monopoly over the control of the value of money and, therefore, the ability to alter its buying power. If these institutions were governed by the 'big Jew', Pound feared, then everyday finance capitalism was in the hands of 'usurers'. This was the well-documented justification of Pound's beliefs regarding his anti-Semitic sentiments at the time. The only way to eradicate usury, Pound believed, was to implement a hybrid economic system based on a combination of C. H. Douglas's theory of Social Credit and Silvio Gesell's Stamp Scrip. For more information on Pound's understanding of economics, see Alec Marsh's *Money and Modernity: Pound, Williams, and the Spirit of Jefferson* (Tuscaloosa: University of Alabama Press, 1998), Leon Surette's *Pound in Purgatory: From Economic Radicalism to Anti-Semitism* (Urbana: University of Illinois Press, 1999), Roxana Preda's 'Economics', in *The Ezra Pound Encyclopedia* (Westport, CN: Greenwood, 2005), pp. 87–9) and *A Companion to Ezra Pound and Economics* (Nordhausen: Verlag Traugott Bautz, 2019), edited by Ralf Lüfter and Roxana Preda.

36 Hugh Witemeyer, ed., *Pound/Williams: Selected Letters of Ezra Pound and William Carlos Williams* (New York: New Directions, 1996), p. 147.

37 Hutchison expressed his disillusionment with the Nazis in his 1946 novel, *The Red Colonel* (London: Hutchinson & Co).
38 Bowd, *Fascist Scotland*, p. 50.
39 Lockhart, *The Diaries*, p. 257. Bowd's research on Hutchison draws heavily from Richard Griffiths' *Fellow Travellers of the Right: British Enthusiasts for Nazi Germany 1933–39* (Oxford: Oxford University Press, 1983). Griffiths was the first to draw connections between Hutchison, Lockhart's *Diaries*, and Rosenberg's *Political Diaries*. See *Fellow Travellers of the Right*, pp. 101–3.
40 Lockhart, *The Diaries*, p. 257. The mention of Hutchison's pamphlet on Silesia, the historical region now belonging to southwestern Poland, is, I believe, a reference to the Lieutenant-Colonel's work *Silesia Revisited, 1929* (London: Simpkin Marschall, 1929). In this study, Hutchison writes of what he considers to be the problems with the partition of Silesian territory and sympathizes with the Germans, following their defeat in the First World War.
41 Rosenberg was notorious for having claimed that the Jews are an 'antirace' (*Gegen-Rasse* in German), a term he borrowed from Arno Schickedanz's *Sozialparasitismus im Völkerleben* (Leipzig: Lotus-Verlag, 1927) according to Jürgen Matthäus and Frank Bajohr (*The Political Diary of Alfred Rosenberg and the Onset of the Holocaust*, n. 13, p. 5). In 1928, Rosenberg founded Combat League for German Culture (*Kampfbund für deutsche Kultur*) in order to fight against 'degenerate' art (Alan E. Steinweis, *Art, Ideology, and Economics in Nazi Germany: The Reich Chambers of Music, Theater, and the Visual Arts* (Chapel Hill, NC: University of North Carolina Press, 1996), p. 23). He was tried in Nuremberg, found guilty, and subsequently hanged.
42 Alfred Rosenberg, *The Political Diary of Alfred Rosenberg and the Onset of the Holocaust*, ed. Jürgen Matthäus and Frank Bajohr (Lanham, Maryland: Rowman & Littlefield, 2015), p. 18.
43 Rosenberg, *The Political Diary*, p. 18.
44 Ibid.
45 From 1920, the Saar territory was administered by the French and the British under the League of Nations' mandate and was only returned to Germany in the 1935 referendum. See Stefan Wolff, *The German Question Since 1919: An Analysis with Key Documents* (Westport: Greenwood Publishing Group, 2003), p. 62.
46 Letter from GSH to EP, 27 June 1934.
47 Holger H. Herwig, *The Demon of Geopolitics How Karl Haushofer 'Educated' Hitler and Hess* (Lanham: Rowman & Littlefield, 2016), p. 71.
48 A brief description of Haushofer's papers can be found in Colin S. Gray and Geoffrey Sloan's *Geopolitics, Geography and Strategy* (London: Routledge, 2014), p. 238. A more detailed and up-to-date discussion is documented in Herwig's *The Demon of Geopolitics*, pp. 250–5.
49 Herwig, *The Demon of Geopolitics*, p. 77.
50 Douglas-Hamilton, *The Truth About Rudolf*, p. xxxxiii.
51 Letter from EP to GSH, 2 July 1934.
52 Letter from GSH to EP, 5 July 1934.
53 Letter from EP to GSH, 24 June 1934. The complete line reads 'Adolf's BEST propaganda is [ill del] economic LIGHT'.
54 Letter from EP to GSH, 2 July anno XII [1934].
55 Letter from EP to GSH, 24 June 1934.
56 Letter from EP to GSH, 24 June 1934.
57 Letter from EP to GSH, 7 July 1934.

58 Letter from EP to GSH, 17 August 1934.

59 I thus agree with Tim Redman, who has argued in *Ezra Pound and Italian Fascism* (Cambridge: Cambridge University Press, 1991) that 'Pound *was* anti-Semitic and [...] it [is] useless for Pound scholars to pretend otherwise or to see in his distinction between "big jews" and "poor yitts" some basis for exoneration' (4–5). For more information on Pound's anti-Semitism also see Peter Nicholls's *Ezra Pound: Politics, Economics, and Writing: A Study of The Cantos* (London: Macmillan, 1984) and Surette's *Pound in Purgatory*.

60 Letter from EP to GSH, 7 July 1934.

61 Letter from EP to GSH, 8 July 1934.

62 Redman, *Ezra Pound and Italian Fascism*, p. 5.

63 Christian Goeschel and Nikolaus Wachsmann, eds., *The Nazi Concentration Camps, 1933–1939: A Documentary History* (Lincoln: University of Nebraska Press, 2012), pp. 1–70.

64 Clarence Lusane, *Hitler's Black Victims: The Historical Experiences of European Blacks, Africans and African Americans during the Nazi Era* (London: Routledge, 2004), p. 185. Similarly, during Mussolini's attack on Abyssinia, Pound claimed to Nancy Cunard in a 1935 letter that 'the Abyssinians are BLACK JEWS'. For the letter itself see Hugh D. Ford, ed., *Nancy Cunard: Brave Poet, Indomitable Rebel, 1896–1965* (Philadelphia: Chilton Book Co., 1968), p. 359; for further information refer to Aldon Lynn Nielsen, *Reading Race: White American Poets and the Racial Discourse in the Twentieth Century* (Athens: University of Georgia Press, 1990), pp. 71–2.

65 The exact date of this letter is handwritten and illegible. I believe that it was sent in the beginning of June 1934 because the date of Hutchison's response is 20 June 1934.

66 Michael H. Kater, *Different Drummers Jazz in the Culture of Nazi Germany* (New York: Oxford University Press, 2003), p. 32.

67 Kater, *Different Drummers*, p. 130.

68 H. J. P. Bergmeier and Rainer E. Lotz, eds., *Hitler's Airwaves: The Inside Story of Nazi Radio Broadcasting and Propaganda Swing, Volume 1* (New Haven: Yale University Press, 1997), p. 314. Bergmeier and Lotz list a total of seventy-nine songs (pp. 293–342), which show the extent of Goebbels's propaganda machine.

69 J. J. Wilhelm, *Ezra Pound: The Tragic Years 1925–1972* (University Park, PA: The Pennsylvania State University Press, 1994), p. 171. The unpublished Pound/William Joyce correspondence is among the holdings of the Yale's Beinecke Library, though excerpts have been published in Humphrey Carpenter's *A Serious Character: The Life of Ezra Pound* (New York: Dell, 1988), pp. 592–5, and Carpenter's '"This Is Ole Ezra Speaking!" Ezra Pound's Wartime Broadcasts from Rome' (*Encounter*, LXXI, June 1988), pp. 3–15.

70 Lorna Waddington, *Hitler's Crusade: Bolshevism, the Jews and the Myth of Conspiracy* (London: I.B. Tauris, 2007), pp. 21–6.

71 Barnes became an Italian national in 1953, only two years before his death. See James Strachey Barnes, *A British Fascist in the Second World War: The Italian War Diary of James Strachey Barnes, 1943–45*, ed. Claudia Baldoli and Brendan Fleming (London: Bloomsbury Academic, 2014), p. 24.

72 For more information on MI5's files on Pound, see Nadel 'Ezra Pound and MI 5', *Paideuma* 40, (2013), pp. 327–48.

73 As documented by David Bradshaw and James Smith, 'Ezra Pound, James Strachey Barnes ("the Italian Lord Haw-Haw") and Italian Fascism', *Review of English Studies* 64/266, 2013, p. 677.

74 Barnes, *Diary*, n. 240, p. 213.

75 Barnes's *Diary* entry for 14 September 1943, pp. 104–5.
76 For more information, see Matthew Feldman, *Ezra Pound's Fascist Propaganda, 1935–45* (London: Palgrave Macmillan, 2013), pp. 143–65; Bradshaw and Smith, 'Ezra Pound, James Strachey Barnes', pp. 672–93. For information on 'Nazi Eugenics and Pound', see Alec Marsh's *John Kasper and Ezra Pound: Saving the Republic* (London: Bloomsbury Academic, 2015), pp. 72–86.
77 In her astute review of Herwig's *The Demon of Geopolitics*, Catherine Epstein raises a pertinent point which transgresses boundaries between history and literature; in Epstein's words: 'But does Haushofer deserve more damning judgement [than Herwig's eschewing words]? An anti-Semite in love with his Jewish wife. A passionate advocate of geopolitics unable to define his discipline. An inspiration to a murderous regime that executed his son. Unable to think through and resolve the paradoxes of his lived experience, Haushofer was more than just morally complicit in the Nazi regime. His failure of thought makes him, and others like him, responsible for enabling the Third Reich' ('Review of *The Demon of Geopolitics: How Karl Haushofer "Educated" Hitler and Hess* by Holger H. Herwig' n.p.). Indeed, if we consider the nature and extent of their involvement, are we not complacent ourselves if we do not pass judgement on the individuals who were complicit with as well as those who actively contributed to the Nazi Reich even after Kristallnacht – Haushofer and Pound included?
78 I am grateful to Jim McCue, a co-editor of *The Poems of T. S. Eliot: Collected and Uncollected Poems* (London: Faber & Faber, 2015), for bringing this information to my attention. The evidence cited above comes from Ricks's and McCue's commentary regarding T. S. Eliot's corresponding note in *Triumphal March* on p. 825.
79 [Otto Katz], *The Brown Book of the Reichstag Fire and Hitler Terror* (London: V. Golanz, 1933), pp. 291–2. For information on historical disputes regarding the burning of the Reichstag, see Anson Rabinbach, 'Staging Antifascism: *The Brown Book of the Reichstag Fire and Hitler Terror*', *New German Critique* 35/103 (2008), pp. 97–126.
80 Martin Gilbert, *Kristallnacht: Prelude to Destruction* (New York: HarperCollins, 2007), p. 16.
81 These include CasaPound, The London Forum, and The Vortex Londinuim.

4

WILL THIS YOWLING NEVER CEASE? THE POUND/AGRESTI CORRESPONDENCE AND THE CHANGING SCOPE OF EZRA POUND STUDIES

Alec Marsh

Archie Henderson's *'I Cease Not to Yowl' Reannotated* is a canto-sized volume of more than 800 pages and the most important work of scholarship on Pound produced so far this century.[1] It is especially helpful as a gloss on the poet's cryptic late cantos. Henderson's reannotation was made necessary by the strangely obtuse notes attending the otherwise extremely valuable, *'I Cease Not to Yowl': Ezra Pound's Letters to Olivia Rossetti Agresti*, edited and annotated by Leon Surette and Demetres Tryphonopoulos, published twenty years ago by Illinois University Press – published and then allowed to fall out of print.[2] The correspondence between the poet and Agresti – she of the artistic Rossetti family – is much more than the letters exchanged by two significant literati, but the conversation of two sometime Fascist intellectuals engaged in reassessing their commitments to the Fascist movement and its head, Benito Mussolini. Surette and Tryphonopoulos's work is a landmark in Pound studies because it brought an unrepentant Pound to our attention, forcing Pound scholarship to look into Pound's extensive rightist affiliations before, during and after the war. The Ezra Pound we have been historicizing ever since has emerged as an increasingly frightening right-wing figure.

Reviewing the book when it came out, I said that it 'will be a source of distress and morbid fascination to all Pound scholars in the future'.[3] It has been more than that. *I Cease Not to Yowl* was a harbinger of more disturbing revelations to come as scholars mine the Pound archives to discover the extreme right-wing activist beneath the benevolent, misunderstood sage most Pound scholars – including myself – had once hoped to redeem. There is a straight line in Pound scholarship to be drawn from *I Cease Not to Yowl* to Matthew Feldman's *Ezra Pound's Fascist Propaganda: 1935–1945* (2013)[4] and to my own *John Kasper and Ezra Pound: Saving the Republic* (2015), a book that grew out of an aborted project by Henderson and me to annotate and publish John Kasper's scores of letters to the incarcerated poet. Kasper played a notorious role as a segregationist agitator, KKK ally, and dynamiter defending racial segregation against the rising tide of racial integration, which Kasper, and Pound, saw as a Jewish/ Communist plot. He was, I conclude, Pound's most perspicacious reader in the 1950s,[5] fully recognizing that the esoteric surface of *The Cantos* concealed a hard, activist core.

Before discussing *'I Cease Not to Yowl'* and its annotation problems, let me remind you of the situation before it was published. Already, it's hard to remember the old narrative of Fascist fall, purgatory in the cage at Pisa, repentance at St. Elizabeths, leading to paradisal redemption that was the consensus among Poundians in the 1970s. Outside the lysoled hallways of St. Elizabeths on the lawn in some mild, endless autumn, the benevolent, if feisty, retired sage was imagined to have produced elegiac verses; that's the all but indelible impression Hugh Kenner gave in his inspiring masterpiece, *The Pound Era* (1971), which taught us that literary criticism could also be great, and creative, writing. Talk about creative! Kenner knew better, much better than almost anyone else, how partial his account was, how much he was leaving out, how much distasteful material he was repressing.

It wasn't just Kenner; it was New Directions as well. Pound's US publisher, James Laughlin, was keenly aware that the charge 'anti-Semite' meant social death in post-war America. The dust jacket of *Section Rock-Drill 85–95 de los Cantares* (1955) says love is its major theme as the *Cantos* move into their third and final phase: 'the domination of benevolence'. And yet, that same dust-jacket claims that the 'purpose of these Cantos is to give the true meaning of history as one man found it … The lies of history must be exposed; the truth must be hammered home by reiteration, with the insistence of a rock drill.' The true meaning of history as Ezra Pound found it was the history of the Jews versus humanity; destroyers versus men; or, as we find in this slogan that was part of the fevered discourse among Pound's 'kindergarten', as he called his circle of young admirers: 'The children of Moses take pleasure in breaking/ What the children of Ovid take pleasure in making.'[6] This outlook leads directly to the final word of *The Cantos*, 'To be men not destroyers'.[7] It cannot be made benevolent.

By the 1990s a counter-argument to the repentant 'good, grey poet' narrative had become fitfully evident. Massimo Bacigalupo's *The Forméd Trace: The Later Poetry of Ezra Pound* (1980), with its then outrageous claim that *The Cantos* were meant to be the poem of 'the Nazi-Fascist millennium', was still a book to be kept at arm's length. Bacigalupo was considered a man of the Left, an Italian with an axe to grind. He claimed, presciently, if cruelly: 'Pound was militantly pro-fascist and anti-Semitic from about 1930 onwards … in many ways the *Cantos* belong in those shops that sell swastikas and recordings of Mussolini's speeches.'[8] Then there was Robert Casillo's *Genealogy of Demons* (1988). Casillo – ironically, a former student of Kenner's at Johns Hopkins – charged that 'criticism has failed to weigh Pound the poet, and Pound the anti-Semite and fascist in a single balance. Nor has it even attempted to investigate in a thorough, systematic and truly serious fashion the relationship of anti-Semitism and fascism to Pound's poetic techniques and language, his cultural vision, and his politics',[9] an investigation his *Genealogy* bravely attempted. Although his work seems prophetic now, Casillo's courageous book was premature. Pound scholars did not want to read it – not because it was bad, but because it wasn't. Casillo was a sourpuss. To parody Pound's *Hugh Selwyn Mauberley*, the non-esteem of self-styled 'his betters' seems to have led to Casillo's final exclusion from the world of Pound letters. He drifted off to the tawny foreshores of the University of Miami to write about Italy and Modernity, the mafia and the movies. Belatedly, his work on Pound is now being supplemented and confirmed.

If the New Criticism dominant in the 1950s seems in retrospect to have been developed specifically to de-politicize Pound and exclude the problematic *Cantos* (though not the early poetry) from university study, one result was to make Pound an exciting counter-cultural figure, who seemed, in my youth, to be closer to Bob Dylan than T. S. Eliot. But, in the 1980s, what in the United States is called 'New Historicist' and in the UK 'Cultural Studies' began as a critical movement in response to the old formalism (called in the United States, the New Criticism) *and* French post-structuralism. New Historicism's emphasis on context provided a theoretical justification for study of Pound's anything-but-autotelic poem, with its myriad references, languages and boundless curiosity. Eventually, the poem's activist, even fascist, investments were bound to come to light.

Since then the superb archive in the Beinecke Library at Yale, lovingly curated and organized by the poet's daughter, Mary de Rachewiltz, and staffed by generous librarians, offers up seemingly limitless projects. The Ezra Pound papers at the Beinecke in MSS 43 consist of 8328 folders in 276 boxes, to which must be added another 513 folders of oversized material. Today, MSS 43 is supplemented by forty-six boxes and another 1021 folders in MSS 53, the Ezra Pound Papers addition. Now the Beinecke also holds the papers of Pound's long-time lover Olga Rudge in two collections (MSS 54 and 241) that share a further 2000 folders, much to do with Pound. Then there is the relatively unsifted material in Sheri Martinelli's papers (MSS 868), which features eight bulging boxes of Pound letters and the Norman Holmes Pearson papers (MSS 899) – both held off-site – which also have much to do with Pound. In brief: a gold mine. No wonder then, that the last few decades have produced and will continue to produce a wealth of important volumes of Pound correspondence.

To date, none of these many volumes have been more important than Surette's and Tryphonopoulos's edition of the Pound/ Olivia Agresti letters, problematic as it is. But who was Olivia Rossetti Agresti? Briefly, Agresti belonged to one of the most distinguished literary and artistic families in England. She was the daughter of William Rossetti, founding member of the pre-Raphaelite brotherhood, editor of their organ, *The Germ*, and the man who published Walt Whitman in England.[10] His more famous brother, Gabriel Dante Rossetti, Olivia's uncle, was the painter and poet who had more influence over Pound's early poetry than anyone else; he was 'Ezra's God', as Basil Bunting noted. Moreover, Agresti was niece to the poet Christina Rossetti and cousin to Ford Maddox Hueffer (later Ford), who came of age next door.

If Olivia Rossetti's artistic roots were pre-Raphaelite, her political roots were anarchist. Her *roman à clef*, *A Girl among the Anarchists* (1903),[11] is her account of printing the famous anarchist journal *The Torch* with her siblings in her parents' basement while still a teen-ager. Later she married an Italian, Antonio Agresti, the anarchist son of a wealthy industrialist.[12] Apparently disillusioned with anarchism, after her husband's death she was involved with David Lubin, a brilliant, utopian and Jewish agronomist who also died young. His International Institute for Agriculture, Surette argues, was the 'first modern international organization and a significant forerunner of the League of Nations'.[13] Agresti wrote Lubin's biography in 1922: *David Lubin: A Study in Practical Idealism.*[14] It spoke to Pound's interest in agriculture, and as the letters show, he read it at St. Elizabeths with interest, while vehemently deploring Lubin's Jewish affiliation. During the *era Fascista* Agresti had been Mussolini's English translator, and sometime speechwriter, yet she became quite critical of *Il Duce's* alliance with Germany and, in hindsight, of the regime in general. A devout Catholic and no anti-Semite, her side of the correspondence forced Pound to more fully examine and loudly justify his various positions, political, religious and literary. The correspondence covers the years of 1937–59, from Pound's pre-war propaganda to his release from St Elizabeths.

Henderson observes of *I Cease Not* that 'No other single volume of Pound letters is as dense, meaty and rich in the themes that it treats. The letters need to be unpacked like Cantos.'[15] The letters show 'a line of continuity' from his prewar thinking, his radio broadcasts and post-war beliefs; to be clear, there were no realization and repentance in the cage at Pisa or at St. Elizabeths. Yes, Pound's thinking evolved with the historical context and his personal situation – but the anti-Semitism and conspiratorial thinking did not. Of course, in the letters Pound denied any active fascism and tried to reinvent himself as a Cold War-style anti-Communist. He sounds, in the fifties, much like an American right-winger of a well-known John Birch Society type; pro-McCarthy and a firm believer that the US government remained infiltrated by Communists; and a States' Rights-style segregationist. In Henderson's words, he 'adopts the preoccupations and attitudes of the American extreme right in the 1950s; opposition to the Federal Reserve Bank; to the UN and UNESCO'; he's anti Yalta, anti-Potsdam; he fears fluoridation in the water and adulterated food as Communist plots.[16]

Make no mistake: in publishing the Pound/Agresti letters Surette and Tryphonopoulos were not setting out to redeem Pound from himself. Of the major Poundians besides Bacigalupo, Surette was always the most sceptical of the Master and his supposedly universal genius. In his 'Introduction' he is forthright about Pound's faults. His letters, Surette says, leave 'no doubt that he believed that the genetic endowment of Jews somehow renders them greedy, unprincipled and destructive of civilized values'.[17] It is still controversial to speak of Pound as a biological (genetic) racist, as he certainly became after reading *Mein Kampf* (in Italian) in 1942.[18] His study of Louis Agassiz with John Kasper in the early fifties, which led to Kasper's publication of *The Gists of Agassiz* (1953),[19] only confirmed Hitler's harsh eugenic views. In 1998 it was provocative to say, as Surette did, that 'It is painful to confront the magnitude of Pound's misreading of history. That is an intellectual failure, but his failure to recognize the unspeakable crimes of the Nazis is surely a moral failure of the greatest magnitude – and one for which no palatable excuse is imaginable.'[20] Till very recently, Pound's fascism was carefully insulated from any Nazi taint. Pound was, in Tim Redman's words, 'a left-fascist'.[21] Only now, thanks to archival scholarship by Henderson, Bernard Dew, Matthew Feldman, Catherine Paul and others, are we prepared to see he was a 'right-fascist' too.[22]

On first reading *I Cease Not*, Pound's 'yowling' seems ceaseless indeed, his obsession with Jewish/Communist conspiracies unremitting; it is the best look we have into Pound's views during his incarceration 1945–59, shedding much-needed light on the obscure 'Washington Cantos', *Rock-Drill* (1955) and *Thrones* (1959). By the time they began corresponding in earnest, Pound was locked up and Agresti had lost her enthusiasm for *Il Duce*; still, the correspondence confirms, unequivocally, Pound's adherence not only to Italian-style fascism, but even to Hitler during his thirteen years' confinement at St. Elizabeths.

What is interesting and troubling is that, despite Surette's introduction, the Canadian editors, and especially their annotators – who may well have been graduate students unfamiliar with the nuances of American politics – seem not to believe what they are reading, so their notes constantly resist the meaning of Pound's texts or are simply absent. The resulting fiasco inspired Archie Henderson to create his massive reannotation. Henderson's project was, he says, 'accidental'. As he made his way through the letters, he 'found that all too often the editors' notes threw up obstacles to understanding, the notes and identifications are frequently wrong, misleading, incomplete, or nonexistent where they need to exist. Many notes ignore or are unaware or under-aware of the political context.'[23] By the fall of 2006 Henderson was already deep into his own reannotations. On 1 June 2008 he wrote me that he had decided 'to go all out on the EP/ORA notes', to write a book. 'I have added four appendices', he continued, 'and am now up to 243 pages. It's amazing how densely packed these letters are. I can't imagine how ORA could have caught half the references.' A few days later he had added thirteen more pages and was realizing that no one had ever read – 'really read' – these letters.[24]

Henderson's book is not an attack on Surette and Tryphonopoulos, nor is this essay; the very fact that they published their book is a significant achievement and a gift to Pound scholarship and they get a lot right. But the ideological tensions that 'throw up obstacles to understanding' in the book are a textbook case of ideological repression. The first, most important and least interesting obstacle is the unwillingness of most publishers to tolerate thorough annotation of their editions. The reasons are, of course, economic, an instance of what Pound correctly identified as 'usura'. As we know to our sorrow, even university presses, like the University of Illinois Press, have their eyes on the bottom line, not scholarship. The editors of '*I Cease Not to Yowl*' rightly lament that they 'wanted to present the complete record' of the Pound/ Agresti correspondence, but 'that would have required a book of some eight hundred pages' presumably including notes.[25] The 327-page book that they were allowed to print includes 'approximately 75 percent' of Pound's letters to Agresti, and excludes all but a few of hers to him, preserved as 'samples' of her writing.[26] Of the 127 letters included, six are from Agresti plus a short article titled 'Political Immaturity' that Agresti wrote in 1948 for Dallam

Simpson's 'Four Pages'.[27] The editors are explicit that they have not 'dropped any letters because they may place Pound in an unfavorable light' and assert that their 'objective throughout is to give as accurate an impression as we can of an important friendship'.[28] Their stated goal, then, is primarily biographical, not political or literary; but the contents of the letters being what they are, this objective too seems something of a swerve; indeed, I remain unsure if Pound and Agresti had ever even met. As we would expect, the post-war conversation between two sometime fascist intellectuals – call them media consultants – no matter how literary, was necessarily a reevaluation of their shared experiences of fascism and the World War.

So what is wrong with the annotations to the Surette/Tryphonopoulos volume, especially when we recall the constraints of working for academic presses now reoriented towards profit above scholarship? First, they never correlate remarks in the letters to Pound's published writing. Henderson was able to correlate the letters to over fifty different broadcasts over Axis radio.[29] Worse, the annotations rarely refer us to the *Cantos,* where often enough, something in a letter will be echoed or repeated. Henderson lists 250 correlations to the *Cantos* either in the letters or in the rare editors' notes.[30] Surely, one of the principal uses for the Pound/ Agresti letters is to serve as glosses on those difficult late *Cantos*. Or, even the *Pisan Cantos*; in a letter dated 18 March 1955, we hear Pound complaining about the chronic 'American time lag' – always decades behind Europe, 'AS per Whitman, discovered by W[illiam] M. R[ossetti, [Agresti's Uncle] in 1854/ still regarded as a joke in 1905 by profs in Philadelphia'. Pound continues, 'First time I heard him taken seriously was by a DANE, in 1906 or 7'.[31] It glosses both incident and dialect in Canto 82, where we are given the Dane's name: 'Reithmuller indignant/ "Fvy! In Tdaenmarck efen dh' beasantz gnow him,"/ meaning Whitman, exotic, still suspect/ four miles from Camden.' (82/545–46) But, as Henderson's rich annotation of this moment shows, it is not so simple. Henderson informs us that Riethmueller was an instructor, not a 'Prof' at the University of Pennsylvania and he was not a Dane, but German. The Dane in question was likely someone else.[32] In that same letter we find a remark relevant to Canto 92: 'Bernie Baruch's friend Ike pushed fairly near the edge of a thought' …[33] words which, slightly modified, appear in Canto 97.[34] (97/698) Why *not* make these connections which enrich both the poem and the letter?

Pound frequently referred to items in American newspapers and on the radio, which were quite as baffling to Agresti as they are to us.[35] In his *Reannotations*, Henderson hunts up these sources. Where Pound mentions a newspaper article – including pieces in Italian papers sent to him by Agresti – Henderson has usually run down the article, situated it, quoted it, so one can see exactly what Pound is referring to.

The letters provide a vivid glimpse into Pound's extensive reading during his captivity. Henderson's researches, assisted by Bernard Dew, uncover an encyclopedia of right-wing literature, newsletters and pamphlets saturating Pound's world and influencing his world view. Unfortunately, for the most part the original annotators are unable to deal with this aspect of Pound's thinking. Surette and Tryphonopoulos fail to comment on, or simply do not recognize

Pound's penchant for 'revisionist' history, particularly of the recent war, as books and memoirs began to come out – as Henderson says, 'it is hidden in plain sight'.[36] This lack is significant, because the *Cantos* themselves should be seen as an effort at historical revision. Of note is Pound's taste for political insider narratives; Col. House's *Intimate Papers* to *Hitler's Table-Talk*; Sumner Welles' *Time of Decision* and Fritz Hesse's *Das Spiel um Deutschland.* As Henderson points out, *The Protocols of the Elders of Zion*,[37] while not mentioned in the correspondence, provides a matrix of assumptions without which Pound's view of recent history is inexplicable.[38]

On the subject of 'Revisionism', Pound's rightist outlook and editorial obtuseness: how is it that Tyler Kent, mentioned in a letter dated 1955, gets no note? The case of Tyler Kent, 'a cipher code clerk in the American Embassy in London' who was arrested in 1940 'for turning over to German agents copies of documents stolen from the embassy',[39] was a *cause célèbre* for the American Right for thirty years. Books have been written about his case, which also involved Soviet intelligence, as the USSR was allied with Germany until June 1941. Kent's name should have fairly leapt off the page to even semi-attuned readers.

Pound called Alexander Del Mar 'our greatest historian'. His *History of Monetary Systems*[40] is vitally important to the late cantos, especially to Canto 97. Pound owned many of his other books and even had Square $ publish Del Mar's *Barbara Villiers: A History of Monetary Crimes.*[41] Why, then, do we find buried in a note to a 3 May 1951 letter, *which the editors saw fit not to include*, that Pound had listed Del Mar's books for Agresti and provided commentary on Del Mar's economic insights![42] With typical Poundian effrontery, the poet, having himself just belatedly discovered Del Mar, spitefully supposes 'Lubin was too IGNORANT to have heard of del Mar' intimating that his occlusion is part of the Jewish blackout of useful history.[43] Therefore, the poet's discomfort is palpable when several years later he reports to Agresti John Kasper's discovery that 'Del Mar was kike'. Nevertheless, Pound promises to go on 'reviving his glorious memory' – as he does faithfully in *The Cantos* – even as he nit-picks that Del Mar had 'no guard against centralization and tyranny' and ignored the usury rate.[44] This typically queasy attempt by Pound to square thinking he admires with his racial beliefs is characteristic of many of these letters.

Most surprising are failures to correctly annotate purely literary references. In Letter 92, Pound misquotes from the opening of Cicero's 'First Oration against Cataline', 'Quo tandem abutere usque … ' hardly an obscure reference. In *I Cease Not to Yowl,* Pound's error is unrecognized and so the fragment is clumsily translated as 'Which will be useful in the end' without further comment. Henderson provides the full, famous, paradigmatic rhetorical question: 'Quo usque tandem abutere, Catalina, patientia nostra?' 'How far Cataline, will you abuse our patience?' As Henderson explains, the phrase is a reference to Agresti's written appeal for Pound's release.[45]

No other volumes of letters have provoked reannotation like Henderson's, yet almost all dealing with correspondence from Pound's St Elizabeths period need what Henderson's *Reannotations* provide. Two examples: *Ezra Pound and James*

Laughlin: Selected Letters[46] looks more or less like a heavily redacted FBI document in light of the Pound illuminated by Henderson's research. It should be retitled *Selections* from *Letters between Ezra Pound and James Laughlin*. It matters that the editor, David Gordon, was an integral part of the St. Elizabeth's right-wing, segregationist scene; he worked at Kasper's Cadmus Bookstore; his *Academia Poundiana*, soon to become the *Academia Bulletin*, was a vehicle for Pound's propaganda scarcely less obviously than *Strike*, a more openly political outlet, edited by Pound acolyte Bill McNaughton, to which Pound contributed under various pseudonyms. Gordon's selection not only protects Pound, but shields himself.[47]

Gordon's carefully censored volume was published before the Pound/Agresti letters, but what to make of Zhiaoming Qian's *Ezra Pound's Chinese Friends* (2008)[48] and Qian's decision to leave out David Wang's extensive political correspondence with Pound, some of which I detailed in *Kasper and Pound*?[49] Had he read *I Cease Not* with attention, Qian could have placed Wang's friendship with Pound properly. He does admit that 'some of [Wang's] statements are neo-fascist' quoting a letter of July 1957: 'My impression of the French is that they are of all Europeans closest to the kikes in spirit and nature … I am for a united Europe under the rule of either Germany and Italy. Adolf and Benito were certainly close to saints.' But Qian whiffs badly in his comment: 'Whether he was speaking his mind or aiming for shock value could only be conjectural.'[50] Pound could not be shocked by these remarks – they were, after all, his own thoughts reflected back to him. Qian mentions, but does not include, Wang's programme for his political faction 'North American Citizens for the Constitution', which allies him closely to Kasper and the segregationist 'Wheat in Our Bread Party', which Qian calls a club; in fact, WHIB actually ran candidates for political office in Tennessee.[51]

In a 2009 talk at Hamilton College collected in *Ezra Pound and Education*,[52] Peter Nicholls proposed three phases of Pound's reception – the 'hippy phase' when Pound was seen as a counter-cultural guru and prophet; a second phase in which an abundance of archival material troubled our understanding of Pound and his poem as his adherence to fascism during the 1930s and '40s became known and any recantation of this politics less plausible; finally, there is a third phase in which the 'open form' of *The Cantos* rescued the poem from Pound's 'closed' politics.[53] Although arguably successive, each phase persists – often enough in the same reader, as I myself can testify. We're now in a fourth phase. If we can liken Nicholls' three phases to the seasons, spring, summer and autumn, 'winter is a-comin' in, and Pound scholars may well sing 'Goddam' and clutch at our overcoats. The fourth phase considers closely the question 'just how deeply involved *was* Pound involved with fascism?' – and not only Italian Fascism, but Nazism, segregation, White Supremacy and the American Right? Matthew Feldman has opined: 'up to his neck'.

As of this writing, Henderson continues to add notes – perhaps he should retitle his work, *Will This Reannotation Never Cease*. Since in so many respects, annotation and commentary are what we do, especially those of us interested in the endless task of 'Historicizing Modernism', reannotation *can* never cease – our work is never done.

Notes

1 Archie Henderson, *'I Cease Not to Yowl' Reannotated,* 3rd ed., CreateSpace, 2010. Henderson's project has been added to and revised since 2009, currently surpassing 1,200 pages. It is essential for any scholar working on 'late' Pound.
2 Demetres P Tryphonopoulos and Leon Surette, eds., *'I Cease Not to Yowl': Ezra Pound's Letters to Olivia Rossetti Agresti* (Urbana and Chicago: University of Illinois Press, 1998).
3 Alec Marsh, *American Literary Scholarship 1999* (Durham: Duke University Press, 2001), p. 158.
4 Matthew Feldman, *Ezra Pound's Fascist Propaganda: 1935–1945* (Basingstoke: Palgrave Macmillan, 2013).
5 Alec Marsh, *John Kasper and Ezra Pound: Saving the Republic* (London: Bloomsbury, 2015), p. xvi. Pound knew all about Kasper's terroristic activities – they were front page news across the United States – but did nothing to put a stop to them. They were in personal contact when Kasper was not in prison, yet Kasper was a devoted disciple who likely would have stopped his violent career had the incarcerated poet insisted. The inference is that Pound approved.
6 Sheri Martinelli Papers, Beinecke Library, University of Yale, YCAL MSS 868, Box 12.
7 Ezra Pound, *The Cantos* (New York: New Directions, 1996), p. 823.
8 Massimo Bacigalupo, *The Forméd Trace: The Later Poetry of Ezra Pound* (New York: Columbia University Press, 1980), p. x.
9 Robert Casillo, *The Genealogy of Demons: Anti-Semitism, Fascism, and the Myths of Ezra Pound* (Evanston: Northwestern University Press), p. 3.
10 One detail of the EP/ORA correspondence notes Agresti's sale of proof copy sheets with Whitman's corrections. Tryphonopoulos and Surette, *I Cease Not*, p. 76.
11 The book was published under a pseudonym, Isabel Meredith. See the recent edition by Jennifer Shaddock, *A Girl Among the Anarchists* (Lincoln: University of Nebraska Press, 1992).
12 Tryphonopoulos and Surette, *I Cease Not*, p. xvi.
13 Ibid. p. xvii.
14 Olivia Rossetti Agresti, *David Lubin: A Study in Practical Idealism* (Boston: Little Brown, 1941). Pound was reading the book (presumably this edition) in the summer of 1949. Tryphonopoulos and Surette provide no bibliographical details.
15 Henderson, *Reannotated,* p. viii.
16 Ibid., p. x.
17 Tryphonopoulos and Surette, *I Cease Not*, p. xviii.
18 See Marsh, *John Kasper and Ezra Pound,* pp. 84–5.
19 John Kasper, *The Gists of Agassiz* (Washington, DC: Square $ Press, 1953).
20 Tryphonopoulos and Surette, *I Cease Not*, pp. xviii.
21 Tim Redman, *Ezra Pound and Italian Fascism* (Cambridge: Cambridge University Press, 1991), p. 267.
22 See Catherine Paul, *Fascist Directive: Ezra Pound and Italian Cultural Nationalism* (Clemson, SC: Clemson University Press, 2016). Bernard Dew MD is an independent scholar and film maker.
23 Henderson, *Reannotated,* p. vii.
24 Henderson, personal communications, 1 and 4 June 2008.
25 Tryphonopoulos and Surette, *I Cease Not*, p. xxv.
26 Ibid., p. xxv.

27 "Four Pages' was a Poundian vehicle edited by Dallam Simpson, which failed to publish the piece. Tryphonopoulos and Surette, *I Cease Not,* p. 8.
28 Ibid., p. xxv.
29 Henderson, *Reannotated,* p. ix.
30 Ibid., p. vii.
31 Tryphonopoulos and Surette, *I Cease Not,* p. 183.
32 Pound, *The Cantos*, pp. 539–40. This example of Henderson's annotation gives the sense of the thoroughness and depths of Henderson's notes:

> Possibly the Danish writer Johannes V. Jensen (1873–1950), who, after visiting America, mentioned Walt Whitman in his volume of essays *Den ny Verden* (København: Gyldendal, 1907), https://books.google.com/books/?id=O8ATAAAAYAAJ, translated into German as *Die Neue Welt: Essays* [The New World: Essays] (Berlin: S. Fischer Verlag, 1908; all websites last accessed 15 March 2020). Jensen's *Digte* (København: Gyldendal, 1907) includes 'Oversaettelser fra Walt Whitman', pp. [81]–104. Richard Henri Riethmueller (1881–1942), a German-born instructor in German, 1905–7, and lecturer on German literature, 1907–9, at the University of Pennsylvania, was quoted in Canto LXXXII: 'Reithmuller indignant: /"Fvy! in Tdaenmarck efen dh" beasantz gnow him,' / meaning Whitman, exotic, still suspect / four miles from Camden' (Canto LXXXII/525-526). Riethmueller was the author of 'Walt Whitman and the Germans', *The German American Annals* NS 4.1-3 (January–March 1906), reprinted as Riethmueller, *Walt Whitman and the Germans: A Study* (Philadelphia: Americana Germanica Press, 1906), https://ia800202.us.archive.org/18/items/cu31924022225316/cu31924022225316.pdf. See Terrell, *A Companion to the Cantos of Ezra Pound*, pp. 457–8; 'Richard Henri Riethmueller', *Who's Who in Dentistry: Biographical Sketches of Prominent Dentists in the United States and Canada* (1916), pp. 157–8, https://books.google.com/books?id=7IwEAAAAYAAJ; 'Richard Henri Riethmueller (1881–1942)', *Proceedings of the Twentieth Annual Meeting of the American Association of Dental Schools* (1943), p. 259; 'Obituary. R. H. Riethmueller, D.D.S., 1881–1942', *The Frater of Psi Omega* (1943?), p. 28.

33 Tryphonopoulos and Surette, *I Cease Not*, p. 183.
34 Pound, *The Cantos*, p. 692.
35 Henderson, *Reannotated,* p. viii.
36 Ibid., p. xi.
37 Colonel Edward M. House, *Intimate Papers of Colonel House*, 2 vols. (Boston: Houghton Mifflin, 1928); Adolf Hitler, *Hitler's Secret Conversations* (New York: Farrar Straus & Giroux, 1953), thereafter published as *Hitler's Table-Talk* and known to have been compiled by Martin Bormann, with an introduction by Hugh Trevor-Roper. Sumner Welles' *Time of Decision* (New York: Harper Bros., 1944); and Fritz Hesse's *Das Spiel um Deutschland* (Munich: List Verlag, 1953); *The Protocols of the Elders of Zion,* no copyright. Numerous editions.
38 Henderson, *Reannotated*, p. ix.
39 Ibid., p. 437.
40 Alexander Del Mar, *History of Monetary Systems* (1896) (Orono, MN: National Poetry Foundation, 1983).
41 Alexander Del Mar's *Barbara Villiers; a History of Monetary Crimes* (Washington, DC: Square $ Press, 1956).

42 Tryphonopoulos and Surette, *I Cease Not*, pp. 61–2.
43 Ibid., p. 52.
44 Ibid., p. 204.
45 Ibid., p. 185, Henderson *Reannotated*, pp. 429–30.
46 David Gordon, ed., *Ezra Pound and James Laughlin: Selected Letters* (New York: W. W. Norton, 1994).
47 I can't resist one example. A late 1960 letter to Laughlin from Rome is headed 'CO Dadone' and gets this brief note: 'Dadone: Ugo Dadone, an old friend of EP's and a correspondent for the Angelo di Stefani Agency' (Gordon, ed., *Selected Letters*, p. 274). Dadone was Pound's roommate at the time and as we know from Mary de Rachewiltz's memoir, not an old friend of Pound's but of Boris de Rachewiltz's, 'a brave man but whose head was still too full of the Eia Eia Allalà spirit' (Mary de Rachewiltz, *Discretions: Ezra Pound Father & Teacher* (New York: New Directions, 1971), p. 307). Dadone was better known as a die-hard Fascist and personal friend of Mussolini's, not the poet's. In the thirties and forties Dadone worked the Middle-East inflaming anti-British sentiment in Egypt and Palestine. Dadone has been seen as one of the inspirations behind the Egyptian Brotherhood, originally an Islamist anti-British faction. His book *Fiamme ad Oriente* (1958), describing the plight of displaced Palestinians, was among the first exposés of Jewish terror in Palestine and Israel.
48 Zhiaoming Qian, ed., *Ezra Pound's Chinese Friends* (Oxford: Oxford University Press, 2008).
49 See Marsh, *John Kasper and Ezra Pound*, pp. 205–13.
50 Zhiaoming Qian, *Chinese Friends*, p. 173.
51 See Marsh, *John Kasper and Ezra Pound*, pp. 205–13
52 Stephen G. Yao and Michael Coyle, *Ezra Pound and Education* (Orono, MN: National Poetry Foundation, 2012).
53 Henderson recalls that 'Burton Hatlen was a proponent of the third phase as early as 1985': 'And as we turn from Pound's political ideology to his poetry, it seems to me important to state at once that, however "closed" and regressive the political system to which Pound committed himself, The Cantos remains an "open" text .... In *The Cantos* Pound's "open" poetic method tends to dissolve fascism, itself an amalgam of disparate political tendencies, back into its constituent parts. *The Cantos* may set out to affirm fascism, but in fact the poem "deconstructs" fascist ideology; and this is, I here shall propose, a principal reason why the poem still lives'. (Burton Hatlen, 'Ezra Pound and Fascism', in *Ezra Pound and History*, ed. Marianne Korn (Orono, MN: National Poetry Foundation, 1985), pp. 145–72 (at pp. 158–9)).

5

USEFUL KNOWLEDGE BEYOND THE BEINECKE: GERTRUDE STEIN READING DISCOURSES OF DEMOCRACY AND NATIONALISM IN *LIFE MAGAZINE* AND *THE LITERARY DIGEST*

Isabelle Parkinson

The Gertrude Stein and Alice B. Toklas Papers in the Beinecke Archive have loomed large in Stein scholarship, particularly since Ulla Dydo's painstaking work to situate Stein's writing practice as the nexus of an everyday life reflected in the archive's materiality of drafts, notes and clippings.[1] The significance of the Beinecke material, alongside the important feminist investment in an attention to the personal and the quotidian, means that Stein's private life has often been central to examinations of her work.[2] My discussion here moves from the personal into public culture by following the documents out of the archive with which Stein was engaged as a reader. The weekly magazines *Life* and *The Literary Digest* made important reading for Stein in the production of two works included in the 1928 collection *Useful Knowledge*: the short piece 'A League' (1919) and the longer portrait 'Woodrow Wilson' (1920). *Useful Knowledge* is often understood as representing Stein's late 1920's, and very personal, coming-to-terms with her American identity.[3] I would argue, however, that these two texts, written in the two years after the First World War and during the formation and establishment of the League of Nations, tell us much more about Stein's early interwar reading and reflect an American identity formulated in response to some of the more vehement forms of nationalism expressed in popular weekly papers. *Life* and *The Literary Digest*, indexed in but largely absent from Stein's archive, are refracted in 'A League' and 'Woodrow Wilson', representing her 'everyday' as a reader of the new broadcast print forms aimed at an expanding transatlantic educated class and responding directly to the expansion of mass democracy in the context of debates around the role of internationalism for the democratic nation-state.

These texts engage directly with questions about the status and role of American democracy in the post–First World War geopolitical landscape, drawing us out of the private sphere and into public discourse. In view of their emphasis on the practice of democracy as a historical reality, I want to use 'A League' and

'Woodrow Wilson' to rethink and put pressure on a strand of scholarship that reads Stein's work as possessing inherently 'democratic' properties that reflect an abstract and very personal engagement with democracy. This strand continues the tradition that begins in those readings of Stein's texts that foreground the traces of her intimate daily life, finding in her work a hermetic private 'democracy' manifested as abstract formal experimentation and divorced from the external political realities of the time. This approach to Stein can be seen in the work of Barbara Will, Ulla Dydo, Juliana Spahr and, more recently, Aidan Thompson and Kristin Bergen.[4] This reading of Stein's work is expressed, for example, in Will's argument for 'Stein's profound affiliation with American "democratic" culture', in Dydo's unequivocal statement in *The Language That Rises*, 'all her work is a demonstration of the possibilities of grammar for democracy', and in Aidan Thompson's more recent claim that Stein's use of repetition 'is democratic in its undoing of hierarchical mechanisms'.[5] My argument here is that, in 'A League' and 'Woodrow Wilson', Stein's ideas about democracy directly engage with the political context of post–First World War America. The readings of her experimental work as formally democratic, I would therefore argue, cannot fully account for the ways in which democracy is conceptualized in her writing.

Readings of the democratic character of Stein's work tend to treat democracy conceptually rather than historically, as a broad ideal that includes general notions of egalitarianism, openness or participation identified in a linguistic experimentation that seems to offer the reader agency. Almost invariably, however, the 'democracy' in Stein's writing is set at an awkward angle to the politics of the historical Stein. Juliana Spahr expresses this problematic in her claim 'if Stein is not the democrat that I am arguing her work suggests she could be, still there is much to be learned from the anarchic democracy of the works themselves'.[6] These interpretations often read – and puzzle over – Stein the author as a more troubling presence than the work she produced; as radically democratic in her language experiments, yet conservative and reactionary in her nationalism and anti-democratic in her support for authoritarian regimes, hinted at, for example, in Juliana Spahr's reference to Stein's friendship with the Nazi collaborator Bernard Fäy.[7]

This way of approaching Stein is critically revisited in Barbara Will's more recent book *Unlikely Collaboration* (2011). In a reassessment of her own earlier characterization, Will explores in detail the Stein-Fäy relationship, beginning with an outline of the problem I have identified: 'the very work for which Stein is best known … is significant precisely because it appears so profoundly dissociated from time and place, from an author and her "views"'.[8] Will goes on, 'To this extent, Stein's experimental writing also seems open to the reader in the radically democratic way that Roland Barthes discusses in his famous essay "The Death of the Author"'.[9] The scholars in this tradition, as we see with Spahr, tend to distinguish the texts and their esoteric, private democracy from the public Stein who might express political 'views'.[10] Will's more historicized way out of this is to identify Stein's troubling politics as a later phase, an expression of ideas that had been brewing in inchoate or indirect forms before the 1930s, but do not emerge until Stein's more explicit approval of the authoritarian nationalism that emerges in Europe in the latter part of the interwar period. Will outlines Stein's 1930s nationalism as at some moments 'extreme' and at others 'a basic nationalist credo', identifying it as a dangerous, 'reactionary' nationalist feeling that is formulated 'as the more optimistic decade of the 1920s turned into the hollow years of the 1930s'.[11] Will therefore also marks off Stein's 'democratic' writing from her 'nationalist' ideology by separating her earlier work from her 1930s expressions of nationalism. This is made explicit in Will's methodology: to look for answers to the question of how Stein seems to become a radical nationalist 'not by searching for political ideas in Stein's experimental writing – writing, again, that abstains from "ideas" and "views" – but rather by looking at the principles that guided her through her aesthetic development'.[12] The work of the early Stein does not yet seem to have a 'politics', allowing the texts written before the 1930s to be read as exemplary of a pure linguistic experimentation that is 'democratic' in the most abstract sense of the term. They are thus untainted by the problematic nationalism that appears in the 1930s and the result of a personal, esoteric engagement with an abstract ideal of democracy divorced from the ground-level realities of mass democracy after the First World War.

What I want to argue here is that democracy and nationalism have a far more complex relationship than is suggested by these attempts to mark off Stein's 'democratic' experimental work from her nationalism, and that something of this can be identified in these early interwar texts and in the publication contexts they lead us to. As part of this more nuanced understanding of the relations between democracy and nationalism, I also want to put the forms of nationalism encountered in these texts in the context of American opposition to the internationalism of the League of Nations.[13] Internationalism was understood in large swathes of opinion in the popular weeklies refracted in these two texts as a threat to American democracy.[14] These texts are complex but clearly identifiable criticisms of the internationalism represented by Wilson and the League of Nations, countering the idea that Stein did not directly express political positions in her work before the 1930s. Indeed, 'A League' and 'Woodrow Wilson' indicate that Stein's 1930s 'reactionary' nationalism cannot be marked off from her earlier political positions (or from their imagined lack). Well before the 1930s, Stein's nationalism is apparent and it is influenced by the popular press – here, her American reading of *Life* and *The Literary Digest* – and therefore her work is much more bound up with the political realities of the time than those readings suggest.

'A League' and 'Woodrow Wilson' both appear in the 1928 collection *Useful Knowledge*, a publication often read as Stein's late 1920s reconciliation with her American identity and a significant expression of her commitment to democracy. The most influential example is perhaps Barbara Will's 2000 account of it as 'Stein's idealized resolution of the earlier concerns that had plagued *The Making of Americans*' where she argues that, 'in *Useful Knowledge* "America" serves as a utopian "landscape" which neither subsumes individual "value" nor abandons the larger frame that is integral to the collective'.[15] This reading has the collection as evidence to support the view that Stein's work is democratic, developed, in

Will's interpretation, to argue that at this point Stein's artistic modes are aligned with a new formulation of her American identity where America is reimagined as an idealized egalitarian landscape. 'A League', however, was published in *Life* magazine on 18 September 1919, and 'Woodrow Wilson', unpublished before its inclusion in *Useful Knowledge*, Ulla Dydo dates at 1920.[16] Rather than representing abstract, oblique, conciliatory odes to American democracy written in the late 1920s, these texts are quite precise responses to a particular political moment. 'A League' was written during Wilson's attempts to secure support for America's role in establishing the League of Nations, and 'Woodrow Wilson' was composed around the time of the presidential election for which Wilson did not run because of ill-health and because of internal Democrat concern over his growing unpopularity – itself widely seen as a result of his promotion of the League.

Stein's submission of the 'A League' to *Life* magazine in 1919 reflects her interest in the popular weekly and her belief that the American mass-market publication was the appropriate context for her experimentation. It is also, as we shall see, the expression of an American nationalism that is in keeping with the many articulations of anti-League nationalism represented in *Life*. The significance of the popular weekly for Stein's exploration of American democracy is also gestured to in the 'First Scene' of the 1920 text, 'Woodrow Wilson':

> Here we have Woodrow Wilson born in the state of Michigan.
> Woodrow Wilson was born in Virginia.
> First Memory.
> I can call.
> Second Memory.
> See the scene.
> Third Memory.
> I can recollect another thing.
> Fourth Memory.
> My literary digest.[17]

In this opening moment, an unidentified narrative voice struggles to remember what it knows about Woodrow Wilson, the twenty-eighth president of the United States, in service from 1913 to 1921, a progressive Democrat and a powerful advocate for the establishment of the League of Nations. Wilson's voice appears explicitly in the 'Second Scene', thus distinguishing it from the initial narrative. This opening moment is a scene of extradiegetic narrative recollection, and the line 'My literary digest' indicates that these narrative 'recollections' come from *The Literary Digest*. What is being remembered, and imperfectly, is a knowledge of Woodrow Wilson garnered from the weekly paper. The possessive 'my' offers a glimpse of a world of intimate engagement with these publications, and this familiar reference, along with the presence of the 1926 *Literary Digest International Book Review* in the Beinecke collection, suggests the significance of the popular weekly for Stein's daily reading.[18]

Life and *The Literary Digest* are weeklies aimed at a broad audience. *Life*, predating the photojournalism associated with its later iteration, was a humour magazine, founded in 1883 in emulation of the successful British magazine *Punch*, and sustained in that form until 1936. *The Literary Digest*, an 'influential weekly journal of current events', gathered news reports, opinion and other material from a vast range of regular publications, presenting a 'neutral' stance on a broad set of issues by offering excerpts and clearly signalling writers' affiliations.[19] Both these publications reached their highest distribution in the period after the First World War. *Life* had 'a circulation of nearly one-half million in 1920' and *The Literary Digest* 'reach[ed] a circulation of almost two million in the 1920's'.[20] *The Literary Digest* was also used in schools, with 'wide adoption throughout the American public school system, particularly in the High Schools, for classes in English, public speaking, debating civics and history'.[21] With an adult American population in the period of around 70 million and considering these papers would have likely been bought for the whole household and circulated informally beyond that, this would have meant a significant proportion of Americans were reading them.

Both publications position themselves as important vehicles in the promulgation and maintenance of American democracy. The cover of *The Literary Digest* for 3 October 1920, for example, titled 'As Election Approaches', depicts a group of three men, staged by their dress and demeanour as representative of the spectrum of social class, clustered around a copy of the *Digest*.[22] This image asserts the function of the *Digest* in enabling the democratic participation of the American citizen, emphasizing its broad readership and the levelling effect of both democracy itself and the paper's instrumental role in it. The 18 September 1919 edition of *Life*, in which Stein's 'A League' appears, references its audience in a similar vein, though in a different mode, bordering its subscription advertisement with cameo heads of men, women and children from across the social stratum, with an elaborately coiffured woman, a bowler-hatted businessman, a straw-chewing farmer and a maid in uniform in continuous succession.[23] Stein's 'A League' and 'Woodrow Wilson' mediate the popular discourses of democracy in these American weeklies. The publication of 'A League' in *Life* and the intimate reference to *The Literary Digest* suggest that, as an ex-pat in Paris since 1903, Stein, at least in part, gets her America, her politics and her sense of national identity through this reading. These texts reveal the intimacy of her engagement with her American reading and designate the weekly magazine as a locus where the private and the public intersect, bringing the everyday of social and political conditions and attitudes into the everyday of what is conceived as a private or domestic life.

Although *The Literary Digest* includes excerpts from publications across the political spectrum, and *Life* is editorially in favour of the League, both include much anti-League and anti-Wilson content. In *Life*, these views are invariably expressed in the political cartoons that make up most of the content, and that, in the September 18 edition, contrast sharply with the rather defensive pro-League editorial in the middle section of the paper, which argues that its opponents are 'stupid' and 'brutish'.[24] The cartoons in this edition also tend to be vehemently anti-internationalist in general, offering caricatures of the League of Nations and the Russian Revolution as internationalist movements that present twin threats to American democracy and national sovereignty. Both 'A League' and 'Woodrow Wilson' are critical of Woodrow Wilson's role on the world stage, resistant to internationalism, and express nationalist feeling. These pieces, as with much of Stein's work in this period, also explore contemporary cultural practices across different media, genres and discourse codes through linguistic experimentation. In this period, as we can see in other examples such as 'A Photograph', and 'A Movie', both written in 1920, her texts often experiment with other cultural modes, abstracting their forms and processes in order to examine how they function. In the examples under discussion, the texts investigate the genres associated with the production of knowledge about this political moment. Both engage positively with the discourse of the American weeklies where they reject internationalism, assert American nationalism and lambast both the League of Nations and Woodrow Wilson, whilst referencing and disparaging the forms of political rhetoric attributed to a perceived paternalistic liberal cosmopolitanism associated with Wilson and the League.

'A League', with its facile rhymes and prominent, awkward rhythm – formal features suggestive of the inevitable pratfalls of slapstick humour – satirizes President Wilson's campaign for the League of Nations, part of which took the form of a national tour throughout September 1919.[25] Published during Wilson's tour, it is an experiment in writing the verbal-visual medium of the political cartoon genre. This choice of genre indicates an alignment with the anti-internationalist stance so often reflected in the political cartoons in *Life*. Amongst the raft of anti-internationalist cartoons in the September 18 edition, two target Wilson and the League in particular. In the first example, a depiction of an encounter between Uncle Sam and Woodrow Wilson, Uncle Sam angrily presents his large stovepipe hat, inscribed 'Monroe Doctrine', to Wilson with the exclamation 'Say! Do you know you sat on my hat!'[26] Wilson stands mute, brandishing a smaller hat with 'League of Nations' feather. The implication is clear: the League of Nations is a threat to American sovereignty and heralds the return of the meddling colonial powers that were seen off by the Monroe Doctrine, the 1823 policy designed to protect the Americas from European imperialism. The second, anti-League, example depicts Uncle Sam once again, this time engaged in defending American democracy and national sovereignty by pushing a 'League of Nations' Humpty dumpty off the wall protecting a distant White house from its incursion.[27]

There are other signifiers here, however, that contribute to the national feeling these scenarios evoke. In the 'Monroe Doctrine' cartoon, Wilson is portrayed with hand on hip and carelessly flourishing his feathered hat. This, in conjunction with the small wire-rimmed glasses obscuring his eyes and rather distracted, weak smile, suggests an intellectualism coupled with an effete and simpering politesse distinct from Uncle Sam's simple bluntness and direct gaze, and Wilson's refined, understated attire registers a European style that again contrasts with Uncle Sam's stars-and-stripes brashness. Indeed, the hat Wilson holds denotes at once the properties of an English bowler and a 'Tyrolean'. Uncle Sam is the plainspoken direct American (with, of course, a much bigger hat) and Wilson's urbane carelessness bespeaks a foreign indifference to or disdain of the American national story. The Humpty Dumpty example has Uncle Sam once again as the indomitable, straight-talking spirit of America who has no truck with the League. More significantly, the wall in the nursery rhyme here becomes a border-wall separating American democracy, represented by the image of The White House in the background, from the rest of the world. One could also infer a reference to the nursery rhyme's 'all the king's horses and all the king's men' who might attempt, on the other side of the wall, to put the League together again, evoking a perception of Europe as monarchical in contradistinction to America's democratic republic. Both of these cartoons have the representatives of the League – a foppish scholar and an egg – as weak, flimsy, even degenerate in the face of the strength of American national identity.

As we can see, the political cartoon is a complex genre that has traditionally 'drawn meaning from a broad range of public knowledge and experience', using allegory, metaphor and symbolism and prompting 'readings of the human body' to translate political abstractions into tangible visual representations, often deploying juxtaposition, literary allusion or references to familiar stories and characters, the distortion of recognizable traits in stereotype or caricature, and visual and verbal punning.[28] 'A League' replicates these features in a writing experiment with this form of political discourse. The title 'A League' uses a pun that evokes the familiar folktale trope of seven-league boots, satirizing both the League of Nations and Wilson's gruelling tour of America to promote it – 8000 miles in twenty-two days – as fanciful or absurd quests. In the first line 'Why don't you visit your brother with a girl he doesn't know?', the reference to a 'visit' begins to elaborate the caricature of Wilson's tour, with 'brother' suggesting an American 'brotherhood' to satirize the purpose of the trip in enabling Wilson to get closer to ordinary Americans.[29] It also hints at an idea of national belonging in which the basis of the social contract is not a bond of mutual recognition but what is common to a group by birth.[30] In this context, the 'girl he doesn't know' is not a brother, and, I would argue, is representative of the League, or at least its overseas outsiders. As a replication of the visual form of the cartoon, this line invokes an image of a man being advised to marry his brother off to a girl in a pragmatic transactional arrangement, an analogy that concretizes Wilson's political aims as an attempt to sell America into a loveless foreign marriage.

The following line 'And in the midst of emigration we have wishes to bestow' compounds this imputation of betrayal by implying that Wilson has revoked his American nationality. The tour comes shortly after Wilson's protracted stay in Europe for the Paris Peace Conference. He was the first American president to travel to Europe while in office, and he remained at the Peace Conference for more or less the entirety of its six-month duration, bar a two-week return visit to the United States. The text, representing this as 'emigration' in an exaggerated form typical of the cartoon genre, caricatures the situation by implying Wilson is a president who has given up his citizenship. He is, therefore, no longer a brother, no longer native. It is notable that, here, nationality is conceptualized in terms of purely legal status: emigration is only possible if citizenship is not predicated on birth, and this foregrounds a tension between opposing conceptions of nationality as either brotherhood and belonging or as a status ascribed as the result of an official process. The image this line evokes – of Wilson returning temporarily from Europe to 'bestow' wishes on Americans in order to gather support – implies an arrogance that is also a caricature of internationalist paternalism. The conception of nationality as citizenship conferred purely through a legal process is thus associated with liberal internationalism. Wilson, rather than being part of an American brotherhood, is a member of a global elite who can live anywhere. In the end what this seems to add up to is a reinforcing of the paradigm of nation and birth as the authentic form of nationality in contrast to a sterile legality for which nationality is simply a matter of expediency.

The central section of the text appears to move to Wilson's perspective, characterized as the de-individuated plural of institutional authority: 'We gather that the West is wet and fully ready to flow/We gather that the East is wet and very ready to say so.' These lines indicate the superficiality of Wilson's endeavour, with 'the West' and 'the East' representing a view of the nation as a map of voter preferences that Wilson can 'gather' (in all the senses of 'infer', 'assemble' and 'garner') and that are 'ready' to support him. The map image also reiterates the imputation that Wilson is both disdainful of and separate from ordinary Americans because it evokes an impression of America seen from above or from a distance. The intimation of the superficiality of Wilson's engagement is sustained in the empty phrases that make up the last in this series of four increasingly lengthening sentences, 'We gather that we wonder and we gather that it is in respect to all of us that we think', where the first person plural and the stative verbs recall the hollow gestural forms of a politician's rhetoric. The final line of the text 'Do you want a baby. A round one or pink one' evokes an image of the politician's half-hearted engagement in ordinary lives and so suggests the cynicism of Wilson's attempt to win Americans to his cause by encountering them directly. This grotesque semblance of a baby, reminiscent of the distortions of political caricature, perhaps also embodies the result of that dubious alliance suggested in the first line, shadowing the conception of a nationality of birth and brotherhood with intimations of blood heritage and a horror of miscegenation.

The cartoons in this edition of *Life* indicate that the nationalist stance expressed in 'A League' is a popular position, a circumstance that is also reflected in *The Literary Digest*. An advertisement for '*The Literary Digest* Liberty Map of New Europe', detailing 'How Europe Has Been Remade' in the 3 October 1920 issue, the year Stein wrote 'Woodrow Wilson', attests to this.[31] *The Literary Digest* regularly produced maps delineating the battles and movements of troops and the changing political situation during the Great War, and this tradition continued after the war as the geopolitical landscape was formed and reformed. The 3 October advertisement, following the 'neutral' editorial approach, picks its way carefully between political attitudes and finds the medial line that runs through them to produce an account of the new world order that will make the map, like its predecessors, 'popular in many thousands of American homes'. What is interesting for this discussion is that the resulting position is a paean to nationalism and markedly equivocal about the role of the League of Nations. It represents the post-war situation as one in which 'Out of the wreckage of autocracy new nations of free peoples are building' and celebrates 'the various young republics that have sprung up from the ruins of empires', constructing a picture of national democracies that have broken free from the grip of a dying order predicated on imperial and dictatorial forms of rule rather than on democratic structures. The emphasis on the construction of new nations and on national self-determination as the necessary condition for democracy tells the story of the outcome of the war as a triumph for the idea of nation. Developing its representation of the new picture of Europe (and of Africa, included as an inset map detailing the post-war carve-up of European colonies and protectorates), the *Digest* advertisement asserts that 'This map must necessarily be of intense interest to all those who have come to our shores from Europe and the Near East', and claims, 'To every such representative of the older peoples, it is the official record of the radical change in the status of his mother country, of its rebirth, so to speak, under the New World Order – a tangible evidence of the realization of his dreams that he will always treasure'. This celebration of nationhood writes the history of American immigration as a history of escape from the autocratic regimes the *Digest* advertisement evokes in its earlier declaration, whilst also promoting an idea of nation as the realization of a 'people' for whom the bond to a mother country is immutable and expresses a fundamental origin.

The potentially fraught complex of positions on the League is carefully sidestepped, however, featuring as the noncommittal statement that 'The Human, Political, Business and Educational Value of this splendid map is in keeping with the immense changes it records, which are closely linked with the whole question of the League of Nations'. The pages of *The Literary Digest* throughout 1919 and 1920 reveal the variety of attitudes to the League, including much speculation and opinion on its popularity amongst ordinary Americans. The article 'League Verdicts in the Primaries' in the 25 September 1920 edition, for example, outlines the debate in the papers about whether or not the selection of the anti-League Georgia Democrat Thomas E. Watson for the Senate reflects the American zeitgeist. The opening quip 'There's a Watson now to help all our editorial Sherlock Holmeses who are trying to find in the recent primaries some clue to the popular feeling about the League of Nations' comments on the difficult detective work required to identify a clear strand in the attitudes of the electorate.[32] Thus, whilst the nationalism apparent in Stein's 'A League' is in keeping with the attitudes expressed in the *Digest* as an uncontroversial reflection of the popular mood, the advertisement's hedging around the issue of the League puts her text's rejection of the internationalism of Wilson and the League as a threat to American democracy at the extreme end of a spectrum of electoral opinion.

Stein's 'Woodrow Wilson' reflects a similar scepticism about Wilson's commitment to America as a national project and about his rarefied distance from the average American. The text offers a series of images of Wilson as standing above or beyond ordinary life and outside the lived experience of being American. From the outset, Wilson is 'heartily immersed in the very necessary process of illusion and reason and teaching and surveying', suggesting a cloistered, academic distance from real life, a view that is also intimated in Stein's much earlier representation of Wilson as the philosophy professor Philip Redfern in her 1904 novel *Fernhurst* and in the references in 'Woodrow Wilson' to 'Wooded Princeton' and 'School men'.[33] This scholarly distance comes to characterize the language around Wilson in the portrait, with its proliferation of grand abstractions and generalizations: 'All language is evil'; 'All songs are not songs'; 'In youth we nurse'; 'realisation was personality'.[34] This is augmented with repeated references to the seriousness associated with a staid and patrician rationalism: 'I accuse myself of earnestness of appreciation of reason and of learning'; 'Can you be more solemn than serious more earnest than flagrant'; 'Everyone is earnest in earnest'.[35] The oppositional relationship this text sets up between the ordinary American and the intellectual elite extends in interesting and important ways that shed light on the nature of Stein's nationalism and the form of democracy these texts project. 'Woodrow Wilson', like 'A League', is an experiment with the genre of the American weekly. In this case, it gets inside the genre of the *Digest* itself, reflecting at once its textual structures and modes and the experience of reading it offers. This aspect of 'Woodrow Wilson' is a significant component in the expression of ideas about democracy, nationalism and internationalism.

Stein's experimentation with the genre features of *The Literary Digest* is perhaps most apparent in the proliferation of sub-headings in 'Woodrow Wilson'. Headings such as 'Youth', 'Languages', 'War in Peace', 'Accomplishment' and 'Applause' replicate in abstract and elliptical forms the preponderance of titles and sub-titles used to corral and organize the mass of information in the *Digest*, for example: 'Peace by Resolution', 'Age and Youth at It in England', 'British-American War over Language'.[36] Stein's iterations of quasi-biographical details of Wilson's life in 'Woodrow Wilson' also reflect the mix of serious information with light-hearted factoids and the cut-and-paste formation of the *Digest* extracts. Under the heading 'School men', for example, the text juxtaposes references to the history of Wilson's role in education ('Whose was the last diploma he signed') with rather dramatic speculation about his character and psyche: 'He was restive and resolute he reasoned and he returned.'[37] This feature also extends to the replication of the broader remit of the *Digest* to include a range of topics from diverse areas of knowledge. After the initial news sections such as 'Topics of the Day' and 'Foreign Comment', the *Digest* also included regular sections on 'Science and Invention', 'Religion and Social Service' and 'Current Poetry' along with more occasional segments such as 'Birds, Beasts and Trees' and 'The Lexicographer's Easy Chair'. Traces of the special-interest sections are present in 'Woodrow Wilson' and intersect the meditations on Wilson's biography, his presidency and his character. A stanza early in the piece offers an interlude that seems directly lifted from the slabs of factual information presented in the *Digest*. The informative, didactic mode in 'Woodrow Wilson', for example, in 'Sandwich glass was made in Sandwich, Massachusetts, it was made in Sandwich Massachusetts it was pink and white and often had the form of a dolphin' replicates the kind of material found in the 'Science and Invention' section of *The Literary Digest*, such as 'Cylinders of Window-Glass' in the 9 August 1919 edition which contains 'an explanation from an article on the industries of Pennsylvania, of which glass-making is one'.[38] Another line in 'Woodrow Wilson', 'Men prefer salmon and cod-fish and breasts of ducks and pigeon', suggests a *Literary Digest* article like 'From Adzes to Zwieback in the Mail-Order Merchandising Game', in the 28 August 1920 number, which reports, in a survey of mail-order habits, that 'Codfish and canned salmon are their favorites in fish'.[39]

These large-scale surveys and other research on consumer habits are commonly reported in the *Digest*, a feature that engages with the modernity of both the vast scale of mass consumer society and the processes of an early information age that make their way into Stein's text as a significant residue of the reading experience. Perhaps the most revealing example of this is an extended reference to the status of factual information in the central portion of the text:

> Do you believe that fish live and swim above jewels. Many fish swim above jewels. The presented fish swims above the jewels.
> Jewels are uncut and pink
> Green and yellow in colour.
> Amber and lavender.
> So many freezing breaths.
> A sound is their sound.[40]

This set of beautiful images is preceded by the posing of a question of belief – 'Do you believe that fish live and swim above jewels' – that is answered by a factual affirmative – 'Many fish swim above jewels' – followed by an evidential exemplar – the 'presented fish'. The knowledge of the fact itself is what prompts the move to a suggestive, poignant imaginary: the striking colours of the jewels, the evocation of a cold world teeming with silent life. This part of the work is not necessarily directly influenced by *The Literary Digest* 'Science and Invention' article 'Not So Dismal after All' (7 February 1920), but the relationship between poetry and fact that Stein's text sets up is also suggested in the article in a way that speaks of a common, exuberant enthusiasm for factual knowledge that is engendered by and expressed in the mass-information revolution represented by the *Digest*. The *Digest* article offers a natural history of the Dismal Swamp, an area of marshland that runs across the coastal regions of south-eastern Virginia and north-eastern North Carolina. The *Digest*'s presentation of the reports detailing the natural features of the region is framed by the identification of a problem in cultural attitudes to it that have arisen because 'the stranger's idea of the Dismal Swamp has been largely derived from verses once declaimed by every properly instructed American schoolboy'.[41] The editorial framing presents the press bulletin of the United States Geological Survey as an opportunity to debunk the myth of the Dismal Swamp that is the result of the 'unfortunate impression that may be created by poetry', offering a corrective to the popular American vision of the Swamp and elevating fact above poetry.[42] The gloomy fantasia of the poem in question, Thomas Moore's 1806 'The Lake of the Dismal Swamp', presented in the opening paragraph of the article 'They have made her a grave too cold and damp/For a heart so warm and true' is set against the brighter facticity of both the Geological Survey report and the editorial comment, in which 'rabbits scamper about, muskrats and fish swim in the placid amber waters, brightly plumed birds fill the air with song … snakes come forth from their holes and lie coiled in the sunshine'.[43] The *Digest* retells the poem as fact in a form that consciously constructs a new beauty out of the knowledge of 'the geologist, the botanist and the zoologist'.[44]

As well as getting inside its structures, forms and functions, 'Woodrow Wilson' attends to the experience of reading the *Digest*, a genre that encourages the practices of browsing, scanning and re-reading that this text both registers and references. Along with the inscription of the traces of these practices that I have already outlined, 'Woodrow Wilson' also includes several direct expressions of the pleasures of reading the *Digest*. These begin with the opening intimacy of 'My literary digest' and its associated recollections of knowledge about Wilson, which are defined as 'Not a dream' and 'Not a drama' and thus, of course, suggest a semblance of both.[45] Reading as not quite a dream or a drama does capture the ways knowledge and understanding might emerge in the experience of reading the *Digest*. There are the dreamlike scraps of half-remembered details gathered from the excess of information and there is the *Digest*'s staging of events and instances of dialogue, its juxtapositions of alternative stances that make up the drama of news. More directly, under the heading 'Pleasures', 'Woodrow Wilson' offers the single line 'Reading everything again is one of many pleasures', reflecting the everyday presence of the *Digest* as a reservoir of knowledge the reader returns to over and again throughout the week.[46] The last stanza of the text is a meditation on the relations between reading and truth: 'When you make an ending you end the ending by realizing that no truth is repeatedly read.' As a response to the weekly digest of news, information and opinion, this reflection comments on both the changing status of truth – the same truth is not repeated in the different representations of the weekly news – and on the way the reader's understanding of truth shifts and mutates as she reads and re-reads the paper. This final segment also returns to the possessive intimacy of the opening with 'read my edition in a car' connecting the modern pleasures of consumerism and speed in an image of the reader in a private space borne along by the new technologies of information and motion.

These ideas, offered in the closing sequence, conclude the exploration of the popular weekly by conceptualizing this kind of reading as enabling readers to choose their truths from the drifts of information and opinion, making each reading unique. This represents the reader of the popular weekly as a consumer liberated by the availability of information and free from the imposition of a single, external truth in a way that echoes and emphasizes an earlier meditation in the text on the tedious oppression of received history: 'History is told and the rest is to unfold and the rest is to be retold and the rest leaves us cold.'[47] The final lines of the text seem to rejoice in the thrill of this liberty: 'leaves, leaves are dry, grass grass is wet, creeks creeks are rushing and birds birds whistle./Whistle and I'll come to you my lad'.[48] These phrases abstract and defamiliarize the linguistic factuality of the kinds of definitions provided in 'The Lexicographer's Easy Chair' section of the *Literary Digest*, in which a homely expert answers questions about language sent in by ordinary Americans across the United States, for example, in the query from '"D. S.," Peabody, Kan' in the 8 May 1920 edition, '"What is the difference in meaning between brave and courageous?"' and the *Digest* Lexicographer's response 'Courage is a natural readiness to face danger; bravery is acquired courage'.[49] Again, Stein's text registers a playful delight engendered in the encounter with this easy access to knowledge and an exuberant pleasure in the abundance of factual information.

This experiment with the form of *The Literary Digest* therefore foregrounds the democratization of knowledge, emphasizing the availability of cheap, mass-produced, digestible information and the consumer's ownership of facts that enable a personal structuring of truth as a new way to access power. *The Literary Digest* offers no single truths, but a series of accounts, opinions and debates, ways of telling truth, of creating history, that reveal their instability. This is the 'democracy' her work engages, and it is set in opposition to Woodrow Wilson and 'Wooded Princeton', to Wilson's 'earnestness', that is, to the sincere and intense conviction of 'School men'. In other words, it is opposed to Wilson's perceived scholasticism, and that of the other legislators of the new world order embodied in the League of Nations.

For Stein, Wilson represents the liberal, internationalist, paternalistic democracy she rejects, and the dismissiveness with which 'A League' and 'Woodrow Wilson' present Wilson's agenda attests to this. These texts assert the need to resist an internationalism perceived as a threat to American democracy from a cosmopolitan elite of well-educated men. Stein's commitment to democracy is therefore a populist, isolationist American nationalism, founded on a concept of fraternity predicated on birth that also begins to hint at ties of race and blood. The nationalism these texts express, however, is ordinary; it is everyday; and it is a form of nationalism that is consolidated as America emerges after the First World War as the richest and most powerful democracy in the world, fizzing with excitement about the democratizing possibilities of the mass production, dissemination and consumption of knowledge. In engaging with these texts as a reader and as a writer, Stein engages with the 'everyday' questions of democracy circulating in this popular discourse. *The Literary Digest* and *Life* form part of a contested space constructing a post–First World War American nationalism for the mass-democratic state. Where that is expressed as resistance to Wilson's internationalist agenda, it influences Stein's ideas about national identity, revealing both the power of the popular press in constructing the reading subject as a national subject and the difficulty in cleanly marking off the forms of nationalism that develop out of this period from those that emerge in the 1930s.

Notes

1 See, particularly, Ulla Dydo's important monograph, *Gertrude Stein: The Language That Rises 1923–1934* (Chicago: Northwestern University Press, 2003). In this text, Dydo uses the Gertrude Stein and Alice B. Toklas Papers in the Beinecke Archive to explore her own earlier distinction between what she terms Stein's 'real writing' or 'real voice' and her 'public or audience writing', an approach that had informed the selections and headnotes in Dydo's 1993, *A Stein Reader*, which references Stein's notebooks and other material in the archive throughout. Dydo uses *The Language That Rises* to challenge her own earlier categorization and identifies more of Stein's 'public' texts as 'real writing'. Dydo's claim about Stein's 'real writing', however, as opposed to 'publicity stunts to charm an audience', is a binary that is essentially sustained in *The Language That Rises*, and, I would argue, draws a false distinction that presupposes problematic conceptualizations of a private self and a pure form of experimental writing (Dydo, *Language That Rises*, 5). In the texts under discussion here, the public and the private meet in Stein's reading in a way that reveals the artificiality of a distinction between the private 'real voice' and public 'personality' that might posit the one as more real than the other.

2 Catharine Stimpson is a significant originator of this approach. See, for example, Catharine R. Stimpson, 'The Mind, the Body, and Gertrude Stein', *Critical Inquiry* 3/3 (1977), pp. 489–506, www.jstor.org/stable/1342936 (all websites last accessed 1 March 2020). Other examples include Lisa Ruddick's attempt at ' humanist understanding of the artistic process' (Lisa R. Ruddick, *Reading Gertrude Stein: Body, Text, Gnosis* (Ithaca, NY: Cornell University Press, 1990), 11) and Ulla Dydo's insistence that, 'she wrote of ordinary daily life, and everything she wrote included the writer who shaped it' (cited in Dydo, *Language That Rises*, p. 19).

3 See my discussion of Will's reading below.

4 See Dydo, *Gertrude Stein*; Juliana Spahr, *Everybody's Autonomy: Connective Reading and Collective Identity* (Tuscaloosa, AL: University of Alabama Press, 2001); Barbara Will, *Gertrude Stein, Modernism and the Problem of 'Genius'* (Edinburgh: Edinburgh University Press, 2000); Aidan Thompson, 'Language and Democracy: Meaning Making as Existing in the Work of Gertrude Stein', *Arizona Quarterly: A Journal of American Literature, Culture, and Theory* 69/3 (2013), pp. 129–55; and Kristin Bergen, '"Dogs Bark": War, Narrative, and Historical Syncopation in Gertrude Stein's Late Work', *Criticism* 57/4 (2015), pp. 609–29. See also Peter Quartermain's *Disjunctive Poetics: From Gertrude Stein and Louis Zukofsky to Susan Howe* (Cambridge: Cambridge University Press, 1992), which does not reference the Beinecke Archive but nonetheless represents an important example of this scholarly approach, characterizing her writing as 'thoroughly democratic, resistant to institutionalised power and meaning', p. 43. Quartermain's interpretation continues the significant recovery work undertaken by the Language Poets in the 1970s, 1980s and 1990s, who claimed Stein's work as an important precursor for their critique of capitalist cultural forms.

5 Will, *Problem of 'Genius'*, p. 160; Dydo, *Language That Rises*, p. 17; Thompson, 'Language and Democracy', pp. 130–1. Note that Barbara Will distinguishes between the dialogic, 'democratic' aspects of Stein's text and her 'investment in modernist discourses of aesthetic withdrawal and in a poetics of interiority', arguing for 'unresolved contradictions between her profound affiliation with American "democratic" culture and her inscription within European high culture' and that

Stein's central claim to 'being a genius' is neither elitist nor wholly progressive and democratizing but conflictual, complex, dialectical' (cited in Will, *Problem of 'Genius'*, p. 160, 12).

6 Spahr, *Everybody's Autonomy*, p. 49.

7 In Spahr's reference to, 'her complicated politics (her lack of respect for conventional feminism, her friendship with Bernard Fay)', cited Spahr, *Everybody's Autonomy*, p. 49.

8 Barbara Will, *Unlikely Collaboration: Stein, Fay and the Making of a Friendship* (Columbia University Press, 2011), pp. 12–13.

9 Will, *Unlikely Collaboration*, p. 13.

10 We can see this mechanism at work in Dydo, where the private 'real' Stein is valorized and the public persona is treated with suspicion as generative of the 'publicity stunts' and provocative statements designed to seek public attention (cited in Dydo, *Language That Rises*, p. 5).

11 Will, *Unlikely Collaboration*, pp. 9, 24, 13.

12 Ibid., 15.

13 As David Ayers argues, 'The two forces of internationalism and nationalism emerge at the same moment and as a response to the same events, and their progress is thoroughly intermingled'. See David Ayers, 'Introduction', in *Modernism, Internationalism, and the Russian Revolution* [online]. Edinburgh University Press, 2018), par. 8.4.

14 This does not necessarily reflect the political mood in the Senate. Adam Tooze argues that 'In 1919 other prominent Republicans were still active supporters of the League of Nations … What they demanded was that Congress must have the final word in approving any collective enforcement action. Since the weakly worded Covenant could easily have been interpreted in this direction, it was Wilson himself who presented the ultimate obstacle to compromise. He insisted that the treaty must be accepted whole and complete, or not at all.' The Treaty was narrowly defeated after five months of debate and this hinged on Wilson's refusal to accept the Republican amendment rather than on any trenchant anti-internationalist feeling. See Adam Tooze, *The Great Deluge: The Remaking of World Order 1916–1931* (London: Allen Lane, 2014), p. 335.

15 Will, *Problem of 'Genius'*, p. 121. Other examples that discuss texts from the collection as exemplary of Stein's identification with America include: Elliott L. Vanskike '"Seeing Everything as Flat": Landscape in Gertrude Stein's *Useful Knowledge* and *The Geographical History of America*', *Texas Studies in Literature and Language* 35/2 (1993), pp. 151–67, www.jstor.org/stable/40755007; and Michael Moon, '"Wherein the South Differs from the North": Naming Persons, Naming Places, and the Need for Visionary Geographies', *Southern Spaces* (16 May 2008), www.southernspaces.org/2008/wherein-south-differs-north-naming-persons-naming-places-and-need-visionary-geographies.

16 See Dydo, *Language That Rises*, p. 135.

17 Gertrude Stein, *Useful Knowledge* (New York: Payson & Clarke, 1928), p. 104.

18 Gertrude Stein and Alice B. Toklas Papers, Series VI: Clippings, 1913–1948 (General), Beinecke Library, Yale University, Box 142, Folder 3340.

19 James Playsted Wood. *Magazines in the United States* (New York: The Ronald Press Company, 1971), p. 203.

20 See David E. E. Sloane, ed., *American Humor Magazines and Comic Periodicals* (Westport, CT: Greenwood Press, 1987), 150; and Wood, *Magazines*, p. 203.

21 Ibid., p. 204.

22 Walter Beach Humphrey, 'As Election Approaches', illustration, *The Literary Digest* 67/5 (3 October 1920), cover.
23 *Life* 74, no. 1925 (18 September 1919) p. 482.
24 Unattributed editorial, *Life* 74/1925, p. 500.
25 Stein's text, printed on page 496, is accompanied by an editorial note: 'Miss Gertrude Stein is one of the pioneers of Free Verse. We publish her poem as a fit accompaniment to President Wilson's elucidation of the League of Nations' (*Life* 74/1925, p. 496). This rather tellingly reflects both that, although the editors are in favour of the League, they, too, imagine Wilson's engagement with the ordinary Americans as a failure, and that Stein is seen as being rather less 'of the people' and more like Wilson than her texts might want to suggest.
26 Paul Reilly, 'Say! Do You Know You Sat on My Hat?' *Life* 74/1925 (18 September 1919), p. 506.
27 Paul Reilly, 'Humpty Dumpty Sat on a Wall', *Life* 74/1925 (18 September 1919), p. 498.
28 Richard Scully, and Marian Quartly, 'Using Cartoons as Historical Evidence', in *Drawing the Line: Using Cartoons as Historical Evidence*, ed. Richard Scully and Marian Quartly (Clayton, Victoria, Australia: Monash University Press, 2009), 01.3; 01.4.
29 Gertrude Stein, 'A League', *Life* 74/1925 (18 September 1919), p. 496. All further references to 'A League' are from this page.
30 Pericles Lewis provides a helpful discussion in *Modernism, Nationalism, and the Novel* of the problem, being worked through in the interwar period, 'of whether the nation should be understood as a legal and political unit, defined by the voluntary membership in it of individual citizens, or as an ethnic and social unit, defined by the shared culture, history, and (perhaps) biological inheritance that was thrust upon individuals, not chosen by them'. See Pericles Lewis, *Modernism, Nationalism, and the Novel* (Cambridge: Cambridge University Press, 2000), p. 6.
31 Advertisement for '*The Literary Digest* Liberty Map of New Europe', *The Literary Digest* 67/5 (3 October 1920), p. 5. All further citations of this advertisement will be taken from this page.
32 'League Verdicts in the Primaries', *Literary Digest* 66/13 (25 September, 1920), p. 15.
33 Gertrude Stein, 'Woodrow Wilson', in *Useful Knowledge*, pp. 104, 107, 112. Wilson was President of Princeton from 1902 to 1910. For Stein's earlier presentation of Wilson, see Gertrude Stein, *Fernhurst, Q.E.D. and Other Early Writings* (Virago Press, 1972). For a discussion of the evidence for Philip Redfern's basis in Woodrow Wilson, see Leon Katz's 'Introduction' to Stein's early writings, reprinted in the above edition of *Fernhurst*, p. 198.
34 Stein, *Useful Knowledge*, pp. 104, 105.
35 Ibid., pp. 104, 107.
36 See, respectively: *The Literary Digest* 65, no. 4 (24 April 1920): 10; *The Literary Digest* 67/5 (3 October 1920), p. 31; and *The Literary Digest* 66, no. 3 (Jul 17 1920), p. 35.
37 Stein, *Useful Knowledge*, pp. 107–8.
38 Stein, *Useful Knowledge*, p. 106; 'Cylinders of Window-Glass', *Literary Digest* 62/6 (9 August 1919), p. 22).
39 Stein, *Useful Knowledge*, p. 110; and 'From Adzes to Zwieback in the Mail-Order Merchandising Game', *Literary Digest* 66/9 (28 August 1920), p. 80.
40 Stein, *Useful Knowledge*, p. 108.
41 'Not So Dismal After All', *The Literary Digest* 64/6 (7 February 1920), p. 88.
42 'Not So Dismal', p. 88.

43 Ibid., pp. 88, 90.
44 Ibid., p. 88.
45 Stein, *Useful Knowledge*, p. 104.
46 Ibid. All references here are from this page.
47 Ibid., p. 109.
48 Ibid., p. 114.
49 *Literary Digest* 65, no. 6 (8 May 1920), p. 150.

6

CLASHES OVER TRANSCENDENCE: T. S. ELIOT AND KARL MANNHEIM THROUGH THE LENS OF PROGRAMMATIC MODERNISM

Jonas Kurlberg

Introduction

Crisis is a fertile ground out of which much intellectual creativity flourishes. During the interwar era, intellectuals gathered in formal and informal networks to envision new futures out of the rubbles of modernity. It was in this context that a group of intellectuals known as the Moot (1938–47) gathered. The Moot was set up by theologian and ecumenist J. H. Oldham, who dreamt of laying the intellectual and structural groundwork for a Christian cultural revolution that was to revitalize Western civilization. The archival material this semi-secretive group left behind is a rich hunting ground for historians seeking to reconstruct the social thought of some of the leading thinkers of this period.

The focus of this chapter is a particularly interesting sub-plot of the Moot, namely, the decade-long interaction between two of the more eminent members of the group: T. S. Eliot and Karl Mannheim. Their friendship did not go unnoticed by other members. Alec Vidler was 'struck by the sympathy' between them and 'by the way they impressed and influenced each other'.[1] Ever since Roger Kojecky's treatment of the Moot in *T. S. Eliot's Social Criticism,* it has become commonplace for Eliot scholars to assume that Eliot's view of the Moot was essentially positive.[2] However, Barry Spurr, in his *Anglo-Catholic in Religion,* has correctly problematized Kojecky's conclusions, postulating that Eliot not only attended the Moot out of a sense of obligation to Oldham, but also ultimately held that associations such as the Moot were futile.[3] While Spurr makes a strong case, a more positive note was struck in Eliot's correspondence with his friends during the early years of the Moot, suggesting a more nuanced picture.[4] Stefan Collini's

An extended version of this chapter has previously been published in Jonas Kurlberg, *Christian Modernism in an Age of Totalitarianism: T. S. Eliot, Karl Mannheim and the Moot* (London: Bloomsbury, 2019).

proposal, that Eliot identified himself as a 'man of letters', as one observing the comings and goings of society from a critical distance, makes sense of his engagement with the Moot.[5] For example, in a letter to Philip Mairet, Eliot spoke of the growing influence of Mannheim and Adolf Löwe on the Moot, a situation that 'needs keeping a very critical eye on'.[6] The majority of Eliot's interaction with the Moot was in response to Mannheim's ideas and it is clear that Eliot found Mannheim fascinating and a useful dialogue partner.[7] Nevertheless, despite his personal empathy he felt compelled to 'warn' people from a wholesale acceptance of Mannheim,[8] and regarded 'his ideas as dangerous'.[9]

Eliot's mode of engagement with the Moot stands in contrast to that of Karl Mannheim. If Eliot was guarded, on the outskirts of the group looking in, Mannheim embraced it wholeheartedly and sought to occupy its centre.[10] As Julia Mannheim conveyed in a letter to the Moot members shortly after her husband's sudden death in January 1947, the group had provided a 'free and safe place for the mind, soul and spirit'.[11] The fact that Oldham decided to discontinue the Moot after Mannheim's death bears witness to his significance for the project.[12] Eliot, for his part, praised Mannheim in an obituary for *The Times* for his 'remarkable influence' during his time in England, not least on the 'informal discussion among a small group [i.e. the Moot]', while also qualifying that 'many must be aware of a debt to him, whose points of view are very different from his'.[13]

My aim here is not merely to expound upon the intriguing debate that took place between the two. Their relationship has already been examined to some extent by Collini[14] and Kojecky,[15] amongst others.[16] A new comparative perspective may, however, be found through viewing this interaction and indeed their whole body of social criticism through the overarching interpretive lens of 'programmatic modernism'. This framework derives from literary studies but has in Roger Griffin's reconceptualization been construed as a 'heuristic tool' for the analysis of the socio-political engagement of individuals and movements in the late nineteenth to mid-twentieth century. Griffin points to a pattern, widely discussed in modernist literary criticism, of decadence and renewal amongst modernist writers, poets and artists, stemming from a deep-rooted antagonism towards modernity, and which in turn sparked a number of countervailing visions of renewal. Interestingly, Collini concludes that few writers conform to Peter Gay's account of the Weimar Republic's modernist 'hunger for wholeness' in the face of social disintegration under modernity 'better than T. S. Eliot'.[17] This impulse towards renewal amongst modernist artists is a building block in Griffin's conceptual construction, as he draws a parallel between this outlook found amongst individual modernist writers and that of socio-political movements. Mannheim is certainly not a modernist in the literary and artistic sense of the term. Nevertheless, once the modernist tag has been expanded to include impulses beyond the confines of 'the arts', there is no reason why individual intellectuals could not be considered through this lens.

In isolation, to point to a pattern of decadence and renewal in political thought in Europe during this era is too generic to be interesting. What makes Griffin's thesis potentially fruitful, however, is his emphasis on the interwar crisis as a crisis of transcendence. That is, the perception that the *nomos* of Christianity was collapsing as a consequence of secularization, fuelling an apocalyptic angst of an imminent end to Western civilization.[18] It is from this perspective that I wish to approach Mannheim and Eliot's social criticism. Mannheim and Eliot lived in an age of transition where new ideas emerged, merged and were tested. In response to a sense of anarchic chaos during the interwar decades, they advanced their respective dreams of a new society. The Moot became both a testing ground and a battleground for their ideologies. Mannheim, as an advocate of civilizational planning, was driven by the Enlightenment's faith in human agency, whereas Eliot's confidence in divine providence led him to argue for a more passive eschatological preparation for God's intervention in history.

Common ground

Secularization, eroding canopies and the loss of transcendence

Despite Eliot's critical stance towards Mannheim's ideas, their socio-political outlooks were, as Wolfgang Wicht points out, 'kindred'.[19] To begin with, they both diagnosed modern society as decadent: a modernist angst of cosmic, apocalyptic chaos permeates the social criticism of both Mannheim and Eliot during the 1930s and 1940s. Broadly speaking, their apocalyptic outlook can be understood in the light of Peter Berger's idea of sacred canopies. Berger has argued that all human societies construct their own *nomos*, that is, an overarching sense of meaning as 'a shield against terror' in an otherwise chaotic world. From time to time, and for various historical reasons, the plausibility structures of such worldviews crumble, leading to breakdown and chaos.[20] Arguably, and as pronounced by Nietzsche's madman,[21] such a sacred-canopy-collapse transpired during the late nineteenth century when Christianity, through secularization, lost its dominant position as the social force of Europe.

Eliot and Mannheim's social projects must ultimately be understood from this premise, as responses to the realization of the loss of transcendence in modern society and its, for many, calamitous repercussions. Such themes are readily identifiable in Mannheim's seminal *Ideology and Utopia*, where he investigated the 'breakdown of the unitary world-view with which the modern era was ushered in'.[22] With the loss of the Church's 'intellectual monopoly' – which had guaranteed the unity of the Medieval order – Mannheim recognized a shift towards a condition of fragmentation in which transient and competing worldviews diminished the possibility of a common vision and social cohesion.[23] Congruous with what Zygmunt Bauman would later conceptualize as the 'ambivalence of modernity',[24] Mannheim's social thought was profoundly affected by the predicament of modernity, in that he celebrated the experimental and spontaneous spirit of the renaissance and liberalism, but lamented its resulting 'neutralization of values'.[25] During the 12th Moot meeting, Mannheim suggested that the modern psyche – via Bergson, Hegel and Croce, and ultimately Protestantism – prized change over stability, yet this mentality had resulted in 'an awareness of the abyss … due to removal of all *eternal scaffolding*'. Consequently, modernity was plagued with a sense of 'disintegration and chaos',[26] and in a Moot paper written in 1941, Mannheim dramatically concluded 'that the world is on the edge of an abyss and only a new social order, a new kind of man can help'.[27] Only a radical reorientation would save modern society from a total collapse.

Neither Eliot nor Mannheim believed that a liberal secular society – if by liberal one means neutral – was sustainable. Understood as a disintegrative force, whether in religion or politics, liberalism in Eliot's view 'prepare[s] for that which is its own negation: the artificial, mechanised or brutalised control which is a desperate remedy of its own chaos'.[28] In other words, since liberalism is a negative force, something else must fill the chaotic vacuum it leaves behind. Directly borrowing from Christopher Dawson, Eliot anticipated that the demand for order in the unstable interwar democratic nations would lead to further centralized control and towards a 'democratic totalitarianism'.[29] The vacuum created by liberalism could simply not remain, and as such, the Western world was at a crossroads between 'a new Christian society' and a pagan society.[30] It is clear which option Eliot thought preferable. In a radio broadcast in 1946, Eliot predicted that '[i]f Christianity goes, the whole of our culture goes … You must pass through many centuries of barbarism'.[31]

Both Eliot and Mannheim, then, congruent with Griffin's conceptualization, understood the crisis of modernity as a crisis of transcendence. The crumbling structures of Christian Europe and the crisis in liberalism form the backdrop to which their respective social criticism must be understood.

Culture, religion and renewal

To further understand this theme of the loss of transcendence, we need to explore Eliot and Mannheim's respective definitions of religion. Mannheim's alarm over secularization was informed by an understanding of religion – inherited from Saint-Simon, Comte and Durkheim – as an indispensable force of social integration and cultural flourishing.[32] In *Ideology and Utopia*, Mannheim maintained that 'the magical-religious view' plays an important meaning-making function that 'make[s] coherent the fragments of the reality of inner psychic as well as objective external experience'.[33] Also in his later ideas on a democratically planned society, religion is consistently seen as a necessary social force. In a Weber-esque analysis Mannheim feared that the mechanization of modern society could become a 'prison', enslaving the masses.[34] The appeal of religion was that it added life and spirit to his otherwise technocratic ideas of social and cultural planning, binding society together without compulsion. In a planned society '[t]he only alternative to the concentration camp was the spontaneous giving up of deviations, and only a revival of religion could bring this about'.[35] During his years with the Moot, then, he came to appreciate religion as a means to mitigate the dangers of a planned society.

If Mannheim's definition derived from classical sociology, Eliot inherited the English tradition and Samuel Coleridge.[36] Whilst Eliot would have reacted to Mannheim's pure utilitarianism, he would nevertheless have agreed on the culture-bearing function of religion. Eliot held that the culture of a society – a people's 'way of life' – is the incarnation of its religion.[37] In other words, religion informs and shapes the institutions, habits and behaviour of a people through and through.[38] Accordingly, in a letter to the Moot on 'Christian imagination' Eliot argued that the production of cultural artefacts, such as the arts, derives from religious experience. Artistic imagination is essentially a religious experience, and according to Eliot, the 'capacity' of religious experience is in turn conditioned by social milieu. It follows that in a secular society where culture is deprived of spirituality, imagination 'itself is broken up'.[39] In short, Eliot asserted that culture could not flourish without religion, for '[n]o culture has appeared or developed except together with a religion.'[40]

Revival of Christianity

There is thus significant overlap between Eliot and Mannheim's diagnosis of the crisis of modern society. Both held that the crisis of modernity was a result of secularization, for without a religious vision society had no unifying purpose. Ultimately, they further shared the belief that only the renewal of Christendom could provide the foundations for Western societies. In this way they depart from the Griffinite mould, for in Griffin's conception Christianity is a spent source and not a source of societal renewal. Nevertheless, the 'return to the mythical past' in the desire to reinstate the spiritual empire of Christendom is a prototypically programmatic modernist move.[41]

For Eliot and Mannheim none of the alternative paradigms at hand filled them with much hope. Liberalism was no real alternative, for on their reading it constituted no positive content and represented mere liberation *from* tradition, a *laissez faire*, with no aim to strive towards; it was a negative, disintegrative force. The totalitarian regimes, as replacement religions, did fill the void previously occupied by Christianity, but at the expense of human dignity and freedom.[42] Thus, as the only viable alternative both turned to Christianity as the source of societal renewal.

For Eliot, the hope of a Christian society was tied up with his conviction that the claims of Christianity are true, but also to his assertion that Christianity has produced 'the highest culture the world has ever known'.[43] Mannheim, on the other hand, claimed that Christianity, as the 'religion of love and universal brotherhood', would in his planned democracy offer an alternate sacred canopy to 'the recent philosophy [fascism] with the demonic image of man'.[44] In essence, Christianity had the spiritual resources and value structure to provide his democratically planned society with religious vitality and transcendent purpose.

Clashes on the transformation of culture

Planning versus preparation for the future

Despite this common ground, Eliot and Mannheim repeatedly clashed over centralized planning; the functions of elites; and the definition, transformation and renewal of culture. Principally, they differed on the mechanism by which their desired 'modernist' cultural and societal renewal should be achieved.

Mannheim's idea of 'Planning for Freedom' was one of the central ideas discussed in the Moot. It sought to overcome the chaotic *laissez faire* of liberalism by accepting the inevitability of centralized planning in industrialized mass society, while at the same time finding means to resist the stifling totalitarianism of fascism and communism. Mannheim believed that through extensive socio-scientific investigation and experimentation, and in collaboration with a host of intellectuals from other disciplines, sociologists could address the ills of modern society. Guided by elites the masses would be inculcated with a democratic mindset enabling them to act as responsible citizens. Outlining a detailed course of action, his programme for a democratically planned society was as bold as it was comprehensive and Mannheim believed that the Moot could form the nucleus that could catalyse his vision into reality.[45]

The vision immediately struck a chord with the Moot members and clearly left Eliot provoked. In a circulated comment, Eliot hailed the paper as a 'masterly outline' while his critique was notably guarded.[46] In a private letter to Oldham, however, Eliot professed that '[t]here were so many objections in my mind', but that he was struggling to articulate these.[47] The first public misgiving towards Mannheim came in his review of *Man and Society* for *The Spectator* on 6 June 1940. Having approved of Mannheim's social diagnosis, Eliot expressed his fears of a latent totalitarianism in Mannheim's ideas of central planning.[48] 'What is the alternative?' asked Eliot.

> It can only be … that which we may call the 'dark age attitude' – waiting, perhaps for many generations, for the storm of the machine age to blow over; retiring with a few of the best books, to a small self-contained community, to till the soil and the cow.[49]

While Eliot did submit a vision of the ideal Christian society in *Idea* – which he hoped would inspire a change in 'social attitude' – he did not devise a plan for its realization.[50] Instead his 'dark age attitude' entailed a long-term view of patient waiting. However, Eliot clearly did not suggest idle passivity. In an editorial for the Moot-sponsored *Christian News-Letter (CNL)*, he emphasized the importance of *preparing* for a 'new world' after the war.[51] The initial step of this preparation consisted of prophetically shaking the nation out of its slumber and awakening it to see the consequences of its passive drifting into paganism.[52] It was a wake-up call from delusion and a call to repentance.[53] Furthermore, Eliot's envisioned future Christian society depended upon educating the 'type of man' who aspired to the ideals of holiness and wisdom.[54]

Definitions of culture

The disparity between Eliot's patient waiting and preparation, and Mannheim's active planning, is related to their disputes over the nature of culture, the role of elites and, ultimately, religious conviction. To begin with, Eliot could afford this 'dark age attitude' because he held a cyclical view of culture in which cultures go through cycles of decay and rebirth. Indeed, in a paper for the Moot, Eliot contrasted his own cyclical understanding of history with Mannheim's progressivism which by implication demands greater activism.[55] Their clash in their definitions of culture is further crystallized in Eliot's *Notes*. Here Eliot took issue with Mannheim's proposition that culture originates within the elites and subsequently filters down to the masses.[56] In *Man and Society*, Mannheim suggested that any 'sociological investigation of the culture in liberal society must begin with the life of those who create culture', that is, the 'intelligentsia'.[57] Such an understanding of culture makes sense in the light of Mannheim's attachment to planning. If culture springs from the elites, then culture is all the more conceivable as an outcome of deliberate co-ordination between intellectuals, especially social scientists. Eliot, on the other hand, had for decades come to understand culture as the outcome of processes within different societal segments and classes, merging organically into a total culture of a people. In *Notes* Eliot wrote that culture is made up of those everyday items and activity such as:

> Derby Day, Henley Regatta Cowes, the twelfth of August, a cup final, the dog races, the pin table, the dart board, Wensleydale cheese, boiled cabbage cut into sections, beetroot in vinegar, nineteenth-century Gothic churches and the music of Elgar ....[58]

Cultures, then, are preserved and evolve organically through the often-unconscious actions and habits of a whole people, rather than the outcome of elite interventions and creativity. The implication is that even if a society possesses all the essential 'conditions' for a culture to flourish, these cannot be generated at will or 'fulfilled solely by deliberate organisation'.[59] Culture cannot be planned.

Is there, then, a paradox between Eliot's emphasis on stability and continuation in his conservative social criticism, and the *aufbruch* of his experimental paradigmatic modernist literature?[60] Arguably, while the *form* might differ, consistent themes are recognizable. For instance, the desolation of a society decaying under materialism expressed in *The Waste Land* finds a parallel in the battle between the material and spiritual world in the play *Murder in the Cathedral* (1935), and also in the juxtaposing of religious versus materialistic worldviews in *Idea*. Another identifiable theme is that of suffering and redemption. In the final speech of *Murder in the Cathedral*, the Third Priest breaks out in a doxology in response to Thomas Becket's martyrdom:

> We thank Thee for Thy mercies of blood, for Thy redemption
> by blood. For the blood of Thy martyrs and saints
> Shall enrich the earth, shall create the holy places.[61]

Just as Becket's sacrifice brings redemption and renewal in Eliot's *Murder in the Cathedral,* so the re-Christianization of modern society will only transpire through a purgatory of 'discipline, inconvenience and discomfort'.[62]

The clerisy debate and the nature of elites

A dominant discussion within the Moot relates to the function of the group itself as an exemplary elite. Mannheim advocated for something between a voluntary organization and a political party: 'a combatant order', similar to the 'nervous system' of a social organism that could be 'co-ordinating its activities' and 'spiritualiz[ing] its aims'.[63] He envisioned a group of intellectuals that, through spiritual renewal and mutual support, could offer leadership to the nation or 'revitalize' existing leadership structures.[64] However, Eliot's aversion towards organized corporate action kept him on guard against such developments in the Moot. While Eliot did not in principle reject the idea of an elite, he doubted whether the Moot could establish sufficient common ground to launch such a 'party'. For Eliot, the value of the Moot was its diversity: 'I find in it, not merely agreement achieved and hoped for, but also *significant disagreement*'.[65] These comments reflect Eliot's general reluctance to subscribe to easy solutions such as societal blueprints. Programmes were a superficial solution that did not prepare for the kind of society, saturated with Christianity, that Eliot yearned for.

The tension over elites is most evidently present in the Moot's discussion on Eliot's paper on the idea of 'the clerisy'. In his 1939 *Idea,* Eliot had already drawn upon Samuel Coleridge's term 'clerisy' to describe an elite that would 'form the conscious mind and conscience of the nation'.[66] By the time he wrote 'On the Place and Function of the Clerisy' in 1946, Eliot had considerably altered his definition of the clerisy, downplaying both its educational and spiritual role. The clerisy is here described as an elite consisting of 'any category of men and women who because of their individual capacities exercise significant power in any particular area'. The clerisy capture ideas and 'alter the sensibility, of their time'.[67]

Eliot's clerisy paper was commented upon by both Mannheim and Michael Polanyi.[68] Interestingly, Mannheim's extensive critique of Eliot's paper offers few points of disagreement. In fact, Mannheim argued that Eliot's clerisy comes close to his own use of the term 'intelligentsia', which consists of those who give 'a lead to the change in politically and culturally relevant ideas'.[69] Eliot's response is less conciliatory, taking aim at the apparent contradiction in Mannheim's insistence on the spontaneity of the clerisy whilst also claiming that culture can be planned.[70] Mannheim had suggested that interactions between the clerics would generate new cultural 'patterns'.[71] For Eliot, an implication of such interaction is the unpredictability of the outcome, '[for] I do not see that the "interplay" can be directed or pattern emergent from it be foreseen or planned'.[72] Furthermore, Mannheim had proposed that 'Planning for Freedom' implies that the organizing of elites can be structured by 'unwritten laws' that enable spontaneity and originality.[73] Naturally, Eliot challenged the idea that '"unwritten laws" can be planned'.[74]

The selection of elites, class and the transmission of culture

Mannheim clearly paid heed to Eliot's criticism. Shortly after the clerisy debate Mannheim published an article for the *CNL* in which he argued that the transmission of culture is a task for every class of society. Not only did Mannheim borrow Eliot's ideas, but his use of the phrases 'the whole people' and 'change the sensibility of their time' must be understood as deliberate plagiarism.[75] As a member of the editorial board of the *CNL*, it is probable that Eliot would have seen Mannheim's article. If so, it did little to alleviate his criticism. It was around this time that a combative Eliot wrote the second chapter of his *Notes* that was going to 'blow the Moot up'.[76] The chapter in question, which originally appeared as 'The Class and the Elite' in the *New English Weekly* (October 1945), further seeks to define the role of the elite in cultural transformation, using Mannheim as a sparring partner.[77]

For Eliot, Mannheim exemplifies the problematic push amongst his contemporaries towards a classless society, in which ruling elites were to be selected on the basis of ability, thereby replacing the functions of the dominant classes. As Eliot readily pointed out, even Mannheim had to admit to the difficulty of selecting elites in a democratic society.[78] Accordingly, a classless society gives rise to cultural degeneration, as the vibrancy of culture is dependent upon a stratified society whereby the plurality of classes reciprocally contributes to the whole. Therefore, while the call for elite membership based on ability appears to address issues of justice, its breakdown of classes hinders the processes of cultural transmission.[79]

The implication of Eliot's argument is that although Mannheim's planned society might seek to recover a common purpose, meaning, shared value basis or indeed some reinvigorated 'sacred canopy', it remains an impossible utopia. Without the classes, society cannot maintain a culture or 'a way of life'. The transmission of culture is dependent upon classes, which in turn implies family structures, and the family lies outside of the scope of the planner.[80] In other words, despite his attempt to reconcile his ideas on culture and elites with Eliot's in his *CNL* article, Mannheim had still failed to address a crucial problem: 'that of the *transmission of culture*'.[81]

Planning and religious renewal

Another point of contention in the debate over societal transformation concerned whether a religious renewal could be planned. During his time with the Moot, Mannheim gained a greater appreciation for religion as a positive social force and sought to incorporate this emphasis in his social criticism. In particular, these ideas are worked out in his lengthy two-part paper 'Towards a New Social Philosophy', 'aiming at a re-interpretation of Christian values in the present situation'.[82] A topic Mannheim addressed was the extent to which planning for religious renewal is possible. He argued that since there is a social context for every transcendent experience, there are certain conditions in which religion can flourish. These conditions can in turn be planned. Eliot responded to Mannheim's paper in his notes on 'Christian Imagination', seemingly concurring with Mannheim's assertion that religion flourishes under certain conditions. Eliot proposed that imagination – the stuff of great art and thought – is essentially religious and that religious experiences flourish in environments that cultivate such.[83] It is striking that Eliot here merely hinted at his aversion to Mannheim's proposal.

This omission is all the more puzzling considering Eliot's critical review of *Diagnosis of Our Time.* In 1943 Mannheim published *Diagnosis,* a compilation of articles written during the war, including 'Towards a New Social Philosophy'. The essence of Eliot's rebuff concerns Mannheim's confidence in the sociologist's ability to stage social conditions in which religion, and thus culture, can thrive.[84] For Eliot, it was a question of what comes first: religion or society? As argued in *Notes,* religion is for Eliot the soil out of which culture emerges, and not the other way around. Religion cannot be reduced to religious experience alone, but also carries dogma which precedes culture. The particularity of dogma, as such, informs the shape a society takes on. Ultimately, Eliot did not share Mannheim's optimism for the possibility of a fruitful reconstruction. Just as modern society had no architectural tradition to warrant enthusiasm in the impending reconstruction of war-torn British cities, so there was no shared value basis or common religious vision on which social construction could yield a cultural renewal.

Humanism versus Christian theism

There is another underlying reason for Eliot's sustained antipathy towards Mannheim's ideas of a planned society. That is, Mannheim's outlook, informed by the humanism of the Enlightenment, clashed with Eliot's Christian supernaturalism. Both held that social cohesion demands a religious framework without which society cannot flourish. Where they fundamentally differed was on the question of whether such religious frameworks themselves have any ontological basis.

In his review of *Diagnosis,* Eliot referred to Dawson's critique of Mannheim's *Man and Society.* Dawson had suggested that the remoulding of human nature, which Mannheim aspired towards through planning, 'is a task that far transcends politics'. Such an undertaking would threaten human liberty as '[the] planning of culture cannot be undertaken in a dictatorial spirit, like a rearmament plan … It must … be undertaken in a really religious spirit.'[85] But Mannheim had, as we have seen, in his later writings suggested this exact point. Thus, there is no fundamental disagreement between Mannheim and Dawson on this account. Eliot's review acknowledged this and yet there was in his mind a decisive difference: Mannheim was a sociologist 'with no dogmatic faith such as Dawson's'.[86] This seems to make all the difference for Eliot. His comments in *Notes* that 'no religion can fully be "understood" from the outside – even for the sociologist's purpose' must be seen as implicating Mannheim.[87]

What was subtly hinted at in his review of Mannheim's *Diagnosis* was more plainly stated in a BBC radio broadcast titled 'Towards a Christian Britain' in early 1941. While not directly addressing Mannheim, Eliot pointed to divine providence as the underlying reason for his aversion to centralized planning: 'But we must not forget God, without whom we can do nothing of worth, but with whom we can do everything. It is impossible to make a blue-print of a Christian order, because we cannot fit God into a blue-print.'[88] As Eliot wrote in a letter to Eric Fenn who oversaw the broadcast, he wished to emphasize that '"Christianisation" was anything but a superhuman task, too difficult to be carried out by Picture Post without the help of God'.[89]

Throughout his time with the Moot, Mannheim insisted that his contributions to the group were limited sociological observations that did not concern the truthfulness of religious claims. Mannheim presented himself as an agnostic who would not make judgements on religious beliefs.[90] Nevertheless, his scepticism is evident in a private conversation in which he offended his fellow émigré and Moot member Michael Polanyi, by questioning the compatibility of faith commitments and honest scientific enquiry.[91] Furthermore, despite his self-proclaimed agnosticism of Christian truth claims, Mannheim's rejection of the doctrine of original sin became a source of contention in the Moot.[92] Interestingly, Walter Oakeshott, speaking of the need for the Moot to overcome this 'one doctrinal problem' which 'may prove a real line of division', attributed Mannheim's objection to original sin to his 'humanistic view'.[93]

Religion was for Mannheim real and forceful, but nevertheless a human construction, a historically contingent phenomenon that could be utilized as a tool of social cohesion at the will of the planner – an attitude consistent with the spirit of the Enlightenment ascribing primacy to human agency in shaping one's own destiny. Eliot accepted sociological perspectives on religion to a point, not least since he understood religion as a cultural force. But in contrast to Mannheim, he held that God was more than a mere human projection. His theistic beliefs meant that religion, and thereby culture, could not simply be manipulated by modern scientists. Therefore, he held a strong antipathy towards appropriations of Christianity on functional grounds: 'what is *worst of all* is to advocate Christianity, not because it is true, but because it might be beneficial'.[94] This divergence was most strongly expressed in the interaction that ensued from Eliot's clerisy paper. In response to Polanyi's critique of this paper, Eliot articulated the essence of his disagreement with Mannheim:

> So, while we can say that there is such a thing as 'culture' (we mean something by the term) we cannot make it a direct object of activity; we can only aim at limited ends which we believe contribute to it. *Culture might be described as that which cannot be planned, except by God.*[95]

The implication of his insistence on God as the ultimate planner is that cultural transformation is not entirely within human control. This does not imply that Eliot denied human agency. For instance, in a broadcast in 1937, Eliot called the nation to self-reflection, humility and repentance in preparation 'to receive the grace of God without which human operations are vain'.[96] As we have seen, Eliot embraced a 'dark age attitude' whereby the individual kept the candle burning by whatever he or she could contribute in their sphere of influence. Eliot urged the listeners of the BBC to a virtuous prophetic living in dark times. 'Christian prophets' are those through whom 'God works to convert the habits of feeling and thinking, of desiring and willing, to which we are all more enslaved than we know'.[97]

Implications for Eliot's socio-political outlook

This theistic outlook undermines the attempt to locate Eliot's social criticism within the proto-fascist bracket.[98] As an offspring of the Enlightenment, fascism put a strong emphasis on human agency expressed in the totalitarian drive towards total state control. It is true that Eliot to an extent shared with the fascist movements a commitment to a hierarchical society and authoritarian rule.[99] However, Eliot's theism – implying a waiting upon and living without control – put him at odds with totalitarianism.[100]

Besides, in contradistinction to the dominant interpretation of Eliot's social criticism, Collini argues that from the 1930s onwards, Eliot can be placed within the Anglican social radicalism of the time as well as the Whig tradition.[101] There is a correlation between Eliot's conversion in 1927 and his shifting political outlook. By the time Eliot had joined the Moot, his commitment to hierarchy and order had waivered. For example, at the first Moot meeting Eliot suggested that Christianity had thrived in 'local circles and small groups' within 'natural community life' rather than through hierarchy.[102] My own argument adds to these voices in suggesting that Eliot's theism steers him away from more authoritarian and reactionary ideals. As Erik Tonning suggests, Eliot's 'uncompromising affirmation of Christian supernaturalism' marked a demonstrable shift away from the Right.[103]

It is also, conversely, the implied humanism in Mannheim's 'Planning for Freedom' that was an underlying reason why he never quite managed to convince the Moot members that his scheme was not simply a disguised form of semi-totalitarianism. Eliot made this claim implicitly by referring to Dawson's critique of Mannheim. Dawson used Mannheim to exemplify a trend towards materialistic planning that would result in worse excesses of the repression of freedom than the totalitarian regimes.[104] This was also Michael Polanyi's argument against Mannheim. The logic of materialism is the sovereign state, as articulated in Hobbes' 'Leviathan', for without a religious framework which locates authority in an external morality, the state must be imbued with absolute power; if not, the nation would disintegrate into civil war between competing groups.[105] Polanyi's confrontation with Mannheim must be understood in the light of this line of thought.[106]

Conclusion

The long-running exchange between T. S. Eliot and Karl Mannheim is one of the more intriguing sub-plots of the Moot discourse. There is something incongruous, but arresting, in this battle of ideas between Mannheim, the eminent Hungarian sociologist and secular Jew, and Eliot, famed nationalized American poet and Anglo-Catholic, over the soul of English society. Their interaction, stretching across nearly a decade, reveals both common ground and deep-rooted differences. In the immediate context of the Moot, Mannheim's ideas of socio-political planning were at the heart of their exchange, drawing a strong response from Eliot. Both identified social disintegration under the forces of liberalism as the cause of the perceived civilizational crisis in interwar Europe. However, they differed on the mechanisms of cultural renewal. They battled over the definition of culture and how culture is maintained, nourished and revitalized. These differences led Eliot to repeatedly oppose Mannheim's planned society, for he considered culture to be the product of a whole people, evolving organically from one generation to the next, flourishing through the spontaneous interaction between different social groups and classes. Such mechanisms for cultural transformation could simply not be planned for and in fact any top-down attempts at cultural planning would prove to be oppressive.

I have sought to frame this interaction between Eliot and Mannheim within the 'programmatic modernism' lens to bring to light the underlying rivalling conceptions of the transcendent. Eliot and Mannheim lamented the loss of transcendence through secularization and its colossal impact on social cohesion in Western civilization threatening fragmentation, chaos and nihilism. Considering the alternatives at hand, both deemed a renewed Christian order as preferable to the quasi-religious totalitarian regimes on the continent. As we have seen, this emphasis on Christianity does not imply that Eliot and Mannheim's ideals for a future society concurred. Mannheim argued that by using insights gained by sociological study Western societies could be guided through an age of transition from a *laissez faire* liberal society to a democratic planned society. Christianity would provide this society with a common bond, values and transcendent purpose achieving cohesion without compulsion. Eliot's social criticism in the 1930s and 1940s is dominated by the ideal of a lived Christian faith more than concrete political structures. He was fixed on something 'beyond politics', to borrow Dawson's phrase. As such, and as David Moody suggests, Eliot's political writing must be approached through 'their governing point of view, their metaphysic'.[107]

This rings true of Eliot's engagement with Mannheim, which only makes sense from the vantage point of his religious faith. Whereas for Mannheim religion was a means to an end, Eliot held that Christianity, or worship of the Christian God, was the ultimate purpose of human society. It is this determined theism that accounts for Eliot's strong aversion to Mannheim's societal planning. From Mannheim's humanistic stance, the mission to re-create a 'sacred canopy' was firmly within the grasp of the scientific community in collaboration with intellectual elites, whereas for Eliot the renewal of culture was in the hands of God.

The upshot of investigating Eliot and Mannheim through the 'programmatic modernism' framework is thus apparent: it brings clarity to their respective social criticism, and pinpoints exactly where their differences lie. To what extent can these intellectuals be said to embody the Griffinite modernism? In Griffin's conceptualization, 'programmatic modernism' 'expresses itself as a mission to change society, to inaugurate a new epoch, to start time anew', which leads to a 'rhetoric of manifestos and declarations, and encourages the artist/intellectual to collaborate proactively with collective movements for radical change'.[108] Accordingly, Mannheim epitomizes this mode of modernism, whereas Eliot, arguably amongst the greatest of modernist poets, ironically, only tentatively fits this description. Both were deeply engaged in a 'mission to change society'; however, Eliot, in contrast to Mannheim, offered a solution to the spiritual barrenness of modernity, but no road map.

Notes

1 Alec R. Vidler, *Scenes from a Clerical Life* (London: Collins, 1977), p. 119.
2 For example, Peter Ackroyd, *T. S. Eliot* (London: Hamish Hamilton, 1984); Kenneth Asher, *T. S. Eliot and Ideology* (Cambridge: Cambridge University Press, 1995).
3 Barry Spurr, *'Anglo-Catholic in Religion': T. S. Eliot and Christianity* (Cambridge: Lutterworth Press, 2010), pp. 190–3.
4 T. S. Eliot, 'Letter to John Middleton Murry', 8 February 1938, Charles Deering McCormick Library of Special Collection, Northwestern University, T. S. Eliot Correspondence Collection (NWE)/II/1/33; T. S. Eliot, 'Letter to John Middleton Murry', 11 April 1938, NWE/II/1/33; T. S. Eliot, 'Letter to George Every', 16 April 1938, private collection.
5 Stefan Collini, *Absent Minds: Intellectuals in Britain* (Oxford: Oxford University Press, 2006), p. 312.
6 T. S. Eliot, 'Letter to Philip Mairet', 5 January 1941, Henry Ransom Humanities Research Center, University of Texas, T. S. Eliot Collection (UTE)/5.4.
7 T. S. Eliot, 'The Germanisation of Britain', *New English Weekly*, 29 March 1945, p. 192.
8 T. S. Eliot, 'Letter to Herbert Read', 3 April 1943, University of Victoria, B.C. Special Collections/8/33.
9 T. S. Eliot, 'Letter to Alan Tate', 13 March 1945 as cited in Collini, *Absent Minds*, p. 319.
10 Cf. Karl Mannheim, 'Letter to Louis Wirth', 13 August 1938, Regenstein Library, University of Chicago, Louis Wirth Papers (LWP)/VII/11.
11 Julia Mannheim, 'Letter to the Moot', 19 January 1947, New College Library, University of Edinburgh, J. H. Oldham Archives (OA)/9/7/41.
12 Notes from the meeting held at St Julian's, 19–22 December 1947, OA/13/3/47.
13 T. S. Eliot, 'Professor Karl Mannheim', *The Times*, 26 January 1947.
14 Stefan Collini, 'The European Modernist as Anglican Moralist: The Later Criticism of T. S. Eliot', in *Enlightenment, Passion, Modernity: Historical Essays in European Thought and Culture*, ed. Micale Mark S. and Robert L. Dietle (Stanford: Stanford University Press, 2000); see also Stefan Collini, *Absent Minds*, chapter 13.
15 Roger Kojecky, *T. S. Eliot's Social Criticism* (New York: Farrar, Straus and Giroux, 1972).
16 See also Raymond Williams, *Culture and Society 1780–1950* (Harmondsworth: Pelican Books, 1971 [1958]); Colin Loader, *The Intellectual Development of Karl Mannheim* (Cambridge: Cambridge University Press, 1985); David Kettler and Volker Meja, *Karl Mannheim and the Crisis of Liberalism* (New Brunswick and London: Transaction, 1995); and Wolfgang Wicht, 'Eliot and Karl Mannheim: Cultural

Reconstruction vs. the Destruction of Culture', *Zeitschrift für Anglistik und Amerikanistik* 36 (1988).

17 Collini, 'European Modernists', p. 207. Peter Gay, *Weimar Culture: The Outsider as Insider* (London: Secker & Warburg, 1968), p. 96.

18 Roger Griffin, *Modernism and Fascism: The Sense of a Beginning under Mussolini and Hitler* (Basingstoke: Palgrave, 2007), pp. 116–17.

19 Wicht, 'Eliot and Karl Mannheim', p. 197.

20 Peter L. Berger, *The Sacred Canopy* (Garden City, NY: Anchor Books, 1967), pp. 26–7.

21 Cf. Friedrich Nietzsche, *The Gay Science*, trans. Josefine Nauckhoff (Cambridge: Cambridge University Press, 2001 [1882]), p. 120.

22 Karl Mannheim, *Ideology and Utopia* (New York: Harvest Books, 1968 [1936]), pp. 13, 22.

23 Mannheim, *Ideology and Utopia*, pp. 14–15.

24 See Zygmunt Bauman, *Modernity and Ambivalence* (Cambridge: Polity Press, 1991), p. 4.

25 Karl Mannheim, *Diagnosis of Our Time: Wartime Essays of a Sociologist* (London: Kegan Paul, 1943), p. 100.

26 Keith Clements, *The Moot Papers: Faith, Freedom and Society 1938–1944* (London: T&T Clark, 2010), pp. 422–3 (12th meeting, 1–3 August 1941), my emphasis. The terminology echoes Peter Berger's 'sacred canopy', see *The Sacred Canopy*, pp. 26–7.

27 Karl Mannheim, 'Topics for the Next Meeting of the Moot', undated [1941], OA/14/3/86.

28 T. S. Eliot, *The Idea of a Christian Society* (London: Faber & Faber, 1939), p. 16.

29 Eliot, *Idea*, p. 15. Dawson suspected that the 'social uniformity and the mechanization of culture' in the wake of liberalism would result in a 'democratic totalitarianism'; see Christopher Dawson, *Beyond Politics* (London: Sheed & Ward, 1939), p. 3.

30 Eliot, *Idea*, p. 13.

31 See the appendix of T. S. Eliot, *Notes Towards the Definition of Culture*, 2nd ed. (London: Faber & Faber, 1962 [1948]), p. 122.

32 Mannheim's ideas were particularly influenced by August Comte. See Karl Mannheim, *Freedom, Power and Democratic Planning* (London: Routledge & Kegan Paul, 1951), pp. 285–6.

33 Mannheim, *Ideology and Utopia*, pp. 20–1.

34 Karl Mannheim, *Man and Society: In an Age of Reconstruction* (London: Kegan Paul, 1940), p. 369; cf. Max Weber, *The Protestant Ethic and the Spirit of Capitalism*, trans. Talcott Parsons (London: George Allen & Unwin, 1930), pp. 181–2.

35 Clements, *Moot Papers*, 422 (12th meeting, 1–3 August 1941).

36 Eliot refers to Coleridge's 'Idea' in his *The Constitution of Church and State*, see *Idea*, p. 67.

37 Eliot, *Notes*, p. 28.

38 Ibid., p. 34.

39 T. S. Eliot, 'Letter to Dr. Oldham from T. S. Eliot', undated [1941], Institute of Education, Records of the Moot (IOE)/MOO/68.

40 Eliot, *Notes*, p. 28.

41 Griffin, *Modernism*, pp. 102, 116–17.

42 Cf. Mannheim, *Diagnosis*, 101; Eliot, *Idea*, pp. 18–19.

43 Ibid., pp. 33–4.

44 Karl Mannheim, 'The Crisis in Valuation', undated [1942], IOE/MOO/77.

45 Karl Mannheim, 'Planning for Freedom', undated [1938], OA/14/3/67.

46 T. S. Eliot, 'Comment on Papers by Mannheim and Hodges', undated [1939], Brotherton Special Collections, University of Leeds, Letters and papers concerning the lay Christian ecumenical society 'The Moot' (LM)/SEC3.
47 Ibid.
48 Eliot's antipathy towards planning predates his encounters with Mannheim, see T. S. Eliot, 'A Commentary', *The Criterion* XVII/66 (1937), p. 86.
49 T. S. Eliot, 'Man and Society', *The Spectator*, 16 June 1940. Elsewhere, in his reflections on the 1930 Lambeth Conference, Eliot attached a religious and eschatological dimension to this 'waiting'. See T. S. Eliot, *Thoughts after Lambeth* (London: Faber & Faber, 1931), p. 32.
50 Eliot, *Idea*, pp. 9, 10.
51 T. S. Eliot, 'Editorial for the CNL, 14 August 1940', *Christian News-Letter* 42 (1940).
52 Cf. Eliot, *Idea*, p. 9.
53 See T. S. Eliot, 'The Church's Message to the World', *The Listener* 17/423 (1937), p. 294; T. S. Eliot, 'Towards a Christian Britain', in *The Church Looks Ahead*, ed. J. H. Oldham (London: Faber & Faber, 1941), p. 106.
54 T. S. Eliot, 'Education in a Christian Society', *Christian News-Letter* 20 (1940).
55 T. S. Eliot, 'Notes on Mannheim's Paper', 10 January 1941, OA/14/6/1. Eliot wrote this comment in response to Mannheim's 'Topics for the Next Meeting of the Moot', undated [1941], OA/14/3/86.
56 Eliot, *Notes*, pp. 37ff.
57 Mannheim, *Man*, p. 81.
58 Eliot, *Notes*, p. 31.
59 Ibid., p. 19.
60 Eliot himself did acknowledge a disparity between his prose and literature: see T. S. Eliot, *After Strange Gods: A Primer on Modern Heresy* (London: Faber & Faber, 1934), p. 28.
61 T. S. Eliot, *Murder in the Cathedral* (London: Faber & Faber, 1965 [1935]), p. 91.
62 Eliot, *Idea*, p. 24.
63 Karl Mannheim, 'Planning for Freedom', undated [1938], OA/14/3/67; OL/SEC7.
64 Karl Mannheim, 'Topics for the Next Meeting of the Moot', undated [January 1941], OA/14/3/86.
65 T. S. Eliot, 'Notes on Mannheim's Paper', 10 January 1941, OA/14/6/1. Already at the 2nd Moot meeting Eliot had stated 'that we should not aim at finding a happy formula to which all could agree'. See Clements, *Moot Papers*, p. 113 (2nd meeting, 23–26 September 1938).
66 Eliot, *Idea*, p. 42.
67 T. S. Eliot, 'On the Place and Function of the Clerisy', 10 November 1944, OA/14/6/10.
68 Ibid., The paper was first published in Kojecky, *T. S. Eliot's Social Criticism*. Phil Mullins and Struan Jacobs have published all five texts linked to this debate in full: see Phil Mullins and Struan Jacobs, 'T. S. Eliot's Idea of the Clerisy, and Its Discussion by Karl Mannheim and Michael Polanyi in the Context of J. H. Oldham's Moot', *Journal of Classical Sociology* 6/2 (2006), pp. 147–56. Unfortunately, the only surviving minutes from the 21st Moot weekend are some brief handwritten summaries provided by an unknown writer (Anon., 'Minutes, Manuscripts', 21 meeting 15–18 December 1944, OA/12/3/27).
69 Karl Mannheim, 'Letter from Karl Mannheim', 20 November 1944, OA/9/6/101.
70 T. S. Eliot, 'Comments on Mannheim's by T. S. Eliot', 24 November 1944, OA/14/6/14.
71 Karl Mannheim, 'Letter from Karl Mannheim', 20 November 1944, OA/9/6/101.

72 T. S. Eliot, 'Comments on Mannheim's by T. S. Eliot', 24 November 1944, OA/14/6/14.
73 Karl Mannheim, 'Letter from Karl Mannheim', 20 November 1944, OA/9/6/101.
74 T. S. Eliot, 'Comments on Mannheim's by T. S. Eliot', 24 November 1944, OA/14/6/14.
75 Karl Mannheim, 'The Meaning of Popularisation in a Mass Society', *Christian News-Letter* 227 (1945), p. 7.
76 T. S. Eliot, 'Letter to Mary Trevelyan', 29 January 1945, Houghton Library, Harvard University, T. S. Eliot Papers (HLE)/bMS AM/1691.2/45.
77 T. S. Eliot, 'The Class and the Élite', *New English Weekly* 11/6 (1945).
78 Mannheim, *Man*, p. 91.
79 Eliot, *Notes*, p. 37.
80 Ibid., p. 44.
81 Eliot, *Notes*, p. 40. Author's emphasis.
82 Karl Mannheim, 'Towards a New Social Philosophy: A Challenge to Christian Thinkers by a Sociologist', undated [1941], Centre for Research Collections, Edinburgh University Library, Papers of Professor John Baillie (BA)/5/22; Karl Mannheim, 'Towards a New Social Philosophy: A Challenge to Christian Thinkers by a Sociologist. Part II: Christian Values in the Changing Environment', undated [1941], OA/14/3/94.
83 T. S. Eliot, 'Letter to Dr. Oldham from T. S. Eliot', undated [1941], OA/9/3/25.
84 T. S. Eliot, 'Planning and Religion', *Theology* XLVI/275 (1943), pp. 104–5.
85 Christopher Dawson, *The Judgement of the Nations* (London: Sheed & Ward, 1943), p. 83.
86 Dawson, *Judgement*, p. 103.
87 Eliot, *Notes*, p. 69.
88 Eliot, 'Towards', p. 114.
89 T. S. Eliot, 'Letter to Eric Fenn', 7 February 1941, BBC Written Archives Centre Caversham (BBC)/TSE/SOU1. It is probable that Eliot here refers to the magazine *Picture Post's* publication of a 'Plan for Britain' in January 1941 which called for an extensive welfare system.
90 At a gathering of intellectuals organized by Paul Tillich in Frankfurt during the early 1930s, Mannheim declared that, '[a] personal God has never addressed me .... I cannot say that a personal God has spoken, and I remain silent about it' (see David Kettler and Colin Loader, *Karl Mannheim: Social as Political Education* (New Brunswick: Transaction, 2001), p. 138.
91 A private encounter with Michael Polanyi betrays a certain antipathy or incomprehension of religious faith commitments (Michael Polanyi, 'Letter to Karl Mannheim', 19 April 1944, MPP/4/11; Karl Mannheim, 'Letter to Michael Polanyi', 26 April 1944, MPP/4/11).
92 Clements, *Moot Papers*, 282 (7th meeting, 9–12 February 1940).
93 Walter Oakeshott, 'Notes on the "Order"', undated [1939], OA/14/8/63.
94 Eliot, *Idea*, p. 58. My emphasis.
95 T. S. Eliot, 'Comments by T. S. Eliot on Michael Polanyi's Notes on the Clerisy', 22 November 1944, OA/14/6/13. My emphasis.
96 Eliot, 'The Church's Message', p. 294.
97 Eliot, 'Towards', p. 115.
98 Asher, *T. S. Eliot and Ideology*, pp. 2–3.
99 See for example Eliot's praise of Portugal's Prime Minister António de Olivera Salazar as a benevolent dictator (Eliot, 'Editorial for the CNL, 14 August 1940'). His support for monarchism softened towards to the end of his life; see Eliot's preface to the second edition of *Notes* (p. 7).

100 As shown by Hannah Arendt, authoritarianism cannot be conflated with totalitarianism (Hannah Arendt, *The Origins of Totalitarianism*, 2nd ed. (New York: Harcourt, Brace & World, 1958 [1951]), pp. 460ff.
101 Collini, 'European Modernists', p. 228. In a letter to Mary Trevelyan, Eliot identified himself as a 'Tory (reinforced by a sort of Whig background)' (T. S. Eliot, 'Letter to Mary Trevelyan', 2 January 1945, HLE/bMS AM/1691.2/43).
102 Clements, *Moot Papers*, p. 55 (1st meeting, 1–4 April 1938).
103 Erik Tonning, *Modernism and Christianity* (Basingstoke: Palgrave Macmillan, 2014), pp. 65f.
104 Dawson, *Judgement*, pp. 83, 86.
105 Michael Polanyi, 'Science and the Modern Crisis', 14 November 1944, BA/5/39.
106 Ibid. Since there are no surviving minutes from the meeting it is unclear whether the paper was discussed at the meeting. However, the minutes from the 20th meeting state that Polanyi promised to provide a paper on his views in response to his exchange with Mannheim on 'Planning for Freedom'. See Clements, *Moot Papers*, p. 692 (20th meeting, 23–26 June 1944).
107 A. David Moody, *Thomas Stearns Eliot: Poet*, 2nd ed. (Cambridge: Cambridge University Press, 1994), p. 319.
108 Griffin, *Modernism*, p. 62.

7

METHODS OF MONTAGE IN BECKETT'S 'RESIDUA'

Anthony Paraskeva

In Samuel Beckett's short prose text, *Ping* (1966), translated from the French as *Bing*, permutations of words and phrases, repeated mechanically in various combinations, portray a bare figure confined in an enclosed white cube. A radically impersonal, machine-like structuring agency, indicating the barest rudiments of movement and gesture, is signalled by the frequent recurrence of the metallic word 'ping'. This word appears variously at the beginning, middle and end of sentences, as well as between phrases, joining together shifting patterns of image and close-up gesture:

> Light heat white planes shining white bare white body fixed ping fixed elsewhere [...] White feet toes joined like sewn heels together right angle ping elsewhere no sound [...] all white all over all of old ping flash white walls shining white no trace eyes holes light blue almost white last colour ping white over.[1]

Critics have tended to read the word 'ping' either as an aspect of the text's mechanization, or its optical qualities; it mimics, in these readings, the sound of a typewriter carriage, or the blink of an eye.[2] I would like to propose a novel reading of the word, which brings together both the machine-like and the visual elements of the text: 'ping', in my account, suggests the mechanical sound of a Moviola, the machine Beckett used to edit *Film* and *Comédie*, at the exact point at which an edit is made on a reel of film.

The particular extremity of phrasal structure in *Ping* isolates it, at least to an extent, from Beckett's work of the period; yet in the frame-by-frame precision with which it re-plays minute gestures, together with its complex montage of geometric abstractions, it belongs to Beckett's other prose work of the period, and which can be placed in the wider context of his experiments with camera and editing techniques. The 1962 *Play* marks a shift in Beckett's theatre towards tight framing, focal points, close-ups, as though the performance were recorded and fixed. The film adaptation, *Comédie*, which Beckett directed with Marin Karmitz in 1965–6, also bears its imprint on the brief 'closed space' prose pieces of this period, published in a section Beckett named 'Residua', and a prose style of mechanically impersonal repetitions of phrase, tightly edited into montage-like schemas. He wrote these enigmatic short prose fictions – *All Strange Away* (1963–4), *Imagination Dead Imagine* (1965), *Ping* (1966–7) and *The Lost Ones* (1971) – during and immediately after his detailed technical work in post-production on *Film* and *Comédie.* These texts mark a key shift in Beckett's prose, from the first-person interior monologue of his earlier novels, to third-person optical description, a visual turn which is an aspect, I argue, of his thinking about the mechanical gaze of the camera, and his detailed working knowledge of film editing. This knowledge was both practical and theoretical, and can be situated in a historical period characterized by the industry-wide use of the Moviola editing machine, before it was replaced in the 1970s by the less precise Steenbeck flatbed editing system, and the contemporaneous revival of Eisenstein's montage method in European cinema. Beckett's writing, in this respect, can be understood in relation to the history of technology, and of editing theory and practice.

Beckett's work with the Moviola – modified in the early 1960s to allow for even greater precision and experimentation – significantly influenced his prose style of this period, as demonstrated in the numerous sequences of multiple takes, precisely assembled and replayed with minute adjustments. The montage-like patterns of rhythmic repetition in Beckett's prose also suggest the importance of Eisenstein, who Beckett had discovered in the 1930s and who was undergoing a revival in the early mid-1960s in the cinema of the nouvelle vague. Beckett had read many of Eisenstein's essays on film editing in *Close Up* and *transition,* and his writing on methods such as metric and overtonal montage offered Beckett a series of technical procedures which serve as an overlooked context for his writing of this period.

Beckett began writing the first text in this sequence, *All Strange Away,* in August 1964 (though it was not published until 1976) immediately after returning to his French home in Ussy from New York, where he spent several days editing *Film* with the editor Sidney Meyers and director Alan Schneider. Beckett returned to the edit of *Film* in September 1964, and again in March 1965 (it premiered at the Venice Film Festival in September) while he was writing *Imagination morte imaginez* (January–May 1965), which he translated in July as *Imagination Dead Imagine.* He wrote *Bing* in September 1966 and Les Éditions des Minuits published it in October. The English version, *Ping,* was published in December 1966 by John Calder as a section of *No's Knife,* a collected shorter prose edition (*Ping* appeared in the 'Residua' section alongside *Enough* and *Imagination Dead Imagine*). In January 1966, just a few months earlier, he had completed editing on the film adaptation of *Comédie,* a project in which the technicalities of editing were very much at the forefront of the work's formal intent. According to Karmitz, much of their discussion focused on 'what cinema, image and editing could bring'.[3] Beckett and Karmitz worked very closely with the film's editor, Jean Ravel – highly regarded for his work on Chris Marker's *La Jetée* (1962) – to develop an experimental, cubist approach to editing.

During post-production on *Film,* and over 'detailed technical discussions',[4] he formed a close friendship with the film's editor, Sidney Meyers. Beckett and

Meyers remained friends and correspondents until his death, when Beckett wrote, 'the announcement at his graveside before strangers, of even a small part of what I felt for him, was something I could not bear the thought of'.[5] As well as editing and directing, Meyers also wrote critical essays on the 'subject of literature and editing', where he proposed a book-length study on 'the effect of the cinema and its special qualities on writing'; intriguingly, the book would focus on 'the similarity between literary editing and film editing' and the 'marked cross influence of one medium on the other and a combined interconnected development'.[6] Beckett's discussions and detailed work with Meyers and Schneider, and then his hands-on work with Karmitz and Ravel, transformed his prose of this period, particularly his sense of the possibility of phrasal units arranged within complex, montage-like structural procedures.

Beckett's serious interest in editing dates back to 1936 when he wrote to Eisenstein expressing a primary interest 'in the scenario and editing'[7] element of filmmaking. He discussed with Thomas MacGreevy his developing interest in filmmaking – 'what I would learn under a person like Pudovkin is how to handle a camera, the higher trucs of the editing bench'[8] – and mentions that he has borrowed 'a lot of works on cinema from young [Niall] Montgomery [...] Pudovkin, Arnheim & back numbers of Close Up with stuff by Eisenstein'.[9] *Close Up* published nine of Eisenstein's essays, which included his most significant writing on montage technique, such as 'Principles of Film Form', published in the September 1931 edition of the journal, and the two-part 'The Fourth Dimension in the Kino', in March and April 1930. Eisenstein's essay 'The Cinematographic Principles and Japanese Culture' was published in *transition* in 1930, and Beckett likely saw the essay, as one of his own poems was published in the same issue.

The extent of Beckett's detailed, hands-on involvement during the editing of *Film* is clearly indicated in his letters. He edited the rough cut with Sidney Meyers in his New York studio, discovering what he called the 'organising principles' of the 'montage',[10] and then he worked on the fine cut, alone in Paris on a Moviola, sending detailed notes to Meyers and Schneider. During this time, Beckett developed an intimate working familiarity with the Moviola editing and viewing machine. There are several references in his letters to the Moviola: 'Recovered Film at last and will be movieoling it';[11] 'Saw screening of Film latest cut yesterday [...] Laying on movieola for next Sunday';[12] 'I have now had two screenings of the new cut and a session with such a deficient movieola'.[13]

The Moviola, the film industry standard editing machine up until the 1970s, is

> a machine full of switches and swivels and interlocking parts almost all of burnished steel and aluminum [...] its legs support a waist high base upon which rests the four inch viewer [...] at the back end of the base are two metal arms that are fitted with sprockets for reels.[14]

Prior to the Moviola, there were no standardized editing machines in the film industry. In the early twentieth century, strips of film would either be run through a projector or held over a light box, while the editor would make notes or mark the film with a wax pencil. The earliest devices, which emerged between 1916 and 1924, involved making crude adjustments to the transport mechanism of existing projectors. An electrical engineer, Iwan Serrurier, created the Moviola Editing Machine in 1924, adapting an early projector system he had patented into a smaller viewing device.

By 1930, the Moviola could allow the viewing and editing of picture and sound in sync on separate reels. The editor would run the film onto sprocket holes, while the passage of film through the gate was controlled with a foot pedal and viewed through a lens unit. The machine enabled precise frame-by-frame viewing. The film would be cut one frame ahead of the incoming shot, and this frame would be used to overlap with the next shot and complete the join. With the invention of the tape-joiner in the early sixties, the cut could be made exactly on the frame line. As Don Fairservice indicates, the tape-joiner allowed film to be 'joined and rejoined using unperforated, clear polyester tape with transparent adhesive'. Used in conjunction with the Moviola, it 'significantly altered editing practice' and allowed the editor to 'take risks, try alternative possibilities'. It was the equivalent of moving from a typewriter to a word processor.[15]

After an intensive few days working alongside Sidney Meyers in New York, Beckett returned to Ussy for work on *All Strange Away*. He continued to work long-distance with Meyers and Schneider during the following months, viewing *Film* on a Moviola in Paris, and sending them notes on 'the details, shortening, lengthening, rhythm'.[16] His assiduous repeat viewings, and the minute level of attention at the level of the frame in his notes, overtly declare a highly developed technical knowledge of editing procedures. In Walter Murch's influential account of the process, *A Perspective on Film Editing*, the editor would begin by looking at the rushes, unedited scenes shot several times and from a variety of camera angles, to give enough coverage to match together a range of different shots. The editor assembled the first cut, focusing on the storyline, maintaining spatial and temporal coherence, ensuring that the eyeline – the angle at which the object or person is observed – matched the angle from which the character was looking, and making decisions about where to cut on specific lines of dialogue. As Murch put it: 'I want to be in the wide shot on this dialogue, I want to be on this two-shot for this line, and I'm going to cut to a reaction on this line.'[17]

Beckett clearly understood that cutting from a long or medium shot to a close-up emphasized details, reactions and underlined nuances of feeling. As he wrote in his contemporaneous notes: 'suggest when E comes back to them after leaving O on his way to the corner that scene should begin with close-up of man'.[18] When cutting in from a medium to a closer shot, the editor looked for signs of movement so that 'the outgoing shot initiates the movement and the incoming shot takes over and completes the action [...] For each cut to appear on the beat, they must occur three of four frames before the actual beat point because of the perceptual lag when you cut to a new image.'[19] Again, Beckett demonstrated an understanding of this highly technical rule in editing, as when he wrote: 'O shot of pulse in lobby [...] the hands [do] not match those of preceding E shot'; 'First full face of O in E vision closes on open mouth, second opens with mouth opening.

Cut opening frames of latter so that shot opens on open mouth'; 'Cut opening frames of second and final shot of E in O vision so that opening shot not static but already moving in'.[20]

The next stage in the process involved refining the cut, concentrating on the rhythms, tightening the pace, creating overlaps. The rhythms are determined by cuts – the equivalent of punctuation or line-endings – establishing pace, then altering the tempo at a key moment, breaking or modifying the rhythm. For Ken Dancyger, 'shots should never be all the same length [...] rhythm requires the variation of the lengths of each shot'.[21] In his editing notes, Beckett showed an intuitive sense of rhythmic variety, as determined by shot lengths: 'Quick O shot of couple [...] I feel E shot of the three after collision is too long'; 'cut lovers and prolong pan back down wall as long as possible before appearance of O'; 'prolong close ups of cat and fish's eye'.[22] His notes also signalled a fine-tuned sense that editing involved not just the removal of entire scenes or shots, but also deciding whether a shot, as Murch puts it, should 'end on this frame or 1/24th of a second later on the next frame'.[23] This is exemplified when he writes: 'O vision of flower-woman from crouching position under stairs too long. Start it with hand on flowers or a second before and cut all preceding frames'; or again: 'couple of blurred frames as O goes with cat from basket second time'.[24] According to Murch, an editor often looked for the blink of an eye to determine where the cut should occur; when a person blinks, it separates or punctuates a line of dialogue, a thought or an idea from what follows. Similarly, in film 'a shot presents us with an idea, or a sequence of ideas, and the cut is a "blink" that separates and punctuates those ideas'.[25] This was a principle which also guided the editing of *Film*, as for instance in a sequence attending to the micro-level of the blink of an eye: 'I still feel that the closed eye (reptilian texture) should last a few seconds longer before it opens.'[26]

As indicated above, Beckett began writing the first text in the 'closed space' sequence, *All Strange Away*, in August 1964. The text bears the influence, in my view, of his technical work in film editing with Sidney Meyers in New York that summer. A single figure, first male, Emmo, then female, Emma, is confined inside an enclosed space with shifting dimensions; first a cube, then a rotunda. The body is perceived in a series of geometric compositions based upon precise co-ordinates: 'floor angles deasil a, b, c and d and ceiling likewise e, f, g and h'.[27] Thereafter, the narrative proceeds in shot-like sequences: 'Black shroud, start search for pins. Light on, down on knees, sights pin, makes for it, light out, gets pin in dark, light on, sights another, light out, so on' (170). Sequences of close-up gestures seem to be timed with an editor's precision, from the blink of an eye – 'Light flows, eyes close, stay closed till it ebbs, no, can't do that, eyes stay open, all right, look at that later' (170) – to a hand clenching a rubber ball: 'Left hand clinging to right shoulder ball, right more faint loose fist on ground till fingers tighten as though to squeeze, imagine later, then loose again and still any length, so on' (174). The phrase 'look at that later' in the first quote, and 'imagine later' in the second, implies a return to a finer cut, a minute adjustment of the image, once the initial rough cut has been assembled.

In this way, the narrative eye in *All Strange Away* scrupulously inspects incomplete or unedited rushes of the body in various states of activity and immobility, and various combinations, before decisions are finalized and the final cut is locked in (though it never arrives): 'Sitting, standing, walking, kneeling, crawling, lying, creeping, in the dark and in the light, try all'; 'no stool, no sitting, no kneeling, no lying, just room to stand and revolve, light as before, faces as before' (171). The text lays bare, I argue, the film editor's process, where possible compositions are tested before becoming fixed into a single, coherent image or sequence. Alternative possible scenarios are rehearsed and re-played, adjustments are made, a gesture is momentarily arrested and re-focussed, and the sequence is played again. 'Till halt and up, no, no image, down'; 'eyes glaring, no, no image, eyes closed' (173). Yet the combinations never crystallize into a stable image, ultimately leaving only 'jointed segments variously disposed' (172).

Beckett's writing is interlaced with the inherent automatism of cinema, which requires successive repetitions or takes from multiple angles of coverage. The first part of *All Strange Away* is like the initial cut of a film, where 'all combinations' (179) are inspected: 'Arse to knees, say bd, feet say at c, head on right cheek at a. Then arse to knees say again ac, but feet at b and head on left cheek at d. Then arse to knees say again bd, but feet at a and head on right cheek at c' (172). The second part of the text, sub-titled 'Diagram', then re-cuts the same sequence, reducing combinations in an attempt to achieve closure (or a final cut); as for example here, where the body is edited into its 'corrected pose' (177) by 'temporarily shorten[ing] long segment': 'unwedging crown and arse with play enough to writhe till finally head wedged against wall at a as before but on right cheek and arse against wall at c as before but on right cheek' (179). Despite the reduction of possible combinations, however, the narrative agency refuses to lock in the sequence and thus defers the final cut – 'Last look oh not farewell but last for now' (181) – as adjustments continue to be made.

Beckett's prose style in these shorter works, its cold mechanical neutrality and complex patterns of montage, bears comparison with the work of Alain Robbe-Grillet, a writer whose novels have often been characterized as cinematic. Roland Barthes argued that the destruction of classical literary space in Robbe-Grillet's novels was based on 'the idea of a new structure of matter and movement [...] derived from contemporary arts and sciences such as the new physics and the cinema'.[28] Significantly, it mattered to Beckett that Robbe-Grillet liked *Film*: 'Pleased to hear that Robbe-Grillet liked [Film]';[29] and later to the same correspondent: 'Robbe-Grillet saw Film in Paris and liked it.'[30] He read *La Jalousie* (*Jealousy*) in 1959, and told Barbara Bray that he found it 'very important and remarkable'.[31]

In *La Jalousie*, an unnamed narrator watches his wife and her presumed lover, noting in obsessive detail – as if recorded by a camera – what he sees and what he imagines seeing. Neutral, machine-like descriptions of scenes are repeated and re-edited with shifting emphasis and minor variations, successive takes closely inspected for possible clues, such as the wife writing a letter, a conversation with her possible lover about a novel, or the crushing of a centipede. As in the later *All Strange Away*, an accumulation of overlapping, mismatched and multiple takes of the same event dislocates any sense of coherent, classically constructed unity of space. Figures previously turning rightwards now gaze towards the left; for instance, when the lover's hand first crushes the centipede, the woman's hand reacts by clenching a knife handle. Later, the same scene is replayed, but now the woman's hand clenches into a fist on a white sheet. Robbe-Grillet expanded and refined this method of serial editing in his script for Alain Resnais's 1962 film *L'année dernière à Marienbad* (*Last Year at Marienbad*), one of the key works of the nouvelle vague, a film which transformed the possibilities of discontinuous, non-linear montage by repeating key scenes and gestures, eliminating the distinctions between the tenses and narrative time zones in which those events occur.

By cross-pollinating artistic tendencies in the nouveau roman and nouvelle vague, *L'année dernière à Marienbad* – alongside films by Duras, Marker and Godard – enabled the emergence of a shared cultural network and mutual interactions between literature and cinema, based on principles of montage and the rediscovery of Eisenstein. Beckett saw the film on its release in 1962 – unsurprisingly, given that he admired Alain Resnais: 'I have met Resnais, the most gifted of the lot probably' – and was aware of the 'young cinéastes', as he called the *Cahiers du Cinéma* group, in a 1959 letter to John Manning.[32] For Marin Karmitz, the 1966 film of *Comédie* represented an opportunity to make explicit these shared aesthetic tendencies: 'There was, in the late 50s, an incredible moment in the functioning of the French culture, which has not been dealt with as much as it should; the Nouveau Roman, Beckett's and Ionesco's theatre [...] the Nouvelle Vague in cinema.'[33] After the problems of technique and execution in the earlier production of *Film*, the making of *Comédie* engaged Beckett during a period of exhaustion regarding the management and approval of theatrical productions of his work: 'Making a little film of Play with young technique hogs. Not unexciting.'[34] What most excited Beckett, it appears, was a style of radically discontinuous editing in which the spotlight in the stage version is replaced with a tightly controlled montage along a single plane or axis. While the film contains 250 separate shots, they are edited together to appear in a single frame throughout. Characters are framed in extreme close-up and are brightly lit when they speak; these shots are cut together with medium shots of the silent figures – dimly lit and constantly visible throughout – and long shots, where the figures are barely visible at all. In the film of *Comédie*, it is the editor who assumes the privileged controlling function of the spotlight inquisitor in the stage version.

During the production and editing of *Comédie* in 1965–6, Beckett worked simultaneously on *The Lost Ones* and *Ping*. In the manuscript of the French *Bing*, Beckett indicated a relation between the two texts: 'Though very different formally these two MSS belong together. *Bing* may be regarded as the result or miniaturisation of *Le Dépeupleur* abandoned because of its intractable complexities.'[35] Elsewhere, he notes that *Bing* is 'a separate work written after and in reaction to *Le Dépeupleur*'.[36] The 'flattened cylinder fifty metres round and sixteen high'[37] described in *The Lost Ones* is inhabited by two hundred people, each seeking a way out by climbing a ladder to niches and tunnels in the walls of the cylinder. A similarly described setting is reduced in *Ping* to a single image of a lone figure confined within a small cube. The formal difference, moreover, resides also in the style of narration. The urbane narrative voice of *The Lost Ones*, with its large vocabulary and baroque varieties of syntax, is stripped down to a limited number of repeated words and phrases in *Ping*. Verbs and personal pronouns have been excised, and all that remains are blunt specifications of a scarcely animated body, seen in partial views, enclosed by floor and ceiling, each a yard square and united by walls two yards high each.

In my view, *Ping* is an intensification of those qualities of repetition, mechanism and impersonality already present in *The Lost Ones*, and which have been characterized as having been influenced by Beckett's work in the cinema. As James Knowlson notes in his authorized biography:

> *Le Dépeupleur* and some of the other short prose texts of the 1960s owe a lot to his recent work in film and television. A determined effort is made to "see" the entire structure and organisation of the cylinder and to describe the workings of the "abode" as precisely as the "eye of the mind" (or the lens of a camera) will allow.[38]

Hugh Kenner also noted the 'constant unemphatic repetition of details from other sections, again in the manner of film shots which establish themselves with respect to one another by bits of overlapping information'.[39] In *Ping*, the scenario is much more strictly associated with a machine-like inquisitor, like the light in *Play* or the camera eye in *Film*. The single eye, 'black and white half closed' observing the figure brings to mind the opening black-and-white close-up of the hybrid mechanical-human eye in *Film*. Yet the image of an eye 'half closed', in mid-blink, also asserts the structural importance of frame-by-frame editing patterns which in my account are the text's organizing principle.

The recurring word 'ping' appears thirty-four times in the text, providing a structuring pattern which sutures the phrases together. For Susan Brienza, the word 'suggests the blink of a human eye'.[40] According to Dan O'Hara, by contrast, it is 'a specifically onomatopoeic word that is and has always been echoic of the metallic noise of machines'.[41] In the latter's view, 'ping' may suggest the sound of an electrocardiograph, deriving from the latter's fact that Beckett underwent surgery in the early 1960s when ECGs were in general usage. In my account, this metallic sound, which comes from outside the discourse of the text, organizing repetitions of phrase into rhythmic patterns, resembles the sound of the interlocking metal parts of the Moviola editing machine as a cut is made in a strip of film. As with a cut in a reel of film, which joins together the same movement or gesture in two separate shots – often with a shift in scale or framing – so does the word 'ping' apparently splice together movements of the lone body in the cube. This can be observed in the variations of 'bare white body fixed ping fixed elsewhere', where the difference between 'fixed' and 'fixed elsewhere' registers a shift in spatial dimension.

Another of the recurring phrases explicitly foregrounds the task of getting the timing of one image in relation to the next exactly right on a Moviola: 'Ping image only just almost never one second light time blue and white in the wind' (195); 'Ping a nature only just almost never one second with image same time a little less' (195). The word also apparently instigates cuts between moments of vocal sound and silence, from 'ping murmur' to 'ping silence'. The word appears to organize the cell-like phrases, exerting a mechanical control over the visual descriptions, implying the presence of an editor figure – the 'black and white' eye which coldly inspects the figure's tiniest movements – scanning and re-scanning a series of takes for the exact point to make the cut. The most frequently occurring word, 'white', which appears ninety-one times, could, in this reading, represent the clear white frame on a reel of celluloid. This is visible on a Movieola at the end of each take when light has entered the camera.

Beckett wrote *Bing* in September 1966 (it was published in October, with the English version appearing in December), just a few months after working on the complex montage in the film adaptation of *Comédie.* During this period – from the late fifties to the mid-sixties – there was a great revival of the Eisensteinian montage method. For instance, *Cahiers du Cinéma* and other journals published translations of his essays, and he was constantly cited by the nouvelle vague as a chief inspiration for the new style of discontinuous editing, such as by Godard, who described the overlapping cuts in a scene in his film *Les Carabiniers* as 'proud, moving, Eisensteinian'. As David Bordwell rightly observes, 'Eisenstein's heirs were Resnais, Chris Marker, and Godard'.[42] For Eisenstein, 'the essence of cinema does not lie in the images, but in the relation between the images'.[43] The theory and practice of montage, which held such a deep fascination for Beckett, was the principal technique defining the Soviet cinema of Eisenstein, Pudovkin and Kuleshov. The original meaning of montage – 'machine assembly' – clearly inflects Eisenstein's notion that 'one does not create a work, one constructs it with finished parts, like a machine [...] Montage is a beautiful word: it describes the process of constructing with prepared fragments'.[44]

In Eisenstein's work, this machine-based sense of the assemblage of individual fragments involves techniques of dissonance, juxtaposition and collision. His montage practice goes beyond Kuleshov's early definition of montage in 1917 as a form of continuity editing, the assembly of 'separately filmed fragments, disordered and disjointed, into a more advantageous, integral and rhythmical sequence'.[45] It also surpasses Pudovkin's method of editing footage to reflect 'the guidance of the attention of the spectator to different elements of the developing action in succession',[46] using cross-cutting and parallel editing to advance narrative and develop character arcs. For Eisenstein, cinematic montage is primarily a formal system of recurring motifs, graphic patterns in dynamic conflict, and rhythmic variations determined by the length of individual shots, and separate from the construction of plot. This formal structure, in his words, depends upon film-shots which demonstrate an 'abstraction of the lifelike', and on 'close-ups [...] isolated from naturalism and abstracted in the necessary direction'.[47] The montage construction in *Ping*, I contend, is an intensification of the inherent abstraction in this system.

Eisenstein's major 1929 essay appearing in *Close Up*, 'The Fourth Dimension in the Kino', offers a set of editing options which present possible frameworks for the montage construction of *Ping*. Eisenstein's first category, 'metric' montage, is based upon the 'absolute length'[48] of each shot, whereby the content of a shot is secondary to its duration. Furthermore, metric montage allows the development of a scheme involving repetition of shots with minor variations to develop rhythmic measures, creating formal tension through 'the effect of mechanical acceleration by shortening the pieces'.[49] Eisenstein gives as an example of metric cutting a dance sequence in *October*, where a limited number of shots of feet and spinning faces of varying lengths are repeated and accelerated in an abstract rhythmic pattern. Likewise, *Ping* is primarily constructed according to rhythmic repetition at the level of word, phrase and sentence. As David Lodge notes in his early close analysis: '*Ping* is a text of permutations, of limited words repeated in various combinations.'[50] In fact, *Ping* consists of 120 words which recur in approximately 100 different phrases or montage cells. These are then configured and reconfigured within the text, each time in a differing pattern. The first sentence, for instance, is broken down into phrases that repeat and modify in slight adjustments and with additional phrases through the text:

> bare white body fixed one yard legs joined like sewn [...] Bare white body fixed only the eyes only just [...] bare white body fixed ping fixed elsewhere [...] Bare white body fixed white on white invisible [...] Legs joined like sewn heels together right angle [...] Bare white body fixed one yard ping fixed elsewhere [...] White feet toes joined like sewn heels together right angle invisible. (193–4)

As Alys Moody observes, each rhythmic unit also functions as a syntactic unit. Thus, the dominant rhythm in the text is characterized by 'regular pairings of stressed syllables', which are then 'interrupted by unstressed syllables' or 'additional stressed syllables'.[51] The reduction of verbs and prepositions allows this metric patterning to frame and re-frame each phrase in fluid and shifting spatial contexts. These then intersect and overlap, suspending a unified image or phrase through an accumulation of modifying clauses. In this respect, the text resembles one of Eisenstein's key montage methods, the overlapping edit, where an event or image is shot from several angles, and each of those shots overlaps so the event is repeated. In this way, the 'action on screen is prolonged beyond its presumed duration',[52] as for instance the scene where the movement of a wheel strikes the foreman in *Strike*, or the breaking of the plate in *The Battleship Potemkin*, where the same action is shown from contrasting and clashing angles. Helpfully, Erik Tonning notes a similarity between Eisensteinian overlapping cuts and the dialogue in *Play*, where there is 'clearly a great deal of overlapping editing at work as scenes are presented from three conflicting angles; the focus here is the juxtaposition of three hermetic solitudes'.[53] This is a method also at work in *Ping*, where individual elements of a phrase are arranged in overlapping patterns from line to line, and partial views, fragments and close-ups collide and overlap from various angles:

> legs joined like sewn [...] Legs joined like sewn heels together right angle [...] White feet toes joined like sewn heels together right angle invisible [...] white mouth white seam like sewn invisible [...] White feet toes joined like sewn heels together right angle ping elsewhere [...] mouth white seam like sewn invisible [...] Head haught nose ears white holes mouth white seam like sewn invisible over. (193–4)

The reduction of the narrative to extreme scenic fragmentation, alongside a formal logic of close-up gestures, constantly revised and re-edited with slight increments and additions, chimes with Eisenstein's notion of the 'disintegrated event'. Here, individual 'montage units' are 'broken up' and re-form into 'multiple chains',[54] forming a 'new quality of the whole from a juxtaposition of the separate parts'.[55] In Eisenstein's editing scheme, 'the film-frame can never be an inflexible letter of the alphabet, but must always remain a multiple-meaning ideogram. And it can be read only in juxtaposition'.[56] In his films the body is 'dismembered' into close-ups that are also 'montage-phrases', which acquire their effect through repetition in different spatial-temporal contexts.[57] In *October*, a woman's hands express sorrow by covering her eyes; another pair of hands tightly grasp a cap in anger; hands are clenched into fists and raised into the air, with each gesture repeated and modified; the grieving woman in the first shot then grasps her handkerchief. As in the second shot, her hand becomes a fist in the third shot and the same gestures are then repeated by other members of the crowd. In *Potemkin*, the motif of a single eye in extreme close-up is repeated and modified in a variety of contexts, echoing the rhythmic repetition of the 'black and white eye' in *Ping*. Elsewhere in *Potemkin,* a single eye inspects some rotting meat; during the mutiny a priest opens one eye in close-up; a soldier's eye widens in extreme close-up as he fires at one of the mutinous sailors; the woman in the Odessa Steps sequence suffers a traumatic wound to the eye. Eisenstein's graphic patterns and recurrent objects or gestures, as in *Ping*, displace narrative, thus creating a complex network of visual associations enclosed within a highly compressed formal structure.

For Eisenstein, the idea of 'the conflict of two pieces in opposition'[58] is absolutely central to montage construction. These conflicts between two or more shots include a range of possibilities, which extend to the following:

> Conflict of graphic directions. Conflict of scales. Conflict of volumes. Conflict of masses. Conflict of depths [...] Close shots and long shots. Pieces of darkness and pieces of lightness. Conflicts between an object and its dimension – and conflicts between an event and its duration.[59]

A cognate range of conflicting elements serves as a structuring principle of *Ping*, such as the repetition of opposing terms 'never' and 'always', 'all and almost', 'within' and 'without', 'all known' and 'known not', and 'over and unover'. The central tension in *Ping* is between the construction of an image of a lone body and the dissolution of that image into visual indistinctness, or between the tentative definition of a body and the featureless planes of whiteness which surround and threaten to subsume it. In this respect, the formal structure of *Ping* evokes Eisenstein's method of overtonal montage, a theory he elaborates upon in 'The Fourth Dimension of the Kino', as published in the 1930 *Close Up*, and with reference to his film *The Old and the New*, also titled *The General Line*. The latter is a film Beckett discussed in a 1936 letter to Arland Usher: 'I do not remember ever having seen any of [Cecil's poems] before. One in which the rime mouth-drouth occurs repeatedly is most remarkable, like the bull let loose among the cows in Eisenstein's General Line.'[60]

The Old and the New tells the story of a female farmer and her attempts to collectivize her region, encouraging her fellow farmers to form a cooperative and adopt tractors and mechanical cream separators, in the face of resistance from kulaks and hostile bureaucrats. According to Eisenstein, the film's chief innovation resides in what he calls, in 'The Fourth Dimension of the Kino' essay, 'overtonal montage': '*The Old and New* is the first film edited on the principle of the visual overtone.'[61] Orthodox montage, Eisenstein explained, involves cutting on what he calls 'the dominant', or the primary expressive qualities of a sequence. This 'dominant' includes such qualities as pictorial composition, 'tempo', 'the chief tendency within the frame' and 'the length of the shots'.[62] Consequently, the overall tone is indicated through light values, focus and graphic patterns. The overtone is 'a sensuous quality subordinate to the overall expressive cast of the shot'.[63] Within each image or shot, 'the central stimulus [...] is attended always by a whole complex of secondary stimuli'.[64] In overtonal montage, these secondary pictorial or sensuous aspects of the composition are organized into patterns that might reinforce or exist in tension with the primary elements, sometimes displacing the dominant aspects of the sequence.

Eisenstein offered an example to illustrate the function of the overtone in a hypothetical series of shots in a montage sequence: 'A gray old man/A gray old woman/A white horse/A snow-covered roof'.[65] This overtone of 'whiteness' displaces the dominant image of 'old age'. Eisenstein then cited the religious procession in *The Old and the New* as a key instance of his overtonal method. In this scene, the primary theme and dominant action involve a procession of priests, icon bearers and prostrating worshippers. Nonetheless, the scene is edited to emphasize secondary sensuous qualities of heat, drought and parching thirst, through accelerated cutting on overtonal shots of the white of the sun, the intense gleam of the belfry cross, extreme close-ups of melting candles, and the dust. The mounting intensity of the overtonal cutting creates a near abstract line of 'whiteness' and 'heat saturation', which eventually overwhelms the central dominant action of the procession of icons, crosses and banners.

In *Ping*, the dominant line – the image of the figure, 'head haught', 'legs joined like sewn', 'heels together right angle' – is frequently displaced by overtonal sensuous qualities of whiteness, light and heat:

> white bare white body fixed one yard legs joined like sewn. Light heat white floor one square yard never seen [...] Traces blurs light grey almost white on white. Hands hanging palms front white feet heels together right angle. Light heat white planes shining white bare white body [...] All white all known murmurs only just almost never always the same all known. Light heat hands hanging palms front white on white invisible. (193–4)

This central image in *Ping* is interlaced with sensuous abstraction, which undercuts and displaces the dominant line. A conflict emerges between the line of the 'body fixed one yard legs joined like sewn' and the overtonal 'Light heat white planes shining white', which together threaten to dissolve the body into indistinct traces and blurs: 'all white all over [...] shining white [...] ping white over'. The function of the recurring words 'white', 'light' and 'heat', which join together the dominant image, extends and enhances the formal strategies of the earlier 'Residua' text, *Imagination Dead Imagine*, particularly as regards the application of this putative Eisensteinian overtonal montage.

Like *All Strange Away*, Beckett's later text envisions a man and woman curled in fetal positions in two adjoining semi-circles, inside a closed white rotunda, suspended in a white vacuum: 'Diameter three feet, three feet from ground to summit of the vault. Two diameters at right angles AB CD divide the white ground into two semicircles ACB BDA. Lying on the ground two white bodies, each in its semicircle.'[66] *Imagination Dead Imagine*, as with its predecessor, is structured around recurring geometrical motifs of gesture. These are repeated, and repeated again, with minor variations as successions of multiple takes: 'the head against the wall at B, the arse against the wall at A, the knees against the wall between B and C, the feet against the wall between C and A' (182). Yet *Imagination Dead Imagine* significantly reduces the dominant line of action, as represented by the two bodies, re-editing the scenario in *All Strange Away* into an alternative cut by bringing into sharp focus overtonal qualities of light and heat: 'The light that makes all so white no visible source, all shines with the same white shine, ground, wall, vault, bodies, no shadow. Strong heat, surfaces hot but not burning to the touch, bodies sweating' (182).

The distinctness of the primary image in *Imagination Dead Imagine*, as in *Ping*, dissolves into prolonged abstract sequences of oscillating temperatures, from 'white and hot' to 'freezing-point' (182), and 'convulsive light' (185) from shining white to 'pitch black' (183). These elements in *All Strange Away* are clearly subordinate to the dominant line; in *Imagination Dead Imagine* and *Ping*, extremes of light and temperature collide in complex overtonal patterns, overwhelming the primary action, subsuming the visible bodies into planes of whiteness and either intense heat or cold. This method strongly indicates the importance of Eisenstein to Beckett's short prose fiction of this period. Eisensteinian methods of montage offered Beckett a context of structure for a new style of narrative procedure, no less than a repertoire of means to re-arrange and juxtapose sequences of highly compressed formal and stylistic motifs.

Notes

1 *Ping*, in *The Complete Short Prose 1929–1989*, ed. S. E. Gontarski (New York: Grove Press, 1995), pp. 194–5. All references to Beckett's short prose fiction are to this edition.
2 See Enoch Brater, *The Drama in the Text: Beckett's Late Fiction* (Oxford: Oxford University Press, 1994), p. 91; and Susan Brienza, *Samuel Beckett's New Worlds: Style in Metafiction* (Norman: University of Oklahoma Press, 1987), p. 167.
3 Karmitz interview with Elisabeth Lebovici, in *Comédie/Marin Karmitz/Samuel Beckett*, ed. Caroline Bourgeois (Paris: Editions du Regard, 2001), pp. 72–3.
4 James Knowlson, *Damned to Fame: The Life of Samuel Beckett* (London: Bloomsbury), p. 525.
5 Jay Leyda, 'Vision Is My Dwelling Place', *Film Culture* 58 (1974), p. 27.
6 Ibid.
7 Beckett to Sergei Eisenstein, 2 March 1936, *The Letters of Samuel Beckett, Vol. 1: 1929–1940*, ed. Martha Fehsenfeld and Lois More Overbeck (Cambridge: Cambridge University Press, 2009), p. 317.
8 Beckett to Thomas MacGreevy, 29 January 1936, *The Letters of Samuel Beckett, Vol. 1*, p. 311.
9 Ibid., pp. 305, 309.
10 Beckett to Arigdor Arikha and Anne Atik, 31 July 1964, *The Letters of Samuel Beckett, Vol. 3: 1957–1965*, ed George Craig, Martha Fehsenfeld, Dan Gunn and Lois More Overbeck (Cambridge: Cambridge University Press, 2014), p. 614.
11 Beckett to Alan Schneider, 3 March 1965, *No Author Better Served: The Correspondence of Samuel Beckett and Alan Schneider*, ed. Maurice Harmon (Cambridge, MA: Harvard University Press, 1998), p. 186.
12 Beckett to Barbara Bray, 22 September 1964, *The Letters of Samuel Beckett, Vol. 3*, p. 627.
13 Beckett to Sidney Meyers, 29 September 1964, ibid., p. 629.
14 Don Fairservice, *Film Editing: History, Theory and Practice: Looking at the Invisible* (Manchester: Manchester University Press, 2001), p. 331.
15 Ibid., p. 334.
16 Alan Schneider to Beckett, 13 September 1964, Harmon, *No Author Better Served*, p. 162.
17 Walter Murch, *A Perspectives on Film Editing* (W. Hollywood: Silman-James Press, 2005), p. 36.
18 Beckett to Alan Schneider, 28 October 1964, Harmon, *No Author Better Served*, p. 177.
19 Michael Rabiger, *Directing: Film Techniques and Aesthetics* (Burlington, MA: Focus Press, 2003), p. 103.
20 Beckett to Alan Schneider, 28 October 1964, Harmon, *No Author Better Served*, p. 177.

21 Ken Dancyger, *The Technique of Film and Video Editing: History, Theory and Practice* (Burlington, MA: Focus Press, 1993), p. 376.
22 Beckett to Alan Schneider, 28 October 1964, Harmon, *No Author Better Served*, p. 177.
23 Murch, p. 54.
24 Beckett to Alan Schneider, 28 October 1964, Harmon, *No Author Better Served*, p. 177.
25 Murch, p. 9.
26 Alan Schneider to Samuel Beckett, 21 January 1965, Harmon, *No Author Better Served*, p. 183.
27 *All Strange Away*, in Gontarski ed. *Complete Short Prose*, p. 171.
28 Roland Barthes, 'Objective Literature', in *Critical Essays*, trans. Richard Howard (Northwestern University Press, 1963), p. 23.
29 Beckett to Alan Schneider, 3 March 1965, Harmon, *No Author Better Served*, p. 186.
30 Beckett to Alan Schneider, 13 January 1965, Harmon, *No Author Better Served*, p. 181.
31 Beckett to Barbara Bray, 26 March 1959, *The Letters of Samuel Beckett, Vol. 3*, p. 246.
32 Beckett to John Manning, 15 October 1959, ibid., p. 246.
33 Karmitz interview, Bourgeois, *Comédie/Marin Karmitz/Samuel Beckett*, pp. 70–6.
34 Beckett to Nicholas Rawson, 25 December 1965, *The Letters of Samuel Beckett, Vol. 3*, p. 682.
35 Richard L. Admussen, *The Samuel Beckett Manuscripts: A Study* (Boston, MA: G.K Hall, 1979), p. 22.
36 Quoted in Brian Finney, *Since* How It Is: *A Study of Samuel Beckett's Later Fiction* (London: Covent Garden Press, 1972), p. 10.
37 *The Lost Ones*, in Gontarski ed. *Complete Short Prose*, p. 202.
38 Knowlson, *Damned to Fame*, p. 536.
39 Hugh Kenner, *A Reader's Guide to Samuel Beckett* (Syracuse University Press, 1970), p. 180.
40 Brienza, p. 169.
41 Dan O'Hara, 'What Goes "Ping" in Beckett's *Ping*?', *Notes and Queries* 54/2 (2007), p. 185.
42 David Bordwell, *The Cinema of Eisenstein* (Boston, MA: Harvard University Press, 1993), p. 261.
43 Sergei Eisenstein, 'Bela Forgets the Scissors' (1926), quoted in Jacques Aumont, *Montage Eisenstein* (London: BFI, 1987), p. 146.
44 Ibid., p. 150.
45 Quoted in Bordwell, p. 46.
46 V. I. Pudovkin, *Film Technique* (1926), trans. Ivor Montague (London: Vision Press, 1958), p. 114.
47 Eisenstein, 'Dickens, Griffith and the Film Today', in *Film Form: Essays in Film Theory*, ed. and trans. Jay Leyda (New York: Harcourt, [1949] 1977), p. 242.
48 Eisenstein, 'Methods of Montage', in *Film Form*, p. 73.
49 Ibid., p. 73.
50 David Lodge, 'Some *Ping* Understood', in *The Novelist at the Crossroads and Other Essays on Fiction and Criticism* (New York: Cornell University Press, 1971), p. 173.
51 Alys Moody, 'A Machine for Feeling: Beckett's Posthuman Affect', *Journal of Beckett Studies* 22/1 (2017), p. 90.
52 Bordwell, p. 46.
53 Erik Tonning, *Samuel Beckett's Abstract Drama: Works for Stage and Screen, 1962–1985* (Oxford: Peter Lang, 2007), p. 93.
54 Eisenstein, 'Dickens, Griffith and the Film Today', in *Film Form*, p. 236.

55 Ibid., p. 238.
56 Eisenstein, 'The Filmic Fourth Dimension', in *Film Form*, p. 65.
57 Eisenstein, 'The Cinematic Principle and the Ideogram', in *Film Form*, pp. 29–30.
58 Ibid., p. 37.
59 Ibid., p. 39.
60 Beckett to Arland Ussher, 25 March 1936, *The Letters of Samuel Beckett, Vol. 1*, p. 328.
61 Eisenstein, 'The Filmic Fourth Dimension', in *Film Form*, p. 68.
62 Ibid., p. 64.
63 Bordwell, p. 131.
64 Eisenstein, 'The Filmic Fourth Dimension', in *Film Form*, p. 66.
65 Ibid., p. 65.
66 *Imagination Dead Imagine*, in Gontarski ed. *Complete Short Prose*, p. 182.

Part II

EMERGING THEMES AND APPROACHES

8

DAVID JONES'S 'BALAAM BUSINESS': THE POETICS OF FORGIVENESS AFTER PASSCHENDAELE

Thomas Berenato

Assigned to 'battalion nuclear reserve',[1] the English poet David Jones (1895–1974) saw the worst of the Battle of Pilckem Ridge, in July and August 1917, from behind the front lines. But these grimmest days of the First World War would inspire a poem Jones began in the mid-1930s after completing a draft of his first book, *In Parenthesis* (1937), about the Somme, July 1916, in which he had been wounded. This new work, *The Book of Balaam's Ass*, attempts expiation of survivor's guilt. It celebrates the 'baptism by cowardice' of one Private Shenkin (Private Jones in the drafts), a Chaplinesque antihero who emerges from the horror unscathed thanks to his good misfortune to fall into a shell-hole during the assault.[2]

Jones 'abandoned' the thirty-five-page typescript, 'as it would not come together', but he included two fragments as the first and last items in his final book, *The Sleeping Lord* (1974).[3] Thomas Goldpaugh, the most recent editor of Jones's unpublished poetry, has shown that Jones built his poems from the inside out by splitting them open and stuffing material of other origin inside.[4] Goldpaugh argues that almost everything Jones wrote after *In Parenthesis* belongs to a single vast work the relationship of whose parts to the whole Jones reconceived down the decades. The instance of a new page of verse, and its accompanying footnotes, that Jones added to the *Balaam's Ass* typescript in 1971 serves as this essay's point of departure for a global account of Jones's compositional practice. The argument arises from an analysis of documents in the Jones archives at the Burns Library, Boston College, and the National Library of Wales, Aberystwyth.

Jones's interpolational procedure undermines the analogy that Jones, and most of his commentators taking him at his word, draws between *poiesis*, or artefacture, and *anamnesis*, the action of the priest during the Catholic Eucharistic rite. This essay suggests that the Sacrament of Penance and Reconciliation instead of the Eucharist models more exactly the way Jones's poetry makes its effect. Forgiveness administers a shock to the analogical imagination on which *anamnesis* depends. In forgiveness the past and present are no longer understood as continuous with one another. Rather, in forgiveness, what was is sprung loose from its place in the temporal continuum and confronted directly with what is in the present. Unlike *anamnesis*, forgiveness does not require the mediation of a priest. Any *homo faber* can perform the rite, although it takes great courage (a preoccupation of Jones's) to carry it off. Forgiveness of this kind does not demand assent to the doctrine of Real Presence. Rather, forgiveness itself invents a real presence: the new present that emerges in the meeting of *now* with a historical phenomenon.

The Book of Balaam's Ass opens with a paean to Prudence Pelham, David Jones's closest lady friend of the 1930s. The setting is Sidmouth, Devon, where Jones lived during the second half of the decade. The '*very sudden*' marriage of Prudence to Guy Branch on 25 March 1939 shattered Jones, for whom the loss mingled with a sense of foreboding about the failure of appeasement, an essay in support of which he wrote that spring but left unpublished.[5] His letters of this period indicate the extent to which the personal and political crises converged in his mind. From Campion Hall, Oxford, he wrote to his friend Harman Grisewood on 23 June 1939:

> Over all that political stuff, I believe I've altered a bit – I feel less interested in it somehow at the moment. I feel I can't cope with it – that whatever one thinks or says makes no 'impression' and one's data is anyway so meagre. I'm feeling if I can't get back to my own 'art work,' which is all I really care about, I don't know what I shall do. I also think all the time about Prudence but don't get any clearer about how to face up to it. O dear, this old romantic love, the only type I understand, does let you down.[6]

Too distracted to paint ('it is so "totalitarian," and you DO have to be strong to do it, once you know the snags'), Jones took refuge in writing – *Balaam's Ass*.[7] The poem's first pages celebrate the astringent radiance of an unnamed 'she', whose graceful movement through a room seems in drafts of this passage to reduce a group of men, diplomats and lobbyists, to silence.[8]

> SHE'S BRIGHT WHERE SHE WALKS SHE
> DIGNIFIES THE SPACES OF THE AIR AND MAKES AN AMPLE SCHEME
> ACROSS THE TRIVIAL SHAPES. SHE SHAKES THE PROUD AND
> ROTTEN
> ACCIDENTS; SMALL CONVENIENCES LOOK SHRUNK SO THAT YOU
> HARDLY NOTICE THEM:[9]

The earliest extant draft of these lines is headed 'entry'.[10] Jones is trying to absorb the blow of this woman, a human howitzer, as she makes her way across a room. Like John Ball's first encounter with an incoming shell in *In Parenthesis*, she does not so much stop time as reveal its inner continuity with space, an event that Jones marks as a shrinkage.[11] This will be his image of forgiveness in its aesthetic mode: not covering an evil or blotting it out or bearing it away, but shriveling it to a husk that might be charged with time. Forgiveness is 'a creative interaction with the past' that leads with its destructive face forward.[12] The forgiver, who is also guilty, incurs a fracture between past and present that affords an opportunity for reconstruction on the strength of the insight that what was can be invaded by what is.[13] Forgiveness, a decision that 'befalls' forgiver and forgiven alike, lies beyond both freedom and fate.[14] Not a matter of choice, it remains inconstruable as sacrifice. It is at once 'balls-up' and 'Praise'.[15] To make a work of art as, in Robert Browning's phrase, 'a forgiveness' is to produce a microcosm as a microeon: as, in Walter Benjamin's phrase, 'an organon of history'.[16]

Jones borrows from Gerard Manley Hopkins a verb to honour forgiveness in this sense: 'keep'. The word gets its most memorable workout in Hopkins's song 'The Leaden Echo and the Golden Echo', but it is the sestet of the sonnet 'As kingfishers catch fire, dragonflies draw flame' that Jones quotes in his July 1938 review of Herbert Read's *Poetry and Anarchism*: 'Feeling the temper of his [Read's] mind, I find it difficult to understand why he should seek, in this world, that freedom which is only reflected in the domain of art: We know that " ... the just man justices; [/] Kéeps gràce: ..., "'.[17] These lines compress into a handful of syllables what Jones takes pages of prose to express: his conviction that the poet, exemplary man, has been by tradition 'the custodian, rememberer, embodier and voice of the mythus'.[18] The 'specific task' of the artist is 'somehow or other, to lift up valid signs'.[19] 'Keeping', then, for Jones, is both retention and protention. The poet keeps culture in store by thrusting it continually before the eyes of the cult. Remembrance begins by dismembering the complacencies of the present, and this mortifying moment gives it its anarchic edge. As a keepsake of immemorial anarchy, a poem poses a threat to any power that seeks to impose a new order: 'Poetry is to be diagnosed as "dangerous" because it evokes and recalls, is a kind of *anamnesis* of, i.e. is an effective recalling of, something loved.'[20] In the preface to *The Anathemata* Jones replaces Hopkins's 'keeping' with Pope Gregory XV's 'propaganda': As an embodiment of 'dangerous memory', in Johann Baptist Metz's phrase, poetry 'is inevitably "propaganda," in that any real formal expression propagands the reality which caused those forms and their content to be'.[21] Forgiveness of a poem unfolds first as anamnesis, a recognition that all of the 'contingent and more remote associations' the poem evokes constitute a clear and present danger.[22] Without this realization the shrinkage that is one look of forgiveness in art cannot occur. The artist who succeeds in spatializing his epoch as an artwork restores it to reality, making it available for propagation. The more densely history is packed in the poem, the more anarchic history appears, because the more transmissible it becomes. Or as Jones puts it: 'The more real a thing, the more it will confound their politics.'[23] Forgiveness is pure propaganda: history reduced to 'the zero point of its own content' for the sake of its transmissibility.[24] This is the end of the artist's vast knowledge, an insight that Jones captures in a line from a draft of *The Book of Balaam's Ass*: 'the beneficent artisans know well the keeping.'[25]

In sacrificing the content of tradition for the sake of its transmissibility, forgiveness yields a keeping without a keeper. Jones's poetics may be seen to seek the state caught in a line of Wilfred Bion's 1970 essay 'Container and Contained Transformed': 'All thinking and all thoughts are true when there is no thinker.'[26] Jones gives to this condition, in which thinker is absolved of thought, the names '"pure myth"' and 'permanent mythus'.[27] Jones defines pure myth – his example is 'the myth of the Evangel' – as 'a myth devoid of the fictitious, an utterance of the Word'.[28] In the *logos*, as the Catholic theologian Heinrich Fries presents it shortly after the conclusion of the Second Vatican Council, 'myth is at once abrogated and fulfilled', revelation being 'the crisis of myth and the judgment upon it'.[29] In his prose Jones keeps myth immaculate by enclosing it in inverted commas, setting off its utterance from its utterer. The footnotes from which the lines of Jones's verse rise serve the same purpose: to establish the poem as permanent myth. In *The Book of Balaam's Ass*, which accrued annotation only late in its composition, the non-human mind fulfils the function of scare quotes. Animals and objects absorb the sin of those who regard them, designated by Jones as 'you'. The first beast to appear in the poem is a tiger in a zoo:

> like when pale flanks turn to lace with agile stripes the separating grill – until you quite
> forget the necessary impertinence
> the shackling and iron security
>   by which and
>   in which and
>   through which
>   you indulge your fine appreciation.[30]

Pacing in her cage, the big cat effaces the frame erected by her keepers and becomes pure myth. Only a look at the identification plate 'tells you she's a male born in captivity', a revelation that arrives with the impact of an 'unquote', releasing the reader back into the wilds of impure or impermanent myth.[31]

The feminine 'minstrelsy' of forgiveness then makes its appearance as 'a living sail' that, seen on Lyme Bay from the Sidmouth seafront, 'sets free the constricting esplanade and bends the rigid sea-rail to a native curvature (for space itself, they say, leans, is kindly, with ourselves, who make wide deviations to meet ourselves)'.[32] Both the turning of the tiger and the 'surprising advent' of this vessel Jones designates as 'incomings that lend life'.[33] Less momentous than Rilke's encounters with panther or torso, Jones's assignations with 'influence' involve a slow seduction that causes his world to 'lean' a little rather than swoon away.[34] To the ship offshore one of Sidmouth's grand hotels has 'inclined' herself, and from it she gains 'a passing fulness'.[35] By it, Jones writes, 'she's been conditioned', as if for purgation. Near the end of the poem Jones will note with some sarcasm of the soldiers stationed in what he calls 'the Zone', blissfully ignorant of their predicament: 'They're as mercifully conditioned as a limbo child.'[36] The influx of influence induces a manifestation of the curvature native to the spacetime continuum, a property that Jones elsewhere identifies with Aristotelian 'equity': the equitable, as Jones quotes the *Nicomachean Ethics*, being '"a better kind of justice"'.[37] Art, on Jones's account, courts an aesthetic equity whose function is to feature an otherwise unfelt flexibility proper to tradition. The confrontation with some cattle that occupies the next page of the poem emphasizes the ungentle aspect of the equitable. Bent out of shape, tradition turns loose an energy approaching the anarchic:

> or
> stiff-legged calves who make the gradual fields skip like imagined hills, play erratic circles to accuse the static adults, drifting on stubble-sea, or set heavily like islands humped …[38]

After this Jones reverses the shot to show 'you' from the perspective of the full-grown bulls, who 'almost seem to rumble' the human trespasser on their turf: 'They startle when you come on hind-legs at them; you come fore-paws waved to shoo them off. You subdue imperiously with fragile man's-hand, bellowings and forest-might. You scorn crumpled or bright horn that gored the burning cat with your anthropoid gestures.'[39] This zoomorphizing move returns to man's-hand the boomerang of brutalization. The allusion that follows to the Book of Daniel equates 'the long idiocy of agriculture' to scorn for God's grace: 'Pray stone bulls won't make the stone low his name, who toppled his diadem to reach his fodder / between the irrigation ducts.'[40] The final paragraph of this section tags the poem's title and gives to the talking ass a Christian spin of the type that other parts of the Numbers story have long received: 'Lords of Creation, hierarchy of use and delectation, rational souls, convenient syllogistic cornering of memory and will, and dumb beasts perishing as poor brute-bodies must – She'ld make a Balaam of you to narrow your path, she'ld drag you down on Christmas night into an appropriate attitude till your arse reflected the nine Choirs shining.'[41] The antecedent of 'she' is the 'bull-brain' broached above but also the 'influence' that 'she' embodies.[42] The shiftiness of the referent captures the elusive fluency of influence even as it confers upon the poem, 'by some acid twist', the quickly evaporating coherence that is for Jones the look of grace in art.[43] 'The immediate, the nowness, the pressure of sudden, modifying circumstance' – this is the way forgiveness makes itself felt, as a liberating narrowing of the path to redemption.[44] Shrinkage and constriction are the hallmarks of anarchy for Jones. 'She' is, like Paul in Ephesians 6:20, 'a legate in bonds' who 'bellows loudly as she ought to bellow'.[45] Parrhesia is the prerogative of the imprisoned – prisoners of 'the fantastic hierarchy' whose preservation is the prerequisite of the stress-testing of each link in the chain of being that this poem performs.[46] The poet is bound to transform tradition into 'genuine myth': 'To conserve, to develop, to bring together, to make significant for the present what the past holds, without dilution or any deleting, but rather by understanding and transubstantiating the material … saying always: "of these thou hast given me have I lost none"'.[47] Anarchism and communism, 'two bugbears' of *Balaam's Ass*, break the chain but keep the baggage.[48] Anarchy, the influence of forgiveness in politics, turns the past to account by showing it on the point of perspiration: 'She'ld make your exploiting governance wither away all right – if she could recall him sweating out his chrism, easing his tailless flank under the burning sun-baked terracing.'[49] The agony here belongs to both Nebuchadnezzar in the field and Christ in Gethsemane. Forgiveness has the look of hematidrosis.

Animals, not men, pass down the wisdom in the world of *Balaam's Ass*. But while the burden of the past weighs heavily on their backs, it proves on inspection to be insubstantial. Tradition means nothing anymore to man, yet a whisper of its onetime validity lingers. Forgiveness – an anxiety of influence – is the persistence of such validity in the absence of significance. When he has not let his inheritance slip from his grasp, man has lost the means of making it out. Animals hold the advantage, a kind of innocence, of never having known the cipher in the first place: 'no tail or hairy ear clears the tormenting buzz of memory – the bovine race-myth not unravel'.[50] Were these kine to talk, their drover would not fail to get their drift. Their words would reach them with what Walter Benjamin calls 'the annihilating character of true reconciliation' (*Vernichtende wahrer Versöhnung*), the life-risking reconciliation of an individual with God.[51] 'Could she blink a thought-maze back, there would be a Dialectical incoming for you!'[52] This condition would clinch the 'true reconciliation with God' that, according to Benjamin, echoing Jesus, 'is achieved by no one who does not thereby destroy everything – or as much as he possesses – in order only then, before God's reconciled countenance, to find it resurrected'.[53] From 'true reconciliation' (*wahre Versöhnung*) with God, which Benjamin elsewhere calls forgiveness (*Vergebung*), follows 'conciliation [*Aussöhnung*] of one's fellow men'.[54] True reconciliation Benjamin restricts to the 'supermundane'; as such it resists 'concrete [*gegenständlich*] depiction' in an artwork.[55]

The artist who wishes to depict forgiveness is therefore doomed to deal in its mundane effects alone. Jones mines the 'Book of Balaam' for an alternative tactic. There he finds scriptural authority for the transposition of reconciliation between God and man to forgiveness of the animal in man. This forgiveness shakes man by the root: 'She'ld thrust you on your origins. She'ld break down and nozzle to your foundations and toss high for the windy advent day a thousand middle-walls of partition.'[56] But it is nonetheless comic. Like Kafka, Jones finds his holy fools funny.[57] Their absurd naïveté renders them irreproachable and, as the poem goes on to show, invulnerable. *The Book of Balaam's Ass* is a concrete depiction of the angel that arises from man's reconciliation with his own animality – and of that angel's necessary evanescence in a world for which the 'genuine myth' of forgiveness is too pure.

The third section of the poem presents a scene of conciliation between veterans and those stuck listening to their warmed-over war stories. The party achieves at best 'the semblance of reconciliation' (*Schein der Versöhnung*) because all involved seek forgiveness from God only indirectly through each other.[58] Jones casts their impasse in terms of the fear that keeps the Wedding Guest from making his peace with the Ancient Mariner: 'you couldn't choose but hear'.[59] It soon grows clear that choice must cede to decision if forgiveness is to befall them. (Children, like animals, are decisive to the extent that they find themselves cut off from choice.) Two decades later, in the preface to his essay collection *Epoch and Artist*, Jones will call their 'trouble' – their inability 'to take the particular for no more than it is' – a *felix culpa*.[60] In *Balaam's Ass* their unselfconscious feeling for 'the immemorial formulas' (Jones quotes a folk rhyme repeated by a character in

George Borrow's *Lavengro*) ensures that 'these being dead, speak'.[61] One auditor voices a similar sentiment even as she complains of 'the tedium of twice-told tales': 'But it is inevitable and meet: / while there is breath it's only right to bear immemorial witness.'[62] Jones defends here the mythical method he had deployed in *In Parenthesis* by ventriloquizing and exaggerating its anticipated detractors' scorn:

> Tilly Vally Mr Pistol that's a pretty tale. La! on my body – tell that, sir, below stairs. Gauffer it well and troupe it fine, pad it out to impressive proportions, grace it from the Ancients. Gee! I do like a bloody lie turned gallantly romantical, fantastical, glossed by the old gang from the foundations of the world. Press every allusion into your Ambrosian racket, ransack the sacred canon and have by heart the sweet Tudor magician gather your sanctions and weave your allegories, roseate your lenses, serve up the bitter dregs in silver-gilt, bless it before and behind and swamp it with baptismal and continual dew.[63]

The truth-content of combat experience has been compromised in the interest of allowing it to enter tradition. This passage imputes guilt of the crime of historical forgiveness ('Lime-wash over the tar-brush there's a dear') to Shakespeare, whose righteousness in the act Jones seizes for himself by implication.[64] The fourth part of the poem reveals on whose behalf, and in whose image, Jones performs the sacrifice of truth 'for the sake of clinging to transmissibility'.[65] The inevitable failure of the sacrifice does not nullify its justification.

This central section of the poem depicts the opening attack of the Third Battle of Ypres (Passchendaele), the assault on Pilckem Ridge in the early morning of 31 July 1917. Twelve thousand soldiers died that day. A member of the 15th Battalion (London Welsh) of the 113th Brigade of the Royal Welch Fusiliers (23rd Foot) of the 38th (Welsh) Division, Jones sat out this episode in 'battalion nuclear reserve'.[66] The manuscript of the Passchendaele passage features a Private Jones, his name changed to Shenkin for the typescript, who affords Jones an inner standing-point from which to unfold the action (specifically 'the G.O.C. in C's diversion before the Mill') that he had only heard from a distance.[67] 'Pick-em-up' Shenkin is 'the least sure-footed of men', maladjusted just so to survive in a shifting sea of mud.[68] Out of phase with the battle rhythm, his missteps save him: 'there was in his maladroitness a scheme of self-preservation'.[69] Like Chaplin's, his immediate environment leans in to accommodate his deviations from the standard. Casualties occur on the 'open plain' of Passchendaele in the complete absence of 'cover'.[70] The barrenness of the terrain, Jones recalls in a draft headnote to the poem, made some in his unit wax nostalgic for the 'woods & chalk ways of the Somme'.[71] A shell-hole 'snuggery' kindly swallows Shenkin.[72] A mixture of indifference, haplessness and fear conspires to reduce him to a 'rodent': 'in his burrow of salvation and over his drawn-back ears and unseen to his deflected eyes the missiles wove this way and that a steel hatch for him'.[73] Here Shenkin lies listening to the cries of the wounded around him each calling on his own tutelar, among them

> the Sanctifier and lord who is glorious in operation, the dispositioner, the effecter of all transubstantiations, who sets the traverse-wall according to the measure of the angel with the reed, who knows best how to gather his epiklesis from that open plain, who transmutes their cheerless blasphemy into a lover's word, who spoke by Balaam and by Balaam's ass, who spoke also by Sgt Bullock.[74]

That only Shenkin hears them is Jones's own 'cheerless blasphemy'. If the transmutation he mentions takes place, it is by virtue of the 'dolorous anaphora' that these pages send up.[75] Benjamin writes of Kafka that he 'eavesdropped on tradition'.[76] In his household, revelation communicates itself as white noise. 'There is no doctrine that one could learn and no knowledge that one could preserve.'[77] In Jones's world, too, 'the unknown God' is known by triangulation, as the addressee of an overheard apostrophe who stands convicted of the unknown guilt in general circulation.[78] Jones toys with the idea of Shenkin as a sin offering, but this scapegrace survives as a 'scape-goat' who walks away from the altar as spry as ever, if not unscathed.[79] Shenkin emerges from his 'shallow crater' as 'easily' as he had slipped into it.[80] His caprice marks him out as influence incarnate: 'You have to be agile to trace the fleet-foot doubling Influence', Jones writes in the next section of the poem.[81] As the reagent of forgiveness Shenkin unwittingly embraces his role to hold hope in reserve as despair:

> In his covert he had not been altogether ungraced because of the diverse cries coming up from the earth, and because of the baptism by cowardice which is more terrible than that of water or blood. Remembering the Rocky Mountain goat he leapt from shell-hole to shell-hole (and no one could tell whether he leapt because he feared or feared because he leapt) until he regained the security of the assembly trench. And that is why he is called one of the three who escaped from the diversion before the Mill.[82]

One small voice Shenkin distils from the rumour of war hails 'the God of the philosophers who is not in the fire, who can yet illumine the nature of fire'.[83] Shenkin's special 'baptism' does not allow him to 'escape' incorporating this 'diverted' divinity into the cowardly life that remains to him. Unsinged by the firefight, he reflects its garish light sight unseen as the 'transmission of the impossibility of transmission, transmission of transmissibility itself – that is, the transmission of trauma'.[84] The look of forgiveness is a thousand-yard stare.

Forgiveness is to be found wherever Jones's typographical cues divert his reader's gaze. This 'Passchendaele' section of the poem is notable for the footnotes Jones added to it three decades on for publication in *The Sleeping Lord* in March 1974.[85] (Provisionally entitled 'Assault on the Mill', it is one of two sections of the longer manuscript of the 1930s and 1940s that Jones revised as the last poem, 'from *The Book of Balaam's Ass*', in his final collection, and the only section to receive self-annotation.) These notes fill in Shenkin's shell-hole. If the latter is the look of truth turned 'transmissibility itself', the former pushes 'pure myth' to the point of unreadability. Some notes straightforwardly detail what Jones terms his 'deposits', the *materia poetica* 'of which the poet is himself the product'.[86] 'Cf. Wordsworth's "Goody Blake and Harry Gill"' is a sober example.[87] Others of this sort serve up less public but not quite private information: '"Big Willie", the heaviest type of German trench-mortars were sometimes called by us "Big Willies" after the name of Kaiser Wilhelm II, and those of lighter caliber, "Little Willies" after the Crown-prince.'[88] The self-conscious exotericism of certain notes, however, transforms them into oblique apologies for the form of the 'poem-with-notes' (which Neil Corcoran finely distinguishes from the 'poem with notes') itself.[89] Gesturing at justification of the appearance of the name 'Hycga' in one passage, Jones comments at the bottom of the page:

> In the 1940s, when writing this passage I supposed my source could only be the *A.S. Chronicle*. But on enquiries I'm told that no such entry exists in the *Chronicle*. Jutes in the vicinity of High-Wycombe sounds improbable, but on the other hand, the idea was fixed in my mind and one does not invent tales of this sort, *ex nihilo*.[90]

Jones almost certainly formed this *idée fixe* on reading R. G. Collingwood's *Roman Britain and the English Settlements* (1936), whose mention on page 452 of Buckinghamshire place-names associated with the Saxon (not Jute) landowner Hycga he notes in the *Balaam's Ass* manuscript.[91] His note in the published version of the poem goes out of its way to conjure up a crisis of transmissibility. Whether Jones forgot his source or deliberately ignored or suppressed it, he offers here an apology for his second-hand scholarship when its integrity was never in doubt.

This section of the poem is a litany of lamentation for the naked exposure of the soldiers on Passchendaele's 'open plain'.[92] On their behalf the footnotes oppose the 'negative gradient' of the narrative, mercifully ratcheting up the Zone's rugosity.[93] The 'backgrounds' that the notes purport to share obtrude into the foreground, throwing up speed bumps in reader's road through the Zone.[94] Poetry in the Zone, these notes proclaim by their presence, only appears mediated by prose, which constitutes a continuation of poetry by other means: commentary. The notes echo the voice of the ass, checking like the latter the headlong rush of prophetic revelation along its course to apocalypse. While from one perspective the ass appears to waylay Balaam, from another she seems to overtake him. Jones's prose similarly surges up from under the lines of his poetry, wringing from the white field of the page on which they are printed room for the tradition from which they emerge to make itself heard. Tradition by turns forestalls revelation, enjoining revelation to tarry out tradition, and perfects it prematurely, forming as it were a forcing house for truth.

Jones's notes 'on points of pronunciation' sound the depths of this dialectic with particular sensitivity.[95] Extracting from it, at the end of his life, a piece for inclusion as the last poem of *The Sleeping Lord* sequence, Jones interpolated in the old manuscript of *Balaam's Ass* a page of new verse that approaches unpronounceability.[96] His editors have named this insertion 'the Melchisedec passage', its eponymous priest-king himself hailing from an interpolation, chapter fourteen, in the Book of Genesis, where his mention at verses 18–20 may mark a yet further incursion of 'an isolated source'.[97] Melchizedek had made a memorable appearance in Jones's 1952 preface to *The Anathemata*. The reader should conceive the 'unity' of that poem, Jones writes there, as one would 'a longish conversation between two friends, where one thing leads to another; but should a third party hear fragments of it, he might not know how the talk had passed from the cultivation of cabbages to Melchizedek, king of Salem'.[98] Here, two decades later, Melchizedek enters the verse on a sudden only to find himself immediately caught in a longish conversation carried out in prose at the bottom of the page. He appears on the list of 'those Bright ones' to whom Shenkin hears, in surround sound, stricken soldiers direct devotions with their last breaths.[99] In *The Sleeping Lord* Melchizedek replaces the original manuscript's 'Lord of Noe who contracted with all flesh indifferently', an exchange perhaps inspired by the apocryphal identification of Melchizedek with Noah's nephew.[100] Dai Meyrick makes his 'dolorous anaphora' on 'Magons and Maponus', Celtic deities equivalent with the Roman Mars and Apollo.[101] The elaborate idiom of the Melchisedec passage – Jones's editor calls it 'recognisably in David's later "Anathemata" style' – marks it as the author's own anaphora, and as if reluctant to release it to the heavens Jones shackles its thirty-one lines to six footnotes, running to forty-one lines of prose.[102] The name-check of Melchizedek himself ('MELCHISÉDEC Wledig') rates the most perverse of these annotations, which explains, or perhaps gives the pretext for, the acute accent Jones places on its penult: 'The stress accent on "e" in Melchisedec is merely in accord with the stress on the penultimate syllable in the majority of Welsh words because it seemed to go with the Welsh title Gwledig (a ruler of great eminence). Cf. Cunedda Wledig, Macsen Wledig. Taliesin refers to God as *Gwledig Nef a phob tud*, "Ruler of Heaven and all countries"'.[103] In the preface to *The Anathemata* Jones tells his readers that he intends his poem to be 'said' and advises them to read it aloud slowly: '"with deliberation" is the best rubric for each page, each sentence, each word'.[104] 'It was written to be read in that way.'[105] This word was written to be read 'wrong' at first, that is, in the manner familiar from the missal: 'summus sacérdos tuus Melchísedech'.[106] Jones's eccentric accent and the footnote explaining its placement wrongfoot the reader in a way that sounds more right to the writer, because it causes the reader to stumble upon a network of association otherwise invisible or inaudible.

Rowan Williams expounds the effects of this move in archaeological terms. For Jones, Williams writes, the object of the artist's excavatory activity is connection as such:

> The artist uncovers 'root systems' in human imagination and communication and displays the virtual infinity of ways in which one thing is what it is because of countless others and one word is anchored in entire systems of myth and perception. Everything and every word is thus *for* a whole ecology of meaning, in whose completeness (a completeness that of course resists possession or definitive expression) the unequivocal gift of God is mediated, the gift of both being and bliss.[107]

Jones goes out of his way to accent the makeshift character of his spadework, exposing it as a kind of 'Penelope work' instead.[108] The same annotation that points up the painstaking reticulation of the verse often suggests that the net in question has simply dropped from the sky, that the 'root system' belongs to an air plant.

The epithets 'noswyl duw Gwener' and 'pridie the Ides of Mars' (for Holy Thursday and Good Friday respectively) prompt a long, tortured note on the second page of the Melchisedec passage in which Jones plumbs the shallows of his soil. These designations, he writes, 'are in no sense meant to have any historicity. The year of the Paschal period in which the Passion occurred is unknown.' To ensure that the lunar calendar keep pace with the solar year, its reckoners must intercalate a thirteenth month every two or three years, an operation whose own history is subject to the spotty survival of the relevant documentary evidence.[109] Dating the Crucifixion ('in the first month / of the Romulean year Ab Urbe Condita / seven hundred and eighty-four', as Jones gives it) thus resists frictionless translation from one calendar to another, a difficulty of which Jones signals his awareness:

> I have simply followed the tradition of the Church and supposed the Supper at which the Oblation placed the Offerand in the state of a Victim to be immolated on the morrow, i.e. Dies Veneris, which *if* it was in the Roman month of March would be the day before the Ides and by Jewish reckoning on the eve of the Passover.[110]

Jones could have made no bones about the 'extreme complexities involved', which he says struck him only after the *fait accompli* of composition, but the bones are the chief attraction of the Melchisedec passage. The several extant drafts of the note on dating appear to be of the same vintage as the verse they supplement; it is hard to be sure which came first in the order of conception. The whole two-page prose-verse complex, however, unambiguously postdates the manuscript into which Jones has inserted it by about three decades. In the published version of 1972 the Melchisedec passage arises in 'from *The Book of Balaam's Ass*' like the Jesus of the Letter to the Hebrews: according to the order of Melchisedec, which is to say without genealogy and as if plucked from out of time. It is an intercalary – and, as it turns out, culminating – moment in the tale of Pick-em-up Shenkin, who seems to take advantage of the interruption it constitutes (itself further dilated by its footnotes) to muster up the courage (or is it just redoubled cowardice?) to break the cover of his shell-hole and make it to the safety of the assembly trench.

At the end of a letter of 20 July 1935 to Harman Grisewood touching on his latest 'mental miseries', Jones says he feels 'rather like a Lifeguardsman in a breastplate and spurs without a horse in a mine-crater in a gas attack', a predicament that prefigures Shenkin's in his shell-hole.[111] Jones wonders what this overarmored warrior should do: 'It would be a good question in a military examination paper, for the staff.'[112] It is a draft of the question that Jones, echoing Jeremiah, issues at the end of the early *Balaam's Ass* manuscript: 'Ah, what shall I write.'[113] In the Zone of postwar life-in-death, where 'Pilkem [*sic*] heath seems fragrant to the memory', happiness arises only from a form of remembrance that seeks to render incomplete what feels complete: suffering.[114] The Lifeguardsman would do well to act on Shenkin's impulse: 'He found that his wire mesh slipped away from him easily.'[115] The decision to quit his covert befalls Shenkin spontaneously, and it arrives with the shock of a drive-by baptism – 'by cowardice' rather than 'of repentance'.[116] Shenkin, the unlikely survivor, finds himself persisting in a state of what Georges Bataille calls, in a letter of 6 December 1937 to Alexandre Kojève, 'unemployed negativity' or, more literally, 'negativity without use' [*négativité sans emploi*].[117] History has ended for Shenkin, and he has nothing left to do but inhabit the end of time as if it were the time of the end that it has been, he suddenly recognizes, all along.[118] It is this realization – an animal insight, or an insight into his own animality – that recalls to him 'the Rocky Mountain goat', a force of creatureliness whose embrace ejects him from his shell-hole.[119] Shenkin leaps out of his human skin, projected into an orbit indifferent to 'project'.

This kingdom, animal or messianic, is the site of 'happiness' as Jones defines it in some notes on painting he made for his doctor, William A. H. Stevenson, on 8 October 1947: 'Painting odd in that one is led partly by what evolves as the painting evolves, this form suggesting that form – happiness comes when the forms assume significance with regard to this juxtaposition to each other – even though the original "idea" was somewhat different'.[120] The temporality of this process is the time of forgiveness, in which the artist soldiers on hapless with happiness, impatient of 'project'. Forgiveness here comes unhinged from both subject and object. Neither God nor sin plays a role. The 'happiest' paintings 'seem to make themselves', Jones writes.[121] And since 'the felicity of forms' is what Jones is 'really after', the 'themes' of an artwork acquire the cast of *anathemata*, preserved as containers emptied of content: 'Subject is *everything* in one sense and nothing in *another*'.[122] The happiness forgiveness entails grows indistinguishable from despair. The end-time marks a new start, but 'the time of the remainder' will also run out.[123] Shenkin has leapt from the shell-hole into the assembly trench; he has not left the front and may never.

In the penultimate section of the poem, Jones puts grace and disgrace (golden and leaden echoes, respectively) in the scales and finds the equation hard to throw off balance: 'Who shall say the measure, and the price?'[124] Gauging the net effect of 'the fleet-foot doubling Influence' proves impossible – 'The tare is wheat within your pruning fingers' – and so the soundest counsel is to trust its strength, which means for Jones to do it homage.[125] 'You'll be out of grace not to praise …', warn the *disciplinae* of both art and war.[126] The artist must 'bend' to influence, and the cost of contortion could not be higher: 'That drought and all dead for peculiar splendour of this one withered tree to eke-out a half-line for this poet in his poverty.'[127] At the end of *In Parenthesis*, Jones dismisses 'Life the leveller' for her 'impudent equality', ushering her on to 'less discriminating zones' where she might meet hierarchy with anarchy more openly.[128] Instead of life, the casualties of the Somme, an 'elect society', receive a 'fragile prize' according to hidden merits that establish among them an order of 'precedence'.[129] A year later and seventy miles north at Ypres, artillery have so undermined the grounds for discrimination that life finds it favorable to flood in, her impudence intact as forgiveness. The zoning laws could not be laxer here, where all zones partake of the Zone.

The last section of the poem introduces the Zone as the place where the hard fate that 'our frailty should use us' becomes apparent.[130] Jones exposes the Zone as the antitype of both Salisbury Plain, where the Fusiliers practised for Passchendaele, and the 'Forward Zone' north of the Ypres Salient itself.[131] The Zone extends forward, as in a Nash landscape, to England in 1919–22, but not, significantly, back to Mametz Wood, the 'King Pellam's Launde' of which 'it would be difficult to think meanly' and the fragrant memory of which persists as an antidote to the antitype.[132] The Somme stands awkwardly in parenthesis between the 'blasted heath' that stretches from Farnborough to Flanders and back.[133] After July 1916, Jones writes in the preface to *In Parenthesis*, the war became more of a 'mechanical affair'.[134] '"Mechanization" in the widest sense' links the training camp at Winnall Down of August through November 1915 to the 'glassy towers' of London immediately after the armistice, and with the advent of mechanization connection to 'a less exacting past' began to wither away.[135] *The Book of Balaam's Ass* sets out to set off the Somme as an improbable but irresistible irruption of 'influence' in the Zone of 'unshared background' that lends to modern life its groundless character.[136]

In Parenthesis ends as the 'Queen of the Woods' bends her 'influential eyes' on the dying at Mametz, but the more 'discriminating zones' that Jones addresses in *Balaam's Ass* seem impervious to her project.[137] In a draft headnote to the poem, dated 1972, Jones acknowledges her absence in order to offer her role to an unnamed understudy: 'There was no "Queen of the Woods" to garland the dead at Passchendaele but no doubt her equivalent found a way for Villon reminds us that the Queen of Heaven & Mundi domina is also Imperatrix of the infernal marsh.'[138] Her 'equivalent', no doubt, is Balaam's ass, who survives in the last section of the poem as a piece of shagreen for sale in the Zone: 'You can be sure of spun buck, sir, you can't improve on our spun buck, my love.'[139] On the heath, where 'Art and Industry have kissed', the angel and the ass, 'freed from love's constraint', combine to form a fine leather accessory.[140] The prophetic voice that howls the poem's final lines sees the skin as of a piece with all commercial products 'conceived outside love's covenant' and as natural to a world in which 'the habitations of Peace and War' alike share freedom from 'love's constraint'.[141] Like his footnotes, which Jones wished to keep here 'to the barest minimum' required by 'courtesy' to put the reader 'on the scent' of the right reference, the ass's hide cures tradition, preserving it by desiccation.[142] Opening his heart to 'sterility' and travailing for influence's 'adamant surfaces', Jones's Jeremiah finds forgiveness under the aspect of wizened wisdom, the look it adopts in the Zone.[143]

Notes

1 Thomas Dilworth, *David Jones in the Great War* (London: Enitharmon, 2012), p. 161.

2 David Jones, *The Roman Quarry and Other Sequences*, ed. Harman Grisewood and René Hague (New York: Sheep Meadow Press, 1981), p. 201.

3 See Jones's letter of ?11 December 1973 to René Hague in David Jones, *Dai Greatcoat: A Self-portrait of David Jones in His Letters*, ed. René Hague (London: Faber & Faber, 1980), p. 250.
4 See David Jones, *David Jones's The Grail Mass and Other Works*, ed. Thomas Goldpaugh and Jamie Callison (London and New York: Bloomsbury Academic, 2018).
5 See Jones's letter of 11 April 1939 from Jones to Jim and Helen Ede in Jones, *Dai Greatcoat*, p. 91; see also Oliver Bevington's edition of Jones's letter of 18 December 1938 to Neville Chamberlain, in Jones, *David Jones on Religion, Politics, and Culture: Unpublished Prose*, ed. Thomas Berenato, Kathleen Henderson Staudt and Anne Price-Owen (London and New York: Bloomsbury Academic, 2018), pp. 11–43.
6 Jones, *Dai Greatcoat*, p. 93.
7 Ibid., p. 92.
8 David Jones Papers, National Library of Wales, LR 7-1 (1), pp. 125–6; David Jones, *The Book of Balaam's Ass*, in Jones, *The Roman Quarry*, p. 187. René Hague, whose work Harman Grisewood completed after Hague's death in 1981, presents an edition of the manuscript catalogued as LR 7-1 as Jones, *The Book of Balaam's Ass*, in *The Roman Quarry*, pp. 187–211; manuscript page numbers are the archivists'.
9 Jones, *The Roman Quarry*, 187; LR 7-1 (4), p. 8; Jones, *The Roman Quarry*, p. 187.
10 LR 7-1 (1), p. 123.
11 See David Jones, *In Parenthesis* (London: Faber & Faber, 2014), p. 24.
12 Walter Benjamin, 'Literary History and the Study of Literature' (April 1931), trans. Rodney Livingstone, in *Walter Benjamin: Selected Writings, Volume 2, Part 2: 1931–1934*, ed. Michael W. Jennings, Howard Eiland and Gary Smith (Cambridge, MA, and London: The Belknap Press of Harvard University Press, 1999), p. 463. Hereafter cited as *SW* II.2.
13 See Paul Tillich, *Systematic Theology: Three Volumes in One* (Chicago: University of Chicago Press, 1967), Vol. 2, p. 174: 'In all human relations he who forgives is himself guilty, not only generally, but in the concrete situation in which he forgives'.
14 Walter Benjamin, 'Goethe's Elective Affinities' (written 1919–22, published 1924–5; Goethe's novel's title not italicized in Benjamin's essay's title), trans. Stanley Corngold, in *Walter Benjamin: Selected Writings, Volume 1: 1913–1926*, ed. Marcus Bullock and Michael W. Jennings (Cambridge, MA, and London: The Belknap Press of Harvard University Press, 1996), p. 332. This volume hereafter cited as SW I. See William Blake's song of innocence 'Infant Joy' for an uneasy rhyme between the actions of 'calling' and 'befalling' that catches the ambivalence of the decision to 'be fallen' that forgiveness entails. To call down the joy of innocence is to 'befall' forgiveness.
15 It is the function of forgiveness to recognize as open to the future what has been sealed by sin or death in the past. Jones's mission – what he calls his 'Balaam business' – is to bring to bear this open relationship with time on those things, including corpses, long or lately left for dead. See Jones, *Dai Greatcoat*, p. 91; William Blissett, *The Long Conversation: A Memoir of David Jones* (London: Oxford University Press, 1981), p. 67. *The Book of Balaam's Ass* conducts this 'business' in the course of describing it. Jones's earliest mention of the poem, his second after *In Parenthesis* (1937), comes in a letter of 31 May 1938 to Harman Grisewood. Jones has been struggling to get the manuscript to hang together ('A very rambling affair – sometimes it all seems balls and sometimes I like it in places.'), but he has no trouble telling Grisewood what it is 'about': 'It is about how everything turns into something else, and how you can never tell when a bonza is cropping up or the Holy Ghost is going to turn something inside out, and how everything is a balls-up and

a kind of "Praise" at the same time.' See Jones, *Dai Greatcoat*, p. 86. The relationship of the events that inspired *In Parenthesis* to the composition of that poem was more 'straightforward' than that between the content and composition of this new writing. *Balaam's Ass* is 'about "ideas"', whereas *In Parenthesis* had a story to tell: the fate of Jones and his friends on the Western Front between December 1915 and July 1916. See *Dai Greatcoat*, p. 86.

16 See Richard Gibson, 'Browning's "A Forgiveness": A Grammatical Reading', *Literature Compass* 11/2 (February 2014), pp. 74–83; and Walter Benjamin, 'Literary History and the Study of Literature', in *SW* II.2, p. 464.

17 David Jones, 'Poetry and Anarchy', *The Tablet* (16 July 1938), p. 77. The grave accent on 'gràce' here is Jones's or his editor's intervention. Jones's copy of Hopkins's *Poems*, a gift at Christmas 1930 from his father, was Charles Williams's second edition, published November 1930 by Oxford University Press, which reads 'Kéeps gráce:' (p. 53). For a history of Jones's reception of Hopkins up to 1968, see Thomas Berenato, 'A "re-cognition" in "the exact sense of that word": David Jones's Unfinished Essay on Gerard Manley Hopkins', in Jones, *David Jones on Religion, Politics, and Culture: Unpublished Prose*, pp. 101–18. Jones mentions Hopkins's 'The Leaden Echo' in *The Book of Balaam's Ass*. See Jones, *The Roman Quarry*, p. 205.

18 David Jones, *The Anathemata: Fragments of an Attempted Writing* (London: Faber & Faber, 2010), p. 21. That poem and its preface were first published, by Faber, in 1952.

19 Jones, *The Anathemata*, p. 23.

20 Ibid., p. 21.

21 Johann Baptist Metz, *Faith in History and Society: Toward a Practical Fundamental Theology*, trans. and ed. J. Michael Ashley (New York: Crossroad, 2007), p. 88; Jones, *The Anathemata*, p. 21.

22 Jones, *The Anathemata*, p. 21.

23 Ibid., p. 22.

24 Gershom Scholem, discussing Kafka, in a letter of 20 September 1934 to Walter Benjamin, in *The Correspondence of Walter Benjamin and Gershom Scholem 1932–1940*, ed. Gershom Scholem and trans. Gary Smith and Andre Lefevere (Cambridge, MA: Harvard University Press, 1992), p. 142: 'You ask what I understand by the "nothingness of revelation"? I understand by it a state in which revelation appears to be without meaning, in which it still asserts itself, in which it has *validity* but *no significance*. A state in which the wealth of meaning is lost and what is in the process of appearing (for revelation is such a process) still does not disappear, even though it is reduced to the zero point of its own content, so to speak. This is obviously a borderline case in the religious sense, and whether it can really come to pass is a dubious point.' This volume hereafter cited as *C*.

25 LR 7-1 (1), p. 126 (verso).

26 Wilfred Bion, 'Container and Contained Transformed', in *Attention and Interpretation* (London: Karnac, 1984), p. 117. Compare Benjamin, 'The Task of the Translator', in Walter Benjamin, trans. Rodney Livingstone, *SW* I, p. 252: 'In appreciation of a work of art or an art form, consideration of the receiver never proves fruitful. Not only is any reference to a particular public or its representatives misleading, but even the concept of an "ideal" receiver is detrimental in the theoretical consideration of art, since all it posits is the existence and nature of man as such. Art, in the same way, posits man's physical and spiritual existence, but in none of its works is it concerned with his attentiveness. No poem is intended for the reader, no picture for the beholder, no symphony for the audience.'

27 Jones, *The Anathemata*, p. 40, 82.
28 Ibid., p. 40.
29 Heinrich Fries, 'Myth', in *Encyclopedia of Theology: The Concise* Sacramentum Mundi, ed. Karl Rahner, trans. John Griffiths, Francis McDonagh, and David Smith (New York: The Seabury Press, 1975), p. 1016.
30 Jones, *The Roman Quarry*, p. 187.
31 Ibid.
32 Ibid., p. 188.
33 Ibid.
34 See the line later in the poem: 'O Mrs Balaam if you want a long thirst to quench after a long burden of prophecy – go to the Zone, you won't be troubled by the sweet influence in the Zone.' Jones, *The Roman Quarry*, p. 209. Jones takes the phrase 'sweet influence' from Job 38:31 in the King James Version: 'Canst thou bind the sweet influences of Pleiades, or loose the bands of Orion?'
35 Jones, *The Roman Quarry*, p. 188.
36 Ibid., p. 208.
37 David Jones, 'A Note on Mr. Berenson's Views', in David Jones, *Epoch and Artist*, ed. Harman Grisewood (London: Faber & Faber, 1959), p. 277. For a fuller discussion of this essay, see Thomas Berenato, 'David Jones and the Influence of Analogy', in *David Jones: A Christian Modernist?*, ed. Jamie Callison, Paul S. Fiddes, Anna Johnson and Erik Tonning (Boston: Brill, 2018), pp. 209–23.
38 Jones, *The Roman Quarry*, p. 188.
39 Ibid.
40 Ibid., p. 189.
41 Ibid.
42 Ibid., p. 188.
43 David Jones, 'Art in Relation to War', in David Jones, *The Dying Gaul and Other Writings*, ed. with an introduction by Harman Grisewood (London: Faber & Faber, 1978), p. 140.
44 Jones, *In Parenthesis*, p. 28.
45 Jones, *The Roman Quarry*, p. 189.
46 Ibid., p. 204.
47 David Jones, 'The Myth of Arthur', in *Epoch and Artist*, p. 243. Jones quotes John 18:9 (KJV).
48 Jones, *The Roman Quarry*, p. 189.
49 Ibid.
50 Ibid.
51 Walter Benjamin, 'Goethe's Elective Affinities', in *SW* I, p. 343; and Walter Benjamin, 'Goethes Wahlverwandtschaften', in *Gesammelte Schriften*, ed. Rolf Tiedemann and Hermann Schweppenhäuser (Frankfurt am Main: Suhrkamp, 1972–91), I.1, p. 184. This edition hereafter cited as *GS*.
52 Jones, *The Roman Quarry*, p. 189.
53 Walter Benjamin, 'Goethe's Elective Affinities', in *SW* I, p. 342; *GS* I.1, p. 184. See Matthew 19:21 and Luke 18:22.
54 Walter Benjamin, 'Goethe's Elective Affinities', in *SW* I, pp. 287, 343; *GS* I.1, p. 184. On 'Vergebung' see 'Die Bedeutung der Zeit in der moralischen Welt', in Walter Benjamin, *GS* VI, p. 98.
55 Walter Benjamin, 'Goethe's Elective Affinities', in *SW* I, 343; *GS* I.1, p. 184.
56 Jones, *The Roman Quarry*, p. 189.

57 See Blissett, *The Long Conversation*, p. 93.
58 Walter Benjamin, 'Goethe's Elective Affinities', in *SW* I, p. 342; *GS* I.1, p. 184.
59 Jones, *The Roman Quarry*, p. 191. On Jones and the doctrine of Original Sin, see Thomas Berenato, 'David Jones and the Ancient Mariner', *Religion & Literature* 49/1 (2018), pp. 131–40.
60 David Jones, 'Preface by the Author', in *Epoch and Artist*, p. 14.
61 Jones, *The Roman Quarry*, p. 190.
62 Ibid., pp. 191–2.
63 Jones, *The Roman Quarry*, p. 193. On the sarcasm of this passage, see Neil Corcoran, 'Spilled Bitterness: *In Parenthesis* in History', in *David Jones: Man and Poet*, ed. John Matthias (Orono, ME: National Poetry Foundation, University of Maine, 1989), pp. 209–25.
64 Jones, *The Roman Quarry*, p. 193. On Jones's reception of the *Henriad*, see Adrian Poole, 'The Disciplines of War, Memory, and Writing: Shakespeare's *Henry V* and David Jones's *In Parenthesis*', *Critical Survey* 22/2 (2010), pp. 91–104.
65 Walter Benjamin, discussing Kafka, in a letter of 12 June 1938 to Gershom Scholem, in *C*, p. 225. See also Benjamin's letter to Scholem of 11 August 1934, *C*, p. 135.
66 Dilworth, *David Jones in the Great War*, 161; see also *A History of the 38th (Welsh) Division, by the G.S.O.'s I of the Division*, ed. Joseph Ernest Munby (London: Hugh Rees, 1920), p. 25. Jones heavily annotated his copy of this book, which he autographed in July 1929. See item 295 of Jones's personal library in the National Library of Wales.
67 LR 7-1 (7), pp. 25, 27; Jones, *The Roman Quarry*, p. 199.
68 Ibid., p. 198.
69 Ibid., p. 199.
70 Ibid., p. 193.
71 David Jones Papers, John J. Burns Library, Boston College, MS 1986-1, Box 3, Folder 1, p. 8 of 9.
72 Jones, *The Roman Quarry*, p. 199.
73 Ibid.
74 Ibid., p. 200.
75 Ibid., p. 201.
76 Walter Benjamin, letter of 12 June 1938 to Gershom Scholem, in *C*, p. 224.
77 Walter Benjamin, letter of 12 June 1938 to Gershom Scholem, in *C*, p. 224.
78 Jones, *The Roman Quarry*, p. 201.
79 Ibid., p. 192.
80 Ibid., pp. 199, 201.
81 Ibid., p. 203.
82 Ibid., p. 201.
83 Ibid., p. 200.
84 Rebecca Comay, *Mourning Sickness: Hegel and the French Revolution* (Stanford, CA: Stanford University Press, 2010), p. 80.
85 See Thomas Dilworth's biography, *David Jones: Engraver, Soldier, Painter, Poet* (Berkeley, CA: Counterpoint, 2017), p. 350.
86 Jones, *The Anathemata*, pp. 14, 20.
87 David Jones, *The Sleeping Lord and Other Fragments* (London: Faber & Faber, 2017), p. 103. Faber first published this book in 1974.
88 Jones, *The Sleeping Lord*, p. 104.

89 Neil Corcoran, 'The Man Who Wrote the Book: Some Recent Work on David Jones', *PN Review* 37/4 (March–April 1981), p. 64.
90 Jones, *The Sleeping Lord*, p. 102.
91 LR 7-1 (6), pp. 9 of 15.
92 Jones, *The Sleeping Lord*, p. 104.
93 W. G. Sebald, *The Emergence of Memory: Conversations with W. G. Sebald*, ed. Lynn Sharon Schwartz (New York: Seven Stories Press, 2010), p. 41. Sebald is speaking of the function of the photographs in his books: 'possibly that of arresting time', p. 41.
94 See Elizabeth F. Judge, 'Notes on the Outside: David Jones, "Unshared Backgrounds," and (the Absence of) Canonicity', *ELH*, 68/1 (Spring 2001), pp. 179–213.
95 Jones, *The Anathemata*, p. 43.
96 LR 7-1 (16), p. 13 of 17; p. 17 of 17 bears the date 26 July 1971. This is a manuscript inscription on a typescript dating to the 1940s.
97 Jones, *The Roman Quarry*, p. 200, editors' footnote 3; *Genesis*, 2nd ed., ed. and trans. E. A. Speiser (Garden City, NY: The Anchor Bible, 1964), p. 105.
98 Jones, *The Anathemata*, p. 33.
99 Ibid., p. 200.
100 Ibid., p. 200; see the commentary on the Letter to the Hebrews in *The Jewish Annotated New Testament*, 2nd ed., ed. Amy-Jill Levine and Marc Zvi Brettler (New York: Oxford University Press, 2017), pp. 471, 473.
101 Jones, *The Roman Quarry*, p. 201; Jones, *The Sleeping Lord*, p. 110; Jones, *David Jones's* The Grail Mass *and Other Works*, p. 150, Jones's footnote 1.
102 David Jones Papers, National Library of Wales, LS 9-2, p. 1 of 32.
103 Jones, *The Sleeping Lord*, p. 108.
104 Jones, *The Anathemata*, p. 35.
105 Ibid., pp. 35–6.
106 *Latin-English Booklet Missal for Praying the Traditional Mass*, 4th ed., twelfth printing (Chicago: Coalition in Support of Ecclesia Dei, February 2015), p. 36.
107 Rowan Williams, foreword to Jones, *David Jones on Religion, Politics, and Culture: Unpublished Prose*, p. xvii.
108 See Walter Benjamin, 'On the Image of Proust' (June–July 1929, revised 1934), trans. Harry Zohn, in *Walter Benjamin: Selected Writings, Volume 2, Part 1: 1927–1930*, ed. Michael W. Jennings, Howard Eiland and Gary Smith (Cambridge, MA, and London: The Belknap Press of Harvard University Press, 1999), p. 238: 'For the important thing to the remembering author is not what he experienced, but the weaving of his memory, the Penelope work of recollection [*Eingedenken*]. Or should one call it, rather, a Penelope work of forgetting?'
109 See Sacha Stern, *Calendar and Community: A History of the Jewish Calendar, 2nd Century BCE to 10th Century CE* (New York: Oxford University Press, 2001), especially chapter 2, 'The Intercalation', pp. 47–97.
110 Jones, *The Sleeping Lord*, p. 109.
111 Jones, *Dai Greatcoat*, p. 76.
112 Ibid.
113 Jones, *The Roman Quarry*, p. 209.
114 Ibid. See Walter Benjamin, *The Arcades Project*, trans. Howard Eiland and Kevin McLaughlin (Cambridge, MA, and London: The Belknap Press of Harvard University Press, 1999), entry N8,1, p. 471, which begins, 'On the question of the incompleteness of history … ' and ends: ' … history is not simply a science but also and not least a

form of remembrance [*Eingedenken*]. What science has "determined," remembrance can modify. Such mindfulness can make the incomplete (happiness) into something complete, and the complete (suffering) into something incomplete. That is theology; but in remembrance we have an experience that forbids us to conceive of history as fundamentally atheological, little as it may be granted to us to try to write it with immediately theological concepts.' On happiness, see also Walter Benjamin, 'Theological-Political Fragment', in *Walter Benjamin: Selected Writings, Volume 3: 1935–1938*, ed. Howard Eiland and Michael W. Jennings, trans. Edmund Jephcott (Cambridge, MA, and London: The Belknap Press of Harvard University Press, 2002), pp. 305–6, and Peter Fenves's commentary, 'Completion Instead of Revelation: Toward the "Theological-Political Fragment"', in *Walter Benjamin and Theology*, ed. Colby Dickinson and Stéphane Symons (New York: Fordham University Press, 2016), pp. 56–74.

115 Jones, *The Roman Quarry*, p. 201.

116 Ibid.; see Luke 3:3.

117 Georges Bataille, *Guilty*, ed. and trans. Stuart Kendall (Albany, NY: State University of New York Press, 2011), p. 111; Georges Bataille, *Œuvres Complètes*, tome V (Paris: Gallimard, 1973), p. 369; Alex Dubilet, *The Self-Emptying Subject: Kenosis and Immanence, Medieval to Modern* (New York: Fordham University Press, 2018), p. 230, note 41.

118 On this distinction see Giorgio Agamben, *The Time That Remains*, trans. Patricia Dailey (Stanford, CA: Stanford University Press, 2005), p. 62, and Dubilet, *The Self-Emptying Subject*, p. 234, note 78.

119 Jones, *The Roman Quarry*, p. 201.

120 Jones, *Dai Greatcoat*, p. 137.

121 Ibid.

122 Jones, *Dai Greatcoat*, p. 138.

123 Dubilet, *The Self-Emptying Subject*, p. 171.

124 Jones, *The Roman Quarry*, p. 206.

125 Ibid.

126 Ibid., p. 207; and Jones, *The Anathemata*, p. 34, note 1.

127 Ibid., pp. 211, 204–5.

128 Jones, *In Parenthesis*, p. 185.

129 Ibid.

130 Jones, *The Roman Quarry*, p. 206.

131 David Jones Papers, John J. Burns Library, Boston College, MS 1986-1, Box 3, Folder 1, p. 6 of 9.

132 See Jeremy Hooker, 'Mametz Wood: The photographs of Aled Rhys Hughes', in *Mametz*, ed. Aled Rhys Hughes (Bridgend: Seren, 2016), pp. 88–9; David Jones Papers, John J. Burns Library, Boston College, MS 1986-1, box 3, folder 1, pp. 2 and 6 of 9; Jones, *The Roman Quarry*, p. 209.

133 Jones, *The Roman Quarry*, p. 207.

134 Jones, *In Parenthesis*, p. ix.

135 David Jones Papers, John J. Burns Library, Boston College, MS 1986-1, Box 3, Folder 1, p. 7 of 9; Dilworth, *David Jones in the Great War*, p. 52; Jones, *The Roman Quarry*, p. 211; Jones, *In Parenthesis*, p. ix.

136 See Jones, *The Anathemata*, p. 14; cf. the David Jones Papers at the John J. Burns Library, Boston College, MS 1986-1, Box 3, Folder 1, p. 4 of 9; see also C. S. Lewis's

commentary on Charles Williams's Arthurian poetry in Charles Williams, *Arthurian Torso: Containing the Posthumous Fragment of* The Figure of Arthur (London: Oxford University Press, 1948), p. 189: 'An example of difficulties arising from Unshared Background would be *The Waste Land*.'

137 Jones, *In Parenthesis*, p. 185.

138 David Jones Papers, John J. Burns Library, Boston College, MS 1986-1, Box 3, Folder 1, p. 7 of 9. See Kathleen Henderson Staudt's brief commentary in her *At the Turn of a Civilization: David Jones and Modern Poetics* (Ann Arbor: University of Michigan Press, 1994), pp. 100–1.

139 Jones, *The Roman Quarry*, p. 210.

140 Ibid., p. 209.

141 Ibid., pp. 202, 209.

142 David Jones Papers, John J. Burns Library, Boston College, MS 1986-1, Box 3, Folder 1, pp. 4–5.

143 Jones, *The Roman Quarry*, pp. 210, 211. One of the travailed-for 'surfaces' is that of the page on which the poem is to be printed. A draft of a 1966 letter to Eric Walter White, one of the first editors of 'A, a, a, DOMINE DEUS', the short stand-alone lyric that Jones fashioned from the end of his *Balaam's Ass* manuscript and would later publish as the first poem in *The Sleeping Lord* sequence, shows the author taking extraordinary pains to ensure that his intended blocking of its prose and verse elements is clear to the typesetter. See David Jones Papers, National Library of Wales, LS 2-1. The letter as Jones sent it, dated 3 November 1966, is among the Eric Walter White Papers at the Harry Ransom Center, University of Texas at Austin.

9

Modernist Studies and the Networking of Digital Collections: Lessons from the Social Sciences

Archie Henderson

If we go online to search the phrase 'Pound Archive', we find out that it refers almost exclusively to the Ezra Pound Archive in the Collection of American Literature at the Beinecke Library, Yale University, with an occasional reference to the Pound collection at the Harry Ransom Humanities Research Center, the University of Texas at Austin.[1] The collection at the Beinecke has been informally called the 'Pound Archive' ever since press coverage of its acquisition by the library in 1973.[2] If finding aids are any indication, however, the Beinecke collection is officially the Ezra Pound Papers, and the UT collection is designated the Ezra Pound Collection.[3] So neither collection, considered individually or collectively, can be considered the 'Pound Archive'. In fact, as Mark Byron writes,

> Pound left a formidable archive of literary documents, letters, executive correspondence with literary journals, social and political essays, and swathes of notes taken from an extensive array of sources across very many fields. Much of this archive is housed in the Beinecke Rare Book and Manuscript Library at Yale University, with important holdings in other locations such as the Lilly Library at Indiana University, the Harry Ransom Humanities Research Center at the University of Texas at Austin, and Schloss Brunnenburg – the home of Pound's daughter, Mary de Rachewiltz, and her family.[4]

Looking at correspondence alone, the exact number of letters written by Pound is unknown, but it is estimated to run into the hundreds of thousands.[5]

The 'Pound Archive' may more broadly be considered a subset of the 'modernist archive', which, like the Pound Archive itself, is scattered across the globe. As Amy Hildreth Chen has written, 'The modernist archive does not live in one collection at one repository, such as a single university special collections department or one pivotal private library. Rather, the modernist archive is a term used to conceptualize a networked set of collections across many repositories in the United States or abroad.'[6] An author's archive needs to be seen, likewise, not as a self-contained collection or collections of documents at one or at most a handful of libraries, but as a 'virtual' archive distributed across many discrete locations. As my recent guide to archives of the right-wing and the extreme right makes clear, materials by or about modernist authors frequently extend across dozens or, in some cases, hundreds of archives and collections.[7]

The global networking of the scattered resources – that is, the cross-linking of artefacts so as to be able to search and analyse them all at one time – is an ideal rather than an actuality as applied to any single modernist author's archive. To the extent that networking may be said to have been accomplished, it has been through two primary means: the growth, in terms of both quantity and detail, of the electronic finding aid, on the one hand, and on the other, the rise of digital collections, both freely accessible and commercial. As for electronic finding aids, the rapid proliferation on the internet of readily accessible, detailed finding aids marks an 'archival turn' that will spur the examination of modernist authors in unprecedented (and unforeseen) ways. As regards digital collections, Finn Fordham writes that 'archives and "the archive" are under increased scrutiny not only because of historical and materialist turns, but also because of the technological revolution which is currently under way and gathering momentum through the digitization of knowledge and of archives in particular'.[8] Digital collections which aggregate smaller collections are also widely available as both open-source and proprietary databases.[9]

Suzanne Marchand has defined an 'archive' as 'a collection of data brought together to resist its being lost to memory'.[10] Collective memory will naturally decay over time as public attention turns to new or different objects. Some cultural artefacts will remain in the collective memory longer than others. It has been argued, for example, that 'biographies remain in our communicative memory the longest (20–30 years) and music the shortest (about 5.6 years)'.[11] What is of concern, however, is the evidence that public attention to cultural artefacts across the board shows a constant decline.[12] A team of authors who conducted a quantitative analysis of culture using millions of digitized books has even commented, 'We are forgetting our past faster with each passing year'.[13]

This trend might be attributed to various causes. The fact that our collective memories are getting shorter relates, in part, to the fact that we live in an era when the collective attention span is collapsing. Distraction and diversion have replaced concentration in all aspects of daily life. In the same way that mobile phones store the telephone numbers of our family and friends that we used to memorize, archives have become, to a greater degree than ever, the repositories of our collective memories. At the same time, the distractions that produce the short cultural attention span mean that there is not enough time to explore the archives where the memories reside – not enough time to locate them, to visit them, to study what is there. Compounding the problem of time, or the lack of it, is the ever-increasing volume and availability of material. In terms of looking for the 'archival needle-in-the-haystack', the haystack gets bigger, but the needle stays the same size. As more finding aids and digital projects go online, there is more to sort through to find the essential and to weed out the non-essential, and less time in which to do it.

If the archive is 'a collection of data brought together to resist its being lost to memory', a 'meta-archive' adds a further layer of resistance. The meta-archive, or what Philipp Rößler calls the 'deep archive', collects the collections into a more unified, if virtual, whole. For Rößler, the 'deep archive' is

> an imagined totality, imagined like 'the canon', consisting of all those documents which are archived somewhere and are accessible in principle, but are generally not so de facto because they are invisible to the currently common research search strategies and/or access to them requires expenditure on a deterrent scale. Thus deep archive documents are characterized precisely by not being visible online. As in the case of the deep web, there is an immeasurable amount of documents which remain hidden for our common search strategies. More often than not it is a matter of coincidence, or Serendipity, if a document of the deep archive is taken note of after all.[14]

With the idea of creating such a 'deep archive', the late musicologist Sabra Statham envisioned an online database for the American composer George Antheil, who was Ezra Pound's protégé for a time in the 1920s. This database would, in her words,

> effectively "collect" dispersed archives into one virtual space where they can be accessed individually or mined for source information, revealing relationships and networks from the past that would otherwise go uncovered.[15]

My *Conservatism, the Right Wing and the Far Right: A Guide to Archives* bears the subtitle 'A Guide to Archives', with 'archives' bearing the primary meaning of discrete repositories of physical or electronic documents or objects. The book, however, may also be seen as a guide to the meta-archive or deep archive of the 'imagined totality' or 'one virtual space' of all archival materials pertaining to the political right. Its primary objective is to cut a path through the thicket of the internet by facilitating the use of archives in its areas of interest: conservatism, the right wing and the extreme right. The book pulls together relevant archival materials from online finding aids for collections scattered across the globe into a fully indexed master list. In so doing, it seeks, in effect, to network the finding aids, to be a 'finding aid of finding aids'. All mentions of a person, topic or organization can be viewed in an instant in the index.

Turning to the field of modernist literature, the same technique could be applied to individual authors, or to modernism as a whole, to create a comparable finding aid of finding aids. For a given topic – whether in the social sciences, the humanities or otherwise – the universe of existing finding aids is an answer looking for a question. It is a form of crowdsourcing or community sourcing where the crowd – in this case, the archivists and librarians who write the finding aids – has already answered a question not yet asked. The question is: What can

I learn about such and such a topic or field from this archive and from all other archives that link with it in some way? To query the finding aids requires, first, that they be connected like a massive database. Secondly, to be searched, databases need an interface. There is no online website that does a completely satisfactory job of meeting either of these requirements.[16] My book was designed to fulfill both purposes for its topic in a nondigital way. The model of the book is that archives (more than 4000 are listed) are arranged alphabetically by name. For each archive, the location, description, published references to the archive, and links to finding aids or other information pertaining to the archive are given. The description may go all the way down to the level of an individual item (or occasionally even beyond, by describing the contents of that item). As an example of a 'deep' description, the entry may make mention of a book, whose contents may be further described by me, with links from individual items within that description to electronic copies of the items in question, which may not be present in the original archive at all. The main body of the two-part index is arranged alphabetically by name or topic and, within each entry, by the numbers assigned to the individual archives containing material on that name or topic. A separate part of the index lists all repositories and their holdings by geographical location. The index is, in essence, the interface to the database of the main text.

Although by no means a book on modernism, my book does include listings for a number of modernist authors who fit within the parameters of its subject matter. Examples include T. S. Eliot and Ezra Pound, who are represented in the index with 125 and 180 entry numbers, respectively. These numbers represent the number of archival collections containing material pertaining to the authors. A complete global list of archival holdings for Eliot and Pound would be considerably longer. Taking into account, however, that these are not intended to be comprehensive lists for Eliot and Pound, but merely reflective of the extent to which materials relating to these authors can be considered right-wing in nature or are found in collections with significant right-wing-related materials, it is still a remarkably long listing. Unquestionably, there is much yet unexplored in the archives, considered in the broadest sense, for these authors as well as other modernist writers.

Linking archival holdings of individual authors is but one kind of cross-linking, or 'networking', in the field of Modernist Studies. Another kind, and one that could benefit equally from both online finding aids and digital collections, is the analysis of periodicals by topics. This has already been done in social studies and, in particular, in the area of the right wing and the extreme right. One of the earliest listings of right-wing periodicals is *The first national directory of 'Rightist' groups, publications and some individuals in the United States (and some foreign countries)* (3rd ed. San Francisco: Liberty and Property, 1957).[17] True to its name, many of the entries are devoted to publications, including periodicals of the political right, which, like the organizational listings, are classified where possible according to the topics of concern to the periodicals. The topical classification system is based on a 'Key to Letter and Other Symbol Designations' at the front of the pamphlet. The corresponding designations are given parenthetically at the end of many entries for such topics (using the directory's own terminology) as states' rights, Negro nationalist (back-to-Africa or anti-NAACP), anti-communist, anti-fluoridation, anti-internationalist, Libertarian, religious, anti-socialist, right to work, and so on. Some periodicals have multiple designations representing various parts of the periodical's programme or philosophy. As the entries also contain addresses for the periodicals, it would be possible to map out the periodicals according to the place of publication (city, state and in some cases country) and the topics addressed.

There is also Christian Davenport's online list of American extreme right organizations, 1970–83, available online in a spreadsheet format.[18] While most of the listings are for organizations, there is a grouping for periodicals, with complete addresses and codes that correspond to the orientation of the periodicals (Anti-Abortion, Anti-Communist, Conservative, Free Market, Patriotic and so on). The information in the spreadsheet is taken from Laird Wilcox, *Guide to the American Right: Directory and Bibliography* (1991).[19]

Topical classification systems have been developed not only for periodical listings in books, but also for several finding aids for large collections of right-wing periodicals. At least three archival collections consist in whole or part of periodical issues whose finding aids are keyed with subject categories. One example is the well-known Right Wing Collection of the University of Iowa Libraries, which is a microfilm collection based on several related collections at various libraries including the University of Iowa.[20] Subject 'types' assigned to the periodicals include Anglo-Israelite, Anti-Black, Anti-Communist, Anti-fluoridation, Anti-Semitic, Christian-Fundamentalist, Conservative and Libertarian. A second example is the Southern Poverty Law Center Intelligence Project Collection at Duke.[21] 'Anti' tags include anti-Catholic literature, anti-Communist literature, anti-homosexual literature, anti-immigrant literature and anti-Semitic literature; other tags are white supremacist literature, survivalist literature, and so forth. A third example is the Russell G. Benedict Collection of political ephemera at Cal State Fullerton, whose tags include abortion, anti-Semitism, eugenics, fascism and the Ku Klux Klan.[22]

In *The Textual Condition* (1991), his attempt 'to sketch a materialist hermeneutics', Jerome J. McGann describes 'the text as a laced network of linguistic and bibliographical codes'.[23] This is a lesson that, as mentioned above, has been learned in the analysis of periodicals in at least some of the social sciences. The notion of 'bibliographical codes' in social science periodicals applies equally well to literary periodicals and is only beginning to be explored as part of the larger subject of periodical studies. In the view of Sean Latham and Robert Scholes, progress in this area of study 'is being driven by the cultural turn in departments of language and literature, by the development of digital archives that allow for such studies on a broader scale than ever before, and by what the producers of the Spectator Project have called "the special capabilities of the digital environment" (Center)'.[24]

Although the analysis of bibliographical codes in literary digital archives is still in its relative infancy, some preliminary efforts have been undertaken. For example, Amardeep Singh has created a network visualization of semantic tags assigned to the poems in Ezra Pound's early volume *Personae* (1909). In his visualization of the book, individual poems are represented by dots color-coded in light orange, and the tags are represented by dots color-coded in pink. Tags include Intertextual, Love, Medieval, Nature, Poetry, Religion, Space, and Time. Paths connect the poems to their tags. Clicking on a poem will pull up a hypertext version of the poem; clicking on a tag will pull up a list of poems to which that tag is assigned.[25]

Modernist correspondence has also been the subject of network analysis. In 2017, a group of four undergraduate students at Hope College in Holland, Michigan, used a digitized copy of *The Letters of Ezra Pound 1907–1941*, edited by D. D. Paige (Faber & Faber, 1951) to construct a nodal network map of seventy-nine of Pound's correspondents.[26] The nodes represent the correspondents; the size of the nodes reflects the number of published letters to that recipient. The Hope College research group concedes that 'one of the shortcomings of this data is that while the network shows who he wrote, it does not reveal anything about the content of the letters'. Another shortcoming, not noted, is that *The Letters of Ezra Pound 1907–1941* contains only a small sample of Pound's vast correspondence and cannot serve as the basis for judging the relative importance to him of the recipients (or his importance to them).

As a second example of correspondence, using the digital 'Calendar' of Willa Cather's letters developed by Andrew Jewell and Janis P. Stout, Gabriel Hankins has created a nodal map to represent her correspondents, with larger nodes for the more frequent addressees. Hankins notes 'the dominance of her relationship to her editor at Houghton Mifflin, Ferris Greenslet, and the secondary prominence of a range of female writers and friends. Even more telling are the *hapax graphomena*, the cloud of once-written correspondents that immediately surrounds Cather in the visualization, indicating her attention to a wide public audience'.[27] The map contains information about the sender, recipient and relative frequency of epistolary communication; however, only twenty-two recipients are named. The 'Calendar' on which the map is based has additional search fields for repositories holding original letters, works and characters created by Cather, people referenced in the letters, and other names and titles (places, books, organizations, etc.).[28] A more complex visualization using these fields and others as tags would further the process of 'reconstructing complex networks of sociality and of epistolary cultures'.[29]

In my final example of correspondence, what might be called a 'social network map' in Modernist Studies is the social network map of H.D. and her correspondents. Celena E. Kusch has created a node map of the people in H.D.'s archives of correspondence at the Beinecke. Unlike the approaches taken in the above-cited Pound and Cather examples, Kusch's approach is to sort the 213 individual correspondents in H.D.'s archival records 'in nodes based upon the people who introduced H.D. to members of the wider network. Major nodes are anchored by Frances Gregg Wilkinson, Ezra Pound, Richard Aldington, Bryher, Edith Sitwell, Sylvia Dobson, and Norman Holmes Pearson.'[30] Viewing the full map requires downloading the VUE (Visual Understanding Environment) application, developed by Tufts University, which is used to open a downloadable file called HDCorrespondenceNodes.vue. The node map which opens in VUE can be saved as an HTML file, a PDF or several other formats. The instructions in the map are to 'click any name to expand and explore further connections. Contacts are nested under the people who introduced H.D. to them. Click the arrow pointing up in the map or at the bottom of the screen to return to H.D.'

Modernist periodicals have also attracted network analysis. One such approach to the analysis of modernist periodicals is to focus on the subject matter of the periodicals themselves, considered in isolation from their editorial or cultural contexts. Reporting on a class analysis of the September 1918 issue of the *Little Review*, Jeffrey Drouin remarks that he and his students assigned as topic tags Aesthetics, Ageing, Art, Death, Dissolution, Fiction, Gender, Greatness, Immortality, Irony, Labor, Literature, Mediocrity, Memorial, Music, Poetics, Poetry, Praise, Religion, Women, World War and Writing.[31] Topic tags, of course, represent only one of many periodical codes that could be analysed. A second possible approach to the analysis of modernist periodicals is to view the contributors or editors associated with literary magazines as forming their own network. In analysing the field of 'high modernism as network', Richard Jean So and Hoyt Long have created a network visualization of thirty-five major American poets, arranged according to which US-based periodicals they published in between 1917 and 1918. The operating assumption was that 'publication in a specific periodical can be taken as a measure of a poet's objective relation to other poets publishing in that periodical for a given time span'.[32] In the network visualization, poets and journals are represented by nodes or clusters, and the fact of publication in a journal forms the lines or edges linking one type of node to another.[33] The thicknesses of the lines and the sizes of the nodes are adjusted to indicate the relative weight of each. The result is a network visualization 'which suggests that the more a subset of poets has had their work published in a shared subset of periodicals, the closer they should appear in the represented network and vice versa'.[34] This method could be extended beyond merely a list of contributors to show multifaceted connections among the journals based on other 'codes' (some of which are listed below).

For more sophisticated querying of a network visualization, So and Long propose the use of the concepts of 'brokerage' and its opposite, 'closure', which are terms borrowed from sociology and organizational studies.[35] In sociology, 'brokerage facilitates the flow of ideas and the creation of new ones through the meeting of disparate opinions and worldviews'.[36] According to So and Long, 'brokers' are mediators who link nodes that otherwise might remain 'disparate and unrelated'.[37] Ezra Pound comes to mind as a 'literary broker' *par excellence* if the field of poets and periodicals is extended beyond the United States. Pound was described by one of his correspondents as a 'maker of connections'.[38] A visual analysis of Pound's role as a mediator among periodical nodes could reinforce and dramatize the prevailing New Modernist Studies view of him as less a poet and more 'an ideologue, a facilitator and an influencer – always in correlation with his peers, his time, and his environment'.[39] For the opposite concept, closure in poetic networks – that is, 'the tightening of circles of like-minded writers' – So and Long point to the cohesiveness of a manifesto-based literary movement.[40] Cohesiveness may be temporary or fleeting. To illustrate the fluidity of the movement from 'closure' to 'brokerage', So and Long cite the example of the Fugitives, who 'shortly after the peak of their group's cohesion in 1925 … quickly disperse to disseminate their ideas to a broader group'.[41] There is no reason, then, that a poet could not take on both roles at different times or even at the same time but under different circumstances.

A third possible approach to the analysis of modernist periodicals is to study the cultural network of which a periodical is a part. This is, in fact, one of the most important periodical codes. The cultural network consists of all of the periodicals with which a given periodical is linked in some manner. Sean Latham and Robert Scholes write that

> Anyone who studies periodicals soon discovers that they are frequently in dialogue with one another …. Periodicals thus create and occupy typically complex and often unstable positions in sometimes collaborative and sometimes competitive cultural networks. Uncovering these sorts of connections – which are inevitably lost in the process of anthologization – adds new layers of density both to magazines themselves and to the work of individual contributors.[42]

The uncovering of the periodical nodes in the cultural network, which are not as obvious as the names of contributors or editors, may reveal larger issues of culture and identity that tie the periodicals together or around which they cluster. For example, T. S. Eliot's journal *The Criterion*

> was part of a network of European periodicals with a shared perception of European culture and European identity. Examples of other reviews in the *Criterion* network were the *Nouvelle Revue Française* from France, *La Fiera Letteraria* and *Il Convegno* from Italy, the *Revista de Occidente* from Spain (edited by José Ortega y Gasset), and *Die Neue Rundschau*, the *Europäische Revue*, and the *Neue deutsche Beiträge* (edited by Hugo von Hofmannsthal) from Germany.[43]

British Poetry Magazines 1914–2000: A History and Bibliography of 'Little Magazines', compiled by David Miller and Richard Price (2006), is the only book to date which, to my knowledge, indexes twentieth-century literary magazines by geographical location, subject, name and title.[44] 'Names' are defined as 'the names of authors, artists, editors, publishers and associated organisations, including poetry workshops and publishers associated with little magazines'.[45] The magazines are divided into five chapters, each representing a somewhat arbitrary interval of time: 1914–39, 1940–9, 1950–9, 1960–75, 1976–2000.[46] Among the periodicals represented in the first chapter is entry A15 for *Blast: Review of the Great English Vortex*, edited by Wyndham Lewis (London: John Lane, The Bodley Head, volume

1 (20 June 1914)–volume 2 (July 1915)).[47] *Blast* is in fact the periodical which inaugurates the period with which the book opens.[48] For this example, the place of publication in the Geographical Index is London. In the separate Subject Index, subjects are visual poetry and Vorticism. Names in the Name Index are Seamus Cooney, Paul Edwards, T. S. Eliot, John Lane, Wyndham Lewis, Bradford Morrow and Ezra Pound. Obviously, neither the list of subjects nor that of names strives for completeness – Drouin's sample topical analysis of the *Little Review* vastly exceeds *British Poetry Magazines 1914–2000* in scope – but the lists adequately cover the contents of the rather brief description allocated to the periodical in the main body of the book.

Further development in the analysis of bibliographical codes – which will allow for more extensive coverage of periodical contents – requires digitization of periodical runs and the creation of tags to code and analyse them. The digitization process is well under way for titles out of copyright, with new titles falling out of copyright every year:[49]

> The diversity of these resources reveals that one of the key elements for the creation of periodical studies is already falling into place: the assembly and dissemination of a core set of objects. Now that they are readily accessible, we are prepared to begin work on a second essential element for this field: the creation of typological descriptions and scholarly methodologies.[50]

Precision of description can be increased not only by greater completeness of subjects and names, but also by the addition of tags to describe other latent bibliographic codes in the periodicals. As Peter Brooker and Andrew Thacker write,

> We can also make McGann's bibliographic codes more precise by discussing a particular subset, the periodical codes at play in any magazine, analysing a whole range of features including page layout, typefaces, price, size of volume (not all 'little' magazines are little in size), periodicity of publication (weekly, monthly, quarterly, irregular), use of illustrations (colour or monochrome, the forms of reproductive technology employed), use and placement of advertisements, quality of paper and binding, networks of distribution and sales, modes of financial support, payment practices towards contributors, editorial arrangements, or the type of material published (poetry, reviews, manifestos, editorials, illustrations, social and political comment, etc.). We can also distinguish between periodical codes internal to the design of a magazine (paper, typeface, layout, etc.) and those that constitute its external relations (distribution in a bookshop, support from patrons).[51]

Networking-related codes that could be added to the analysis of a publication include the publisher or publishers (they sometimes changed); the journal's organizational affiliation (if any); the names of, and extent of support from, individual or institutional patrons or benefactors; references made to other periodicals (by way of reviews; mutual exchanges of journals, news notes or announcements; mutual advertisements or publicity;[52] the reprinting of another journal's material or excerpts from it or descriptions of its contents; mentions in contributor's notes; and a sharing or overlapping of publishers, editors, patrons, financial supporters, or grant-making institutions, etc.); type of publication (newsletter, bulletin, one-off manifesto-like production, house organ, glossy magazine, etc.); range of years of publication; thematic concerns, subject matter and ideological or political positions; changes of subject matter or editorial policy over time; and changes in the size or makeup of the audience across space or time. While much of this information can be gleaned from an examination of the periodicals themselves, finding aids, participants' memoirs, preserved editorial files and secondary literature might provide additional details not otherwise available.[53]

Besides network visualization by nodes or clusters as described by So and Long, and as exemplified by H.D.'s network of social acquaintances, another kind of visualization – one that might be more appropriate to far-flung networks such as the *Criterion* network – is geographical mapping of authors and periodicals. This kind of mapping in effect assigns geographical coordinates to certain nodes and clusters. With a mapping programme and a more refined and detailed topical classification system, an author's connections with cities, his or her connections with various magazines, and the magazines' connections with one another, could be laid out for view. Interactive maps could indicate some of the changes through time in subject matter, format and audience. In the case of right-wing periodicals, such geographical and topical analysis and mapping have already been carried out for the Southern Poverty Law Center Intelligence Project Collection at Duke University. In the SPLC example, the cities of publication for the extremist literature in the collection are represented by green circles on a map of the United States and Canada, showing a concentration of circles along the coasts, in the South, and in the Midwest around Chicago and Detroit.[54] Hovering the mouse over a circle will reveal a box containing the number of titles in that city, the location, the genre, associated names (usually the editor or publisher), and a link to the record for the periodical (if there is only one in the city). In the database below the map, highlighting the names of all cities and then hovering over the column will reveal a grid icon; clicking the icon will open up a link to 'View Data', from which the data for all periodicals in spreadsheet format is downloadable as a text file. The spreadsheet contains columns for City, Country, State, ATTR(Assoc Names), ATTR(Genre), ATTR(Link), ATTR(Title), CNTD(System number), Latitude (generated) and Longitude (generated).

For the Modernist Journals Project, Mark Gaipa has created a series of maps showing where contributors to *Poetry* and *The Little Review* lived during the time of their contributions.[55] For example, the map 'Where "Poetry" Contributors Lived, 1912–1922' marks geographical locations with red pins. 'The number in each red circle indicates the number of contributors at that location (while red pins without numbers indicate that only one contributor came from that location). The names of individual contributors and the number of their contributions to the magazine can be found by clicking on each pin and then scrolling through the multiple contributors at that location.'[56] To date, there does not seem to be a mapping project for individuals associated with modernist periodicals along the lines of the Chicago Modernism project described above. However, a map of Ezra Pound's 'connectedness', drawing on his network of periodicals viewed geographically, has been envisioned by Gabriel Hankins:

> As in my visualization of responses to G. L. Dickinson, a Neatline edition of Scholes and Wulfman's account might allow the reader to see different paths through the archives, presses, and little journals to which Pound contributed. A scholar might narrate the trajectory of Pound's engagement with the magazines through the neighborhoods in London he inhabited, through the extended network of the addresses of editors, or through the lens of proximity, in a question parallel to that of social network mapping: how 'connected' was Pound to London, to the international reviews, to wealthy benefactors? The dense imagined geography of Pound's *Cantos* might well reward a spatial reading of his implied poetic landscape, from 'Cathay' to Malatesta's Italy to John Adams's New England. The dense place-names of *A Draft of XVI Cantos*, for example, narrate a voyage from Greece to Italy to Confucian China and Revolutionary Russia, in a series of shifting, interpenetrating, yet concretely realized locales that invite the reader to reread familiar topography. So too with spatial humanities mapping: rather than mere illustration or compendium, we see these new spatial humanities tools as potential pathways into new and unknown kinds of argument, analysis, and spatial defamiliarization.[57]

Returning to finding aids, another possible approach to modernist archives is to use finding aids to list and index the themes and leading issues, including but by no means limited to the political and esthetic questions that absorbed and preoccupied the modernists, and then link them across finding aids for various authors. How many writers took up a given issue? How did they communicate among themselves on that issue? How did the issues change through time and place? How important were the issues in the context of the culture at large? The issues could then be mapped geographically, temporally, nodally or in a number of other ways.

In summary, the study of networks is getting off the ground in the field of literary modernism as it has in many other fields. This has been made possible by the rapidly expanding availability of online finding aids to archival collections, as well as by the gradual increase of digitized periodical runs (hampered, however, by the slow lifting of copyright restrictions for the early decades of the twentieth century[58]). Networks can take many forms: linked archival holdings for authors or among authors, topical links among poems in a book or among periodicals in a network, and networks of correspondents or social acquaintances of a given author. Visualizations of the data can take the form of graphs or maps. Literary networks are, in a sense, networks of codes. By a sophisticated assignment of codes to authors and periodicals, network analysis can probe the extent and strength of the nodes that form the network, leading to a better understanding of the relative cohesiveness and influence of the network as a whole, along with the relative roles of individual authors and periodicals. Recent applications of network analysis in the social sciences can illuminate the path forward for modernist scholars.

Notes

1 For an example of the latter, see Richard Parker, '"The Most Disliked Periodical in England": Ezra Pound in Ronald Duncan's *Townsman*', in *Revues modernistes, revues engagées*: 1900–1939, ed. Hélène Aji, Céline Mansanti and Benoît Tadié (Rennes: Presses Universitaires de Rennes, 2011), 221–32, https://books.openedition.org/pur/38421?lang=en. Outside the field of literature, 'Pound Archive' may also refer to the Richard W. Pound Olympic Collection, held at McGill University in Montreal.

2 'Yale Acquires Archive of Poet Ezra Pound', *Bridgeport Post*, Bridgeport, Connecticut, 30 September 1973, 14, https://www.newspapers.com/newspage/60786093/.

3 The online finding aids for these collections are at https://archives.yale.edu/repositories/11/resources/1584 and https://norman.hrc.utexas.edu/fasearch/pdf/00110.pdf, respectively.

4 Mark Byron, '[A Cross in the Margin]: Inscription and Erasure in Jacques Derrida and Ezra Pound', in *Understanding Derrida, Understanding Modernism*, ed. Jean-Michel Rabaté (London: Bloomsbury, 2019), 157–77, https://www.academia.edu/39537309/A_Cross_in_the_Margin_Inscription_and_Erasure_in_Jacques_Derrida_and_Ezra_Pound.

5 According to Demetres P. Tryphonopoulos, 'in his lifetime, Pound wrote a total of approximately a quarter of a million letters'. (Demetres P. Tryphonopoulos, 'Letters', in *Ezra Pound in Context*, ed. Ira B. Nadel (New York: Cambridge University Press, 2010), 55.

6 Amy Hildreth Chen, 'Finding the Modernist Archive: Why UX [user experience] Matters', *Modernism/Modernity Print+* 3, Cycle 2, 25 August 2018, https://modernismmodernity.org/forums/posts/finding-modernist-archive.

7 Archie Henderson, *Conservatism, the Right Wing and the Far Right: A Guide to Archives* (Stuttgart: ibidem-Verlag, 2018, 4 vols.)

8 Finn Fordham, 'The Modernist Archive', in *The Oxford Handbook of Modernisms*, ed. Peter Brooker, Andrzej Gąsiorek, Deborah Longworth and Andrew Thacker (Oxford and New York: Oxford University Press, 2010), 45–60.

9 For some examples, see note 51.

10 Suzanne Marchand, 'Ancient History in the Age of Archival Research', in *Science in the Archives: Pasts, Presents, Futures*, ed. Lorraine Daston (Chicago: University of Chicago Press, 2017), 139, as quoted in Eric C. Stoykovich, *Review of Science in the Archives: Pasts, Presents, Futures*, ed. Lorraine Daston (Chicago: University of Chicago Press, 2017), '*RBM: A Journal of Rare Books', Manuscripts, and Cultural Heritage* 18/2 (Fall 2017): 134–6 (at 135), http://rbm.acrl.org/index.php/rbm/article/view/16823/18406 and http://rbm.acrl.org/index.php/rbm/article/view/16823/18413.

11 Cristian Candia, C. Jara Figueroa, Carlos Rodriguez-Sickert, Albert-László Barabási and César A. Hidalgo, 'The Universal Decay of Collective Memory and Attention', *Nature Human Behaviour* 3/1 (January 2019), pp. 82–91, https://static1.

squarespace.com/static/5759bc7886db431d658b7d33/t/5c1129b5c2241b7d0c8d672c/1544628763785/CandiaEtAl_NHB_2018.pdf.

12 Alin Coman, 'Predicting the Decay of Collective Memory', *Nature Human Behaviour* 3/1 (January 2019), pp. 18–19, https://www.nature.com/articles/s41562-018-0480-7.

13 Jean-Baptiste Michel, Yuan Kui Shen, Aviva Presser Aiden, Adrian Veres, Matthew K. Gray, The Google Books Team, Joseph P. Pickett, Dale Hoiberg, Dan Clancy, Peter Norvig, Jon Orwant, Steven Pinker, Martin A. Nowak, and Erez Lieberman Aiden, 'Quantitative Analysis of Culture Using Millions of Digitized Books', *Science* 331/6014 (14 January 2011): 176–82 (at 179), http://www.uvm.edu/pdodds/teaching/courses/2009-08UVM-300/docs/others/2010/michel2010a.pdf and http://www.uvm.edu/pdodds/research/papers/others/2011/michel2011a.pdf.

14 Philipp Rößler, '1924, Introducing "Modernism": The Deep Archive in the Age of WWWisibility' (11 October 2017), 2, https://edoc.hu-berlin.de/handle/18452/19131 and https://edoc.hu-berlin.de/bitstream/handle/18452/19131/1924%20Introducing%20Modernism.pdf?sequence=1.

15 Sabra Statham, 'The George Antheil Digital Edition: Methods and Editorial Techniques', *voiceXchange* 4/1 (Summer 2010): 25–33, https://letterpress.uchicago.edu/index.php/voicexchange/article/download/39/77.

16 The most useful online resources are Social Networks and Archival Context (http://snaccooperative.org) and ArchiveGrid (https://beta.worldcat.org/archivegrid/).

17 *First National Directory of 'Rightist' Groups, Publications, and Some Individuals in the United States (And Some Foreign Countries)*, 2nd–6th ed., published by Liberty and Property (4th ed., http://catalog.hathitrust.org/Record/009629756).

18 Please see: https://radicalinformationproject.weebly.com/uploads/2/6/8/2/26824616/extreme_right_70-83.xls.

19 Laird M. Wilcox, *Guide to the American Right: Directory and Bibliography* (Olathe, KS: Laird Wilcox, 1991). I am grateful to Professor Davenport for details.

20 *The Right Wing Collection of the University of Iowa Libraries 1918–1977: A Guide to the Microfilm Collection* (Glen Rock, NJ: Microfilming Corporation of America, 1977), https://www.roosevelt.nl/sites/zl-roosevelt/files/right_wing_collection_of_the_university_of_iowa.pdf and https://archive.org/download/GuideToRightWingCollectionUnivOfIowa/Guide%20to%20Right-Wing%20Collection-Univ%20of%20Iowa.pdf.

21 Katrina Martin, 'Mapping Alternative and Extremist Literature', 11 March 2015, http://blogs.library.duke.edu/rubenstein/2015/03/11/mapping-alternative-and-extremist-literature/and https://public.tableau.com/profile/laurenreno#!/vizhome/SPLCDukeFinal/SPLCdashboard. Genre terms are derived from *Genre Terms: A Thesaurus for Use in Rare Book and Special Collections Cataloging*, http://rbms.info/vocabularies/genre/alphabetical_list.htm. The finding aid is Guide to the Southern Poverty Law Center Intelligence Project Collection, 1940s–2010, RL.10135, Human Rights Archive, David M. Rubenstein Rare Book & Manuscript Library, Box 90185, Duke University, Durham, North Carolina 27708-0185, https://library.duke.edu/rubenstein/findingaids/splc/.

22 Russell G. Benedict Collection of political ephemera, 1920–1980, FC-06, Freedom Center, University Archives and Special Collections, California State University, Fullerton, 800 N. State College, PLS-352, Fullerton, CA 92834-3599 [transferred from the University of Nevada, Reno, where it was called the Contemporary Issues Collection], http://archives.fullerton.edu/repositories/5/resources/1.

23 Jerome J. McGann, *The Textual Condition* (Princeton: Princeton University Press, 1991), 13.
24 Sean Latham and Robert Scholes, 'The Rise of Periodical Studies', *PMLA* 121/2 (March 2006), pp. 517–31 (at 517), https://seeeps.princeton.edu/wp-content/uploads/sites/243/2015/03/Scholes-Latham-rise-periodical-studies.pdf.
25 Amardeep Singh, 'Visualizing Pound's Early Poetry', *Lehigh University Scalar*, 25 July 2017, https://scalar.lehigh.edu/ezra-pound/index.
26 Rachel Brumagin, Annika Gidley, Joshua Kam and Katrin Kelley, 'The Influence of Ezra Pound', *Little Modern Magazines*, 2017, http://littlemodernmagazines.hopedla.org/our-project/map/. The only correspondent omitted is Alice Serly, who was one of the two recipients of a letter addressed to Tibor and Alice Serly.
27 Gabriel Hankins, 'The Weak Powers of Digital Modernist Studies', *Modernism/Modernity Print+*, Vol. 4, Cycle 1 (27 February 2019), https://modernismmodernity.org/articles/weak-powers.
28 Andrew Jewell and Janis P. Stout, 'A Calendar of the Letters of Willa Cather: An Expanded, Digital Edition', Willa Cather Archive, updated July 2019, https://cather.unl.edu/index.calendar.html.
29 Hankins, *op. cit.*
30 Celena E. Kusch, 'Using a Visual Understanding Environment to Understand H.D.'s Networks of Influence', H.D. International Society, 18 November 2016, https://hdis.chass.ncsu.edu/using-a-visual-understanding-environment-to-understand-h-d-s-networks-of-influence/.
31 Jeffrey Drouin, 'Close- and Distant-Reading Modernism: Network Analysis, Text Mining, and Teaching the *Little Review*', *The Journal of Modern Periodical Studies* 5/1 (2014), pp. 110–35, Appendix: Table 1 Nodes, categories, and their counts, 131–2, https://seeeps.princeton.edu/wp-content/uploads/sites/243/2015/03/Druin_Network-Analysis-Text-Mining-and-Teaching.pdf. Of these topics, Drouin finds that Death is the editorial and thematic focus of this issue (pp. 111, 113, 114).
32 Richard Jean So and Hoyt Long, 'Network Analysis and the Sociology of Modernism', *boundary* 240/2 (Summer 2013): 147–82 (at 148), http://pdfs.semanticscholar.org/319b/33a2e1c14fe4ebfe422c129f98dab54f92c7.pdf. Full-color versions of all figures in the essay are available at https://lucian.uchicago.edu/blogs/literarynetworks/files/2012/10/NetworkAnalysisImages.pdf.
33 So and Long, 'Network Analysis and the Sociology of Modernism', p. 156.
34 Ibid., p. 157.
35 Ibid., p. 162.
36 Ibid., p. 166.
37 Ibid., p. 163.
38 Margaret Bates, 'EP: Maker of Connections' *Paideuma* 6/1 (Spring 1977): 114–15.
39 Michael Coyle and Roxana Preda, *Ezra Pound and the Career of Modern Criticism: Professional Attention* (Rochester: Camden House, 2018), p. 138.
40 So and Long, 'Network Analysis and the Sociology of Modernism', pp. 166–7.
41 Ibid., p. 169.
42 Latham and Scholes, 'The Rise of Periodical Studies', p. 529.
43 Jeroen Vanheste, 'The Reconstruction of the European Mind: T. S. Eliot's *Criterion* and the Idea of Europe', *Journal of European Periodical Studies* 3/2 (Winter 2018): 23–37 (at 23), https://ojs.ugent.be/jeps/article/view/9716/9370 and https://ojs.ugent.be/jeps/article/download/9716/9370. 'These other periodicals were discussed in a

special "Foreign Reviews" section in which notable contributions were mentioned and sometimes translated' (29).

44 *British Poetry Magazines 1914–2000: A History and Bibliography of 'Little Magazines, Compiled by David Miller and Richard Price* (London: The British Library; New Castle, DE: Oak Knoll Press, 2006) includes four indices: Geographical Index, Subject Index, Name Index and Title Index.

45 *British Poetry Magazines 1914–2000*, p. 368.

46 The compilers explain that 'The book is divided by periods which seem to us meaningful in terms of the history of the little magazine and which allow the dedicated poetry reader a reasonable chunk of time through which to browse' ('How to Use This Book', *British Poetry Magazines 1914–2000*, xv).

47 *British Poetry Magazines 1914–2000*, p. 10.

48 Ibid., p. ix.

49 'At midnight on New Year's Eve [2018], all works first published in the United States in 1923 will enter the public domain .... Much the same will happen every January 1 until 2073, revealing long-overlooked works from the Harlem Renaissance, the Great Depression, World War II and beyond. (After 2073, works published by authors who died seven decades earlier will expire each year.)' (Glenn Fleishman, 'For the First Time in More Than 20 Years, Copyrighted Works Will Enter the Public Domain', *Smithsonian Magazine* (January 2019), https://www.smithsonianmag.com/arts-culture/first-time-20-years-copyrighted-works-enter-public-domain-180971016/).

50 Latham and Scholes, 'The Rise of Periodical Studies', p. 519.

51 Peter Brooker and Andrew Thacker, 'General Introduction', in *The Oxford Critical and Cultural History of Modernist Magazines. Volume I: Britain and Ireland 1880–1955*, ed Peter Brooker and Andrew Thacker (New York: Oxford University Press, 2009), 1–26 (at 6), https://seeeps.princeton.edu/wp-content/uploads/sites/243/2015/03/Brooker_Thacker_Intro_Mod_Mags.pdf

52 On the phenomenon of 1920s avant-garde magazines advertising each other, see Gábor Dobó and Merse Pál Szeredi, 'Network Diagrams in Futurist and Other Avant-Garde Magazines: The Creation and Self-Positioning of an Imaginary Community', in *International Yearbook of Futurism Studies*, Vol. 10, ed. Günter Berghaus (Berlin: De Gruyter, 2020), pp. 68–94.

53 Some (but not all) of these tags are included in the advanced search fields of aggregation databases which collect and cross-search peer-reviewed digital objects from federated sites. Examples include NINES (https://nines.org/search), 18th-Century Connect (https://18thconnect.org/search), MESA (https://mesa-medieval.org/search), ModNets (https://modnets.org/search) and Studies in Radicalism Online (SiRO) (https://studiesinradicalism.org/search).

54 Katrina Martin, 'Mapping Alternative and Extremist Literature', 11 March 2015.

55 Mark Gaipa, 'Chicago Modernism: The Importance of Chicago to *Poetry* and the *Little Review*', Modernist Journals Project, 2020, https://modjourn.org/chicago-modernism/.

56 Mark Gaipa, 'Chicago Modernism (Section 3): Visualizations of the Data', Modernist Journals Project, 2020, https://modjourn.org/chicago-modernism-section-3-visualizations-of-the-data/.

57 Gabriel Anderson Hankins, 'Visualizing Modernist Magazines with Geographic Information Systems (GIS): New Approaches in the Spatial Humanities', *Journal of Modern Periodical Studies* 5/1 (2014): 69–93 (at 86–7).

58 See, for example, Roxanne Shirazi, 'A "Digital Wasteland": Modernist Periodical Studies, Digital Remediation, and Copyright', *Creating Sustainable Community: ACRL 25 March 2015–28, 2015, Portland, Oregon: Conference Proceedings*, ed. Dawn M. Mueller (Chicago: Association of College and Research Libraries, A division of the American Library Association, 2015), pp. 192–8, https://academicworks.cuny.edu/cgi/viewcontent.cgi?article=1000&context=gc_studentpubs.

10

MODERNIST (DIS)LOCATION: THE CASE OF KATHERINE MANSFIELD

Gerri Kimber

Introduction

This essay discusses the background to the genesis and development of the four-volume *Edinburgh Edition of the Collected Works of Katherine Mansfield*,[1] incorporating a broader discussion on the repositioning of Mansfield within the modernist literary canon as a result of the edition. Until the Edinburgh edition, there had never been a true scholarly edition of Mansfield's writing, with the exception of the five volumes of her letters (OUP, 1984–2008). This state of affairs led to my devising the Edinburgh edition and becoming the Series Editor, with the publication, in 2012, of the two volumes of fiction with co-editor Vincent O'Sullivan. The fiction volumes were followed by a third, non-fiction volume in 2014, comprising all of Mansfield's essays, reviews, translations, parodies and poetry, co-edited with Angela Smith. The fourth and final volume appeared in 2016, co-edited with Claire Davison, which remaps Mansfield's personal writing. A significant amount of new material was uncovered and incorporated into all four volumes.

Prior to the publication of the Edinburgh edition, the sheer quantity of books required to provide an overall view of Mansfield the writer had been a frustrating experience. There have been countless editions of her stories, but these have always tended to replicate the volumes edited by Mansfield's husband John Middleton Murry after her death, from which nearly all subsequent 'collected' editions derive. For many years Mansfield's diaries and personal writing presented an equally frustrating problem. Murry's three editions of his dead wife's personal writing – the so-called *Journal* (1927, 1954) and *Scrapbook* (1939) – were in fact fabrications, worked up and heavily edited from a mass of notebooks and loose papers used indiscriminately by Mansfield throughout her lifetime, with

A much shorter version of this essay was first published in the *Journal of New Zealand Literature*, 31/2 (2013).

some notebooks abandoned and then reused years apart.[2] New Zealand scholar Margaret Scott took on the awe-inspiring task of trying to decipher this mass of manuscript material – as well as Mansfield's notoriously illegible handwriting – and subsequently published the two-volume *Katherine Mansfield Notebooks* in 1997.[3] However, the contents were placed in only loose chronological order, with the sparsest of annotations, and no meaningful index. The situation was so far from ideal that it seemed bizarre that no one had ever thought of compiling a complete edition of Mansfield's writing. Murry had been in control of Mansfield's estate for so long, but he had also been dead since 1957, and more than fifty years after his death seemed more than long enough to make her work available in the scholarly editions it deserved.

Volumes 1 and 2: The fiction

It took over two years to assemble the stories and fiction fragments for the first two volumes of the edition. Not all Mansfield's stories had been collected by Murry when he compiled his own story collections and it soon became clear that the fiction would require two large volumes. This may explain why Antony Alpers's 'definitive' edition of the stories from 1984 omits many stories under the guise that he did not think them good enough.[4] In a definitive edition, one would expect to find everything, but it is entirely possible he may also have been constrained by his publishers because of issues regarding length. His volume contained eighty-five stories in one volume; the Edinburgh edition of the fiction contains 225 stories and fiction fragments in two volumes – a significant difference.

Some curious omissions in the Alpers edition include 'A Fairy Story' (no reason given), which is one of the many highlights of the Edinburgh edition. It was first published in the *Open Window* in December 1910 and signed 'Katharina Mansfield'. It is a story written in the fantasy genre, yet with thoroughly modern metropolitan sections incorporated into the rather strange plot – a story years ahead of its time – and yet this is the first time it has been collected in any Mansfield fiction edition. Other stories omitted by Alpers include 'A Marriage of Passion' (1912), which he believed to be 'a coarse progenitor of Bliss';[5] 'New Dresses' (1912), which he felt was too 'sentimental';[6] 'The House' (1912), which he felt had 'some biographical but little other interest';[7] 'Old Tar' (1913); 'Brave Love' (1914–15); 'The Aloe' (1916); 'A Cup of Tea' (1922), amongst many others. There did not seem to be a specific editorial policy for these omissions, but rather they seemed to follow subjective personal opinion.

It is in the early period of Mansfield's writing life that the difference in content to previous editions is most marked and where an exciting and innovative writer emerges. Four unknown stories were discovered in the King's College London archives in 2012 by Dr Chris Mourant, then a PhD student working on another project. Three of them are stories for children – part of a book Mansfield was working on in 1908 whilst still in New Zealand. Nothing came of this project, and these stories ended up in the possession of Mansfield's life-long friend Ida Baker, from whom they were somehow acquired by Miron Grindea, editor of *ADAM* magazine, the archives of which are now held at King's College.

However, the most significant story in this find was the fourth one, titled 'A Little Episode', which can be dated to 1909, and which offers perhaps the most detailed picture of events during the period in 1908–9, when Mansfield fell in love with Garnet Trowell, became pregnant and was rejected by him. In order to provide respectability for herself and her unborn child, she subsequently married George Bowden, a singing teacher. The firm biographical evidence for this personal history was, however, systematically destroyed by Mansfield herself. 'A Little Episode', written whilst still in England in spring 1909 and before she was taken by her mother to Bad Wörishofen in Germany, hints at her bitterness over Trowell's abandonment of her and their unborn child, as perceived in the callous portrayal of Jacques and his duplicitous behaviour towards Yvonne. The sentence 'By Lord Mandeville's pillow she saw a large bottle of Eucalyptus and two clean handkerchiefs' (1/543) also hints at her distaste for the fastidious Bowden and the reason for her escape on her wedding night. The years 1909–12 have always proved challenging for biographers, since Mansfield destroyed most of her personal papers from this difficult and painful time of her life – what she referred to as her 'huge complaining diaries' (4/203). And so what we are left with is scant information, pieced together by successive biographers. However, thanks to the new edition, we now have more of a sense of her inner turmoil during this period.

In addition, two unfinished novels – *Juliet* from 1906 and the even more significant *Maata* from 1913 – unpublished in these versions until our edition, also contain significant biographical resonances. Mansfield began writing *Juliet* while still a student at Queen's College in London in 1905, aged seventeen. The date at the opening of 'Chapter I, October 14th', as our note states, 'makes it clear that the narrative was set on her birthday, reinforcing the fact that this is an early self-portrait' (1/60). The surviving fragments of the intended novel depart considerably from her own synopsis, and are transcribed by Scott in the *Notebooks*, with no attempt to present them sequentially. Although puzzles remain, they are rearranged in the *Collected Fiction* to preserve the time-line Mansfield intended. This new version presents a unique glimpse into Mansfield's mindset at this difficult time, containing her memories of the most painful period of her life up to that point: her relationship with Garnet Trowell and the pregnancy and subsequent still birth of the baby she conceived by him. Taken together, both *Juliet* and *Maata* represent two of the most exciting rediscoveries of the edition. And once the bitterness and despair of 'A Little Episode' are added to the mix, a remapping of Mansfield's relationship with the Trowell family and the horror of the subsequent fall-out can now be made.

As noted above, perhaps the most remarkable aspect of these two volumes is that it permits us to see – for the first time – the genesis of Mansfield the writer. We can watch her development, and see germs of ideas, first drafts, tentative beginnings, transformed into some of her most recognizable and important works. For example, the ending of 'The Dolls' House' (1922), one of the very last stories Mansfield wrote before her death: 'I seen the little lamp,' she said, softly. 'Then both were silent once more' (2/420) has become one of the most famous lines in New Zealand literature. But that 'little lamp', which appears so magnificently and so unforgettably in that line, is in fact the mature fruit of a seed that was sown many years before, where it appears in five much earlier stories, now observable for the first time.

In both volumes, lamplight is gentle, calming, seductive, comforting, warming, a metaphor for security and 'home', which reaches its apotheosis in 'The Dolls' House', whose defining, most memorable feature is its 'little lamp'.

Equally exciting is the number of Māori-related themes, words and characters revealed, particularly in volume 1.

Table 1 Stories which feature a 'little lamp'

'Les Deux Étrangères' (1906): 'The house was very quiet. Only the nursery clock went on doing arithmetic and **the little dark lamp** with its one bright eye had no conversational powers.' (1/35)

'Vignettes' (1907): 'Down below, in the Mews, **the little lamp** is singing a silent song. It is the only glow of light in all this darkness.' (1/78)

'The House' (1912): She stripped off her gloves and sat, hands folded in her lap, looking up at the green blistered door, and a **little octagonal lamp** hanging over the doorway. (1/305)

'The Aloe' (1915): 'Ooh!' Kezia flung out her arms – The Grandmother had appeared on the top step – she carried **a little lamp** – she was smiling. (1/477)

Volume 2

'Prelude' (1917): 'Ooh!' cried Kezia, flinging up her arms. The grandmother came out of the dark hall carrying **a little lamp**. She was smiling. (2/61)

Table 2 Stories with Māori references

Volume 1

'A True Tale' (1903): There were no white people living there, but tall, stately, copper coloured men and women, who sailed all round their country in great, carved canoes, and hunted in the woods for game, and very often, I am afraid, human people, whom they killed with aké-akés. (1/15)

'"I was never happy", Huia said' (1906): 'I was never happy', Huia said, leaning back wearily and closing his eyes. Radiana laid her hand lightly against his face. 'That is because you do not know the secret' she said. [...] The scent of the flowering jessamine clung round them with almost mystical sweetness. (1/61)

'Summer Idylle' (1907): 'See, Hinemoa, it is hair, and know you not, should a warrior venture through the bush in the night they seize him and wrap him round in their hair and in the morning he is dead. They are cruel even as I might wish to be to thee, little Hinemoa.' (1/69)

'Vignette: Sunset Tuesday' (1907): A young Māori girl climbs slowly up the hill – she does not see me, I do not move. She reaches a little knoll and suddenly sits down native fashion, her legs crossed under her, her hands clasped in her lap. She is dressed in a blue skirt and white soft blouse. Round her neck is a piece of twisted flax and and [*sic*] a long piece of greenstone is suspended from it. Her black hair is twisted softly at her neck, she wears long white and red bone ear-rings. (1/93)

'Vignette: By the Sea' (1908): Across the blue sea a boat is floating with an orange sail. Now the Māori fishermen are sailing in, their white sail bellying in the wind. On the beach a group of them, with blue jerseys, thick trousers rolled to their knees. The sun shines on their thick crisp hair, and shines on their faces, so that their skins are the colour of hot amber. It shines on their bare legs and firm brown arms. They are drawing in a little boat called 'Te Kooti', the wet rope running through their fingers and falling in a mystic pattern on the foam blown sand. (1/112)

'Rewa' (1908): Rewa heard the sweet wild song of the pipiwharauroa. She walked rapidly, her head thrown back. She tore off a great branch of briar berries and swung them in one hand. (1/128)

'The Woman at the Store' (1912): 'The only people who come through now are Māoris and sundowners!' (1/272)

'How Pearl Button Was Kidnapped' (1912): There were some men on the floor, smoking, with rugs and feather mats round their shoulders. (1/286)

'Old Tar' (1913): 'By gum!' the old man would mutter, lifting his worn head. 'It's a durn fine place … it's a place to shake yer lungs out in – yer know, boy, my Pap bought this from the Māoris – he did. Ye–es! Got it off Ole Puhui for a "suit of clothes an' a lookin'-glass of yer Granmaw's."' (1/341).

'Young Country' (1913): 'Hallo, Mrs Bead' said Rachael. She buried her head in the Māori woman's neck and put her teeth in a roll of soft fat. Mrs Bead pulled Ray between her knees and had a good look at her. (1/368)

'The Beautiful Miss Richardson' (1915): We are making cheap flannelette chemises for the Māori Mission. They are as long as nightdresses, very full, with huge armholes and a plain band round the neck – not even a lace edging. Those poor Māoris. (1/434)

'The Aloe' (1915): He had one saying with which he met all difficulties. 'Depend upon it, it will all come right after the Māori war.' (1/486)

Volume 2

'Toots' (1917):
I don't want the poor soul to feel that he has fallen amongst absolute Māoris. (2/16)

The table above reveals how Māori characters are prevalent in early stories but have completely disappeared by 1913, except for minor generic references. In those early stories, Mansfield's sense of place, of her roots in her native New Zealand is striking. Modernism's early desire for the 'raw' and the 'savage' brought memories of Mansfield's homeland to the fore, enabling her to depict a darker underbelly to the accepted notion of colonialism: what we now, of course, call postcolonialism. These are real characters being drawn here, with Mansfield's acute eye detailing clothes, surroundings, shapes, to bring them to life.

And of course there is the fragment of her novel, *Maata*, named after her childhood friend, the Māori princess Maata Mahupuku, where Mansfield herself takes on the Māori persona of the protagonist. Mansfield's father had been an amateur Māori linguist and she herself had been on a six-week camping trip to the Ureweras in the North Island of New Zealand in 1907, where she had experienced at close hand the life of the Māori in the bush, almost the last place in the North Island at that time which colonial expansion had not yet touched. These stories reveal Mansfield's search for the authentic, in a world where she increasingly felt herself isolated and 'false'. Again, it is only here, in the *Collected Fiction*, that the significance of this Māori-inspired thread can be discerned. Indeed, as a professional writer, she would draw on her rich memories of her rural Karori childhood to fashion some of the most memorable stories ever written by a New Zealand author, using innovative, experimental techniques that we now associate with literary modernism. The modernist revelation of character through narrative voice – through suggestion and symbolism – would become her method, where she would offer glimpses into the lives of individuals, families, captured at a certain moment, frozen in time like a painting or snapshot. The Māori thread offers us a particular glimpse of this early modernist innovative experimentation in her fiction.

One of the original aims of the edition was to strip out any editorial intrusions by Murry. Mansfield published three collections of stories during her lifetime, but after her death in 1923, Murry went on to publish two further collections of stories from the mass of manuscripts and notebooks bequeathed to him after her death: *The Doves' Nest and Other Stories* (1923) and *Something Childish and Other Stories* (1924). In addition, as noted earlier, further fiction fragments made their way into both editions of the *Journal* (1927 and 1954) and the *Scrapbook* (1939). Where Mansfield had not proposed a title for these stories or fragments, Murry simply made one up, and sometimes did the same even when she had clearly given her own title. He also occasionally altered the names of characters, for no discernible reason.

An example can be found in a story clearly titled by Mansfield 'The Boy with the Jackdaw' (1918); in the *Scrapbook*, Murry renamed it 'The Quarrel'. Another story titled by Mansfield as 'To the Last Moment' (1918) was published by Murry in the *Scrapbook*, without the final two paragraphs, and retitled 'The Scholarship'. The list is endless. 'The New Dresses' was originally published by Mansfield in *Rhythm* in October 1912. She used German names, although the story was clearly based on her own family life in Wellington. In giving her characters German names, she was presumably either intending it for publication in her first collection of stories, *In a German Pension*,[8] or to be consistent with other stories she published in the magazine the *New Age* at that time. Murry later republished the story in *Something Childish and Other Stories* and gave the characters English names, changing the surname Binzer to Carsfield.

The editorial intention for the *Collected Fiction*, then, was not just to draw from those previously published collections as every edition of her fiction had done to date, but to map Mansfield's development as a writer, which could only be done by including every scrap of fiction she wrote, good or bad, long or short. As Kirsty Gunn noted in a review of these two fiction volumes in the *London Review of Books*:

> By giving us every draft and fragment in the order of their production – including schoolgirl jottings, ideas that never made it into print [...] the editors [...] are able to show us, on the page, the craftswoman learning what she needs to learn

> in order to be published and become well known, and then learning from those lessons in order to forget them. [...] there are [stories] that slowly, piece by piece, in version after version, arrive at the full expression of her ambition, where Mansfield can be seen for who she is: one of our great modernists, the creator of a narrative form so familiar to us that we barely think of it as one at all.[9]

This is perhaps the most important achievement of the fiction volumes – to situate Mansfield even more firmly within the canon of experimental modernist writers. They illustrate how Mansfield is present at the beginning of this movement as one of its most exciting and cutting-edge protagonists; they furthermore reveal how radical and innovative Mansfield's narrative writing would become during her lifetime, ultimately placing her at the forefront of modernist short story writers.

Volume 3: The poetry and critical writings

As we worked on compiling the manuscript for volume 3 – the poetry, critical writings, essays, pastiches and translations – the more astonished we became at the sheer diversity of Mansfield's literary life. At 750 pages, this large volume comprises nearly 200 poems, over 300 pages of translations, a good number of parodies and pastiches, and over 200 pages of reviews and essays. It seemed all the more remarkable given Mansfield's constant ill health, her early death at thirty-four, and the fact that all this activity was *secondary* to her main occupation as a fiction writer. The body of work assembled was particularly exciting because of the new material which was presented in this volume for the first time, and in every section.

The poetry section was considerably enlarged from any previous publication, revealing how, for Mansfield, poetry was an easy form of artistic expression. Eighty of the poems were written before she left New Zealand at the age of nineteen to return to England to become a writer. These are frequently juvenile in form and content, yet the sheer number attests to Mansfield's absolute need to find an expressive outlet for her burgeoning creative talent. The earliest extant poems, written in 1903 when she was fourteen, are particularly inventive and glimmers of the later mature writer are evident. One of these, 'Friendship', with its first line: 'He sat by his attic window' (3/7), is situated within a domestic arena which features so prominently in Mansfield's short stories, where at least one character will, at some point, be looking out of a window. These myriad references to windows by Mansfield reveal for Alpers how a 'trick of her mind is evident: she is constantly inhabiting one space while observing another, and has her characters doing the same'.[10] This anticipates the modernist concept of liminality in Mansfield's short stories; how the view from a window – a *place-in-between* – can alter perceptions from the present to the past, from the past to the future, and invite the crossing of a metaphorical threshold to an event yet to be realized or understood. It is a concept which runs through much of her creative writing and reveals its innovative nature from the outset.

The translation section offers perhaps the most exciting new aspect of Mansfield's work in the entire volume since this had never been collected in any publication before. With the assistance of Dr Mirosława Kubasiewicz and Professor Claire Davison, we assembled, for the first time, over 300 pages of Mansfield's translations. Apart from Alphonse Daudet's story 'M. Seguin's Goat', which Mansfield translated directly from the French herself, all her translations were from the Russian, and were collaborations with the Russian émigré S. S. Koteliansky, a well-known figure in literary London in the first decades of the twentieth century. He would become one of her closest confidantes, and played a decisive role in foregrounding Mansfield's interest in Russia for almost ten years. Indeed, her letters and notebooks are crowded with references to Chekhov, Dostoevsky, Tolstoy and other Russian writers.

Koteliansky was a Russian Jew from the Ukraine, who emigrated to England in 1911, following political harassment by the then Tsarist government. In 1914, he came into the sphere of Mansfield and Murry, having been introduced by D. H. Lawrence. Although literature was where his real interest lay, he was by then working in an office known as 'The Russian Law Bureau', translating Russian legal documents. During the winter of 1914, Koteliansky and Murry decided to collaborate on a series of translation projects for a publisher called Maunsel, translating Russian works into English for £20 a piece (dividing the fee between them), with Koteliansky doing the initial translation and Murry polishing and perfecting the English; their first such venture was *The Bet and Other Stories* by Anton Chekhov (1915).[11] Over a number of years this method would result in many books of Russian translations, with a variety of collaborators in addition to Murry – for example, Leonard and Virginia Woolf, and D. H. Lawrence – and, of course, Mansfield herself, who was thrilled at the prospect of these new translations: 'When you think that the English literary world is given up to sniggerers. Dishonesty, sneering, DULL DULL, giggling at Victorians inside whiskers and here is this treasure – at the wharf only not unloaded.'[12] In 1915, she worked with Koteliansky on a translation of the short story 'Colonel Ribnikov', from Alexander Kuprin's collection, *The River of Life and Other Stories*, though her translation was not acknowledged when the book was published.[13] As Claire Davison notes, 'Koteliansky later paid tribute to this contribution, admitting that her name had been dropped "because she was not then known as a writer"' (3/142). In 1922, the pair worked on a translation of *Gorky's Reminiscences of Leonid Andreyev*, which was eventually published in a limited edition in 1928, five years after Mansfield's death.[14]

However, perhaps the collaboration with Koteliansky which influenced Mansfield the most – and also gave her the most pleasure – was the translations of Chekhov's letters, which appeared as a thirteen-part series in the *Athenaeum* beginning on 4 April 1919. She wrote to Koteliansky on 6 June of that year:

> *I do my very best* always with these wonderful letters & can do no more. Wonderful they are. The last one – the one to Souverin about the duty of the artist to *put* the 'question' – not to solve it but to so put it that one is completely

> satisfied seems to me one of the most valuable things I have ever read. It opens – it discovers rather, a new world. May Tchekov live forever.[15]

In the autumn of 1919, ensconced on the Italian Riviera for health reasons, Mansfield's first letters home were to Koteliansky and spoke about their plan to extend and publish a translation of these Chekhov letters in book form. Koteliansky sent her a pile of manuscripts he had been working on with the following note: 'My ambition is to see our Tchekhov letters in book form [...] I want this book as a token of our perhaps uncommon friendship.'[16] The edition was never finished in Mansfield's lifetime, Koteliansky completing and publishing the volume with Philip Tomlinson in 1925.

In addition, previously unpublished translation manuscripts are presented here for the first time. *The Judges*, Mansfield's translation of Stanisław Wyspiański's play from 1904, painstakingly transcribed for the edition by Polish scholar Mirosława Kubasiewicz, was a collaboration Mansfield undertook with a former Polish lover, Floryan Sobienowski, in 1917. A small section of the translation ended up in the New York Berg library, the rest in the National Library of New Zealand. In addition, the Harry Ransom Center in Texas holds the manuscripts of Mansfield's collaborative translation with Koteliansky of 'The Dream', a poem in prose by Leo Tolstoy, together with 'The Creative History of "The Devils"' by Dostoevsky. All in all, then, the body of work that comprises this section, never collected in one place before, offers us a new vision of Mansfield as a proficient – and prolific – translator.

Mansfield's sense of humour – an important feature of all her writing – is particularly evident in the section containing the parodies, pastiches and aphorisms. Most of the pieces date from 1910 to 1913, and reflect the influence of Beatrice Hastings, the partner of A. R. Orage during the early period 1910–12 that Mansfield was publishing work in the *New Age*. Both women had a mischievous and frequently mordant sense of humour, and while Hastings would end up taking her parodying to vindictive extremes later in life, Mansfield retained a more measured, literary approach. Two other pieces in this section had never been published before: 'Sumurun: An Impression of Leopoldine Konstantin' (1911), discovered by myself in New Zealand in February 2013, does not easily fit into any category, being, as it states in the title, an 'impression' of an actress performing in a silent play-pantomime that Mansfield saw on the London stage at the beginning of 1911; secondly, the group of aphorisms called 'Bites from the Apple' (1911). The latter was another discovery made in the archives at King's College London by Chris Mourant, who suggests that they were again influenced by her relationship with Hastings and Orage, and intended for publication in the *New Age*. A third piece, the parody 'Virginia's Journal' published under the pseudonym 'Virginia' in *Rhythm*, in 1913, is here definitively attributed to Mansfield for the first time, a typed manuscript having been discovered by myself amongst her papers in New Zealand in early 2013. Two New Zealand scholars had for many years asserted it could not possibly have been penned by Mansfield, though Clare Hanson disagreed, and made an excellent case for its provenance as a 'clear hit back at the *New Age* and its circle of contributors'.[17] Her decision was vindicated by my discovery of the manuscript. There are clear references to Orage and other writers, including, as Hanson points out, an early criticism of Bennett ('Rennet'), who wrote for the paper under the pseudonym Jacob Tonson, thus demonstrating how criticism of Bennett 'was common, or commonplace, by 1913, long before the publication of Woolf's "Mr Bennett and Mrs Brown"'.[18]

Many of Mansfield's book reviews were published by Murry in his edited collection *Novels and Novelists by Katherine Mansfield* (1930), and subsequently edited and republished in Hanson's 1987 volume *The Critical Writings of Katherine Mansfield*.[19] Neither volume, however, reflects the entirety of Mansfield's critical writing. Where needed, we restored original manuscripts, omitting Murry's frequent small editorial changes and/or inaccuracies and added other reviews written in numerous other magazines and papers, several of them overlooked until now. As Hanson notes of Mansfield's copious reviews for the *Athenaeum*:

> Mansfield put 'her all' into these reviews, and devoted nearly two years of her short writing life to them, at the expense of her fiction. [… H]er critical writings represent a genuine attempt to take on the literary establishment on its own terms. Mansfield wanted to 'preach', to convert, and could and would take up the opposition's weapons in order to do this. The extent to which she at the same time subverted and undercut contemporary literary-critical forms must by the same token be recognised.[20]

What volume 3 ultimately demonstrates is the scale of Mansfield's intellectual achievement, with intelligence and imagination vigorously interacting. As a young woman she relished the border-crossing of the *Rhythm* group, where women were empowered, gender roles became unstable, and any member of the group with a passionate interest could express it without being an 'expert', as, for instance, when Anne Estelle Rice reviewed the Ballets Russes's *Schéhérazade*. Her subsequent involvement with Virginia Woolf and the Bloomsbury Group not only provided intriguing discussions of the art of fiction but also extended her skill in parody. Aldous Huxley would describe a skit she wrote for a house-party at Garsington in a letter to his brother Julian: 'We performed a superb play invented by Katherine, improvising as we went along. It was a huge success, with Murry as a Dostoevsky character and Lytton as an incredibly wicked old grandfather.'[21] And of course, her preoccupation with Russian writing would evolve into a collection of finely honed translations.

Volume 4: The diaries

Volume 4 presents, for the first time, an unexpurgated and chronologically ordered version of Mansfield's personal writing. As mentioned in the introduction, Murry was the first editor of some of this material in his various edited volumes pertaining to be either Mansfield's *Journal* (1927), her *Scrapbook*

(1939) or her *Definitive Journal* (1954). The very misleading impression given was that Mansfield had assiduously kept such things as a 'journal' or a 'scrapbook' during her lifetime and that Murry had simply published what she had written. But as critic Philip Waldron noted as early as 1974: 'The [manuscript] material consists of four diaries which, like most diaries, are copious in early January but quickly peter out; some thirty notebooks and exercise books; and several hundred loose sheets of paper.'[22] Murry must have known that one day his clever patchwork-quilt methodology for these volumes would be revealed, yet was seemingly not deterred.

A useful example of Murry's editorial principles can be seen in one of the most significant and well-documented episodes in Mansfield's adult life: her brief love affair with French author Francis Carco in February 1915. In her notebooks of the time, Mansfield, having temporarily suspended her love affair with Murry, recounts the journey she undertook to the occupied war zone at Gray in north-west France in order to visit Carco, using the pre-arranged excuse of an aunt's illness to get her through the checkpoints. (She would make use of these notes in her semi-autobiographical story 'An Indiscreet Journey', written in May 1915.) In the 1927 *Journal*, the Carco episode fills four pages, in the form of a couple of unposted letters, together with a long description of her arrival in Gray and initial meeting with someone called 'F'. It was not until 1954, when the *Definitive Journal* was published (the 'Carco' episode now extending to six much larger-formatted pages), that it was possible to see how much had been expurgated by Murry from the original edition. Details of a sexually explicit nature, anything which would have revealed that Mansfield had journeyed illegally to a war zone for a brief sexual liaison with a Frenchman she barely knew, the calculating tone of this 'experience' – all this had been removed from the 1927 edition. Our version restored Mansfield's original, unexpurgated text, with none of the style embellishments to be found in either of Murry's editions.

In 1939, more loose manuscripts were used by Murry to create the volume known as *The Scrapbook of Katherine Mansfield*, an 'intermediary' edition of the *Journal*. In the introduction to the volume, he writes:

> It is possible that I attach an exaggerated importance to these [fragments]. But [...] European opinion has received her [Journal] as a minor classic [...]. There are now many people in many different countries [...] who take a peculiar personal and loving interest in all that pertains to Katherine Mansfield. In their eyes, I know, this book needs no apology.[23]

In fact, much of the book is filled out with extracts of unfinished stories, falsely creating the idea of Mansfield owning and writing in a specially designated 'scrapbook' of ideas.

The second editor of all this manuscript material was Margaret Scott, who, in 1997, produced her magisterial two-volume edition of the notebooks. On publication, these volumes revealed just how selective Murry's editorial principles had been. In nearly 700 pages of text, Scott painstakingly transcribed all the extant notebooks and loose manuscripts from which Murry had created his editions of the *Journal* and *Scrapbook*, but with uneven chronological ordering. Nevertheless, Mansfield scholars were at last able to ascertain how disparate these various documents were, and how false was the sense that Mansfield had ever really written a 'journal' as such, intended for publication. Of course, it is to Murry's credit as an editor that he was able to create such a seamless text from so many bits and scraps, but this should not detract from the essentially duplicitous nature of his endeavours, which allowed for a false impression of the legacy of Mansfield's personal writing to last for over three-quarters of a century.

Chronologically ordered for the first time and unexpurgated, our own volume of Mansfield's personal writing reveals the minutiae of her daily life – encompassing art, music, contemporary history, personal finances, observation, memory, testimony, imagination and emotion. What emerges is her creative imagination, made visible in the quirkiness of her style or the meandering pattern of her thought processes. When read alongside her fiction, and illuminated by biographical information, the personal writing reads as a testimony to Mansfield's other, secret life – when her aspirations to authorship, creative and economic autonomy, imaginative and stylistic originality, her keen ear for the material world around her, all attest to the brilliance of a pioneering proto-modernist voice, often well in advance of the heavyweights and highbrows with whom she has tended to be compared.

This volume also contains the complete manuscript of Mansfield's unknown poetry collection, *The Earth Child*, unearthed by myself following a research trip to the Newberry Library in Chicago in May 2015, sadly too late to be included in the poetry section of volume 3. The manuscript was bequeathed to the Newberry Library in Chicago, by the estate of Jane Warner Dick (1906–97) in 1999, where it remained unnoticed until my discovery.

The little volume manuscript was compiled by Mansfield in 1910 and sent to the London publisher Elkin Mathews in the second half of that year. Of the thirty-five poems in the cycle, which date from 1909/10, when she was just twenty-two, only nine were previously known. This is a time of her life when biographical information is at its most scant, since, as noted earlier, Mansfield systematically destroyed all her personal papers from this difficult, youthful period. They arguably represent some of the finest poems Mansfield ever wrote, whilst also containing information about people, places and events for which almost no other biographical evidence is available. Furthermore, read as a poem-cycle as she herself intended, since the poems are all numbered, the sequence acquires a very different literary style and shape. It shows the development of Mansfield's youthful lyrical voice and poetic persona as she moved away from the influence of Wilde and *fin-de-siècle* symbolism, towards the more complex early modernism of continental Europe. In addition, the cycle provides a fascinating bridge from her earliest poems, sketches and vignettes through prose-poetry to narrative, offering new insight into her evolution and apprenticeship as a writer. It reveals that just when Mansfield's stories were beginning to be accepted for publication in London journals, she was also taking herself seriously as a poet, providing an incisive illustration of her ability to forge a new literary voice made from personal memory, intercultural experimentation and contextual echoes.

Conclusion

Modernism did not arrive in Britain in the early years of the twentieth century as a ready-made concept. It was a response to a variety of stimuli – cultural, political, historical and literary. In the case of Mansfield, the cultural landscape she had grown up with in New Zealand and chose to dislocate herself from enabled her to view modernity from a postcolonial viewpoint. In much of her early work she merged both concepts, as she experimented and honed her skills as a writer. In incorporating everything Mansfield wrote, whether complete or incomplete, the Edinburgh edition is able to chart Mansfield's development as one of Britain's key exponents of literary modernism, redefining her status within the modernist canon, and regenerating scholarship in this iconic New Zealand writer.

And the journey is to continue, as in 2018 Claire Davison and I were awarded a four-volume contract with EUP to completely re-edit Mansfield's letters, currently only available as a five-volume print on demand edition from OUP, the first volume dating from 1984 and the final one twenty-four years later, in 2008. My recent research has uncovered much new material pertaining to Mansfield's life, including new letters. Time has moved on, and there is much that is new to be said about Mansfield – for example, her focus on poetry in 1910, over and above the short story, as evidenced by the 'Earth Child' collection, her important European cultural contacts, as well as new research into the final weeks of her life near Fontainebleau, which has uncovered several new eye-witness testimonies. The sometimes sparse annotations in the OUP volumes seem outdated and insubstantial in the light of so much new research.

There will be four comprehensively annotated volumes in total, arranged by recipient, rather than chronologically. This means that scholars working on, for example, the relationship between Mansfield and Virginia Woolf, will be able to see all Mansfield's letters to her in one place, without the need to obtain or consult multiple volumes at a time, affording a much deeper understanding of each epistolary relationship. For in the case of Mansfield, her letters do not just complement her oeuvre; they are an essential part of it. As many scholars have noted, some of the letters are as finely written and crafted as the stories, and even illustrate the stylistic, imaginative and expressive scope of Mansfield as a writer better than certain stories composed with the publishing market and commercial readerships in mind. As Alpers notes of Mansfield's period away from Murry between September 1919 and the end of April 1920: 'Soon Katherine was back in London, having written to Murry since September some 110,000 words in letters, or twice as many words as are in her whole *Collected Stories*. Some passages in those letters are more worthy to endure than many of her stories.'[24] Overall, the letters double Mansfield's oeuvre, and thus constitute an essential body of works for today's readers.

Notes

1 Gerri Kimber and Vincent O'Sullivan, eds., *The Edinburgh Edition of the Collected Works of Katherine Mansfield*: vols. 1 and 2 – *The Collected Fiction* (Edinburgh: Edinburgh University Press, 2012); Gerri Kimber and Angela Smith, eds., *The Edinburgh Edition of the Collected Works of Katherine Mansfield*: Vol. 3 – *The Poetry and Critical Writings* (Edinburgh: Edinburgh University Press, 2014); Gerri Kimber and Claire Davison, eds., *The Edinburgh Edition of the Collected Works of Katherine Mansfield*: Vol. 4 – The Diaries of Katherine Mansfield, including Miscellaneous Works (Edinburgh: Edinburgh University Press, 2016). Hereafter references to all four volumes are placed directly in the text: (volume/page number).
2 John Middleton Murry, ed., *Journal of Katherine Mansfield* (London: Constable, 1927); John Middleton Murry, ed., *The Journal of Katherine Mansfield 1904–1922: Definitive Edition* (London: Constable, 1954); and John Middleton Murry, ed., *The Scrapbook of Katherine Mansfield* (London: Constable, 1939).
3 Margaret Scott, ed., *The Katherine Mansfield Notebooks*, 2 vols. (Canterbury: Lincoln University Press, 1997).
4 Antony Alpers, ed., *The Stories of Katherine Mansfield – Definitive Edition* (Auckland: Oxford University Press, 1984).
5 Alpers, *The Stories of Katherine Mansfield*, p. 550.
6 Ibid., p. 552.
7 Ibid.
8 Katherine Mansfield, *In a German Pension* (London: Stephen Swift, 1911).
9 Kirsty Gunn, 'How the Laundry Basket Squeaked', *London Review of Books* 35/7 (11 April 2013), pp. 25–6.
10 Antony Alpers, *The Life of Katherine Mansfield* (London: Viking, 1980), p. 53.
11 Anton Tchekhov, *The Bet and Other Stories*, trans. Samuel Solomonovitch Koteliansky and John Middleton Murry (London: Maunsel, 1915).
12 Vincent O'Sullivan and Margaret Scott, eds., *The Collected Letters of Katherine Mansfield*, 5 vols. (Oxford: Clarendon Press, 1984–2008), Vol. 2, p. 341. Mansfield to Koteliansky, *c.* July 1919. Hereafter referenced *as Letters*, followed by volume and page number.
13 Alexander Kuprin, *The River of Life and Other Stories*, trans. Katherine Mansfield and S. S. Koteliansky (London: Maunsel, 1916).
14 Maxim Gorky, *Reminiscences of Leonid Andreyev*, Katherine Mansfield and S. S. Koteliansky (London: Heinemann, 1928).
15 *Letters*, 2, p. 324.
16 Koteliansky to Mansfield, 26 September 1919, cited in Irene Zohrab, 'Katherine Mansfield's Previously Unknown Publications on Anton Chekhov, Journal of New Zealand Literature 6 (1988), p. 143.
17 Clare Hanson, *The Critical Writings of Katherine Mansfield* (Basingstoke: Macmillan, 1987), p. 148.
18 Hanson, *The Critical Writings of Katherine Mansfield*, p. 148.
19 John Middleton Murry, ed., *Novels and Novelists by Katherine Mansfield* (London: Constable, 1930).
20 Hanson, *Critical Writings*, pp. 1–2.
21 Grover Smith, ed., *Letters of Aldous Huxley* (London: Chatto & Windus, 1969), p. 118.
22 Philip Waldron, 'Katherine Mansfield's Journal', *Twentieth-Century Literature* 20/1 (January 1974), pp. 11–18 (cited p. 11).
23 Murry, *Scrapbook*, pp. v–vi.
24 Alpers, *The Life of Katherine Mansfield*, p. 314.

11

GOSSIP FROM ABROAD, OR, WHY HISTORICIZE MODERNISM?

Alexander Howard

The creative output of the second-generation modernist poet, little magazine editor and occasional experimental filmmaker, Charles Henri Ford (1908–2002) has much to tell us about the historical shift away from predominantly impersonal and heteronormative models of modernist aesthetic praxis, to more demotic and often overtly non-normative instances of postmodern cultural production. Over the past ten years or so, I have charted the manner in which the openly queer Ford moved to shape or make fun 'out' of the various movements, artists and materials he encountered and engaged with over the course of his rich and varied career.[1] When writing about this unfairly marginalized figure, I sought to place his myriad contributions to modernism in their proper historical context. To put the matter in the simplest terms possible: I looked to 'historicize' Charles Henri Ford. In order to do so, I scrutinized a wide range of germane archival and unpublished documentary resources housed at research centres and libraries based in the United States, especially the Harry Ransom Center at the University of Texas, Austin. The archival materials held at those institutions not only provided me with an opportunity to better understand what it was that Ford hoped to achieve in his life and career, but also provided me with a suitable means with which to analyse and interpret Ford's numerous creative interactions, artistic achievements and career moves.

This methodological insight did not arrive overnight. I want first to reflect on some of the initial research methodologies and related close-reading practices I utilized when getting to grips with Ford's work. Where appropriate, I will also look to discuss some of the materials I unearthed and analysed in the course of my research. Having done so, in the latter stages of this disputation, I will consider: What might we stand to gain if and when we choose to historicize modernist cultural producers of Ford's ilk?

Charles Henri Ford was born into a family of Southern Baptist hoteliers based in Brookhaven, Mississippi. It was in the so-called 'Magnolia' State that the adolescent Ford launched his first literary venture: the second-generation modernist little magazine, *Blues: A Magazine of New Rhythms* (1929–30). Edited and published in Columbus, Mississippi, the relatively obscure *Blues* is useful when trying to understand Ford. Adam McKible reminds us that modernist little magazines matter. McKible suggests that if we want to understand literary history, we need to emphasize that history's 'difference from our present moment. Collections and anthologies cannot do this; they de-contextualize past writing and make it familiar in ways that little magazines resist.'[2] Peter Marks would likely concur with such an appraisal, arguing as he does that modernist little magazines 'provide unrivalled contemporary documentation of [various] ongoing literary developments, of rivalries and collaborations, of short-lived enthusiasms and failed projects, and of rich and illuminating work of lasting value'.[3] Accepting this, we might also posit, to borrow a critical formulation coined by Suzanne W. Churchill, that 'little magazines are intimate and social: they bring together an ensemble of writers into a small space, staging a performance for a familiar audience of like-minded people, who read each issue during the same limited time period'.[4] Churchill also writes of how modernist little magazines prove capable of framing 'distinct literary spaces that [make] new forms of poetry possible'.[5]

These assertions certainly help us understand what Ford hoped to achieve with his modernist little magazine, which was conceived and presented to the general reading public as 'a haven for the unorthodox in america and for those writers living abroad who though writing in English have decided that america and [the] american environment are not hospitable to creative work'.[6] In equal measure, however, it now strikes me that modernist little magazine theory, for all its talk of bosom closeness and affective conviviality, sometimes misses the mark when getting to the bottom of the intimate workings – and some of the more intimate aspects – of modernism. And this is where the modernist archive comes into it. Consider the following letter, in which an uncharacteristically downbeat Ford sent to his mother on 7 July 1930:

> Truly dear,
> It is nice & very nice to know that you'll be here Xmas …
>
> Yes I AM trying to eliminate the obnoxiousness of my environment by partially excluding it from my consciousness! I'm doing a large amount of reading: last night and this morning I read a book called Class Reunion by Franz Werfel translated from the German & found it superior if not superb; also Proust's Within a Budding Grove, then there's Sherwood Anderson's Poor White, 2 books by Nietzsche, a novel by Turgenev, and other things by Walter Pater, Remy de Gourment and Virginia Woolf … Shall I send you something? I could send you Confessions of a Young Man by George Moore for one thing …
>
> Our business too is very poor, yesterday the lowest of all … I'm not spending a cent on clothes or anything to wear I've bought one lone pair of suspenders ($1.50) and that was because the ones I had were falling apart.

> I think I'll break even on this number of Blues … number 9 is now being printed, the gallery proofs should be here tomorrow and the finished magazines the first part of next week at the latest.., it's really a brilliant number and I want you to read every word of it.
>
> Philadelphia is our team too for the series but I risked a dollar on St. Louis one game and won.
>
> Now sit down and write me another letter swanlovely.[7]

I quote at length from this letter, which Ford wrote while living in Columbus, Mississippi, for a number of interrelated reasons. Most obviously, this unpublished epistolary document offers us insight into Ford's literary interests and extra-literary passions. That is to say, the letter contains a wealth of information and anecdotal detail that we can use when striving to get a better sense of the man himself. Significantly, it also provides insight into the conceptual remit underwriting *Blues*. Recall, here, those previously cited lines about Ford's modernist little magazine being 'a haven for the unorthodox in america and for those writers living abroad who though writing in English have decided that america and [the] american environment are not hospitable to creative work'. A quick glance at the letter above reveals that Ford's call to create an environment 'hospitable' to modernism in the pages of *Blues* was, in a sense, biographically inflected: founding and editing a modernist little magazine appealed to Ford as it provided him with a concrete means to assuage the sense of isolation caused by geographical surroundings that he perceived – rightly or wrongly – to be both 'obnoxious' and unconducive to creative production. In this way, then, access to archival materials helps us understand both the man who created the modernist little magazine, and the modernist little magazine that the man created.

Knowing this, it seems to me that the modernist archive trumps modernist little magazine theory – at least in certain regards. To be clear: this is not to suggest that modernist little magazine theory has nothing to offer. Indeed, the rigorous and nuanced critical methodologies associated with modernist little magazine theory can give us a better sense of the various historical circles and textual 'havens' in which groups of modernists once huddled together. But little magazine theory doesn't necessarily give us an accurate sense of what those assorted movers, shakers and huddlers actually thought and felt about the moving 'ensemble' otherwise known as modernism. This, I want to argue, proves to be the case when it comes to modernists like Ford. Hence, again, the significance of the modernist archive.

Charles Henri Ford said on more than one occasion that he wanted to be extremely famous. Here is Ford at the tender age of eighteen, in an overwrought and presumably unintentionally hilarious journal entry of 30 May 1926:

> As for me, gradually I am coming to see that I will be, something, yea famous, in this stupid world. The niche I will carve is becoming more distinct in outline tho the actual carving has not been commenced. I have something I know to tell people or something beautiful to give them that will live. I believe I am a genius, and from now on …[8]

Now fast-forward a couple of years. The following journal entry, which is dated 30 July 1928, demonstrates that Ford had taken it upon himself to 'carve' out a niche in what was by then a decidedly overcrowded modernist sphere:

> What writers have influenced me most? Wilde, perhaps; and Shaw, Mencken and other iconoclasts in my ways of thinking. Perhaps I would have been happier had I never seen a book … never known the intensity of poetry … the thirst to create … the hunger for fame and life … hence the realization of the futility of it all … hunger again … fire and ice, fire and ice.[9]

Some seven months after this journal entry appeared, Ford published the first issue of his modernist little magazine. Ford thought that *Blues* might help him to make an immediate impact on the modernist scene. But things didn't pan out as hoped by this self-professed iconoclast, who began to wonder, a couple of decades later in life, as to whether 'being famous posthumously [would be] any fun'.[10] Witness the journal entry that an older – though by no means necessarily wiser – Ford jotted down sometime in November 1951: 'Fashions in poetry will change – my poetry will be recognized, my name will be exalted. And so at this point in my history I must not betray my heritage to be. The words, a flesh that lives on, as spirit, after we are gone'.[11] And here he is again – this time on 17 November 1951. The following extract appears in a letter addressed to his confidante and collaborator, the queer second-generation modernist poet and noted film critic Parker Tyler:

> I admit that my poetry is a time-bomb as far as audience disturbance on a grand scale is concerned. I do take some joy in knowing that one-day my name will be exalted; let those of contemporary fame rejoice, too. Your citing [of Ezra] Pound and [William Carlos] Williams is not exciting – Pound leaves me cold and Williams, I say, is that Chinese emperor – he's unclothed (with greatness).[12]

Ford found himself at something of a crossroads at the start of the 1950s. As this rather tetchy letter to Tyler attests, his poetry had failed to make much of an impression in literary circles. Judging by the general tenor of much of the correspondence he churned out in the early 1950s, Ford seems to have taken his relative lack of poetic success quite hard. He intimates as much to Tyler in a letter written on 7 May 1952: 'I feel no urge to write anything – not even a diary. Not even a diary. Not even Great Examples in literature inspire me to emulation. What is it? A running up of Knowledge, or a running down of the libidinal creative fluid?' Yet in the very same breath, a clearly confused Ford concedes that he does in fact

> WANT to do something, create something. But imaginative literature, aside from the prose poem, bores me. Perhaps a movie camera will be the answer … Co-incidence that you shd mention suicide in your last letter … <u>God or Suicide</u>,

> I told Pavlik [Tchelitchew], might be a title for something ... And I've thought of how I shd be capable of suicide, if the time came when life had no more novelty. It would be novel to have a son. Or to have lots of money. Or fame through poetry or plays – or anything ... The unbearable thing, I guess you've tasted it, is to go on being as you are when you're dissatisfied.[13]

By his own admission, the profoundly 'dissatisfied' Ford struggled to get much in the way of substantive work finished – or printed – in the first half of the 1950s, which he spent in various parts of Europe. As he put it to Tyler on 26 December 1952: 'Ideas erupt here as the dead volcano must have ONCE (the Monte Cavo which I see from my room) – when will I ever finish any – or, what is even more remote, see them produced in book form'.[14] It seems, to all intents and purposes, as if the increasingly exasperated Ford was suffering from something approximating a severe case of writer's block: 'Call it indecision or wavering or inconsistency or lack of will or confusion. The passion is perverted, diluted'.[15]

That was Ford in July 1953. Statements of this sort help to explain why he decided to refocus his creative attention on visual matters. Ford now began to experiment with film and paint. His decision to do so eventually paid off: in 1955, an exhibition of Ford's photography was held in London, at the Institute of Contemporary Arts; in 1957, a collection of Ford's drawings and gouaches was displayed at the Paris-based Galerie Marforen. Not long after, however, personal disaster struck: on 31 July 1957, Ford's partner of twenty-three years, the noted Neo-Romantic painter, Pavel Tchelitchew died of a heart attack. Tchelitchew's death, untimely and tragic as it most undoubtedly was, seems to have triggered something in Ford. He started thinking seriously about poetry again, and in 1962 he decided to return to the United States. Before he moved back, a now upbeat Ford told the trusted Tyler: 'I think the cycle has revolved. I'm back where I started – or almost. So tell me if anything is available around Beatdom'.[16]

Ford's timing was, in this instance, remarkably fortuitous. In his absence, a younger generation of North American poets had discovered his work. We see proof of this in Ford's archive. The second-wave New York School poet Ted Berrigan was – to take but one example – particularly effusive in his praise of Ford's modernist achievements:

> About reading at Le Metro, how about the first Wednesday in June [1965]? It's free admission, and contributions, you wouldn't make more than maybe twenty-five dollars (or less), but there a lot of us who sure would like to hear you read. Your poetry and your old magazine, VIEW, paved the way for so much of what many younger poets feel is <u>really</u> happening now, when so many other poets were being so boring and so ordinary.[17]

Nor was Berrigan the only New York School poet to single Ford out for praise. Now held at the Harry Ransom Center (HRC), Ford's personal library includes a host of books written by and about the loosely aligned New York School group of poets. Tellingly, each volume contains a warm, handwritten inscription. Ford's copy of Kenneth Koch's *The Publications* (1977) is one such volume, featuring as it a dedication from Koch to Ford as the man 'who inspired [his] poetry at its start'. Keeping all that in mind, then, a word or two more about the contents of Charles Henri Ford's archive. In 1968, the HRC, which is housed at the Austin branch of the University of Texas, acquired Ford's papers. A mere year before that acquisition took place, the New York-based poet, dancer and photographer Gerard Malanga had cause to pen the following lines about Ford:

> Genitals are flashing by and then colors.
> In the next year summer will be
> good to you with the young
> friends beside you.
> The matter is the dream that guides you into a life
> time of sunlight over your head
> And relations get younger.
> Rain has begun to fall and tears, also.[18]

This poem features in the *Screen Tests/A Diary* (1967) volume that Malanga put together with his and Ford's mutual friend, the seminal postmodern artist Andy Warhol. It is worth emphasizing at the outset that Malanga thought fondly and highly of Ford, who he referred to as 'Dear Charlie Pop Candy Pop'.[19] This is worth bearing in mind as we approach Malanga's ambivalent poetic account of 'Charlie' Ford. Malanga begins by correctly foregrounding the overtly sexual quality – 'Genitals are flashing by' – of large swathes of Ford's creative output. Malanga also, in the sixth line of the poem, makes passing reference to Ford's life-long interest in Surrealism. Elsewhere in the poem, the younger writer suggests that a definitive sort of tipping point has been reached in Ford's life and career. Malanga seeks, on the one hand, to reassure his older friend and poetic mentor that there are many more summers to come. On the other, Malanga emphasizes the gulf between Ford and 'the young/friends' who continue to gather around him. While Malanga's 'diary' entry serves as a marker of respect, it also serves to situate the nearly sixty-year-old Ford against a discernibly melancholic poetic backdrop – in a rain-sodden setting where artistically inclined friends and creative 'relations' only ever seem to get 'younger'. Written two years later, 'Malanga's Life of Ford' suggests in a similar manner that the gulf separating 'Candy Pop' and the younger generation continues to widen. In this poem, Malanga debates his friend's position in the annals of literary history:

> but whether his life merely circulated as a hot foot note in the business
> world of poetry i don't know
>
> for that he should go around
> with the aura evolving about him stories passed along as a hearing aid whisper
> among strangers and friends
> he is like the night of jupiter and lives in that fashion[20]

Malanga's poetic treatment of Ford is certainly well intentioned. By the same token, however, the connotations of physical decrepitude associated with Ford's apparent 'hearing aid whisper' have always struck me as more than a little melancholy. I have always wondered, too, about the 'aura' that seems to evolve around and 'about' the ageing Ford. Both these things should be kept in mind as we turn to another poem written by Malanga. This final example opens with a depiction of the master street photographer Henri Cartier-Bresson walking amidst a cluster of exuberant schoolchildren, primed with his trusted Lecia camera. But then he disappears into the poetic ether. Ford's lover, the Neo-Romanticist painter Pavel Tchelitchew, who is sunning himself on the glimmering 'sand of a beach in winter vanishes'. Gertrude Stein and Paul Éluard soon follow suit. So, too, does Ford's close collaborator, the queer modernist novelist and film critic, Parker Tyler. Not long after that, the artist Joseph Cornell, whose work Ford showcased in the pages of his influential *View*, also vanishes. The exact same thing then happens to the American expatriate Paul Bowles, who is initially set against the backdrop of a side street in Tangiers. The famous British fashion photographer Cecil Beaton also features. Malanga has him waving adieu 'through the rear window of a taxi'. In its final stages, the poem becomes increasingly elliptical and sombre. An elderly woman, who is dressed in black, 'vanishes as the shadow of a building falls upon her'. Ford's cherished sister, the actress Ruth, is the last to leave. She takes her leave while sleeping, and yet 'another life vanishes'.[21]

Appropriately enough, this poem is entitled 'Charles Henri Ford's Archive Vanishes'. Many of the people Ford loved and collaborated with enter into and then withdraw from Malanga's poem. Without a doubt, the content of this suggestively titled poem is discernibly melancholic. What else might we say about it? To begin: we could say something about Malanga's use of epistrophe. People and things are continually disappearing – or 'vanishing' – in these elegiac verses. We are left with the prevailing impression that this is very much a poem about personal loss and the inexorable passage of time. The rich social and creative milieu these lines evoke – which were written sometime after Ford departed this sorry veil of tears – has undoubtedly faded into the historical ether. I wonder though: Are things quite as lachrymose as they might appear on first inspection? To all intents and purposes, it would seem so. Yet I can't help but think back to something Ford felt moved to mention in November 1951. I have in mind here that previously cited journal entry about a textual sort of 'flesh' that somehow proves capable of enduring long 'after we are gone'. I mention that here because the more time I spend with Malanga's poem, the more I come to appreciate the fact that Malanga's poem – which could itself be described as an idiosyncratic kind of textual refuge or haven – proves capable of preserving something of the 'spirit' of the modernist milieu of which Ford was a small, though undoubtedly significant cog. And this, in turn, brings me back to the question of the modernist archive.

I want now to bring this enquiry to a close by suggesting that access to the modernist archive not only affords us the opportunity of preserving the 'spirit' of Ford's historical milieu, but helps us – in a way that Malanga's lugubrious and historically removed poem simply cannot – to put some critical 'flesh' on the bones of that same milieu. Gavin Butt reminds us of the fact that, in a turn of phrase indebted to the tonally ambiguous ruminations of the queer post-war American poet John Giorno, 'gossiping is a social activity which produces and maintains the filiations of artistic community'.[22] A draft document held at the HRC helps to illustrate precisely this point. Written by a certain 'Hobo Peep' in the summer of 1936, the breathless and exuberant 'Gossip from Abroad' is full to the brim with anecdote and intimate detail about the various comings and goings of modernism's best and brightest.[23] The singular Jean Cocteau is, for example, reported as having returned from a trip around the world, 'with a new coiffure to match his new face (youthified by the painful burning process which has kept the Hon Mrs Reginald Fellowes more beautiful than her daughters, who have children of their own) consisting of a high clip, with curls in front a la Hepburn'.[24] Not all that long after this, the inimitable Salvador Dalí makes a suitability theatrical entrance. Hobo Peep recounts, how, at a decidedly raucous lecture in London,

> Dali appeared in a deep-sea diver's costume, leading from two large-wolf hounds. SALLLLLLVADOR DALI! came from the loud-speaker in the back of the room, the microphone on the platform receiving Dali's opening words, his own name. He went on (in French, with a heavy Spanish accent) to tell of his pictures, speaking of one that represented the cadaver of a jackass, and a fly buzzing in a Bacchic dance around the rotting matter, but instead of flashing on the screen his picture, appeared the portrait of his wife and chief source of inspiration, Gala: the trembling old gentleman operating in the magic-lantern got his slides mixed.[25]

Having waxed suitably poetic about all things accented and Bacchic, Hobo Peep goes on to describe how, on the other side of the English Channel, '<u>Andre Breton</u> and <u>Paul Eluard</u> have quarrelled but <u>Eluard</u> continues to be <u>May Ray</u>'s best friend'.[26] How best to approach this unpublished document, which also hints at the role that acts of financial patronage played in the development and promotion of modernism?[27] To be sure, the general tenor of Hobo Peep's missive is both – as mentioned not all that long ago – ebullient and agog. Having said that though, I think there is something more to be said about this particular communiqué. There is, for one thing, something to be said about the lack of critical judgment on display in this document. I mention that here as Hobo Peep makes it clear from the outset that he has no interest whatsoever in passing anything even remotely approaching the condition of properly evaluative or 'critical' judgement on the various creative personages and cultural happenings that are being described in this most gossipy of international bulletins.[28] As to why Hobo Peep chose not to put the critically evaluative boot in? It is difficult to say with any degree of certainty. What we can say with something approximating the condition of relative certainty is this: Hobo Peep seems fascinated by the various sorts of social and creative networks that enabled much if not all modernist cultural production.[29] Critically evaluative or not, the fact remains: archival materials of this type are clearly of great interest to modernist scholars of an overtly historicist bent. Unpublished documentary texts of this sort will always be of great interest to scholars invested in methods and processes of historicization because it affords fresh insight into and information about certain of the social dynamics and commercial imperatives underpinning the networked and historically situated artistic circles in which modernists such as Ford once moved and participated. Overlooked archival materials such as Ford's epistolary tête-à-tête, as well as the larger archives in which such documentary materials are now to be found, are in this concrete fashion of vital critical importance: they serve to move critical conversations about modernism along.[30] That is, they furnish us with unique, lively and often intimate records that help us to more accurately and thoroughly historicize modernism. Having done so (and only having done so), we might then go about setting ourselves the equally important task of picking up the critically evaluative slack (as left behind by the aforementioned Hobo Peep), of theorizing some fresh, inventive and rigorously historicized interpretations and reimaginings of what we have come to recognize as modernism.

Notes

1 See Alexander Howard, *Charles Henri Ford: Between Modernism and Postmodernism* (London: Bloomsbury, 2017); 'Keep on Waking: Charles Henri Ford, Camp, and Surrealism', *Miranda* 14 (2017), http://miranda.revues.org/9812 (all websites last accessed 12 June 2019); 'Camp, Modernism, and Charles Henri Ford', *Modernism/modernity* 23/1 (2016), pp. 9–13.

2 Adam McKible, *The Space and Place of Modernism: The Russian Revolution, Little Magazines, and New York* (London: Routledge, 2002), p. 10.

3 Peter Marks, 'Making the New: Literary Periodicals and the Construction of Modernism', *Precursors and Aftermaths: Literature in English, 1914–1945* 2/1 (2004), p. 37.

4 Suzanne W. Churchill, 'The Lying Game: *Others* and the Great Spectra Hoax of 1917', in *Little Magazines and Modernism: New Approaches*, ed. Suzanne W. Churchill and Adam McKible (Aldershot: Ashgate, 2007), p. 179.

5 Suzanne W. Churchill, 'Introduction?' in *The Little Magazine 'Others' and the Renovation of Modern American Poetry* (Aldershot: Ashgate, 2006), p. 10.

6 Anonymous, 'Out of a Blue Sky', *Transition: An International Quarterly for Creative Experiment*, 16–17 (1929), n.p.

7 Charles Henri Ford, *I Will Be What I Am: A Documentary Portrait*, [n.d.], 134, Series 1, Box, 3, Folder 1, Charles Henri Ford Papers, Harry Ransom Center, University of Texas at Austin, p. 135.

8 Ford, *I Will Be What I Am*, p. 76.

9 Ibid., p. 116.

10 Charles Henri Ford to Parker Tyler, 19 April 1951, Container 8, Folder 5, Parker Tyler Papers, Harry Ransom Center, University of Texas at Austin.

11 Charles Henri Ford, *Water from a Bucket: A Diary, 1948–1957* (New York: Turtle Point Press, 2001), pp. 126–7.

12 Charles Henri Ford to Parker Tyler, 17 November 1951, Container 8, Folder 5, Parker Tyler Papers, Harry Ransom Center, University of Texas at Austin.

13 Charles Henri Ford to Parker Tyler, 7 March 1952, Container 8, Folder 5, Parker Tyler Papers, Harry Ransom Center, University of Texas at Austin.

14 Charles Henri Ford to Parker Tyler, 26 December 1952, Container 8, Folder 5, Parker Tyler Papers, Harry Ransom Center, University of Texas at Austin.

15 Ford, *Water from a Bucket*, p. 159.

16 Charles Henri Ford to Parker Tyler, 7 July 1960, Container 9, Folder 1, Parker Tyler Papers, Harry Ransom Center, University of Texas at Austin.

17 Ted Berrigan to Charles Henri Ford, 26 April 1965, Series 2, Box, 12, Folder 2, Charles Henri Ford Papers, Harry Ransom Center, University of Texas at Austin.

18 Gerard Malanga and Andy Warhol, *Screen Tests/A Diary* (New York: Kulchur Press, 1967), p. 17.

19 Gerard Malanga to Charles Henri Ford, 24 April 1964, Series 2, Box 14, Folder 3, Charles Henri Ford Papers, Harry Ransom Center, University of Texas at Austin.

20 Gerard Malanga, *10 Poems for 10 Poets* (Los Angeles: Black Sparrow Press, 1970), p. 29. The last line of this extract alludes to a collection of short stories that Charles Henri Ford edited: *The Night of Jupiter and Other Fantastic Stories* (New York: View Editions, 1945).

21 Gerard Malanga, *No Respect: New and Selected Poems, 1964–2000* (Santa Rosa: Black Sparrow Press, 2001), p. 288.

22 Gavin Butt, *Between You and Me: Queer Disclosures in the New York Art World, 1948–1963* (Durham, NC: Duke University Press, 2006), p. 1.

23 On 8 August 1936, Ford told Parker Tyler that he had just written 'a gossip-from-abroad letter to [the New York printer] Lew Ney for his Hobo Number in case its not off the press signed anonymously HOBO-PEEP but what you don't already know in it maybe wont hurt you'. Charles Henri Ford to Parker Tyler, 8 August 1936, Container 8, Folder 3, Parker Tyler Papers, Harry Ransom Center, University of Texas at Austin. NB. Original spelling and punctuation preserved.

24 Charles Henri Ford, 'Gossip from Abroad', [1936], series 1, Box, 2, Folder 4, Charles Henri Ford Papers, Harry Ransom Center, University of Texas at Austin, p. 1.

25 Ford, 'Gossip from Abroad', pp. 1–2.

26 Ibid., p. 2.

27 The issue of financial patronage comes to the fore in the opening paragraph of the draft of the letter: 'The Paris season opened and closed with the Concert written and conducted by Igor Markevitch, the much talked [about] new genius of music, first discovered by Diaghilew about 8 years ago. His newest work is a symphony, Le Paradis Perdu, with a chorus of 250, which sing the poetry not of Milton but of Mr. Markevitch, perhaps with the aid of Milton and the Bible. The money for this particular evening was said to have been furnished by Mr. Edward James (Tilly Losch's ex) and since this is a gossipy foray, your Hobo Correspondent will not attempt to give any critical evaluation.' Ford, p. 1.

28 Ibid.

29 We get a sense of this in the final paragraph of the free-wheeling letter. Note, in particular, how Ford goes to significant lengths when describing the role that social networking played in the pre-publication history of Djuna Barnes seminal *Nightwood* (1935): 'Edith Sitwell writing a first novel in the country in England … Djuna Barnes, returned from London where T. S. Eliot's enthusiasm for her latest work incurred its

acceptance by Faber & Faber, reports that Englishmen should have sailed for America at the age of 5 …. Emily Holmes Coleman has a flat in Chelsea, loves poetry, and was responsible for Djuna Barnes' MS getting into Eliot's hands … H.D. also has a flat in London but Bryher is in Switzerland … '. Ford, p. 3.

30 Unpublished documents of this sort also, in a neat turn of phrase that should be familiar to the editorial team behind the 'Historicising Modernism' series, reach beyond the familiar rhetoric of intellectual and artistic 'autonomy' employed by many modernists and their critical commentators.

12

EXPANDING QUEER ARCHIVES: RICHARD BRUCE NUGENT'S UNPUBLISHED MODERNISM

David Deutsch

Handsome, talented and courageously queer, even for his generally tolerant, avant-garde New York social circles, Richard Bruce Nugent (1906–87) worked during and after the cultural flowering of the Harlem Renaissance. An acquaintance of Langston Hughes and Zora Neale Hurston, and consequently a frequent byline in cultural histories of the Renaissance, Nugent achieved some early prominence through his sensual drawings for little magazines and for his explicitly pan-erotic prose piece 'Smoke, Lilies and Jade', published in the scandal-making artistic journal *Fire!!* (1926). Following *Fire!!* Nugent's critical sidelining was due partly to contemporary unease over his sexual and gender non-conformities and partly to his comfort with producing art in relatively ephemeral or private mediums, such as in magazines and in unpublished manuscripts, many of which now reside at Yale's Beinecke Library alongside documents relating to his long eclectic life.[1]

Yet, if long overlooked after 'Smoke', by the mid-1980s scholars and artists began to excavate Nugent's work in groundbreaking anthologies and in cinema focusing on queer black men, such as Joseph Beam's *In the Life* (1986), Isaac Julien's *Looking for Langston* (1989), and Beam and Essex Hemphill's *Brother to Brother* (1991). Thomas Wirth added fuel to this new fire through his compilation of Nugent's work in *Gay Rebel of the Harlem Renaissance* (2002) and his publication of Nugent's Renaissance-era novel *Gentleman Jigger* (2008). These latter works illustrate how Nugent's prose ranges from a decadent symbolism to modernist techniques of fragmentation to fashion a variety of homoerotic narratives. As Wirth argues, by 'refusing to accept the supposition that homosexual themes, modernist forms, and "decadence" were off-limits to black writers', Nugent fought 'to expand his contemporaries' conceptions of blackness' and to create a formally and thematically queer multiracial aesthetic for American fiction.[2] Nugent's narratives certainly form an important part of American queer literature generally, but they should also be understood as vitally 'quare', to borrow E. Patrick Johnson's term for a queer hermeneutic that accounts for 'the material existence of "colored" bodies'.[3] Thanks to writers such as Beam and Hemphill and to Wirth's generous executorship of Nugent's archive, including leaving it in the public domain in 2014, scholars can increasingly understand the extent to which Nugent engaged and even shaped cosmopolitan traditions into an explicitly quare modernist American tradition.

In this chapter, I want to use Nugent's archive to show how he stylistically and conceptually engages a key theme of a queer American modernism, namely that of same-sex desiring angelic characters. While twenty-first-century audiences might recognize this theme thanks to Tony Kushner's *Angels in America* (1991–2) and to Jonathan Larson's *Rent* (1994), with its gender-fluid heroine Angel, these plays expand work from the 1920s onwards by authors such as Countée Cullen (in 'The Shroud of Color' (1924) and 'The Black Christ' (1929)) and Langston Hughes (in 'The Trouble with Angels' (1935) and 'The Little Virgin' (1927)) who represent the racial diversity of queer US subcultures through angelic figures. Significantly, Nugent's work connects to but stands apart from that of Cullen and Hughes because of his willingness to emphasize overtly queer themes that he refused to temper for professional or social reasons and that he explored in little magazine stories and in initially unpublishable manuscripts. In his work, moreover, Nugent defiantly mixes sacred and profane angelic imagery to depict same-sex desiring and gender nonconforming men as angelic rebels, as mixtures of humanity and divinity and thus as embodiments of what I call 'bad beatitudes'. By 'bad beatitudes' I mean behaviours, such as same-sex sex, and identities, such as quare subjectivities, that create hybrid states-of-being in which the conventionally profane becomes the unconventionally sacred and vice versa, with both inverted concepts held in tension. Often such bad beatitudes explicitly revise Miltonic or Blakean paradigms to insist on the moral, spiritual and even patriotic value of racial and sexual rebels who frequently thrive despite their nominally degraded circumstances. Combining contemporary African American intellectual and religious tropes with earlier European aesthetic traditions, quare angels in African American writing work within their own analogous yet more racially aware and more uniquely cosmopolitan traditions.

Nugent's engagement with literary bad beatitudes and his stylistic versatility come across most complexly in 'Uranus in Cancer', an all but complete novel that critiques the multifaceted constituents of a queer multiracial America.[4] Begun in the 1920s and expanded from around 1955 to 1965, Nugent composed 'Uranus' in four parts, 'Exposition', 'Lunatique', 'Letters into Limbo' and 'Sing a Dream'. In each section, he uses a new narrator to examine the evolving love life of Angel Stuartti, a young man with African, Hispanic, Italian and US heritages, born in Puerto Rico, raised in New Jersey, and a relation to Aeon and Stuartt of *Gentleman Jigger*. Wirth published a slightly abridged version of the highly romantic 'Lunatique' section in *Gay Rebel*, but a consideration of the whole manuscript illuminates Nugent's thoughtfully sustained prismatic modernism, his representations of continually shifting and concurrent perceptions, simultaneously affirming and disparaging, of queer individuals in the mid-twentieth century from the perspectives of Angel himself, his conventionally masculine lovers or 'trade', a female lover, and his friends. This approach shows how Nugent intentionally disrupts what Siobhan Somerville has described as the 'intertwined' and 'simultaneous efforts to shore up and bifurcate categories of race and sexuality' between 'black' and 'white' and 'homosexual' and 'heterosexual' during 'the late nineteenth and early twentieth centuries'.[5] Nugent performs this disruption through the complex trope of a quare Angel-ic rebel against a Caucasian heteronormative ideal of masculinity and of US nationalism.

While Wirth's slightly abridged version of 'Lunatique' launches directly into the surreal perspective of the adolescent Angel, in his manuscript Nugent invites a more critical reading of this section by balancing out its dream-like prose with the pragmatic concreteness of his opening 'Exposition'. This 'Exposition' provides a frame narrative that describes the novel's sections, including 'Lunatique', as remembrances of Angel collected by his cousin Aeon. Having intended to write a history of their family in the United States, Aeon quickly shifts focus to the fascinating life of Angel, thereby unusually centring a family's and even a nation's experiences around a queer multiracial individual. Aeon begins by tracing Angel's cosmopolitan background, describing how his grandfather left the United States for Italy, rejecting 'this land of opportunity that somehow could always find the black blood in no matter how pale a person and use the stigmas against him'.[6] By introducing the grandfather's pragmatic move to Italy to avoid discriminatory American hierarchies, a move reversed when Angel's mother repatriates her own family, Nugent encourages a reading of the grandson's dreamlike perceptions as an analogous means to de-centre a world hostile to individuals with mixed racial heritages as well as with non-normative genders and sexualities. If Nugent employs a purplish prose to signal the escapist fantasies of an adolescent beginning to explore the romantic overtones of sensual desire, an echo of his grandfather's Italianate flight, Angel's perspective also encompasses a real world mixed with metaphors and literalism. This perspective angelically blurs the poles of dreams and reality, as well as racial, sexual and gender classifications. If at times this dreamy, angelic perspective risks lunacy, it also evokes a rebellious reordering of existence, one that resists any too static or discrete categorizations and that evolves toward more affirmative, if at times frightening, identity formations.

Nugent begins 'Lunatique' with Angel going through puberty and thus an in-between state that explains his intense blurring of internal and external identities. At the age of 'sixteen', while living in New Jersey's Palisades in the 1930s, Angel prefers to think in his mother's 'Italian old-country idioms' and in his father's 'Spanish aphorisms', and while 'other boys were playing pool' or 'learning loitering on the streets, he was living dreams'.[7] Perceiving the world through a distancing European poetry, Angel skirts alienating American conventions of blackness, so hated by his grandfather, as well as the unpoetic, rough masculine habits of his mixed-race male peers. Yet Angel's environment nonetheless affects him as even his fleeting encounters with his peers influence his eroticized gender expressions. When encountering girls, the local boys usually offer comments on their erotic 'possibilities', which while clearly harassment also lends an 'insolent and stiffly-proud lilt to the girls' walk' and so functions as a problematic tribute to which the girls respond with self-assertive pride. A similar process occurs with Angel, whom the boys also 'bait' in ways that break through his fugue-like state. Although Angel 'never' consciously 'heard' the boys, the 'sight and sound of them' sparked in his movements 'a touch of the same coquetry that painted the girls' (251–2). Whether Angel's effeminate flirting is innate or learned, like the boys' loitering and white misconceptions of blackness, the girls' behaviour provides a clear comparison for Angel's that emphasizes his combination of masculine and feminine traits.

Consequently the boys perceive Angel as an erotically charged variant of the more feminine and eccentric facets of their already diverse community. Although at first they consider Angel only a 'mildly interesting topic', their 'conversation' about him accumulates an orgasmic charge as it 'spattered around … into tepid curiosity as to his sex life' and they imagine that '[i]f he were a girl, they could all have a good time' (252). Angel inspires the boys to engage in pleasurably poetic fantasies, not so different from his own, which lead them away from imagining sex with girls and toward an exciting contact with the effeminate Angel. Nugent creates here a community that readily accepts intermingling Puerto Rican, Spanish, Italian and African heritages to suggest that an easy blurring of sexual and gender classifications by boys already charged with surging hormones could be fairly plausible. Within this social schematic, flexible categories of sexuality and gender become part of these boys' psychologically and geographically multiracial American landscape.

Still, as part of this poetic blurring, the boys' imagined sexual encounters with Angel occasionally veer towards an aggression analogous to their harassment of women. Nugent raises the interrelated degradations of misogyny and queer-phobia to acknowledge their reality and to contradict their seeming inevitability. The boys initially consider Angel to be 'like a dog to tease (and pet) but never harm'. This animalistic characterization allows the boys to trivialize an uneasy sensuality, a teasing and petting, with a distancing superiority not explicitly designed to hurt a peculiar yet familiar member of their society. This dehumanization, however, Nugent insists, risks veering into threatening behaviour as the boys consider whether Angel might be 'a *pato* like they had met down at the ferry terminal' and 'whom they had chased after they had used him. Scared the hell out of him'. The boys have a clear conception of a disgraced effeminate queer man, a *pato*, equivalent to a fairy, hinted at by the homonym 'ferry', whom they 'used' sexually and then terrorized. This violence hovers at the edge of the boys' relationship with Angel. The boys refuse to see someone close to their age and in school with them as a *pato*, but they enjoy imagining that Angel is 'so nuts' that he might be tricked into touching them for a cheap trinket, 'for an apple-on-a-stick or a dime. That would be fun. And convenient too, if it worked. That was how it all began' (252). To any reader familiar with the conventionally tragic endings of 1930s same-sex narratives, the phrase '[t]hat was how it all began' following the juxtaposition of the story of the ostensibly normal boys who 'used' and then abused the *pato* raises an ominous cloud which the rest of the narrative subtly resists.[8] The boys never physically attack Angel as a fairy or for being queer, but this scene raises the consistent potential for male violence against effeminate and same-sex desiring men, as well as the multifaceted limits of queer identifications that did not readily encompass conventionally masculine, same-sex behaviours and longings.[9]

This scene broadens then an exploration of Angel's same-sex desires to include the desire of these relatively masculine boys to entice an effeminate male without considering themselves to be at all queer. George Chauncey has noted that effeminate mannerisms rather than same-sex erotic interactions generally, although not always, connoted queerness in the 1910s and 1920s, and Eric Garber has detailed how a similar interpretive process occurred in African American culture in blues songs and in Harlem in the 1920s and 1930s.[10] Nugent draws on these contexts in his depictions of these boys in New Jersey. In addition to courting girls, these wilfully masculine boys with a mixture of African, European and American heritages often visit spaces that represent provincial versions of the racially mixed, occasionally homoerotic urban 'interzones' detailed by Kevin Mumford.[11] The boys first visit the ferry/fairy bathroom and then spend hours voyeuristically watching one another flirt with Angel by the local river: they watched, for instance, 'while one [boy] went over and talked to [Angel]. Watched while he tried all the obvious tricks unsuccessfully, watched him cradle his crotch', and watched him 'take a curving leak' and 'with a little difficulty put his semi-hard self away again and ostentatiously zipped his fly'. The physical and psychological excitement in these scenes flows most strongly through the boys who find it 'fun' and like a 'game' to try, and to watch each other try, to seduce Angel 'night after night' as he remains distracted by 'other things entirely' (252). This process continues, courting and avoiding both same-sex sex and violence in unexpected ways, until most of the boys' interest in Angel wanes.

Nugent offers a romantic twist, however, by having Adorio, the local heart-throb, continue to pursue Angel, initially using this 'game' to prove his superior attractiveness to the other boys and subsequently as an excuse to pursue a loving same-sex intimacy. Nicknamed 'Cano', a reference to 'his pale hair' which contrasts 'provocatively with his Puerto-Rican being and complexion', Adorio exudes a magnetism that makes him the boys' 'acknowledged leader' and that causes a 'vision of him' to linger in the 'girls' eyes' (251). After the boys fail to seduce Angel, Cano asserts his own allure by claiming that '*he* could get' Angel. Cano's motivations prove far more complex though than simply enhancing his public reputation, for '[e]ven after the others lost interest … he continued' to meet with Angel, as this had become 'a habit' for him, 'like praying' (252, 253). Cano and Angel's relationship takes on a highly romantic, emotionally charged and spiritual idealism. Rather than exposing his 'crotch' to Angel, Cano uses more poetic techniques in their nightly encounters. 'Look at the sky', he tells Angel, 'then the stars will be in your eyes, and I can have one for the asking. And if you look closely enough, you'll see them in *my* eyes, taken from yours'. Rather than starting with crude lust, the two share romance and poetry, using metaphorical techniques and identities which through repetition normalize their relationship and communicate their shared desire for closeness. Cano becomes the 'Moon' for Angel and this poetic fancy enables Cano to share with Angel what 'a man smothers inside himself and has lonesome feelings about', while Cano learns to interpret Angel, who likewise now feels as if he 'had no secrets' (253). If such poetry prevents them from overtly acknowledging their love both to themselves and to each other, this distance nonetheless allows their companionship to develop a shared spiritual rhetoric that enables a psychological and emotional intimacy.

This shadowy poetic perspective allows both boys private room for exploration, but it becomes problematic as Nugent indicates that a healthy romance must also exist in a pragmatically clear-cut, even public sphere. While Angel fantasizes that Adorio is the 'Moon', Adorio wonders whether his suppressed interest in men can sustain his love for Angel, 'I couldn't love you, could I, Chicito?' Cano tests this hypothesis, as 'the moon kissed [Angel] sudden-and-long', then 'spoke on in tentative tones … half frightened and half calculating, half conqueror and half conquered' as they 'made love', with Angel fellating Adorio (257). This semi-private space on the Palisades perceived through anthropomorphic celestial mythologies allows for a negotiation of frightening and deeply longed for connections, as well as a strategic and spontaneous surrendering to romantic and sexual desires on both sides. Cano moves past his resistance to romantic same-sex sex by emphasizing Angel's youthful gender ambiguity and Angel responds to Cano's sensuality by turning him into a fantasy that would not mock him at school or chase him as a *pato*. A conventional reality, however, inevitably intervenes. After sex, Angel falls asleep and Cano leaves, perhaps not wanting to disturb Angel but in effect abandoning his lover naked and alone out in nature. When Angel wakes, he succumbs to the psychological trauma of abandonment after physical and romantic closeness and his body and mind respond with a fever that makes him '[d]elirious' and causes 'hallucinations', which a doctor warns might lead to a '[n]ervous breakdown' (258–9). Only when Cano visits Angel in his sickbed, in a public light, in the presence of his lover's mother, does Angel break the bounds of his fantasy heightened into fever to acknowledge that 'the moon was Adorio' and begin to grow 'well' (259).

Physical and mental illnesses of course play a significant metaphorical role in much early twentieth-century queer literature. Such sicknesses represent the influence of contemporary American medical, legal, religious and social authorities that pathologized same-sex desires and gender nonconformities, a perspective that individuals had to discount in order to consider themselves healthy, moral and sane.[12] Racial inequalities frequently intensified any large-scale senses of dis-ease for same-sex desiring or gender nonconforming people as racism seeped in to even the most accepting of Harlem's homoerotic 'interzones', a trend that Wallace Thurman represents in *Infants of the Spring* through the depression of Stephen and Raymond and through Paul Arbian's suicide. Vaguely defined maladies and volatile nervous conditions also then represent the effects of this pathological thinking as sexual and gender nonconformists of all races were made to feel feverish or delusional as repressions and as the threat of arrest combined with the very real risks of losing jobs, families, status and legal rights could easily cause a nervous breakdown. The best cure in these cases would be an inclusive and equitable role for queer individuals in a more diversely welcoming subculture or social circle. Along such lines, the potential for allegedly pathological thought patterns, in particular, to actually signify unconventional dreams of social reorganization helped to validate queerness and to facilitate the formation of more welcoming subcultures. The stakes of these mutually influential cultural comparisons among sickness, queerness, and race would change drastically in the 1980s with the advent of and societies' shifting reactions to HIV/AIDS across American racial spectrums. But in early instances, a shift of social perspectives on sexual and gender nonconformities, albeit more easily conceptualized than achieved, could help to begin a cure.

In 'Lunatique', Nugent draws on these representational traditions but he emphasizes the creative value of queer thinking even while acknowledging its risks. He stresses how Angel's reputation for being 'nuts' stems from poetical perceptions and feelings that valuably refute too rigid categorizations and classifications. Extending the plurality of an already cosmopolitan American society, evolved from African, Puerto-Rican, Spanish, Italian, and English cultural and linguistic influences, Angel blurs the lines restricting what constitutes a permissible romantic relationship. Granted, this refusal to abide by accepted relationship structures can go too far, as when Angel excessively distorts actual identities and mistakes metaphors for actualities. Angel's lover is of course only ever *like* the moon, although his identifying characteristics might shift to reflect 'Adorio' in more personal circumstances and 'Cano' in more public ones. Taking any poeticism too far, Nugent suggests, can lead to the very real pain and suffering of physical and psychological illnesses, but being able to see the elasticity of seemingly discrete categories valuably recognizes the expansiveness of both individual and communal identities.

Nugent illustrates this elasticity by having Angel and Adorio establish a relatively healthy balance of private and public classifications. If far from an ideal openness, the boys adapt to their age and environment and shift pragmatically between a personal romance and a public friendship. These shifts prove mutually influential for all involved: 'When Angel was well, he went with Adorio to the block and the guys soon accepted him, because he was Cano's friend.' The boys even grow to appreciate Angel as he 'saw things they didn't see until he showed them and said things they never said until they heard them from him' (259). If initially the boys accept Angel because of his friendship with Cano, a familiarity expands to a welcoming acquaintance, and the boys incorporate into their consciousness Angel's perspectives. Granted such poetic incorporations are limited, for the boys never recognize or accept explicitly a mixed-race same-sex romance. They do, however, learn to accept a softer, less-crude version of male friendship and even perhaps an open secret that enables the continuation without social ostracization of Angel and Adorio's relationship. If tragic from the point of view of inclusion and equity for queer individuals, the situation presents a pragmatic solution for two teenagers, one that enables them to feel less isolated and that allows their romance to continue fruitfully if never quite safely in the too-slowly changing world of 1930s New Jersey.

More problematic is the effect of this social assimilation on Angel's personality and sexuality as his public persona adopts some of the boys' misogynistic crudeness.

Nugent signifies such troubling differences in evolving private and public identities through names that indicate the importance of social classifications and yet resist their totalizing power. Alone, Adorio and Angel call each other by their given names, yet their friends recognize them as 'Cano' and 'Chico', respectively, nicknames that hide the softer, more loving, spiritual intimacy of their private romance. As such, Nugent writes, 'Chico went with the guys … when they stood and watched the girls' and 'Chico watched and said things, too' (260). Nugent presents 'Chico' harassing the girls to critique the learned misogyny so prevalent in most male cultures. In doing so, Nugent signals how, despite Angel's effeminacy, his biological maleness offers him some access, no matter how partial, to dominant social groups should he sufficiently conform to popular masculine norms, which he unfortunately does as Chico.

As this analysis suggests, Nugent uses 'Cano' and 'Chico' to explore the compromises that queer men make with themselves and with each other as they sustain and deviate from deeply rooted paradigms of heterosexuality and masculinity. Despite Angel's general disinterest in erotic relations with women, as Chico he allows Cano to teach him

> how to make love to women … because [Cano] wanted everything for Chico that he wanted for himself. For Adorio loved Angel … more completely than he had ever loved anyone before. Loved him the same way he wanted to love a woman, but at the same time differently, too, for … there was manhood to share and have with him. (260)

Nugent indicates the boys' give-and-take in their careful shaping of their innate desires for gender and sex. This considered process echoes what Boone has called 'Nugent's achievements' in 'Smoke' wherein Nugent represented 'an African-American character under the sway of [a queer] libidinal desire that avoids the pervasive racist equation of the Negro with instinctual, "animalistic" sexuality'.[13] A similar process happens in 'Lunatique', albeit with additional concessions by both boys to a learned heteronormativity. Reinforcing heterosexuality as a quasi-demeaning model and cover for their relationship, Cano teaches Chico what he thinks women want from men, which provides an initial way for Adorio to justify having his own libidinal intimacy with Angel. This also enables Adorio to teach Angel about a form of masculinity that he wants for himself and for his lover, just as Angel encourages Adorio to think poetically. As they learn and adapt to each other's needs, these pedagogical sessions offer both boys paths to love each other and to self-love. Such adaptations also enable new discoveries of what might constitute same-sex love and diverse versions of masculinity that enable them to enjoy both innate and learned desires.

This compromising process nonetheless entails several severe drawbacks. It often, Nugent implies, engages an abusive manipulation, as both boys use unwitting women as a means to draw closer together, enacting one more form of misogyny. It also self-destructively coerces the boys into socially ordained roles that they only gradually learn to modify for their own purposes. Adorio 'wanted to love a woman', presumably due to social pressure bolstered by some limited heterosexual attraction, despite his chief intellectual, emotional and physical needs drawing him towards the quasi-effeminate, quasi-masculine Angel/Chico. Likewise 'Chico' agrees to pursue women, but largely to satisfy Cano's expectations, as Nugent reports that 'Angel lived only for Adorio' (260). Lastly, while the vagueness that surrounds their relationship offers opportunities for togetherness, it also discourages any consideration of themselves in larger social terms, which could offer them a comfortingly stable, intellectually and emotionally useful tool to understand themselves and to prepare themselves to connect to an effective sociopolitical queer network.

Angel and Adorio thus adapt to and suffer from the requirements of their larger community, even as they contribute to it on local and national levels. If Angel usefully expands the town boys' perspectives, Nugent signals the value of queer individuals and queer lovers to the nation by having Angel and Adorio enlist together when the United States enters the Second World War. During the war, the lovers find their relationship obliquely idealized within the intense male bonding enabled by the massive movement and mingling of men in the armed forces. As part of the army, the lovers engage both ideals of Hellenic lover-soldiers and contemporary American circumstances. Angel and Adorio's fellow soldiers, for instance, think of them enviously in terms of the 'buddy system' that developed in the United States' military during the 1940s. Allan Bérubé has observed that this system accorded a 'respectability to devoted male couples, whether or not they included gay men' and allowed the manifestation of an 'open affection' between socially and institutionally valued companions.[14] In Nugent's novel, this publically respectable affection enables the intensification of the young men's private romance. After a 'decimating encounter' in Italy, Adorio and Angel's fellow soldiers watch them walk off together and reflect 'what buddies Cano and Chico were and how always when any of them needed help, one of the two would appear as if by magic, and then the other would be there, too' (260). As their fellow soldiers admire them from a distance, the two men engage in personal symbolic marriage gestures. Angel gives Adorio his mother's ring, thereby initiating him into a larger family relationship, after which Adorio 'made his kind of love to Angel' (261). Nugent overloads this scene with irony as the soldiers praise the pair's friendship, their value to their unit, and by extension to the nation, even as the lovers have to hide the precise nature of their intimacy, which the military frequently considered to be disruptive to a unit's cohesiveness and worthy of a dishonourable discharge and/or confinement.[15] Race, of course, adds an additional irony since multiracial citizens, such as Angel and Adorio, often fought overseas for the United States only to be exploited in the military and back at home.[16]

As such, the violence that Nugent introduced and then resisted early in 'Lunatique' resurfaces with heightened symbolism during wartime in more national and international contexts. The local boys refrained from terrorizing Chico and Cano like the more overtly queer *pato* whom they hypocritically use and abuse, but an analogous hypocritical violence resurfaces in world events as the United States deploys same-sex desiring and gender nonconforming soldiers to fight European fascism while abusing these soldiers and their larger communities through its own legalized authoritarian repressions. This underlines the horrific connections, although not equivalencies, between American tyranny and the very fascism that the United States sent its queer and racially diverse soldiers to fight.[17] Nugent illustrates this duplicitous national exploitation on both queer and racial levels by describing how Adorio gets killed in battle and Angel subsequently returns to New Jersey, 'where he was honored as a hero, and Cano was honored posthumously', with everyone being 'proud and sad' for 'they all knew that Angel was alone' (261). These townspeople, like US citizens at large, benefit from and often take pride in the achievements and sacrifices of individuals whose rights they restrict and whose identities and relationships they marginalize or disavow even as they intuit, if they do not entirely admit, the intensity of the distress, the sickness and the loneliness that this alienation causes.

In his edition of 'Lunatique', Wirth ends the narrative at this point, thereby stressing Nugent's salient critique of US hypocrisy, with society eagerly benefiting from but refusing to give full equality to quare minorities. In his manuscript, however, Nugent closes this section with a greater resiliency by detailing how Angel moves beyond this personal and national impasse. Rather than return to his provincial life, Angel refuses to give in to a decadent fascination with staticness and death, and at twenty-one he leaves for New York City, where he 'lived rapidly'.[18] Once there, he adopts a gregarious and active resistance to the crudely violent world around him by assuming the name Riccie Ricordi, signalling his growing independence, Riccie being a shortened version of Ricardo, signifying a firm leader who remembers his past, *ricordi* meaning 'memories' in Italian. Without forgetting Adorio, Riccie explores the new intimacies and more varied queer points of view available in New York in the 1940s.

Combined with the 'Exposition', this shift at the end of the manuscript of 'Lunatique' signals that one key facet of Nugent's project in 'Uranus' is to create a plentitude of narrative scopes, like interlocking celestial and terrestrial spheres, which represent quare lives from a multitude of Miltonic or Blakean perspectives. In the 'Exposition', Nugent introduces Aeon as a biographer and an anthologist of sorts who compiles diverse characters' reflections on Angel. 'Lunatique' is the first reflection after the 'Exposition', which turns out to be an autobiographical letter sent to Aeon and signed 'Riccie'. The final manuscript page of 'Lunatique' thus requires readers to shift their understanding of it as a story blending decadent and surrealist traits into a favourable retrospective impression of how Riccie perceived his early years from a more mature standpoint. Nugent pairs this with a diametric derision of Riccie in the next section, entitled 'Letters into Limbo', which comprises letters written by Riccie's one-time housemate Aldo. In these documents, Aldo asserts his normative masculinity by critiquing Riccie as not dreamy or nationally valuable but as a 'bitch' and he reports that their cross-class, multiracial housemates dislike Riccie's 'flippant manner' (21, 23). Aldo presents Riccie's effeminate facetiousness as disruptive to their communal house. Here sexual, gender and racial denigrations collide as Aldo claims to quote certain white associates' aversion to Riccie's alleged social disruptions.

This multifaceted epistolary narrative structure creates a prismatically indeterminate intimacy. Voices encountered always via second- or third-hand reports reflect erratic modernist identities, such as those explored by Djuna Barnes or Sam Selvon. In 'Uranus', Nugent uses such fragments to explore the phobias, desires and mental acrobatics engaged in by so-called trade or masculine men who desire effeminate men but who often admit this only indirectly so as to retain their socially superior, ostensibly heteronormative self-identity.[19] Aldo, Nugent eventually suggests, lashes out at any semblance of queerness to reassert his questionable normality and to resist his own craving for Riccie. After spending pages lambasting Riccie in letters to Aeon, Aldo admits that they once had an affair and he recalls with an anxious yearning 'how adeptly Riccie' performed various 'love-techniques' (69). Aldo's scorn for Riccie, Nugent implies, stems from his regret or resentment over their split, from his anxious need to reject any queer intimacies, and from his desire to punish Riccie for accepting same-sex desires so easily, which Aldo misinterprets as a dissipated promiscuity.

In actuality, Nugent portrays most of his characters as sexually spontaneous, which in effect highlights Riccie's intense emotional restraint, an extension of his loyalty to Adorio. By the end of 'Letters', Riccie has had sex with several male characters and with a woman named Cynthia, thereby illustrating a promiscuity analogous to his intellectual and social open-mindedness. Yet on Riccie's part these physical encounters avoid emotional intimacies, as Cynthia notes that Riccie can sleep with a person with 'nothing personal done' (98). Riccie remains emotionally unattached to his male and his female sexual partners and these disconnections result from Riccie's lingering grief for Adorio. Refusing to equate physical and emotional intimacies, Riccie challenges denigrations of same-sex promiscuity and of a queer glibness by manifesting an enduring loyalty to his first love.

Nugent evolves this quare loyalty in 'Sing a Dream', the final section of 'Uranus', as Riccie returns to being Angel and fills the emotional void left by Adorio's death with a new relationship with a Hispanic man named Jesus. This new virile lover overtly reaffirms Nugent's tendency to use character names to insist on the spiritually and physically rebellious value of same-sex romances, presenting as sacred what mainstream early and mid-twentieth-century society too often presented as profane. Nugent signals this rebellious bad beatitude by strategically queering the name 'Jesus', which US society generally reserves for a messiah but which Hispanic cultures use as a more quotidian name, like Angel or Angelo. Nugent's archive, for instance, contains pictures of his friend Jesus S. and nude photos of Angelo P., men who likely served as models for the fictional Jesus and for Angel's occasional lover Angelo in 'Uranus'. In 'Uranus', as in these pictures, a spiritual same-sex eroticism merges happily with a more prosaic yet still exciting material reality.

In acknowledging Angel and Jesus's spiritually and physically exciting relationship, Nugent imagines a certain queer loyalty. After Angel and Jesus declare their mutual love, for instance, Jesus encourages a quasi-open relationship, observing that his brother Angelo loves his wife but that he 'needs' Angel 'too' for certain erotic and emotional fulfilments (252). Angel agrees but signals that his 'love' for Jesus will take precedence. This loyalty complicates non-monogamy by exploring a hierarchy of emotional and physical fidelities, as Angel and Jesus will love others but will give first preference to each other. Nugent suggests via this final note the potential for individuals and for US society to reject a same-race, cross-sex monogamous ideal, if this proves too mutually restrictive.

Without stretching parallels between approaches to romantic relationships and to scholarship too far, I will close by suggesting that Nugent can help to theorize a certain queer loyalty to archival research. Nugent's manuscripts inspire a loyalty that defies engaging an archive through totalizing or monogamous approaches to literary classifications and to resultant interpretations. The analytical approach I have outlined with regard to 'Uranus' exemplifies what I mean. Following Wirth, Julien and the placement of Nugent's archive within Yale's James Weldon Johnson Memorial Collection, I agree that it seems right to emphasize Nugent's relationship with black queer identities and with the Harlem Renaissance. Yet a queer loyalty to Nugent's archive should also value the intermittent pursuit of other critical liaisons. José Muñoz has noted that since 'archives of queerness' are often 'makeshift and randomly organized, due to the restraints historically shackled upon minoritarian cultural workers', more conservative intellectuals have often critiqued 'queer scholarship's claim to "rigor"'. Yet challenging too narrow definitions of 'rigor', Muñoz argues that queer archives can in fact lead to new forms of scrupulous analysis, which result in queer intellectual acts that '*contest and rewrite the protocols of critical writing*'.[20] A queer loyalty to Nugent's archive can indeed help to rewrite the protocols of critical writing. It can encourage an eclectic scholarship that prioritizes Nugent's relationship to the Harlem Renaissance and to quare black culture while also acknowledging that other literary traditions need Nugent too, as Angelo occasionally 'needs' Angel. Nugent's interest in Hispanic culture should encourage us to connect his work to writers such as John Rechy or Luis Zapata, while we should connect his Angelic characters to Ginsberg's or William Burroughs's same-sex desiring angelic hipsters and to drama by Kushner and Larson. While some academics familiar with Nugent's critical reception will prove reticent towards such temporally and culturally unconventional pairings, a queer loyalty to Nugent's archive should encourage readers to acknowledge Nugent's contributions to a wide range of queer post–Second World War cultural activities. Rather than partition off and isolate queer literary traditions, this approach will discover more polyvalent swathes of US cultures. It will value peripheral aesthetic associations while also honouring the heterogeneous even promiscuous aesthetic associations of many queer or quare American authors. In the end, finally, it will enrich our understanding of our (broadly construed) queer American archives.

Notes

1 'Given his sexual explicitness', Schwarz notes, 'the majority of Nugent's works remained unpublished during the Renaissance era'; see A. B. Schwarz, 'Transgressive Sexuality and the Literature of the Harlem Renaissance', in *The Cambridge Companion*

to the Harlem Renaissance, ed. George Hutchinson (Cambridge: Cambridge University Press, 2007), p. 145. Undoubtedly, 'Uranus" queer themes and sexual references ensured that the novel stayed in manuscript form only, even well after the Renaissance era.

2 Thomas Wirth, 'Introduction', in *Gay Rebel of the Harlem Renaissance: Selections from the Work of Richard Bruce Nugent*, ed. Thomas Wirth (Durham, NC: Duke University Press, 2002), p. 45.

3 E. Patrick Johnson, '"Quare" Studies, or (Almost) Everything I know about Queer Studies I Learned from My Grandmother', in *Black Queer Studies: A Critical Anthology*, ed. E. Patrick Johnson and Mae G. Henderson (Durham: Duke University Press, 2005), p. 136.

4 With the exception of scenes from 'Lunatique', which I cite from Wirth's published excerpt in *Gay Rebel* so that readers can follow up with greater ease, I quote from the first extant ribbon copy of 'Uranus', which is the most complete draft of the novel. Nugent reworked several portions over time but the changes were small. I cite portions that remained almost entirely consistent from draft to draft. Wirth notes that 'a handwritten version [of "Lunatique"] appears in one of Nugent's early notebooks from the twenties' (*Gay Rebel*, 248); the Beinecke dates the ribbon copies to c. 1955–65.

5 Siobhan Somerville, *Queering the Color Line: Race and the Invention of Homosexuality in American Culture* (Durham, NC: Duke University Press, 2000), p. 3.

6 Bruce Nugent, 'Uranus in Cancer (ca. 1955–1965)', Bruce Nugent Papers, Series III: Long works of fiction, novels 1929–85, box 42, folders 1 and 2, James Weldon Johnson Memorial Collection, Beinecke Library, Yale University, New Haven, Connecticut.

7 Nugent, *Gay Rebel*, p. 251. Further references to the edition of 'Lunatique' from *Gay Rebel* will be made parenthetically in the text by page number, unless otherwise noted.

8 See, for instance, the violent ends of queer characters in Thurman's satire of Richard Bruce Nugent as Paul Arbian (R.B.N.) in *Infants of the Spring* (1932) and in Blair Niles's *Strange Brother* (1931).

9 Examining the roughly contemporary Newport Naval Training Station incident in 1919–20, Chauncey has noted that even adults consciously engaged in articulating sexualities had difficulty agreeing on terms to define 'the relationship between homosexual behavior and identity in the cultural construction of sexuality. Even when witnesses agreed that two men had engaged in homosexual relations with each other, they disagreed about whether both men or only the one playing the "woman's part" should be labelled as "queer"'; see George Chauncey, 'Christian Brotherhood or Sexual Perversion? Homosexual Identities and the Construction of Sexual Boundaries in the World War One Era', in *Hidden from History: Reclaiming the Gay and Lesbian Past*, ed. Martin Duberman, Martha Vicinus, George Chauncey (New York: New American Library, 1989), p. 295.

10 See Chauncey, *Gay New York: Gender, Urban Culture and the Making of the Gay Male World, 1890–1940* (New York: Basic, 1994), p. 56; and Eric Garber, 'A Spectacle in Color: The Lesbian and Gay Subculture of Jazz Age Harlem', in *Hidden from History: Reclaiming the Gay and Lesbian Past*, ed. Martin Duberman, Martha Vicinus and George Chauncey (New York: New American Library, 1989), p. 320.

11 Kevin Mumford, *Interzones: Black/White Sex Districts in Chicago and New York in the Early Twentieth Century* (New York: Columbia University Press, 1997), pp. 79–80, 85–6.

12 For conflations of queerness as sickness, sin, and crime, see, for instance: Jonathan Katz, *Gay American History: Lesbians and Gay Men in the U.S.A.* (New York: Thomas

Y. Crowell Company, 1976), pp. 129–34; and John D'Emilio, *Sexual Politics, Sexual Communities: The Making of a Homosexual Minority in the United States, 1940–1970* (Chicago: University of Chicago Press, 1983), pp. 17–18, 45–52.

13 Joseph Boone, *Libidinal Currents: Sexuality and the Shaping of Modernism* (Chicago: University of Chicago Press, 1998), p. 223.

14 Allan Bérubé, *Coming Out under Fire: The History of Gay Men and Women in World War II* (Chapel Hill: University of North Carolina Press, 2010), p. 188.

15 Bérubé has detailed how many men and women in the United States' armed forces found new freedoms and queer communities even as the military and government offered an evolving series of horrific punishments for queer men and women who served their country; see his chapters 'The Gang's All Here' for the former and 'The Fight for Reform' for the latter.

16 For a discussion of such exploitations, see, for instance, Douglas Blackmon, *Slavery by Another Name: The Re-Enslavement of Black Americans from the Civil War to World War II* (New York: Doubleday, 2008), pp. 376–9.

17 Citing German news sources, Stefan Kühl reports that in the 1930s, 'Nazi propagandists reacted to American criticism by arguing that ethnic minorities in the United States were treated in a similar way as were Jews in Germany', a situation that was particularly true for black individuals; see Kühl, *The Nazi Connection: Eugenics, American Racism, and German National Socialism* (New York: Oxford University Press, 1994), pp. 98–9.

18 Nugent, 'Uranus in Cancer', Bruce Nugent Papers, Series III: Long works of fiction, novels 1929–85, box 42, folders 1 and 2, p. 15. Further references in this section to the unpublished 'Uranus in Cancer' edition will be made parenthetically in the text by page number.

19 For roughly contemporary definitions of 'trade', see Chauncey, 'Christian Brotherhood', p. 303.

20 José Muñoz, 'Ephemera as Evidence: Introductory Notes to Queer Acts', *Women and Performance* 8/2 (1996), p. 7.

13

Q. D. LEAVIS, ARCHIVES AND THE 'ART OF LIVING'

Miranda Dunham-Hickman

Even in a post-Derridean era sensitized to the hazards of a desire for origins, much work with archives unfolds from the assumption that there is much to be gained from awareness of traces provided through the archive of the materials and environment from which something emerges and takes form, its originary matrix. This essay maintains that the work of Q. D. Leavis (QDL) – well-known Cantabrigian figure, spouse of F. R. Leavis (FRL), co-founder of *Scrutiny* and author of *Fiction and the Reading Public* (1932) – itself represents such a formative matrix. Q. D. Leavis's research comprises a still generally unrecognized body of conceptual material importantly shaping the cultural contributions of the group associated with the periodical *Scrutiny* and its legacy. Moreover, through its impact on the *Scrutiny* circle, I would argue, in still little acknowledged ways, Q. D. Leavis's work significantly influenced what Terry Eagleton famously calls 'the rise of English' – the field this group did so much to build.[1] Finally, this line of thought informs preliminary notes on how we might, today, approach a trove of newly available archival material on 'QDL' herself and, more generally, how the case of Q. D. Leavis might offer ways to think beyond what Derrida calls (in an enigmatic footnote of *Archive Fever*) the 'patriarchive' – patriarchal understandings of the archive and the patriarchal logic of the archive as generally understood.[2]

That archives witness and keep cultural memory through their artefacts provides good reason to read them at times through the concept of a 'matrix' (*OED*): 'a place or medium in which something is originated, produced, or developed; the environment in which a particular activity or process begins; a point of origin and growth'. A matrix points to the past of an organism; archival material can register a text's past and genesis. From this flows the customary cultural gendering of the archive. Relevant here is the Aristotelian distinction as articulated by Judith Butler between 'matrix' and 'form' – in the received cultural binary, respectively gendered feminine and masculine. Butler comments on

> the classical association of femininity with materiality [which] can be traced to a set of etymologies which link matter with *mater* and *matrix* (or the womb) ....

> In Greek, *hyle* is the wood or timber out which various cultural constructions are made, but also a principle of origin, development and teleology .... The matrix is an originating and formative principle which inaugurates and informs a development of some organism or object. Hence, for Aristotle, 'matter is potentiality, form actuality'. In reproduction, women are said to contribute the matter; men, the form.[3]

An 'archive' construed as making legible through its documents a matrix of 'some organism or object' thus may easily be read as merely 'feminine' and 'maternal', subordinated in that classical way – yet as latter-day archival scholars, we are equipped to deconstruct and challenge that familiar cultural hierarchy and to address how and why archives matter. Indeed as Derrida's 'patriarchive' suggests, the archive and the archival are generally read as womblike, but this analogy need not be read through feverish psychoanalytic and patriarchal suspicions about the desire for the womb.[4]

These reflections emerge from work pursued over the last decade on the genesis of this discipline we still call 'English'. In a course I've designed on early-twentieth-century criticism, we seek to thicken and complicate received narratives on the 'rise of English' (articulated by such sources as Eagleton's *Literary Theory* and Gerald Graff's *Professing Literature*) with dusty documents from the cultural archives. Pace Derrida, I'll admit to the wish for the story of origins of how we 'do' English as a field of study now, since this is behind the curtain for so many. Students read I. A. Richards on his protocols, follow Empson into the wilds of ambiguity, and consider the Leavises on 'real culture'; then we cross the water to later critics taking a page from these figures, American New Critics such as Cleanth Brooks and John Crowe Ransom, then Canadian successors such as Northrop Frye and Marshall McLuhan. We also read Q. D. Leavis, by whose pioneering 'anthropological' method my students are often caught. We follow her commentary on the habits of the British reading public, or publics, of her time, her diagnosis of their typical reading matter, levels of taste and the cultural factors conditioning these.[5]

My thinking on Q. D. Leavis also relates to ongoing work on what I shorthand now as the 'making of the female public intellectual' in the early twentieth century, initially spurred by Toril Moi's study of Simone de Beauvoir.[6] In this context, the idea of 'making', which I often link to 'poiesis' in the context of verse, points to the concepts of matrix, formation and resources, conditions of possibility shaping development. In this spirit, this essay considers the 'making' of English as a discipline and addresses what QDL herself read as vital resources for the 'making' of intellectual practice.[7]

Again, Q. D. Leavis's early research, especially for *Fiction and the Reading Public* (1932), based on her dissertation, often now feels somewhat like a hidden archive sourcing and shaping early vanguard work in the field of 'English'. What spurred this line of thought was discovering that, surprisingly, Canadian media guru Marshall McLuhan had credited Q. D. Leavis's work in the 1970s with a foundational impact on his thought. To capture the significance of QDL's *Fiction and the Reading Public* on his work, McLuhan used a pair of tropes derived from Gestalt psychology and communications, 'figure and ground'. Stepping off from this dichotomy, and from the concept of 'ground' in particular, this essay divides into three parts: first, it explores the implications of McLuhan's use of 'ground' with regard to Q. D. Leavis's work and the development of the field of English; second, it considers the place of such a concept of 'ground' in Q. D. Leavis's own thought, and then, finally, it frames a cluster of methodological questions about how in future, on the one hand, we might handle and read archival materials associated with Q. D. Leavis herself and, more generally, explore an avenue for re-theorization of the archive.

In recent commentary on what Mark Krupnick calls the 'intellectual provenance' of McLuhan's work,[8] there has been emphasis on its wellsprings at Cambridge, where after pursuing both a second BA and MA,[9] McLuhan earned a doctorate in 1943.[10] There he encountered I. A. Richards, in whose experimental protocols he participated, William Empson and F. R. Leavis. Although he is often linked to the 'New Criticism' in the United States, and though he cultivated relationships with the American New Critics in the late 1930s and 1940s,[11] it was Cambridge that most significantly shaped McLuhan's sense of intellectual practice and critical vision. He later styled himself 'the only man in the USA who had a thorough grounding in the techniques of Richards Empson and Leavis at Cambridge'.[12] McLuhan would read the Cambridge group as surpassing the New Critics in their awareness of the larger post-Arnoldian cultural missions informing the work of early twentieth-century criticism. At one point McLuhan even critiqued F. R. Leavis in a letter for being so concerned with such 'important' cultural work that he neglected what McLuhan called the 'sun in the egg-tarnished spoons on the daily table':[13] more on this idea later.

It would be Cambridge-inspired methods that McLuhan would deploy in *The Mechanical Bride*, his first book, in 1951, which directs techniques of close reading to the phenomena of popular culture – advertising, journalism, comics, radio, film. When first teaching in the United States, McLuhan noted that he was keen on 'getting Leavis across to my classes'.[14] McLuhan would later observe of his influences, crediting modernists as well as the Cantabrigian critics by way of a Blakean phrase: 'Richards, Leavis, Eliot, Pound and Joyce in a few weeks opened the doors of perception on the poetic process, and its role in adjusting the reader to the contemporary world. My study of media began and remains rooted in the work of these men.'[15] Yet one of these 'men' turns out to be a woman.[16]

McLuhan first met both Q. D. Leavis and F. R. Leavis in 1935, shortly after arriving at Cambridge: 'This afternoon, ... I called for tea with Dr. and Mrs (also Dr.) Leavis. He is the editor of Scrutiny, a highbrow English journal.'[17] McLuhan encountered the Leavises three years after the annus mirabilis for their circle, in 1932, when they had founded *Scrutiny*. Although QDL never appeared as official editor of *Scrutiny*,[18] she was constantly involved with its preparation and contributed a wealth of its articles.[19] In 1932, QDL would also publish *Fiction and the Reading Public*, begun as a dissertation under the supervision of I. A. Richards. She would earn her doctorate in 1931, at the age of twenty-five.

In 1933, a Leavisite book called *Culture and Environment* appeared.[20] Co-authored by F. R. Leavis and Denys Thompson, this 'experimental' book, as Leavis and Thompson put it, directed the 'training of critical awareness' that the Cambridge critics were pursuing in the literary classroom to the 'immediate cultural environment – and the ways in which it tends to affect taste, habit, preconception, attitude to life and quality of living' (4–5), so as to help readers to 'discriminate and resist' (5). This book would essentially 'close read' advertising and journalism, much as McLuhan later would in his first book, *The Mechanical Bride* (1951). Acknowledging his theoretical debt, McLuhan even titled a 1944 course he designed 'Culture and Environment' (Letters 157).[21] While not publicly recognized, QDL's work was central to *Culture and Environment*. As Chris Baldick notes, 'Years later, F. R. Leavis was to insist that the enormous influence of *Culture and Environment* derived from its debt to Q. D. Leavis's work in *Fiction and the Reading Public*. Using her research as a basis, F. R. Leavis had been able to write *Culture and Environment* in a week.'[22] In *Culture and Environment*, QDL's *Fiction and the Reading Public* is quoted (see 'Substitute Living', 100–1), and several other examples are clearly drawn from QDL's research, although without explicit acknowledgement.[23] As F. R. Leavis's biographer Ian MacKillop observes, F. R. Leavis and Denys Thompson 'had so much help from QDL that it is surprising that her name did not appear on the title page' (208).[24]

It would be *Fiction and the Reading Public* that McLuhan would credit years later with major theoretical influence on his work. In a 1973 letter, McLuhan registered respect for the way that, rather than consider the novel in isolation, QDL had studied the cultural environment out of which novels were written and the 'publics' (21) who read them. Here McLuhan invokes the metaphor of figure and ground: 'Communication theory for any *figure* requires the including of the *ground* for that figure and the study of the interplay between the *figure* and its *ground* .... QDL's *Fiction and the Reading Public*', he noted, was 'the only study ever made, in English, of a reading public. That is, the study of *ground* for the *figure* of the novel. The ordinary study concentrates on *figure* minus ground, i.e. the content of the novel is studied and the kinds of reader and their relation to the novel are ignored'.[25] In a letter of 19 June 1975 to John Culkin, he presents his interest in 'figure' and 'ground' and the interplay between them as an interest in 'formal cause'.

> I realized that the audience is, in all matters of art and expression, the formal cause ... e.g. Plato's public is the formal cause of his philosophy. Formal cause is concerned with effects and with structural form, and not with value judgments. My own approach to the media has been entirely from formal cause. Since formal causes are hidden and environmental, they exert their structural

> pressure by interval and interface with whatever is in their environmental territory. Formal cause is always hidden, whereas the things upon which they act are visible.[26]

In this context, McLuhan reads as addressing the 'reading public' Q. D. features as such a 'ground' and 'formal cause', but given the language here (a 'formal cause' as 'hidden' and 'environmental', exerting 'structural pressure'), his language also suggests the forces witnessed and carried by the material of an archive. And insofar as Q. D. Leavis's work often seemed to be the source, usually 'hidden', of much of the work of the *Scrutiny* group, 'ground' as McLuhan uses it (suggesting 'formal cause'), this train of thought also pertains to the role of Q. D. Leavis in the cultural system that gave rise to the development of English as a field. That McLuhan uses 'formal' here is striking: in the Aristotelian line of thought McLuhan uses, while such 'hidden' forces might be interpreted as material that is then formed so as to be visible, here they are further read as involved in and shaping that which is 'formal'. Also notable is that McLuhan uses 'environmental' in his remarks, given the 'grounding' in QDL's work of *Culture and Environment*, which clearly exerted such formative impact on his own thought.

McLuhan again used 'ground' in a 1977 letter to New Critic Cleanth Brooks describing his methodology. As he said, the 'pattern used by all phenomenology began with Descartes in selecting *figures* without *ground*, the Norrie Frye style of classification without insight'. In contrast: 'My media studies work entirely by *figure* and *ground*, both the input and the consequences.'[27] 'Input' suggests that for McLuhan, 'ground' sometimes designated not only the 'reading public' or audience (which he took as 'formal cause'), but more generally also the cultural environment and resources informing a text. In this formulation, 'ground' both informs and shapes 'figure', beyond allowing for interpretation thereof. Given this, it is also striking that McLuhan called himself in a letter 'the only man in the USA who has thorough *grounding* in the techniques of Richards Empson and Leavis at Cambridge'.[28] In the light of McLuhan's associational linkages, the term 'grounding' points not only to the Leavis overtly noted here, F. R., but also to the work of QDL. In the lexical subtext is the other Leavis.

With 'ground', McLuhan thus designates both a context against and in relation to which a text can be read, as part of his favoured hermeneutics, and, as his word 'input' suggests, the cultural conditions for the production of a certain figure, which exert shaping and formative pressure: that is, a kind of matrix. In fact one of the definitions of 'matrix' includes the concept of 'ground': 'the ground substance in which structural elements (e.g. of a shell, cell wall, etc.) are embedded'. In view of the figure-ground binary, even what Q. D. Leavis and F. R. Leavis meant by their master term 'culture' begins to read as the crucial cultural 'ground' that classic New Critical readings (famously focused on form and the 'work itself') characteristically elide, in favour of figure. Thus in this force field of tropes, including QDL's work in this narrative as crucial influence on not only McLuhan but also the *Scrutiny* group from which McLuhan drew, in turn pivotal to the evolution of 'English', makes QDL's work read here as part of the often elided 'ground' of 'English' as a field.

Again, one sense of 'ground' suggests context for reading, the other kindred sense a source or basis, a matrix. And both of these map onto significances sometimes attached to the 'archival' – on the one hand, relevant archival material can be used to shed light on the significance of a text (read as 'figure'), and in other cases, archival materials witness, even constitute, the occasion and cultural resources for the making of a certain text, its provenance.

At this point, as inspired by the terms of McLuhan's tribute to Q. D. Leavis, I'll turn to exploring the concept of 'ground' in the thought of Q. D. Leavis herself – how she construed concepts adjacent to what McLuhan indicates by the term – since these prove pivotal to her thinking as well. This then leads to the question of how to reckon with a notable wealth of archival materials now newly available at Girton College, Cambridge, about Q. D. Leavis herself, about what QDL's daughter calls her 'creative domestic life'. The material in this archive brings out QDL's own ideas about the 'grounding' or matrixes for scholarly, critical, and intellectual practice. In my reading, Q.D. Leavis's perspective on this topic, signalled implicitly through her work, notably diverges from, even counters, McLuhan's vision of the gender and positioning of both archive and cultural critic, emerging from his conceptual circuit about 'ground' and 'figure'. If McLuhan's homage to Q. D. Leavis serves to surface her cultural contributions, in some respects her own ideas on such contributions read as McLuhan (to adapt Willmott's phrase) nearly 'in reverse'.[29]

Apart from the kind of research she pursued for *Fiction and the Reading Public,* providing a vital resource for the *Scrutiny* group, Q. D. Leavis clearly valued other kinds of cultural production as important to intellectual work. A salient register of this is her now famous attack on Virginia Woolf's *Three Guineas* (1938),[30] the terms of which suggest her objections not only to Woolf's claims (which she reads as unfortunately emotional rather than rational) but also to the cultural 'ground' from which, in her reading, these arose – Woolf's class positioning and life experience. The review is usually noted for QDL's vitriolic quarrel with the class insularity associated with Bloomsbury. It also, however, articulates QDL's position on what she construes as a vital matrix for intellectual practice. For QDL, what Woolf lacks, crucially, is understanding of what QDL calls, in what feels like a turn on Montaigne, 'the art of living' (208, 210).[31] (Here I think of the comparable emphasis on the concept of 'living' in *Culture and Environment:* one chapter is entitled 'Substitute Living'; the commentary emphasizes ways to improve, through reading and 'scrutiny', 'quality of living'.) For QDL, Woolf's conception thereof (and this stings) is that of an 'idle charming cultivated' woman – a 'parasite'. QDL's vision of what's needed for 'sterling qualities of mind and character' comes through in her reading of Woolf's experiential limitations. When Woolf lauds the heroic achievements of women who managed to think 'while they stirred the pot, while they rocked the cradle', this line of thought taps into what QDL finds important. While in QDL's reading, Woolf knows nothing of this domain, she herself does: 'I myself, however, have generally had to produce contributions for this review with one hand while actually stirring the pot.' QDL's daughter recalls, in the archival notes, 'My mother did much of her thinking while making jam and doing the myriad other household jobs.'[32] What follows reveals more about QDL's quarrel with the direction of Woolfian feminist thought: 'I feel bound to disagree with Mrs. Woolf s assumption that running a household and family unaided necessarily hinders or weakens thinking.' In fact, for QDL, such activities ('living') vitally nourish 'thinking'.

> One's own kitchen and nursery, and not the drawing-room and dinner-table ... is the realm where living takes place, and I see no profit in letting our servants live for us. The activities Mrs. Woolf wishes to free educated women from as wasteful not only provide a valuable discipline, they serve as a sieve for determining which values are important and genuine and which are conventional and contemptible. ('Caterpillars', 210–11)

Thus the engine room of QDL's model of intellectual practice turns out to be the kitchen and nursery. Before letting our minds scroll onwards to thoughts of grease fires and squalling infants, I'd offer that QDL's 'kitchen' and 'nursery' are significantly related to, if not aligned with, the concepts of 'ground' and 'archive', at least if these are construed in certain ways. Again, a term apt for what QDL values here is 'matrix'. Given QDL's accent on kitchen and nursery, the 'maternal' labour of a culture is also clearly germane. For QDL, what counts as essential ground for intellectual practice is very much about the zone of experience suggested by McLuhan's 'egg-tarnished spoons on the daily table', though with a significant (and gendered) difference.

This again indicates the Leavisite sense of 'culture': when the Leavises, in a post-Arnoldian vein, thought of their master term 'culture' (their acute sense of the interwar crisis in which drove their work), they saw what F. R. Leavis tellingly called 'a real culture' as grounded in folkways – dancing, handcrafted products, folk music: these were the practices, customs and traditions, associated with an older village-England lost, vital to what they construed as cultural health.[33] For them, literature, somewhat surprisingly, was in many respects only a 'substitute' for such 'real culture' and 'living culture'.[34] As *Culture and Environment* has it:

> [L]iterary education ... is to a great extent a substitute. What we have lost is the organic community with the living culture it embodied. Folk-songs, folk-dances, Cotswold cottages and handicraft products are signs and expressions of something more: an art of life, a way of living, ordered and patterned, involving social arts, codes of intercourse and a responsive adjustment, growing out of immemorial experience, to the natural environment and the rhythm of the year. (1–2)

The phrases 'art of life' and 'way of living' here resonate notably with QDL's 'art of living' from the review of *Three Guineas.* Given this, it follows that Leavis would privilege the kitchen and the nursery as sites providing the conditions of possibility for the kind of intellectual practice she endorses. If folk songs and dances and handicraft products imply a realm of 'patterned' custom and ceremony, whereas the kitchen implies everyday prosaic details, both of these draw attention to material, sensory realities, daily rhythms and experience derived from these as deeply important to forming what the Leavises see as thinking, cultural commentary and vital judgements about taste. If, for Matthew Arnold, 'culture' qua 'the best which has been thought and said in the world' is needed for 'nourishing' creative work, in the Leavisite vision, English folkways represent a 'real culture' needed for nourishing and grounding these 'best' ideas. Moreover, the ways of such a 'real' culture are themselves practices for which 'literary education' is merely a 'substitute', which makes them not just ground, but in this version of the scheme, figures, practices themselves meriting reading and valuation.

In turn, QDL's emphasis on 'the art of living' for valuable intellectual practice sheds light on the significance of this trove of materials recently gathered and made available by Q. D. Leavis's daughter, Kate Varney, about what Varney calls in her introduction to the archive the 'creative domestic practices' of her mother. This collection of materials shows QDL making the home space in ways that recall such customary, embodied practices as folk songs and dances: her daughter even registers a memory of QDL singing folk songs to children in the family.

I discovered this archival windfall at Girton College: it offered a rich array of information, often in the form of fine-grained memoir from Varney about the rituals and dailiness of her childhood and the physical details of the home at 6 Chesterton Hall Crescent. One category foregrounded in this wealth of notes is headed (3) ECONOMY, FOOD, HOSPITALITY, KITCHEN AND GARDEN. The concatenation of terms here suggests the framework of values within which the family culture understood the work of the 'kitchen'. Kitchen provisions were gathered according to careful 'economies', especially given conditions of the 1930s and 1940s. Varney mentions war rationing. Other comparable headings include (1) Pets and animals, (2) Shopping, (4) Health and illness, (5) Junk shopping and china and (6) Furniture and fabrics. The specificity of Varney's record is compelling:

> There were several greengrocers in Chesterton road, Victoria Avenue and Milton Road. That in Victoria Avenue smelled of the beetroot always on the boil….
>
> We were also registered with Mr Onyett the grocer. Each week a notebook with our order – eg 'fats for 5' (how much butter, marg, lard depended on the grocer's quota that week), back bacon cut at number 4, 'scouring powder' (=VIM) and so on was handed over the counter and a box subsequently delivered to the back door, and either unpacked then or collected next week as containers were in short supply.

Varney's notes detail the particulars of the home space and its daily routines and practices in vivid detail. Here are the spoons on the daily table. Among other things, she remembers the objects her mother loved to acquire from their 'junk shopping', browsing second-hand shops for crockery, sometimes 'blue and white':

> There were 'real' junkshops in [the] 1950s and 1960s where Victorian transfer ware, Edwardian glass etc languished under piles of house clearance items. Our first treasure trove was Mr. Turpin's …. Most items were not priced, so one sought him out to ask him. It was said that he sold Georgian silver at a time when it was not valued. I have a charming blue and white 'Asiatic Plants' pattern soap dish, recently admired by a museum curator.[35]

For me the fine grain of this archival record reads as even more fascinating than a rich account of some of this material Varney provides in an interview in *Women: A Cultural Review.*[36] In another context, I'd like to unpack the distinctive significance and value of such 'textured' accounts of memory, which I read as quintessentially archival, located in and focused on objects and sensory experience. Carolyn Steedman's *Dust* on archival experience comes to mind – especially her chapter 'What a Rag Rug Means', invoking Bachelard's concept of 'topoanalysis', in which the modelled analysis of domestic interiors resonates with the analysis of what one finds in an archive – that is, archival objects.[37]

Derrida famously reads the archive as domicile, wherein objects are under 'house arrest' (*Archive Fever* 2). What Varney has made available in this archive at Girton, in the form of reminiscences about the home life of the Leavises, suggests two related ideas: on the one hand, the idea of domestic space *as* archive, tracing the origins of those who once dwelled there, and on the other, archive as house or room left behind. What I read as QDL's implicit theory of the archive reads the archive as more generative domicile than troubling 'domiciliation', more house than 'house arrest'. Steedman's epigraph to *Dust* offers a memorable passage from the 'Time Passes' section of Virginia Woolf's *To the Lighthouse*, a vision of the house space, from which the people have departed, but whose objects still bear the impressions of their living:

> What people had shed and left – a pair of shoes, a shooting cap, some faded skirts and coats in wardrobes – these alone kept the human shape and the emptiness indicated how they were once filled and animated; how once hands were busy with hooks and buttons; how once the looking glass had held a face.[38]

(The sound play of 'hooks' and 'buttons' here suggests 'books'.) What Varney's archive witnesses is not just archival resources and 'stuff' of the home space, but also the choice-making and thinking arising therefrom. Some of what Varney registers in her reminisces accents conscience and good judgement. As Varney notes, 'My mother was extremely thrifty and resourceful and used to say that in some ways she enjoyed the challenge of the wartime.' In line with the theme of 'hospitality', the sense of bounty made possible through frugality and good judgement is also often vividly on display:

> [My mother] entertained my three cousins .... She was very fond of the girls ... During and after the war she knitted them jumpers and found them little items and food to sustain them while two of them were working in the Land Army ....[39]

Why was Varney moved to add to and curate this new archive on the 'creative domestic life' of her mother? In part, as corrective for the perception that QDL was merely a harsh critical voice, as she is portrayed in many accounts. Varney wants it known that her mother was generous and resourceful, a devoted spouse and parent. Of her notes, she says,

> I hope they will be able to contradict the many snide references bandied around about her. It has to be appreciated that no one endowed with her creative genius, energy and spontaneity could have survived such vicissitudes without at times feeling both depressed and bitter at times.

She notes of further reasons:

> I did not write with the idea of publication but just to put in an archive for future reference the background against which, indeed often despite which, my mother's output of literary criticism was achieved.[40]

McLuhan mentions 'input'; here, as Varney invokes the 'archive', she notes the 'output' of 'literary criticism', whose 'background' in QDL's life Varney accents. Again, carrying on from McLuhan, especially in view of Q. D. Leavis's implicit model of intellectual practice, I would suggest that this 'background' (richly traced through this 'archive') deserves to be read not only as that which facilitates reading the significance of the 'literary criticism', but also as 'ground' and generative matrix for QDL's prolific literary criticism. And for QDL, this was a 'ground' not 'against' or 'despite' which she produced her intellectual work, not so as to foil or cast into relief what she did, but rather *from* which she did. The archive at Girton, in other words, witnesses the 'art of living' that QDL reads as pivotal to critical and intellectual practice.

The extraordinary specificity of Kate Varney's notes rhymes with the lavish sensory specificity with which Q. D. Leavis's own letters and notes typically brim, often about the home space and daily practices.[41] Varney shares with her mother a bent for richly detailed sensory knowledge and memory, grounded, one might say, in particular dense with colour, texture, quantities, precise names, numbers and images, detailed accounts of spaces and solid objects, furniture, and food. QDL's criticism, in contrast, often features a language of rational abstraction, and it's good to discover what feels like a basis of her criticism in such sensory detail.

Striking is that, though she notes in her letters the prospect of the study of her dreams, QDL in the end never enjoyed a room of her own. The Girton finding aid records of Varney's comment, 'Whereas my father worked in the solitude of his study in peace and quiet my mother never had the luxury of her own room.' Varney concedes that about this state of affairs, her mother had mixed feelings. Yet in the light of what this paper addresses, we might also read QDL's situation in the home space as also suggesting a model of female intellectual practice alternative to both that of F. R. Leavis and that of Woolf, which neither needed nor proceeded from a 'room of one's own', one from which she saw women as uniquely (and fortunately) well positioned to benefit. At least some women, those overseeing the kitchen, could access much more readily than their male counterparts the stuff, the ground, of actual 'living' that QDL read as essential to the formation of judgement and taste, and to a critical idiom: these were crucial to the kind of intellectual practice the Leavises valued. This archive, filled with details on domestic dailiness and the daily table, clearly diverges from the usual archive featuring letters and manuscripts: but it literalizes and makes plain the kind of 'matrix' that QDL favoured, not just for making sense of intellectual practice but also for grounding and giving rise thereto. It also suggests the archive as re-theorized by way of QDL's thought.

In McLuhan's thought, in contrast, 'ground' is a matter of structural relation – that which stands in relation to text/figure as illuminating and formative. He takes as complementary the 'ground' and 'figure', genders ground 'feminine', and although he suggests that ground is essential, in his conceptual work, the idea of 'ground' is ultimately subordinated. When aligning the concept of ground and 'formal cause', for instance, McLuhan linked these, in turn, to strains of his religious thought; McLuhan was a devout Roman Catholic. He aligned 'formal cause' and 'ground' with the concept of the 'feminine' congregation – necessary to religious practice, complementary to the priest, who could never become priests – gendered masculine. As he wrote to Marion Hammond on 20 June 1975:

> This is just a note about the ordination of women which concerns 'formal causality', i.e. structural form .... The writer's or the performer's public is the formal cause of his art or entertainment or his philosophy. The *figure/ground* relation between writer and public or between the artist and his making is a kind of interplay, a kind of intercourse .... There is, as it were, a sexual relation between performer and public .... The congregation is necessarily feminine to the masculine role of the priest .... It is, therefore, this inherent sexual aspect of the priesthood that makes the ordination of women impractical and unacceptable to a congregation in their feminine role.[42]

McLuhan's scheme requires the congregation, as ground, 'formal cause', in its 'feminine role', supportive of and subordinate to the priest. In my reading, Q. D. Leavis's thought on the archive turns this logic around. So too to a considerable extent does the *Scrutiny* work on literature and culture. For the *Scrutiny* group whose work was formative for the development of 'English', the 'figure' of literature is merely a 'substitute' for the materials of what functions here as 'ground' and which also constitutes the stuff of 'real living' and 'real culture'. My reading is that if Leavises had had the hierarchy their way, the stuff of the cultural 'archive' would be published rather than concealed and would step forth from the archives rather than remain merely hidden, ancillary and supportive. For them, it was this which counted most, not only as formative force, but even as a set of sustaining cultural practices, figures in their own right.

With Q. D. Leavis's vein of thought on the 'kitchen and nursery' as archive, have we begun to step beyond the 'patriarchive'? My sense is yes – what Q. D. Leavis suggests is archive as maternal space, one not altogether read through patriarchal logic and binaries, nor patriarchal conceptions of the 'feminine'. In QDL's thought, this material, maternal space is not just supportive helpmeet to the 'figure' (whatever her own role was with respect to FRL within their marriage and career). Instead, it is what allows one to decide values and standards, what is 'important' (and what is merely 'conventional' and 'contemptible'), what qualifies as 'the art of living'. Moreover, the work of the kitchen itself represents metonymically the 'art of living', not just that on which 'art' depends. If in McLuhan's scheme the 'feminine' archive is necessary but may never become the priest, in QDL's lines of thought, the 'feminine' archive both provides resources that give rise to the priest and itself becomes a site for cultural work. QDL herself was raised in an Orthodox Jewish household. QDL's thinking, as I read it, suggests that the maternal archival space may itself become the locus for rabbinical cultural work.[43]

Whether or not we accept this line of thought, it guides us to construe the material of this archive at Girton in certain ways and read it as illuminating richly the Leavisite idea of 'real culture' both so central to the 'rise of English' – and underwriting QDL's idea of critical and intellectual practice, the formation of what she calls in *Fiction and the Reading Public* a 'first-class fully-aware mind' (74).[44]

What implications might this have for archival practice more generally? Most archival material, I would suggest, implies this kind of physicality and granularity: Varney's archive only writes large what the archive often makes available through its solid objects: a kind of sensuous scholarship, as Paul Stoller notes.[45] This example from Girton, replete with sensory images and grounding in cultural particulars, right down to the 'junk shop', discoveries from the cultural archive Q. D. Leavis herself loved, again encourages a reading of archive as matrix, as kitchen, as associated with the domestic, familiar and often maternal, the object-oriented. In the information housed in the archive, we are moving through the intimate domestic interiors of Bachelard's topoanalysis such that the notes from Varney herself begin to feel like such domestic objects. The Girton archive thus encourages attention to what, borrowing a term from close reading, I call the 'texture' of the archive – that is, to its objects and sensory particulars, their colours, materials, surfaces, sizes, grain. How might we take such cues into our own practices?

Especially in view of Q. D. Leavis's 'creative domestic practice', and her emphasis on values, this case might heighten our sensitivity to the 'values' by which, as researchers, we create accounts and narratives from what we find in the house of the archive. Hal Foster reads archives as sites of not just excavation but construction.[46] Indeed this case invites us to read archives as a call to construction – to 'making' and intellectual practice. How might our immersion in such archives, their texture, their physicality, sensory particulars, provide what QDL calls in 'Caterpillars' a 'sieve', an alembic, for deciding the 'values' that will inform that construction? How might this process, furthermore, help us guard against mere accumulation, so as to consider and judge what we will include in accounts of what we find and decide what kind of narratives, in our own kitchens, we will make? All this talk of 'ground' may also spur critical interrogation of the definition of this term in any given context: as in gestalt theory, what qualifies as figure or ground depends on the case, and how each of these signifies likewise depends on the instance. For us today, as for Varney when she sifts through materials indicating the 'making' of QDL, the home space that she made and that made her thought, perhaps the poetic 'figures', what deserves reading, will often reside in what we find among the textured particulars of the archive, among the dusty and somewhat tarnished spoons.

Notes

I am very grateful to Kate Varney and the Mistress and Fellows, Girton College, Cambridge for permission to quote from her notes in the archive on the 'creative domestic practice' of Q. D. Leavis (Q. D. Leavis Papers at Girton College, University of Cambridge). Warm thanks also to Hannah Westall, archivist and curator at the Girton College Archive, for expert support.

1 Eagleton, *Literary Theory*, Ch. 1, 'The Rise of English' (Minneapolis, MN: U Minnesota Press, 1983), pp. 15–46.

2 See Derrida, *Archive Fever* (Chicago: University Chicago Press, 1994), p. 4, note 1. I take this phrase to suggest the 'archive' as understood and gendered through patriarchal logics.

3 Butler, *Bodies That Matter: On the Discursive Limits of 'Sex'* (New York: Routledge, 1993), pp. 31–3.

4 In other words, the desire for the womb need not read as thanatotic. See Paul Flaig, 'Supposing the Archive Is a Woman', in *New Silent Cinema*, ed. Flaig and Katherine Groo (Routledge, 2016), pp. 180–99.

5 Q. D. Leavis, *Fiction and the Reading Public* [1932] (London: Chatto and Windus, 1939).

6 See Toril Moi, *Simone de Beauvoir: The Making of an Intellectual Woman*, 2nd ed. (Oxford: Oxford University Press, 2008).

7 In the work on the development of English as a field, I am indebted to the work of Gerald Graff, *Professing Literature: An Institutional History* (Chicago: University of Chicago Press, 1983), Chris Baldick, *The Social Mission of English Criticism 1848–1932* (Oxford: Clarendon Press, 1983), Joseph North, *Literary Criticism: A Concise Political History* (Cambridge: Harvard University Press, 2017), and Christopher Hilliard, *English as a Vocation: The Scrutiny Movement* (Oxford: Oxford University Press, 2012).

8 Mark Krupnick, 'Marshall McLuhan Revisited: Media Guru as Catholic Modernist'. *Modernism/modernity* 5/3 (1998), p. 108.

9 John Guillory, 'Marshall McLuhan, Rhetoric, and the Pre-History of Media Studies', *Affirmations: Of the Modern* 3/1 (Autumn 2015), pp. 78–90.
10 Donald Theall, *The Virtual Marshall McLuhan* (Montreal: McGill-Queen's University Press, 2006), p. 4.
11 Krupnick, 'Marshall McLuhan Revisited: Media Guru as Catholic Modernist', p. 109.
12 Marshall McLuhan, *Letters of Marshall McLuhan*, selected and edited by Matie Molinaro, Corinne McLuhan, and William Toye (Oxford: Oxford University Press, 1987), p. 157.
13 McLuhan, *Letters*, p. 166.
14 McLuhan, Diary 2 November 1937. Qtd. in Terence Gordon, *Marshall McLuhan: Escape into Understanding*, 78. Walter Ong noted that when teaching at St. Louis University in Missouri, during this period, McLuhan 'was an outpost in mid-America for the Leavis school … Cambridge New Criticism', which 'was a tremendous breath of fresh air' (cited in Gordon, p. 79).
15 'Foreword', in *The Interior Landscape: The Literary Criticism of Marshall McLuhan 1943–1962*, ed. Eugene McNamara (New York: McGraw Hill, 1969), xiii–xiv. On McLuhan and Cambridge-inspired close reading, see also Jessica Pressman, *Digital Modernism: Making It New in New Media* (Oxford: Oxford University Press, 2014), especially Chapter 1, 'Close Reading: Marshall McLuhan, from Modernism to Media Studies'.
16 Here I think in terms of what Derrida, referring to Sonia Combe's phrase, calls the 'repressed archive' (cited in *Archive Fever*, p. 4).
17 McLuhan, *Letters*, p. 67. At the time, McLuhan found F. R. Leavis 'an uncompromising idealist, tactless, impatient, vain, and affected'. According to Muriel Bradbrook, QDL said years afterwards that 'McLuhan impressed me … as a rather loud, aggressive person, always running around arguing with everyone' (cited in Philip Marchand, *Marshall McLuhan: The Medium and the Messenger* [Cambridge:. MIT Press, 1998], pp. 39–40).
18 G. Singh, *A Critical Study of Literary Critic Q. D. Leavis's Published and Unpublished Writings* (Lampeter, Wales: Mellen, 2002), p. 2.
19 Ian MacKillop, F. R. Leavis's biographer, suggests that Q. D. Leavis's decision to assist her husband in founding *Scrutiny* the same year that she published her book 'blocked the development' of QDL's own career, 'despite [*sic*] the enthusiasm with which she helped him' (cited in Ian MacKillop, *F. R. Leavis: A Life in Criticism* [New York: St Martin's Press, 1995], p. 132).
20 F. R. Leavis and Denys Thompson, *Culture and Environment: The Training of Critical Awareness* (London: Chatto and Windus, 1933).
21 As Philip Marchand notes, 'F. R. Leavis's book *Culture and Environment*, written with Denys Thompson and published in 1933, showed Leavis's Canadian disciple how the analytic powers of the critic could be exercised not only on literature but on the social environment. Leavis adopted a tone of moral urgency as he lamented the passing of what he termed the "organic community," in which people were educated in folk traditions, crafts, and ways of life based on the soil and cottage industries. This was entirely congenial to McLuhan's outlook', p. 40.
22 Baldick, *The Social Mission of English Criticism 1848–1932*, p. 187.
23 For instance, *Culture and Environment* refers to and relies upon the work of George Sturt (who wrote under 'George Bourne'), *Change in the Village* (1912) and *The Wheelwright's Shop* (1923), on which Q. D. Leavis's work often depends, as an important register of cultural change in England from the late nineteenth to

the early twentieth century (see *Fiction and the Reading Public*, 283; *Culture and Environment*, p. 3).

24 Ian MacKillop, *F. R. Leavis*.

25 McLuhan, *Letters*, p. 467. Marchand notes of this: 'A book published by Mrs. Leavis in 1932 was also seminal in McLuhan's thinking. *Fiction and the Reading Public* took a novel approach to the examination of fiction: rather than viewing it as an entity generated from the brains of writers in a vacuum, Q. D. Leavis studied it as a kind of response to the various reading publics or audiences that demanded fiction. The cultivated and highly literate public of the eighteenth century, for example, called forth from its writers a very different fiction than did the readers of the cheap mass periodicals in which Dickens's novels were serialized. Here was a suggestion that McLuhan also developed in his later years when he began to insist on the audience as a *cause* of any work of art, a cause that should be studied almost as carefully as the work of art itself', p. 41.

26 McLuhan, *Letters*, p. 510. In Aristotelian thought, 'formal cause' is the pattern or design which determines the form taken by something.

27 McLuhan, *Letters*, p. 529.

28 Ibid., p. 157.

29 This idea plays on Glenn Willmott's title, *Modernism or McLuhan in Reverse* (Toronto: University of Toronto Press, 1996).

30 See Q. D. Leavis, 'Caterpillars of the Commonwealth Unite', *Scrutiny* 7 (1938), pp. 203–14.

31 Ibid. See also Q. D. Leavis's comment on where, for her, 'living' actually takes place – in the 'kitchen' and the 'nursery' rather than in the 'drawing room' (211). This calls to mind remarks in *Fiction and the Reading Public* on 'living at the novelist's expense' (235 ff.), suggesting that real 'living' has been replaced by fiction in a fallen modern age, and the parallel concept, 'substitute living', from *Culture and Environment* (99 ff.).

32 Girton College Archive and Special Collections, Girton College Private Papers (Q. D.) Leavis 1/2/1. Section: (3) ECONOMY, FOOD, HOSPITALITY, KITCHEN AND GARDEN, comments from Kate Varney, daughter of Q. D. Leavis. Permission to quote from the notes in this archive, thanks to Kate Varney and the Mistress and Fellows, Girton College, Cambridge.

33 See F. R. Leavis, *How to Teach Reading: A Primer for Ezra Pound* (Cambridge: G. Fraser, Minority Press, 1932), p. 3.

34 See Leavis's and Thompson's recommendation of *Rustic Speech and Folk Lore* by E. M. Wright and *Words and Idioms* by Logan Pearsall Smith. Again, the Leavises also often point to George Sturt, who wrote under 'George Bourne', *Change in the Village* (1912) and *The Wheelwright's Shop* (1923). Sturt was an English writer on rural crafts and village life:

> What we had to do was to live up to the local wisdom of our kind; to follow the customs, and work to the measurements, which had been tested and corrected long before our time in every village shop all across the country ... A good wheelwright knew by art but not by reason the proportion to keep between spoke and felloes; and so too a good smith knew how tight a two-and-a-half inch tyre should be made for a five-foot wheel .... He felt it, in his bones. (Sturt, *The Wheelwright's Shop* [1923] [Cambridge: Cambridge University Press, 1994], pp. 19–20)

35 Girton College Private Papers (Q. D.) Leavis 1/2/1. Section: (3) ECONOMY, FOOD, HOSPITALITY, KITCHEN AND GARDEN, comments from Kate Varney.

36 Kate Varney and Jan Montefiore, 'A Conversation on Q. D. Leavis', *Women: A Cultural Review* 19/2 (2008), pp. 172–87.

37 See Steedman, *Dust* (Manchester University Press 2001), chapter 6. See also chapter 4, 'The Space of Memory: In an Archive', 79, on Bachelard's 'topoanalysis': 'the systematic psychological study of the sites of our intimate lives' (Gaston Bachelard, *The Poetics of Space* (Boston: Beacon, [1958], 1994), p. 8).

38 See Carolyn Steedman, *Dust* (Manchester University Press 2001), epigraph.

39 Girton College Private Papers (Q. D.) Leavis 1/2/1.

40 Girton College Private Papers (Q. D.) Leavis 1/2/1, Introductory note from Varney.

41 For an example, see G. Singh, *A Critical Study of Literary Critic Q. D. Leavis's Published and Unpublished Writings*. Singh quotes this passage from QDL's 'Notes' for a memoir of her husband, detailing their cycling tours:

> 'We naturally took holidays on *bike* ... and this time (summer 1930) we took our cycles on the train to Winchester and then cycled through the New Forest (also comparatively unspoilt then) ... Of course being so hard up we stayed each night at small inns or bed-and-breakfast-for-cyclists cottages or farmhouses. The food always seemed, whether 'tea' or breakfast, to bread and jam (homemade if you were lucky), boiled egg, watercress or lettuce, and ham (at farm-houses, sometimes delicious home-cured and boiled) and a big pot of strong Indian tea. Their coffee we soon learnt was undrinkable (made from a poisonous liquid in a bottle), and many an aspidistra we watered with it to spare our landlady's feelings'. (cited in Singh pp. 7–8)

42 McLuhan, *Letters*, p. 511.

43 As Singh notes in his study of Q. D. Leavis, she 'was born in London in 1907 into a cultivated Jewish family of Polish origin'. When Q. D. Leavis married F. R. Leavis, who was not Jewish, her family cut her off, making of this upbringing and its domestic environment and culture yet another repressed archive. As Singh observes, 'Marriage to a Gentile caused Q. D. Leavis to be ostracised by her family, which she never forgave', p. 2.

44 In forthcoming work, I pursue the implications of the underrecognized impact of QDL's work on historiography of 'the rise of English'.

45 I borrow this concept from Paul Stoller, *Sensuous Scholarship* (Philadelphia: University of Pennsylvania Press, 1997).

46 See Hal Foster, 'An Archival Impulse', *October* 110 (Autumn 2004), pp. 3–22.

INDEX